AMERICAN CLASSICS:
EVOLUTIONARY PERSPECTIVES

Evolution, Cognition, and the Arts

Series Editor
BRIAN BOYD (University of Auckland)

Editorial Board

STEVEN BROWN
(McMaster University)

JILL COOK
(The British Museum)

RICHARD GERRIG
(Stony Brook University)

SARAH HRDY
(University of California, Davis)

MARCUS NORDLUND
(University of Gothenburg)

ALEX C. PARRISH
(James Madison University)

DAVID SLOAN WILSON
(Binghamton University)

AMERICAN CLASSICS:
EVOLUTIONARY PERSPECTIVES

JUDITH P. SAUNDERS

Boston
2018

Library of Congress Cataloging-in-Publication Data

The bibliographic data for this title is available from the Library of Congress.

©Judith P. Saunders, 2018

ISBN 978-1-61811-765-6 (hardback)
ISBN 978-1-61811-592-8 (open access)
ISBN 978-1-61811-767-0 (electronic)
ISBN 978-1-61811-766-3 (paperback)

Book design by Kryon Publishing Services (P) Ltd.
www.kryonpublishing.com

Cover design by Ivan Grave

Published by Academic Studies Press
28 Montfern Avenue
Brighton, MA 02135, USA
press@academicstudiespress.com
www.academicstudiespress.com

for Lynne Liddell Doty

Table of Contents

Acknowledgments — vii
Glossary — viii
Introduction — x

1. *The Autobiography of Benjamin Franklin*: The Story of a Successful Social Animal — 1
2. Nepotism in Hawthorne's "My Kinsman, Major Molineux" — 23
3. Biophilia in Thoreau's *Walden* — 37
4. Bateman's Principle in "Song of Myself": Whitman Celebrates Male Ardency — 61
5. Maladaptive Behavior and Auctorial Design: Huck Finn's Pap — 78
6. Hell's Fury: Female Mate-Retention Strategies in Wharton's "Pomegranate Seed" and *Ethan Frome* — 97
7. Male Reproductive Strategies in Sherwood Anderson's "The Untold Lie" — 126
8. *The Great Gatsby*: An Unusual Case of Mate Poaching — 138
9. Female Sexual Strategies in the Poetry of Edna St. Vincent Millay — 175
10. Philosophy and Fitness: Hemingway's "A Clean, Well-Lighted Place" and *The Sun Also Rises* — 204
11. Paternal Confidence in Zora Neale Hurston's "The Gilded Six-Bits" — 226
12. The Role of the Arts in Male Courtship Display: Billy Collins's "Serenade" — 246

Conclusion — 253
Works Cited — 263
Index — 283

Acknowledgments

I owe a debt to all those who read portions of this book at various stages of its composition, offering much valued editorial counsel: Joseph Carroll, Anja Müller-Wood, Brian Boyd, Mathias Clasen, Patricia Tarantello, and Jonathan Gottschall. Thanks are due also to Charles Duncan and Robert Funk, organizers of many SAMLA sessions on Darwinian Literary Studies; initial versions of several chapters were first tested in that forum. I am grateful as always to my colleague Victoria Ingalls of the Marist College science faculty. Our ventures in collaborative, interdisciplinary teaching have been a consistent source of intellectual stimulation, refining my understanding of evolutionary biology.

Permission to reprint chapters previously published, in whole or in part, by the following journals and presses is gratefully acknowledged:

"Male Reproductive Strategies in Sherwood Anderson's 'The Untold Lie.'" *Philosophy and Literature* 31, no. 2 (2007): 311-22. Reprinted in *Short Story Criticism*, vol. 142, edited by Jelena Krystovic, 114-19. Detroit and New York: Gale Cengage Learning, 2011.

"*The Autobiography of Benjamin Franklin*: The Story of a Successful Social Animal." *Politics and Culture* (Spring 2010): 1-6. https://politicsandculture.org/2010.

"Nepotism in Nathaniel Hawthorne's 'My Kinsman, Major Molineux.'" In *Telling Stories / Geschichsten Erzählen: Literature and Evolution / Literatur und Evolution*, edited by Carsten Gansel and Dirk Vanderbeke, 296-309. Berlin and Boston: De Gruyter, 2012.

"Paternal Confidence in Zora Neale Hurston's 'The Gilded Six-Bits.'" *Evolution, Literature, and Film: A Reader*, edited by Brian Boyd, Joseph Carroll, and Jonathan Gottschall, 392-408. New York: Columbia University Press, 2010.

"Biophilia in Thoreau's *Walden*." *South Atlantic Review* 79, no. 1-2 (2015): 1-24.

"The Role of the Arts in Male Courtship Display: Billy Collins's 'Serenade.'" *Philosophy and Literature* 41, no. 2 (October 2017): 264-71.

Glossary

Adaptation: a change in the structure or functioning of an organism that makes it better suited to its environment (i.e., a heritable characteristic that tends to increase the fitness of individuals possessing it).

Adaptive: tending to increase the individual's fitness (i.e., conferring an advantage in terms of survival and reproduction). Note: any *adaptation* was, necessarily, *adaptive* at some point in an organism's evolutionary history, but changes in environment or ecological niche can reduce the benefits of a formerly advantageous adaptation.

Alloparent: an individual other than a biological parent who helps to care for juveniles.

Altruism: helping behavior provided at a cost to the performer (*See also* **Selfishness**.)

Coefficient of relatedness: the percentage of genes, on average, that two individuals share by common descent. The coefficient of relatedness between parent and child, or between full siblings, is .5 (i.e., they share one-half of their genes). That between aunts or uncles and nephews or nieces, or between grandparent and grandchild, is .25 (they share one-fourth of their genes).

Fitness: the reproductive success of an individual, commonly expressed in terms of the number of copies of his or her genes an individual succeeds in getting into the next generation.

> *Direct fitness*: success resulting from the individual's personal reproductive efforts.
>
> *Indirect fitness*: success resulting from the reproductive efforts of relatives with whom the focal individual shares genes, weighted according to coefficients of relatedness to the focal individual.
>
> *Inclusive fitness*: The sum of an individual's direct and indirect reproductive success. (i.e., personal reproductive efforts and reproductive efforts of kin).

Genotype: the genetic constitution of an individual organism, i.e., the organism's full hereditary information. (*See also* **Phenotype**.)

Hypergamy: marrying someone superior to oneself, typically measured by social status or material wealth.

Hypogamy: marrying someone inferior to oneself, typically measured by social status or material wealth.

Intersexual: between or among members of the opposite sex (i.e., intersexual conflict = conflict between men and women).

Intrasexual: between or among members of the same sex.

Kin selection: selection for genes causing individuals to favor close kin (i.e., selection for behaviors that increase the inclusive fitness of the performer).

Nepotism: any discriminative behavior tending to favor an individual's relatives and hence to contribute to that individual's inclusive fitness.

Parental investment: any investment by a parent in an individual offspring that increases the offspring's chance of surviving (and of future reproductive success) at the cost of parental ability to invest elsewhere.

Phenotype: the manifest nature of an organism, including morphological, physiological, and behavioral attributes. (*See also* **Genotype**.)

Proximate cause of behavior: the internal reinforcing mechanism (e.g., hormonal or psychological) that triggers a behavior. (*See also* **Ultimate cause**.)

Reproductive value: an individual organism's expected future contribution to its own fitness.

Residual reproductive value: an individual's remaining reproductive value, as measured at a given point in time, taking into consideration age, sex, health, environmental conditions, and other pertinent factors.

Selfishness: behavior directed toward maximizing the survival and reproductive success of the performer. (*See also* **Altruism**.)

Strategy: a blind, unconscious behavior program.

Ultimate cause of behavior: the reason why a specific reinforcing mechanism (i.e., the proximate cause) evolved; that is, the survival-oriented or reproductive purpose it serves. (*See also* **Proximate cause**.)

Introduction

This collection of essays offers evolutionary analysis of a dozen works from the American literary tradition. The aim is to create an interdisciplinary framework for examining key features of the chosen texts, offering an accessible introduction to Darwinian literary critical methodology in tandem with new insights into acknowledged classics. No specialized knowledge of evolutionary biology is needed to follow the lines of argument put forward. Essential terms and concepts, together with pertinent scientific research results, are explained in context, and a glossary is provided. Discussion integrates evolutionary analysis with examination of literary elements such as plot, setting, tone, theme, metaphor, symbol, characterization, and point of view. Connections are made throughout to existing commentary on the targeted texts, illustrating how Darwinian scrutiny can enrich, expand, confound, or reconfigure understandings derived from other critical approaches.

A central premise throughout is that literary works reflect—and reflect upon—universal attributes of an evolved human nature. Across genres, literature explores relationships between human organisms and their environments, cultural and physical; it represents reproductively driven activities, both direct and indirect. Characters compete for mates, resources, and status; they are motivated by desire, jealousy, envy, and vengeance. They employ both cooperative and coercive strategies, engage in both straightforward and duplicitous interactions. All these fitness-based manifestations of human striving necessarily find expression in human art. In the arena of literary make-believe, characters confront choices and difficulties mimicking those in real life, enabling readers to rehearse behavioral options, ponder social complexities, and study hypothetical life histories. From problem-solving to wish-fulfillment, art consistently reflects deep-seated human concerns. Prominent among these is a preoccupation with the human condition itself. Literature serves as a forum in which writers and readers can consider, celebrate, question, deplore, and defy the forces constraining their existence. Stories, poems, and plays offer fascinating glimpses into the psyche of an animal intelligent enough to discern and assess the workings of its own mental and emotional processes. Individual texts do not merely illustrate the operations of evolved adaptations, moreover; they probe the workings of those adaptations in specific environmental contexts. Evolution may with reason be said to provide the stuff of art, since it forges the central comedy, irony, and tragedy of the human predicament.

The work of Charles Darwin, augmented by subsequent research in genetics and the behavioral and cognitive sciences, functions as the basis for adaptationist study of human communication, philosophy, and aesthetics. Literary Darwinism is a relatively young but fast growing branch of a multi-disciplinary enterprise. The intellectual rationale for undertaking evolutionary investigation of music, painting, drama, narrative, and poetry has been articulated by aestheticians and critics such as Ellen Dissanayake, Edward O. Wilson, Joseph Carroll, Robert Storey, Brian Boyd, Michelle Sugiyama, Blakey Vermeule, Lisa Zunshine, and Nancy Easterlin, to name some of the prominent thinkers in a growing field. Readers unfamiliar with the historical and theoretical foundations of Darwinian literary study will find useful commentary in works by these writers, who indicate how the explanatory power of evolutionary ideas can be brought to bear effectively on the arts.[1] Theoretical discussion has addressed broad-based questions such as the adaptive value of art or the cognitive basis of prosodic and narrative forms. Practical application has followed hard on the heels of theory. Examining works by authors representing different national

---

1   See, for instance, Ellen Dissanayake, *What Is Art For?* (Seattle: University of Washington Press, 1988) and *Homo Aestheticus: Where Art Comes From and Why* (Seattle: University of Washington Press, 1992); Edward O. Wilson, *Consilience: The Unity of Knowledge* (New York: Alfred A. Knopf, 1998); Joseph Carroll, *Evolution and Literary Theory* (Columbia: University of Missouri Press, 1995) and *Literary Darwinism: Evolution, Human Nature, and Literature* (New York and London: Routledge, 2004) and "An Evolutionary Paradigm for Literary Study, with Two Sequels," in *Reading Human Nature: Literary Darwinism in Theory and Practice* (Albany: State University of New York Press, 2011); Robert Storey, *Mimesis and the Human Animal: On the Biogenetic Foundations of Literary Representation* (Evanston, IL: Northwestern University Press, 1996); Brian Boyd, *On the Origin of Stories: Evolution, Cognition, and Fiction* (Cambridge, MA and London: Harvard University Press, 2009); Michelle Scalise Sugiyama, "Reverse-Engineering Narrative: Evidence of Special Design," in *The Literary Animal: Evolution and the Nature of Narrative*, ed. Jonathan Gottschall and David Sloan Wilson (Evanston, IL: Northwestern University Press, 2005); Blakey Vermeule, *Why Do We Care about Literary Characters?* (Baltimore, MD: Johns Hopkins University Press, 2010); Lisa Zunshine, *Why We Read Fiction: Theory of Mind and the Novel* (Columbus: Ohio State University Press, 2006); Nancy Easterlin, *A Biocultural Approach to Literary Theory and Interpretation* (Baltimore, MD: Johns Hopkins University Press, 2012).

literatures and languages, Darwinian critics have offered evidence in recent decades that evolutionary psychological readings can correct misapprehensions and resolve ambiguities in literary texts, clarifying or revising long held understandings of aesthetic design and psychosocial significance.[2] Asking if, when, and how literary characters' behavior is *adaptive*, that is, whether it directly or indirectly promotes the passing on of genes, is the key to viewing canonical texts in a decisively new light: Darwinian analysis offers thought-provoking alternatives to Poststructuralist assumptions and practices.

The methodology utilized in this book relies on theory and research now current in the field of evolutionary biology rather than on individual authors' reading and interpretation of Charles Darwin's ideas. Authors writing after 1859 had opportunity to study Darwin's writing firsthand, clearly; they were exposed, as well, to public dissemination and discussion of his theories. Since Darwin was hardly the first scientist to take up the topics of fossil records and species extinction, moreover, many authors writing prior to publication of *The Origin of Species* had access to pre-Darwinian conceptions of evolution. A number of biographers and critics have traced the engagement of literary figures with Darwin's thinking and with that of his precursors, interpreters, defenders, and detractors. Bert Bender, for one, has investigated late nineteenth- and early twentieth-century American writers' familiarity with the Darwinism of their day, discussing in detail how "different writers construed evolutionary theory."[3] Such historical-biographical subject matter, interesting and valuable in its own right, does not form part of the project at hand. Darwinian literary analysis is not dependent upon an author's knowledge of evolutionary biology, nor is it undermined by an author's outdated or mistaken interpretations. If there is indeed a "universal human nature," as research in evolutionary

---

[2] Books and journal articles featuring practical application of Darwinian literary critical methods are too numerous to permit individual mention. Joseph Carroll provides a selective survey in "An Evolutionary Paradigm for Literary Study," 9-12. Another useful starting-point is the special edition of *Style* devoted to analyses of individual works from the American French, Russian, and British literary traditions: "Applied Evolutionary Criticism," ed. Brett Cooke and Clinton Machann, *Style* 46, special issue, no. 3-4 (2012). Further illustrative examples are gathered together in Part IV ("Interpretations") of *Evolution, Literature, and Film: A Reader*, ed. Brian Boyd, Joseph Carroll, and Jonathan Gottschall (New York: Columbia University Press, 2010).

[3] Bert Bender, *Evolution and "the Sex Problem": American Narratives during the Eclipse of Darwinism* (Kent, OH and London: Kent State University Press, 2004), 232. See also his earlier book, *The Descent of Love: Darwin and the Theory of Sexual Selection in American Fiction, 1871-1926* (Philadelphia: University of Pennsylvania Press, 1996).

psychology strongly indicates—that is, if "our thoughts, feelings, and behavior are the product of psychological adaptations" that have evolved over a period of millions of years—then literary representation of that human nature will prove susceptible to Darwinian examination with or without an author's conscious focus on evolutionary ideas and themes.[4] The central principle guiding evolutionarily based criticism is that literature inevitably "reflects the structure and character of the adapted mind."[5]

The twelve works selected for discussion represent a fairly wide sampling of well-known American authors and texts, ranging chronologically from Benjamin Franklin to Billy Collins. No such sampling will meet with perfect approval, not merely because of shifting notions of canon but because of the many and inevitable omissions. It would be impossible, clearly, to address all the acknowledged masterpieces of American literature in a single volume of essays. (Why Thoreau and not Emerson? Why Hawthorne and not Melville? Why Twain and not James?) The line-up of selections offered is to some extent arbitrary and accidental. In another lifetime, or in another book, things might fall out differently. It is chiefly the omissions that may rankle: the works chosen are much read, much admired, much taught, and they have attracted considerable bodies of secondary comment. The exception is Billy Collins, a successful contemporary writer whose poetry has yet to be subjected to the judgment of history; he is included in a forward-looking spirit, a nod to the continuously emergent nature of any tradition.

In addition to canonical status, choice of texts was influenced by the goal of illustrating a wide range of adaptationist concerns. Each essay focuses on a clearly defined topic, or cluster of topics, central to a particular literary work (nepotism, mate guarding, reciprocity, cheating, and deception, among others). The goal is not to identify every possible point of evolutionary interest in any one text but to choose a few of the most significant points for close study. Some topics lend themselves to tighter focus than others; for this reason, the essays are not uniform in length. Analyses are self-contained in terms of argument and reference, permitting readers to dip into the book's contents selectively. The collection is unified by the focus on a single national literature, although

---

4 John Tooby and Leda Cosmides, "Conceptual Foundations of Evolutionary Psychology," in *The Handbook of Evolutionary Psychology*, ed. David M. Buss (Hoboken, NJ: John Wiley and Sons, 2005), 5.

5 Joseph Carroll, "Literature and Evolutionary Psychology," in *The Handbook of Evolutionary Psychology*, ed. David M. Buss (Hoboken, NJ: John Wiley and Sons, 2005), 936.

no all-encompassing statement concerning the nature or development of American literary tradition per se is intended. Darwinian literary-critical methodology serves as the main cohesive principle. Looking at a wide range of fitness-driven motives and behaviors, the essays investigate how and why readers respond as they do to the imaginary predicaments of fictive persons and situations. The volume as a whole explores the potential of evolutionary theory to address fundamental questions of literary purpose, effect, and value.

CHAPTER 1

Benjamin Franklin's Autobiography: The Story of a Successful Social Animal

Presented by its author and regarded by generations of readers as a pattern of the successful life, Benjamin Franklin's *Autobiography* illustrates critically important adaptive goals and strategies. It is the story of an individual, rooted in a specific time and place, wrestling with universal human problems. Though very much a man of his own time, Franklin convincingly presents himself as a man for all times. His extraordinary career depends on his ability to assess his eighteenth-century colonial environment perceptively, responding in a canny way to its expectations and opportunities. Beginning with the assumption that wealth and status are objectives motivating much human striving, he offers readers a step-by-step account of the methods he used to acquire "Affluence" and "Reputation."[1] Though focusing thus on his own individual interests, he demonstrates that his personal goals can be achieved only within the framework of a human community. In his optimistically prosocial model of human life, then, distinctions between selfishness and altruism tend to blur. As he presents himself—and in this respect it is impossible to disagree with him—Franklin is a highly effective social animal. He deploys the principle of reciprocal altruism with intuitive insight and practiced skill; he negotiates the intricacies of dominance hierarchies with the utmost shrewdness; he identifies cooperation as a crucial component of his success, repeatedly discovering for readers' benefit that self-interest and collective well-being are inextricably intertwined.

Like any piece of autobiographical writing, Franklin's book represents a "dramatization and selective ordering of the varied materials" of its author's experience: it is, as one of his biographers has observed, "an elaborate fabrication, truthful in its details yet subtly misleading in its overall plan." All memoirists necessarily "project a pattern on their recollections" and hence

---

1 Benjamin Franklin, "The Autobiography," in *Benjamin Franklin's Autobiography: An Authoritative Text, Backgrounds, Criticism*, ed. J. A. Leo Lemay and P. M. Zall (New York and London: Norton, 1986), 1. All citations refer to this edition.

"distort the lives they describe."[2] Indeed, autobiography exercises a special fascination precisely because it offers more than description: analytical and evaluative commentary accompanies the chronicling of events. J. A. Leo Lemay, one of Franklin's most discerning readers, calls his book "a major literary achievement, more complex, and in many ways, more artful, than a beautifully constructed novel."[3] Like other literary artists, Franklin is "trying to make sense of the world, to construct usable models."[4] It would be possible to undertake biosocial examination of his life *as lived*, with results almost certainly different, at least in some respects, from those that emerge from this examination of his life *as written*. Indeed, most twentieth-century discussions of the *Autobiography* note factual inconsistencies between the life and the book. Francis Jennings, for instance, offers a detailed and "strongly revisionist" analysis of Franklin's personal history.[5] The discussion that follows treats the *Autobiography* as a product of conscious design and interpretative intent: it is a vehicle for conveying its author's conceptions of human nature and social community. Discrepancies between auctorial assertion and ascertainable fact (whether caused by omission or embellishment) need not hamper consideration of the evolutionary issues raised, directly or indirectly, in the version of his life Franklin deliberately shaped for "Posterity" (1).

Never denigrating, disguising or disowning his ambitions, Franklin expends no energy on self-justification. He does not pretend, for instance, that the wealth and status he achieves are unsought, or mere by-products of intellectual, ethical, or spiritual questing; he presents them, rather, as deliberately formulated and unquestionably worthy ends.[6] He acknowledges no disadvantages to being rich and powerful, and he takes uncomplicated pride in having become so. The adaptive value of material prosperity and social status has been demonstrated repeatedly by sociological and anthropological

---

2 Ormond Seavey, *Becoming Benjamin Franklin: The Autobiography and the Life* (University Park and London: Pennsylvania State University Press, 1988), 7, 8.
3 J. A. Leo Lemay, Franklin's *Autobiography* and the American Dream," in *Benjamin Franklin's Autobiography: An Authoritative Text, Backgrounds, Criticism*, ed. J. A. Leo Lemay and P. M. Zall (New York and London: Norton, 1986), 349.
4 Joseph Carroll, "Wilson's *Consilience* and Literary Study," in *Literary Darwinism: Evolution, Human Nature, and Literature* (New York and London: Routledge, 2004), 81.
5 Francis Jennings, *Benjamin Franklin: Politician* (New York and London: Norton, 1996), 204.
6 Seavey points out that Franklin's unquestioning endorsement of wealth-building reflects attitudes generally prevalent in his time period: "traditional criticisms of avarice and of the sordidness of trade were muted in the eighteenth century as never before or since. Trucking and bartering were not merely inevitable but laudable." *Becoming*, 36.

research.[7] Resources are obviously an essential component in the successful rearing of human offspring, who undergo a long period of dependency and require instruction in a host of skills, often complex, that will enable them to survive in their physical and social worlds. In consequence, as David M. Buss observes, "the evolution of the female preference for males who offer resources may be the most ancient and pervasive basis for female choice in the animal kingdom."[8] Because access to goods and services depends to a considerable extent upon status, furthermore, a quest for dominance tends to go hand-in-hand with efforts to accumulate wealth. Women seeking mates respond to the current community standing, and probable future status, of potential partners as well as to resources on hand, seeking men who manifest "a strong proclivity to ascend the hierarchy of tribal power and influence."[9] Such men are likely to exercise economic control in their social groups and thus prove able to provision offspring and long-term mates exceptionally well.

In describing his ambition to achieve "Affluence" and "Reputation," Franklin does not specify enhanced mating opportunities as a motivating factor—nor would we necessarily expect him to do so (1). Because it has been selected for throughout human evolutionary history, the inclination to acquire resources and achieve status exerts a powerful effect on human behavior even in the absence of conscious thinking about the likely payoff in terms of fitness. Franklin's ambitions are the proximate expression of an ultimate goal: wealth and power generally translate into more opportunities to pass on genes. This remains true whether or not he articulates the ultimate evolutionary function of his objectives. In taking for granted their universal desirability, moreover, he evinces awareness of their fundamental importance in human endeavors. He acknowledges the centrality of genetic continuity indirectly by formulating his autobiography at the outset as a letter to his son. He begins by asserting the importance of ancestry, emphasizing the general human wish to learn something about one's forebears and, in turn, to pass on to descendents information about the present generation. Thus he is persuaded that his own "Posterity may like to know" how he achieved his success in life (1). He devotes several pages of his book to family history, attempting to define himself and his descendents in the context of preceding generations. He takes particular pleasure in learning that one of his uncles was a notably "ingenious" man who became

---

[7] David M. Buss, *The Evolution of Desire: Strategies of Human Mating*, rev. ed. (New York: Basic Books, 2003), 22-25.
[8] Ibid., 22.
[9] Ibid., 30.

"a chief Mover of all public Spirited Undertakings" (3); clearly he is intrigued and gratified to find that some of the qualities he most values in himself have manifested themselves previously in the Franklin lineage. He comes close to couching this "extraordinary" resemblance in terms of genetic inheritance with a jesting comment about the possible "Transmigration" of personality traits (3).

Other references to family, scattered throughout the narrative, subtly reinforce the importance of kinship. Franklin expresses grief at the loss of a young son to smallpox, for instance, and he makes use of the occasion to offer advice about inoculation to other parents: he takes for granted that all parents will be "bitterly" saddened by the loss of a child, that they naturally seek to protect their offspring from harm (83). He also describes the assistance he renders to his elder brother James by educating the latter's son and helping to establish him in business after James's death. Even though Franklin explains his actions as an effort to make "Amends" to his brother (for having failed to complete the full term of his apprenticeship), his benevolence to his nephew is a clear instance of nepotism (83). In helping a young relative to prosper in life, he helps himself—by maximizing his own inclusive fitness: he increases the likelihood that the genes he shares with that nephew will be passed on. Again he illustrates his implicit recognition of the biological underpinnings of human striving.

He devotes the bulk of his autobiographical energies to illustrating his successes and describing "the conducing Means" he employed to achieve them (1).[10] He highlights, through repetition, the importance of "Industry and Frugality" in building wealth (74, 78, 79). Numerous anecdotes illustrate his willingness to work hard and to minimize expenses in order to achieve financial security. At the same time he underscores the importance of long-range planning. Industrious and thrifty habits help him to achieve prosperity because at every point in his life he has clearly identified goals: to educate himself, for example, to become a good writer, to own a business. Over time his goals expand in a variety of directions: to contribute significantly to scientific research, for instance, to exercise effective community leadership, and even to achieve "moral Perfection" (66): purposefulness is a leitmotiv in the *Autobiography*. For maximum effectiveness, moreover, "Industry and Frugality" must be supported by competence. Franklin offers evidence that his high level of skill (as press-man, compositor, and supervisor) is a key

---

10 Lemay analyzes the famous sentence in which Franklin introduces his purposes, demonstrating how he "carefully reworked" its syntax so as to highlight the phrase "conducing Means." It is not *the nature* of his success, but *the means of achieving it*, that constitutes "the primary subject of his book." Lemay, "American Dream," 354, 355.

ingredient in his rapid rise to proprietorship of his own printing-house. Later, well-orchestrated exhibitions of competence bring in profitable jobs and increase demand for his services. His carefully honed skills as a writer likewise contribute to his rapid rise to prosperity, most importantly by ensuring the popularity of his newspaper and almanac.

In sum, Franklin harnesses exceptional skills, diligent work habits, and a thrifty lifestyle to high aspirations and sound planning. Setting out to develop and maintain this combination of qualities, he exhibits traits associated worldwide with "the sustained acquisition of resources over time." In all societies, Buss observes, "young men are evaluated for their promise," and "key signs" of future success include "education" and "industriousness," along with ambition.[11] Enumerating "tactics" with proven effectiveness, Buss echoes Franklin with startling fidelity: he emphasizes the importance of "putting in extra time and effort at work, managing time efficiently, prioritizing goals." Another strategy Buss identifies as critical is "working hard to impress others" and, unsurprisingly, image building is a recurrent theme in the *Autobiography*.[12]

Indeed, the detailed emphasis Franklin devotes to his arrival in Philadelphia provides a strong clue to the importance he places on community reputation and status.[13] He takes distinct pleasure in contrasting the picture he paints of a disheveled runaway boy with the prominent man he was later to become, that is, to "compare such unlikely Beginning with the Figure I have since made there" (20). From the very start he seeks to position himself advantageously in his community, to make a favorable impression on others. "I took care not only to be in *Reality* Industrious and frugal, but to avoid all Appearances of the Contrary," he confides (54). For maximum effectiveness, an individual's good qualities must be "visible to ... Neighbors" (49). Franklin is straightforward about his strategic efforts to create a good reputation for himself; he points out that those who obtain community regard are likely to have access to resources and influence. Potential customers, partners, and investors choose to do business with him because he wins a reputation for

---

11 Buss, *Evolution of Desire*, 30.
12 Ibid.
13 See Seavey, *Becoming*, 29-30; David Levin, "The Autobiography of Benjamin Franklin: The Puritan Experimenter in Life and Art," *Yale Review* 53, no. 2 (1964): 258-59; Lemay, "American Dream," 355; Robert F. Sayre, *The Examined Self: Benjamin Franklin, Henry Adams, Henry James* (Madison: University of Wisconsin Press, 1988), 19; Robert F. Sayre, "The Worldly Franklin and the Provincial Critics," *Texas Studies in Literature and Language* 4 (1963): 516-17.

efficiency, speed, and cost-effectiveness. Managing his public image so successfully, he proves that he possesses a high degree of social intelligence: the ability to discern cultural norms and to assess probable penalties for deviation.[14] He is "constantly attuned to the expectations of those around him, responding swiftly to ... changing situations."[15]

For the most part, he strives for congruence between his public image and his real self—that is, he wishes to be known for qualities he actually possesses—but there are interesting exceptions. He discusses at some length, for instance, the advantages to be derived from a reputation for humility, a virtue he reports having tried in vain to acquire. He did succeed to a considerable extent, he explains, in achieving "the *Appearance*" of humility (75). Avoiding "all direct Contradiction" and eschewing dogmatic terms such as "*certainly*" or "*undoubtedly*," he trained himself to phrase his opinions more modestly and more tentatively than had been his habit (75). Although these modifications to his style of conversation did not reflect a real character change, he forthrightly admits, he concludes that they proved valuable, nonetheless, because his opinions found "a readier Reception" and he began to have "much Weight with ... Fellow Citizens" in civic and political matters (75, 76). Deliberately attempting to overcome a reputation for being "proud," "overbearing" and "insolent," he consciously forges a humble persona for himself, reaping "the Advantage of this Change in my Manners" (75). Despite the admitted disjunction between self and image, he does not condemn himself for dissimulation. Humble self-presentation may not be as admirable as genuine humility, but it is the next-best thing. Why?—because it fosters positive, productive sociopolitical interactions.

Consistently emphasizing the benefits of cooperative behaviors and attitudes, Franklin clearly indicates a commitment to the principles of reciprocal altruism. Reciprocity works in human communities by permitting benefits to be exchanged over time.[16] In this "very complex system" of human interaction, services or resources are given in the expectation of equal return

---

14 See Steven Pinker, *The Blank Slate: The Modern Denial of Human Nature* (New York: Penguin, 2002), 64-65.

15 John William Ward, "Who Was Benjamin Franklin?", *American Scholar* 32 (1963): 553. For discussion of social intelligence, including its cognitive functioning, adaptive usefulness, and probable origins, see Pascal Boyer and H. Clark Barrett, "Domain Specificity and Intuitive Ontology," in *The Handbook of Evolutionary Psychology*, ed. David M. Buss (Hoboken, NJ: John Wiley and Sons, 2005).

16 Richard Dawkins, *The Selfish Gene*, (Oxford and New York: Oxford University Press, 1989), 183-84.

(equal in value, not necessarily in kind) at a later date.¹⁷ When the system functions properly, both parties stand to reap more in the way of benefits than they expend in costs. Illustration of this idea abounds in the *Autobiography*. Business partnerships are carried out most "amicably," he explains, when "every thing to be done by or expected from each partner" has been "very explicitly settled" (91). He further advises readers: "always render Accounts and make Remittances with great Clearness and Punctuality," since a demonstrated attentiveness to contracted obligations is "the most powerful of all Recommendations to new Employments and Increase of Business" (85). In a variety of contexts, throughout his narrative, Franklin emphasizes reciprocity as a cornerstone of social cooperation. Because undetected cheaters can obtain significant benefits, as Robert Trivers points out, cheating behavior is an inevitable hazard in reciprocal exchange. In consequence, humans have developed complex adaptive mechanisms for keeping track of reciprocal transactions and identifying unreliable exchange partners.¹⁸ Franklin accordingly makes great efforts to win a reputation as a reliably cooperative community member. The emphasis he places on integrity is best understood in this context. He argues repeatedly that there is a positive correlation between the exercise of honesty and the acquisition of wealth. Keeping one's word, paying on time, charging fair prices, treating competitors decently: such practices foster lucrative enterprises in the long run, he counsels, because they provide evidence of a dedication to reciprocal obligation. He models his personal style according to these principles too, observing that it costs relatively little to be agreeable instead of contentious, or modest rather than overbearing, but the payoff in terms of universal friendly regard is potentially enormous.

Franklin acknowledges the importance of tit for tat behavior with particular effectiveness when he reports his occasional lapses from its standards. He designates as *errata*, for example, his failure to fulfill the terms of his apprenticeship, his long unpaid debt to his brother's friend Vernon, and the casual breaking of his tacit engagement to Deborah Read. Whenever possible he attempts to correct these asymmetrical transactions, often long after the fact. He indicates awareness of the human propensity to keep a mental scorecard of favors given and received.¹⁹ Knowing that others will remark and resent any unequal exchanges, he goes to great lengths to prove (to readers as well

---

17 Robert Trivers, *Natural Selection and Social Theory: Selected Papers of Robert Trivers* (Oxford: Oxford University Press, 2002), 25.
18 Trivers, *Natural Selection*, 38-46.
19 Ibid., 38; Dawkins, *Selfish Gene*, 227.

as to his exchange partners) that he remembers his obligations and will not, in the long run, default on them. He offers as a role model for readers his friend Mr. Denham, a man who demonstrates his "good ... Character" by repaying "with Interest" debts incurred under an old bankruptcy and for which he already had "compounded" (39). Established in the Colonies, now far out of the reach of "his old Creditors," Mr. Denham might have kept all to himself the "plentiful Fortune" his exertions in America earned for him, but he chooses instead to repair old reciprocal alliances (39). This, Franklin asserts, is the kind of behavior that enhances an individual's reputation and thus is apt to glean long-term social and financial benefits.

Underlying much of his advice is the unstated premise that the social environment he and his readers inhabit is one in which crude displays of dominance—brute strength, reckless bravado, or ruthless bullying—will not prevail.[20] Describing himself as a natural leader, of an "early projecting public Spirit," he learns to exercise dominance subtly, often from behind the scenes (7). Numerous incidents support his claim that a deliberately adopted pose of modesty assists him in bringing many a "Scheme" to fruition (64). To avoid attracting envy or resentment, he learns to keep himself "out of sight," attributing his plans to "a *Number of Friends*" (64). He determines that it is wiser to lead inconspicuously, foregoing overt bids for power or admiration. Those shrewd enough to make "this little Sacrifice of ... Vanity" will find it "repaid" in long-term good will, he counsels (64): people are more inclined to offer praise voluntarily to those who do not demand it. Illustrating the superior effectiveness of gentle persuasion and indirect leadership, he rejects strong-arm tactics, "dogmatical" styles, and self-glorifying impulses (14). It is worth noting that he emphasizes pragmatic results rather than ethical considerations: one should avoid domineering behavior because it is ineffective.

Franklin's views on this topic accord well with Christopher Boehm's analysis of reverse hierarchies, in which "the united subordinates are constantly putting down the more assertive alpha types in their midst." Societies Boehm describes as "egalitarian" engage in "vigilant suppression" of behaviors that might signal the emergence of despotically inclined leaders.[21] With his condemnation

---

20 See Trivers for discussion of "developmental plasticity," which enables individuals to make behavioral choices suited to the immediate environment: "relevant parameters ... differ from one ecological and social situation to another." *Natural Selection*, 46. Pinker's book offers detailed consideration of "the dialectic between organism and environment," which "constantly changes over historical time." *The Blank Slate*, 127.

21 Christopher Boehm, *Hierarchy in the Forest: The Evolution of Egalitarian Behavior* (Cambridge, MA and London: Harvard University Press, 1999), 3, 169.

of power plays and self-glorification, Franklin demonstrates awareness that he lives in a community committed to egalitarianism as Boehm defines it. When he reports his ascension to important positions of leadership (in "every Part of our Civil Government"—"great Things to me"), Franklin is careful to inform readers that these honors are "entirely unsolicited," "without my ever asking any Elector for his Vote, or signifying either directly or indirectly any Desire of Being chosen" (100-101). His community entrusts him with power precisely because he does not appear to seek it, he reports, thus confirming the value of the strategic modesty and restraint he espouses.

An important feature of his commitment to cooperation is Franklin's disinclination to hold grudges or to respond aggressively to grievances. Even when injured or exploited by others, he displays a "remarkable" and "almost total lack of rancor."[22] Sent on a wild-goose chase to London by the false promises of Governor Keith, Franklin permits himself a few harsh reflections on the man who has "impos[ed] so grossly on a poor ignorant Boy," but he contemplates no retaliation (33). He does not seek the satisfaction of a personal encounter in which he might express his anger, for example, nor does he attempt to broadcast his story in an effort to shame or discredit the man whose "pitiful Tricks" have so inconvenienced him (33). He goes out of his way instead to offer readers a dispassionate summing up of Keith's character and accomplishments: aside from his "Habit" of tricking the naïve with empty "Expectations," he is "an ingenious, sensible Man," "a good Governor" who deserves credit for "several of our best Laws" (33). Here Franklin displays an even-tempered reaction to what most people would regard as extreme provocation. Instead of nursing the flames of righteous indignation, which might lead to futile demonstrations of aggression against a high-status individual, he deals practically with the problems Keith has caused him and then moves on. By responding to ill-use with a spirit of detachment, he avoids the high social and psychological costs of revenge. Thus he is free to channel his energies more positively toward the achievement of long-term goals.

He advises readers to avoid becoming embroiled in personal vendettas, asserting that it is best, whenever possible, to convert opponents into allies. "How much more profitable it is," he counsels, "to remove, than to resent, return and continue inimicable Proceedings" (85). When a new member of the General Assembly opposes the selection of Franklin as Assembly clerk, he does not indulge in self-pity or resentment. He foresees that this man is likely "in time" to wield "great Influence": instead of creating lasting enmity by reacting

---

22 Levin, "Puritan Experimenter," 267.

with knee-jerk hostility to a hostile act perpetrated by a person "of Fortune, and Education," he concocts a successful scheme to win the man's regard (84). Clearly he believes that anyone aspiring to rise in status and assume leadership roles needs a strong base of social support. Thus he avoids quarrels, even when provoked, especially with those in more powerful positions than his own. He also avoids being embroiled in hostilities perpetuated by others. He refuses, for example, to print "Libelling and Personal Abuse" in his newspaper, preserving his disengagement from local strife even at the cost of immediate profits (80). Instead of seeking to dominate those around him with exhibitions of temper or hostile threats (a masculine strategy that has proven effective in some social environments), he adopts a strategy of self-control based on long-term calculation of his own best interest. Implicit in his mild-mannered rejection of aggressive methods of self-defense is this message: it may feel good, briefly, to express rage and indulge in righteous resentment, but such behavior is apt to impede efforts to build wide-based community support.

Franklin does depict himself yielding to resentment on two memorable occasions. On the first of these, he dunks his friend Collins in the Delaware River for refusing to take his turn at rowing. Franklin's atypically hostile behavior in this incident expresses his frustration with a friendship that has grown burdensome: unemployed and "sotting with Brandy," Collins has been borrowing money "continually" (26). Giving way to his resentment decisively and aggressively, as he does, enables Franklin to terminate the friendship. He rids himself of a downwardly mobile companion whose presence in his life has become a social and financial liability. He indulges in rancor again when his courtship of a "very deserving" girl is thwarted by her parents, who refuse to meet his demands for a dowry: "I was forbidden the House, and the Daughter shut up" (55). Since the family had encouraged his suit until this point, he interprets their about-face as manipulative. In his view, they are trying to capitalize on his emotional involvement: they assume that he is "too far engag'd in Affection to retract" and that he will, in consequence, "steal a Marriage," thus freeing them from any formal financial obligation to the young couple (55). Rejecting the role of pawn to which he suspects he has been assigned, he ends his courtship forthwith and refuses to be "drawn … on again" even when the family shows signs of relenting (56). David Levin interprets this episode as a failure on Franklin's part to subordinate temper to long-term advantage: "he seems at last to have obeyed his own feelings of resentment rather than the economic interest that might have been served by allowing the girl's parents to re-open negotiations."[23] Levin evidently overlooks the importance Franklin places on integrity in reciprocal transactions. To marry this girl would mean entering into a long-term alliance with her family, an alliance he is unwilling to forge with people who have tried to cheat him. It is not uncontrolled indignation that motivates his behavior, but self-protective caution.

Cooperation is so essential to economic and social advancement that it is sometimes necessary, Franklin acknowledges, to bow to the force of numbers or circumstance. When, for instance, his companions in the composing-room at Watts's printing-house try to collect double payment for the employee "Drink" fund, he learns that he must meet this unfair demand to protect himself from vengeful harassment: "little pieces ... of mischief" directed against him (36-37). The fact that he is in the right, or that his supervisor supports his initial refusal to pay, does not matter: his antagonists outnumber him, and they have the power to make his workaday life miserable. He yields to the majority in this case, concluding that it is "Folly" to be "on ill Terms with those one is to live with continually" (37). He bends himself to majority opinion on a much larger scale, throughout most of his adult life, by suppressing his iconoclastic religious views. Disposed to "doubt of Revelation itself," he becomes a skeptic by the age of fifteen (45). Realizing that his "indiscrete Disputations about Religion" have caused him to be "pointed at with Horror by good People, as an Infidel or Atheist," however, he gradually begins censoring public expression of his thinking (17). In addition to "avoid[ing] all Discourse that might tend to lessen the good Opinion another might have of his own Religion," he makes monetary contributions to "whatever ... sect" solicits his help (65). Such behavior is calculated to create the socially acceptable image of a man kindly disposed toward the religious institutions flourishing in his immediate environment. There are plenty of hints in his book that the inclination to satirize traditional dogma continued to be strong in him, for example, the "little metaphysical piece" he wrote in London, condemned by his employer as "abominable," and classified by Franklin as a youthful "erratum" (34). He is forthright about the trouble he courts with his apostasy, and he accurately senses that candor on this topic will mark him out for disfavor in his community, hindering financial and social advancement. It is his "accommodation with religion," as Seavey observes, that "made his career in business possible."[24]

---

23 Ibid., 265.
24 Seavey, *Becoming*, 57.

In myriad ways, readers observe, the ability to get along with others emerges as a vital first principle in Franklin's program for personal advancement. He presents himself as "a master of compromise."[25] Because success can be achieved only within the social community, it is counterproductive to exacerbate sources of disagreement. Even when he acknowledges that antagonistic strategies may bring short-term advantage, he underscores the more substantial benefits of civility and generosity. In order to squelch competition, he reports, the owner of the only newspaper in Philadelphia—who also "kept the Post Office"—forbids the mail riders to carry Franklin's papers (55). Years later, when Franklin himself becomes postmaster, he determines not to "imitate" his predecessor's "unkind" behavior (55). What, after all, does his rival's mean-spirited action accomplish? It inhibits a new competitor's efforts to some degree but in the long run succeeds only in triggering the "Resentment" of an up-and-coming young fellow-citizen (55). It does not, in the end, prevent the establishment of a second newspaper. Offering examples such as this one, Franklin emphasizes his conviction that the short-term gains from hostile exercises of power are outweighed by the acrimony they engender. To treat competitors unfairly only destroys opportunities for potentially profitable cooperative alliances in the future.

Arguing for the efficacy of reciprocal symmetry in business and personal relations, Franklin presents no anecdotes in which fraud bests integrity in the long run. His position on this point is significant in that evolutionary biologists have observed that deception for purposes of gain is ubiquitous in human societies: the combination of intelligence and language sets the stage for attempted misdirection and deceit of all kinds. Indeed, Buss lists deception as a tactic frequently employed to obtain status or resources.[26] Ranged against the successful implementation of deceit, however, is the powerful score-keeping mentality that is so integral a part of reciprocal exchange. Franklin's reliance on honesty presupposes the existence of effective cheater-detection mechanisms: he indicates that attempts at deception are very likely to be discovered, resented, and punished. Hence his advice to readers encourages reliance on straightforward methods such as hard work and thriftiness; he condemns false promises and duplicitous dealings as ineffective strategies in the quest for long-term success. It is only in the arena of self-presentation that he appears to embrace a moderate degree of deceptiveness. To comply with principles of social cooperation

---

25 Sayre, "The Worldly Franklin," 518.
26 Buss, *Evolution of Desire*, 30.

(such compliance being essential to secure prosperity and reputation, in his view), he is willing to pretend he is more humble—or more orthodox—than he is. He provides misleading cues about his personality, or about his personal beliefs, in order to avoid community disapprobation. Such deception is self-protective in intent, rather than actively exploitative; its goal is to maintain the community regard essential for success in his chosen enterprises.

The conscious calculation with which Franklin crafts his public image, together with his unabashed candor in describing his efforts in this regard, triggers more hostile response than does any other aspect of his self-presentation. Complaints that he is "engaged in pretending to be someone he really wasn't quite" abound.[27] Such exasperation is inevitable, Leibowitz asserts, since "the image of the self-made winner … invites defacement."[28] Often Franklin has been accused of manipulative and hypocritical behavior.[29] Sayre, Ward, Leibowitz, and Griffith address these criticisms, considering the historical, social, and psychological implications of Franklin's persistent role-playing[30] —a tendency that "inevitably casts unsteadying shadows on his sincerity."[31] Sayre observes that Franklin's "receptivity to new ideas, to new possibilities, and to new roles for himself" enables him to succeed in the prevailing socioeconomic conditions.[32] Ward argues that "Franklin's self-awareness" and "lusty good sense" take much of the sting out of his image-building efforts: "his good humor in telling us about the part he is playing, the public clothes he is putting on to hide what his public will not openly buy."[33] Although Franklin bases much of his behavior upon "a commonsense utilitarianism which sometimes verges toward sheer crassness," he demonstrates its efficacy: "it worked. For this world, what others think of you is what is important."[34] Griffith rightly points out that "playing a role … is in itself morally neutral" and, as twentieth-century psychology has demonstrated, all humans assume a variety of social masks.

27　John Griffith, "Franklin's Sanity and the Man Behind the Masks," in *The Oldest Revolutionary*, ed. J. A. Leo Lemay (Philadelphia: University of Pennsylvania Press, 1976), 126.
28　Herbert Leibowitz, "'That Insinuating Man': *The Autobiography of Benjamin Franklin*," in *Fabricating Lives: Explanations in American Autobiography*, ed. Herbert Leibowitz (New York: Alfred A. Knopf, 1989), 32.
29　Ward, "Who Was," 541-53; Griffith, "Franklin's Sanity," 124-36.
30　Sayre, "Worldly Franklin"; Ward, "Who Was"; Leibowitz, "Insinuating Man"; Griffith, "Franklin's Sanity".
31　Griffith, "Franklin's Sanity," 126.
32　Sayre, "Worldly Franklin," 518.
33　Ward, "Who Was," 549, 553, 549.
34　Ibid., 553.

The examples Franklin offers in his own case (e.g., underlining his industriousness, or disguising his pride) are hardly demonic, Griffith argues: indeed, a "quality of innocence prevails in all Franklin's famous 'deceptions.'"[35]

On the topic of self-deception Franklin is astute and articulate, showing excellent insight into the human animal's capacity to construct self-serving arguments.[36] In the much admired passage in which he describes breaking his "Resolution of not eating animal Food," he draws on his own experience to illustrate the biased workings of supposedly rational thought (28). He describes how commitment to vegetarian principles is subverted by appetite. Convinced though he has been that devouring a living being constitutes "unprovok'd Murder," the enticing smell of fish "hot out of the Frying Pan" causes him to revise his thinking on the spot (28). After all, he argues to himself, the stomach contents of the cod show that *they* have been eating *their* fellow creatures; in dining on cod he will merely be imitating this example. He recognizes that he is using his mental powers to justify actions that contradict his stated convictions, and he gently mocks the ease with which he can shift from one line of argument to another simply to gratify his appetite: "So convenient a thing is it to be a *reasonable Creature*, since it enables one to find or make a Reason for every thing one has a mind to do" (28). He detects evidence of similar obfuscating reasoning, moreover, in those around him. On several occasions he observes members of the Quaker and Moravian sects contradicting their professed views, either by allocating funds for military purposes or by giving tacit support to aggressive self-defense: yet they disguise their deviation from principle with euphemisms (identifying gunpowder as *"other grain"*) or delayed protests: "'thee was willing enough that I should stay and help to fight ... when thee thought there was Danger'" (96, 95).

Franklin's evident disdain for deluded thinking manifests itself in a tendency to present his own motives with disarming candor. He approaches marriage, to name a conspicuous example, with conscious acknowledgement of the cost-benefit calculations that enter into the mate-selection process. As Buss's research indicates, people seek long-term partners with approximately equal mate value to their own, based upon attributes ranging from appearance, health, and personality to status and resources. A successful mate search requires realistic appraisal of one's own assets as well as those of a potential

---

35 Griffith, "Franklin's Sanity," 128, 136.
36 For analysis of mechanisms of self-deception from an evolutionary perspective, including origins and functions, see Trivers, *Natural Selection*, 255-93.

spouse.[37] Franklin describes his search for a wife very straight forwardly, in almost precisely such terms. He presents marriage as a refuge from the dangers of "Intrigues with low Women" and venereal "Distemper," as well as an opportunity to obtain the means of discharging outstanding business loans (56). He discovers, to his chagrin, that his perceived mate value is not as high as he himself has assessed it: "the Business of a Printer being generally thought a poor one, I was not to expect Money with a Wife, unless with such a one as I should not otherwise think agreeable" (56). In these few lines he articulates his understanding that marriage is a transaction to which each partner brings a bundle of assets in the expectation of obtaining equivalent value. The only girls whose parents will meet Franklin's dowry demands are those whose daughters suffer from unstated liabilities. The telling insertion of the word "otherwise" in the phrase "such a one as I should not *otherwise* think agreeable" shows his awareness that a sufficiently large economic inducement might be thought to compensate for other deficiencies (e.g., in appearance, personality, health, or social circumstance). Forced to reassess his own mate value downward, he settles for the distinctly liability-laden Deborah Read, whose marital status is ambiguous and whose runaway husband has left debts that "his Successor might be call'd upon to pay" (56).

His business-like approach to marriage no doubt conflicts with the romantic ideas harbored by many twentieth-century readers, but it is undeniably free from self-deceiving bombast. Franklin is not kidding himself about his motives or methods in seeking a wife. Throughout his book he provides evidence that he is determined to avoid falling, unwittingly, into counterfactual reasoning. Indeed, this goal appears to be just as strong as his desire to avoid consciously deceiving others. He admits, therefore, to weaknesses; he reports shortcomings. Although he hopes to persuade others that he has grown humble, for instance, he is careful not to persuade himself to share in that illusion. While narrating the early events in his life, he pauses to note flaws in his youthful behavior and assumptions: his manner to his brother was "perhaps ... too saucy and provoking" (17); the "ingenious men" who praised his adolescent writing efforts probably were "not really so very good [judges]" as he then thought (15); praise "tended to make [him] too vain" (15). Such self-deprecation is intended to persuade readers that he is committed to honest self-appraisal, and it contributes, consequently, to the impact of his narrative.

---

37 Buss, *Evolution of Desire*, 8-9, 11-12, 284-85.

Admitting that he sometimes yields to narcissistic impulses, moreover, he shrewdly forestalls possible criticism: he disarms readers at the outset by admitting that to write down his personal history will "gratify [his] own *Vanity*" (2). Later, having devoted years to a minutely conceived, "arduous Project" for self-improvement, he gracefully acknowledges that his expectations were naively overweening: in the end, he "fell far short" of the "Perfection" he initially imagined to be achievable (66, 73). Readers are bound to like him better for this admission. He increases the likelihood that some may adopt his plan, in fact, by putting forward modest claims for its merits as well as his own. His consistent insight into his own motives and actions, coupled with his refusal to paint these in unfailingly rosy hues, renders him more fully human to his audience: he appears to be admirably "devoid of hokum."[38] Sensing that a robotically ideal model would inspire neither admiration nor imitation, he skillfully uses moments of candid self-reflection to add credibility to his account.[39] In the relationship between writer and reader, negatively framed self-disclosure becomes yet another mechanism for winning trust and support. Just as he seeks allies in his community, Franklin seeks them in the "Posterity" he addresses in his book.

His commitment to strategic alliance as an important mechanism for realizing his ambitions manifests itself in yet another aspect of his history: his enthusiasm for clubs, formal and informal. In his youth, he twice organizes friends into small groups devoted to improving themselves through reading and writing, stipulating regular meetings and specific assignments. Later he

---

38 W. Somerset Maugham, *Books and You* (New York: Doubleday, Doran, and Company, 1940), 82.

39 Seavey discusses in detail the two-part identity Franklin utilizes in his narrative: young Franklin presented in counterpoint to older Franklin; Franklin as author played off against Franklin as subject. *Becoming*, 38-47. Sayre, too, devotes attention to the double point of view in Franklin's narrative (see "Worldly Franklin," 516-23). "In a sense Franklin was writing to himself as well as about himself, developing correspondences between the past and the present," Sayre suggests: "the older Franklin publicize[s] his youth and also demonstrate[s] to himself a continuity between the retired gentleman who is writing and the boy and young man who was already receiving attention from men like the indulgent writer" (*Examined Self*, 17-19). Levin usefully addresses distinctions "between the *writer* of the book and the chief *character* he portrays. "Puritan Experimenter," 259. Examining evidence from the original manuscript, Zall shows how alterations to the text of various kinds (especially deletions and interpolations) reveal conscious intention on Franklin's part: he "shaped the plot, character, and theme" in his narrative to achieve specific purposes. P. M. Zall, "A Portrait of the Artist as an Old Artificer," in *The Oldest Revolutionary*, ed. J. A. Leo Lemay, 53-65 (Philadelphia: University of Pennsylvania Press, 1976), 54.

forms the Junto, "a club of mutual improvement" (47), exhibiting a gift for the "social networking" Buss identifies as one of the tactics used "to elevate ... position within hierarchies."[40] By preparing and discussing essays on "Morals, Politics, or Natural Philosophy," club members expect to gain knowledge and cultivate their intellectual abilities; perhaps, too, they may heighten their ethical awareness or refine their moral principles (47). At the same time that it fosters intellectual and moral development, moreover, membership offers distinctly material advantages: in addition to increasing their ability to influence "public Affairs" for their collective benefit, those belonging to the group are actively engaged in "exerting themselves in recommending Business" to one another (84, 49). Claiming that the club succeeded in achieving both sets of purposes, Franklin demonstrates his conviction that these are mutually reinforcing.

Without any sense of contradiction or hypocrisy, men can club together in the hope of improving both their knowledge and their finances. Indeed, as Franklin's comments on his own long-term project in self-education demonstrate, he regards education as a significant business asset: men with a sophisticated knowledge base, including mathematics, sciences, history, and modern languages, have tools that can be used to obtain financial success and increased status. If he derives other benefits from his prosocial activities—that is, benefits unrelated to building resources and reputation—he does not state them. He emphasizes the utility of friendships and alliances in achieving critical long-term goals, never mentioning companionship as a benefit in and of itself. Precisely because important life goals are at stake, he does not believe in forming cooperative alliances randomly. As he makes clear later in his history, the Junto is a "Secret" society: "the intention was to avoid Applications of improper Persons for Admittance" (84). Although he does not linger on the point, he clearly indicates that choosing one's exchange partners carefully, with an eye toward long-term advantage, is crucial.

Franklin is convinced that the quest for worldly prosperity and social distinction is fully compatible with other, more seemingly idealistic objectives. To be well educated, socially responsible, ethically aware, and congenially cooperative is to magnify one's opportunities for accumulating resources and building status. Those who win broad-based liking and respect, those whose contributions to the community are valued, expand their range of influence and improve their social standing. Such dominant, high-status individuals are better able to acquire wealth than individuals who are perceived to be negligible, unhelpful,

---

40   Buss, *Evolution of Desire*, 30.

or anti-social. Franklin provides numerous examples to support his conclusion that doing the right thing, in terms of interpersonal and community good, invariably proves to be the right thing in terms of unvarnished self-interest. Ward comments on Franklin's "many-sided" nature, arguing that his personality is riddled with "opposites." Here Adaptationist theory proves its usefulness by helping readers perceive coherent motivation in seemingly inconsistent behavior. Thus Franklin is "an eminently reasonable man who maintained a deep skepticism about the power of reason;"[41] that is, he values his own intellectual capacities but is alert to the ever-present danger of self-deception. He retires from his print shop as soon as he can afford to do so, not because he is hypocritical in promoting a "gospel of hard work," but because industriousness is a means of achieving the goal of prosperity rather than an end in itself. His devotion to "the service of others" does not contradict his dedication to "his own advantage and personal advancement,"[42] since altruistic contributions serve to enhance reputation and raise stature. Apparent contradictions in Franklin's motives or deeds such as those Ward highlights assume coherency when examined through the lens of Darwinian logic.

Because a wide array of goals fits together so seamlessly in the world Franklin inhabits, he radiates a happy confidence that efforts in one arena will bear fruit in others. "The *Autobiography* is deliberately optimistic about mankind and about the future," as Lemay observes; it communicates "a philosophy of hope."[43] To devote time and energy to projects such as an improved fire department, more efficient street cleaning, or a broad-based book-lending system must be deemed altruistic, but the altruist himself, as a member of the community, stands to benefit from the improvements he initiates. Franklin celebrates the fact that social animals can serve self-interest and collective interests at one and the same time. Even a penchant for specialized research, like his personal passion for astronomy, is conducive to discoveries with potential long-range benefits to the public.

His famous project for "arriving at moral Perfection" similarly combines idealistic and worldly aims (66). He creates and defines his own list of ethically "necessary or desirable" attributes instead of accepting any pre-existing "Catalogue" (67). The "Virtues" he identifies emphasize socially useful traits, those likely to promote cooperation (67). They are not "the ends that Franklin

---

41 Ward, "Who Was," 541.
42 Ibid., 541.
43 Lemay, "American Dream," 357.

aims at," Lemay accurately points out, but "merely the means of discipline that will allow the ends to be achieved."[44] *Silence*, for example, supports talk that "may benefit others or yourself" (67). *Frugality* authorizes expense "to do good to others or yourself" (67). *Sincerity* condemns "hurtful Deceit" and encourages "just" thinking; that is, it enforces reliably reciprocal attitudes and behaviors (67). Following up on the theme of reciprocal obligation, *Justice* admonishes against "doing Injuries, or omitting the Benefits that are your Duty" (67). *Industry* reinforces the importance of working hard at "something useful" (67). *Moderation* highlights the importance of cooperation even in the face of hostility. In describing this virtue, Franklin underlines his conviction (well illustrated, as already noted, by his own behavior) that it is important not to use moral righteousness as an excuse for aggression: "Forbear resenting Injuries so much as you think they deserve," he counsels (67).[45] Readers observe that several of these virtues mention duty to self—right along with duty to others: Franklin's conception of moral perfection obviously includes responsible self-interest. Like everything else in his life, this project is predicated upon his insight that personal advantage is the wellspring of human motivation. He asserts that it is "our Interest to be completely virtuous," reiterating his conviction that ethical principles are useful and necessary to those who seek worldly success (66). Viewing the matter the other way around, he is consistent in his reasoning, arguing that some degree of material security and comfort provides the necessary foundation for moral behavior: "it being more difficult for a Man in Want, to act always honestly" (79). His conviction that economic advancement and moral advancement are mutually reinforcing goals no doubt contributes to his generally optimistic stance in life.

The intertwining of economic and moral ambition extends itself to his metaphysics. "The most acceptable Service of God," he assures readers, is "the doing Good to Man" (65). Observing the plethora of religious sects thriving in the American colonies, he labels as harmful only those doctrines that "divide us and make us unfriendly to one another" (65). He condemns as "unedifying" sermons whose aim is "rather to make us Presbyterians than good Citizens" (66). In effect, he asserts that social cooperation is the wish of the Almighty. Thus the *Autobiography* brings good news: the principles of reciprocity that ensure vocational success, create favorable reputation, and enhance social status also serve as the foundation of human morality and the core of human

---

44 Ibid., 355.
45 See Trivers, *Natural Selection*, 47, 276.

religious belief. There is no conflict between spiritual and material goals. Readers are apt to be heartened by Franklin's conviction that human purposes, seemingly so multifold and so incompatible, fit together coherently. Confident that it is not necessary to sacrifice one ambition in order to achieve others, he puts forward a view of human aspiration that is all-of-a-piece. This, together with his conviction that honest reciprocity inevitably trumps cheating, helps to explain the upbeat appeal of his book.

The particular historical context in which Franklin writes explains, at least in part, the source of his optimism. In a boom economy it is true to say that every competent, hard-working person can prosper. A rapidly increasing population, together with the availability of cheap and arable land, creates a continually increasing demand for goods and services; hence there is no need to employ devious tactics with competitors. As Franklin notes elsewhere, "the rapid increase of inhabitants takes away that fear of rivalship"; "there is room for them all."[46] Since everyone can do well, there is no downside to choosing cooperation as a *modus operandi*. Clearly the *Autobiography* celebrates some of the chief advantages the American colonial experience offered eighteenth-century Europeans, advantages that have remained an enduring theme in American national identity even though the circumstances fostering them have ceased to exist. His narrative depicts an individual analyzing his environment astutely, particularly its "openness" and "fluidity," shaping his own behavior in response to existing opportunities and constraints;[47] thus he maximizes his success. His book might have proven even more useful to future generations if he had articulated this point explicitly and advised his readers accordingly: *study your environment and adapt your strategies to accommodate prevailing conditions.* Instead he writes as if the environment he inhabits were unchanging and the "conducing Means" he utilizes were universally applicable. Ormond Seavey comments astutely on this point:

> Other writers of autobiography have been overtly aware of the character of their times as they wrote—Gibbon, Wordsworth, and Henry Adams, for example. For Franklin the age is almost entirely excluded from consideration. He was not disposed in the Autobiography to treat the eighteenth century as a distinctive period, burdened with its own limitations

---

46 Benjamin Franklin, "Information to Those Who Would Remove to America," in *The Norton Anthology of American Literature*, vol. A: *Beginnings to 1820*, 7th ed., ed. Nina Baym et al (New York and London: Norton, 2007), 467, 464.
47 Ward, "Who Was," 551.

and proclivities. He was conscious all along of addressing posterity; he would be read not by his contemporaries but by the unforeseeable future. So he was unwilling to suggest that there have been large differences from one historical period to another, for fear of being trapped in a period himself.[48]

Franklin "presents his accomplishments not just as the product of one particular personality but as the natural human response to his circumstances"; throughout his book, therefore, he indicates his "belief in the existence of natural human responses."[49] Because its author subscribes to an idea of universal human nature that meshes well with current Adaptationist thinking, the *Autobiography* lends itself with particular ease to an evolutionary approach. Beginning with the assumption that every individual wishes, if possible, to acquire wealth and status, Franklin urges readers to adopt cooperative strategies in pursuing these aims. Long-term planning, goal-oriented initiative, genuine competence, and persistent diligence—supported by self-knowledge and social intelligence—lay the foundation for eventual success. Consistently prosocial strategies are crucial: being agreeable, getting along, supporting local customs and norms. Public image matters: community reputation must be intelligently managed. Hostile, ungenerous, or resentful behavior nearly always proves counter-productive, as do conspicuous efforts to gain power or prominence. Commitment to reciprocal obligation is essential. Contributions to group welfare, undertaken with careful modesty, embed the individual securely in a social network, while alliances and coalitions, wisely chosen, are efficient mechanisms for creating strong social and business supports and for extending personal influence.

From one point of view the *Autobiography* is "a self-portrait of the Enlightenment man," based upon a number of centrally important eighteenth-century ideas about human nature.[50] The book is a reflection of a particular time and place, and its author interprets his experience in light of values and assumptions shared by his contemporaries. "It points to Franklin's great capacity to respond to the situation in which he found himself and to play the expected role, to prepare a face to meet the faces that he met."[51] At the same time, however, Franklin's history shows an individual confronting

---

48 Seavey, *Becoming*, 38-39.
49 Ibid., 10.
50 Ibid., 38.
51 Ward, "Who Was," 548.

adaptive problems that have characterized human life since Paleolithic times. Like every individual, he is influenced in his choices and in his cost-benefit calculations (conscious or unconscious) by numerous factors: his own inherited phenotypic qualities (physical, mental, and emotional); his physical environment (its resources and threats); his social community (its customs, norms, and power structures); his position (economic and social) in his community. The sheer complexity of interaction among these variables explains why people living in the same time and place fail to display uniformity in their conduct or in their thinking. From the available possibilities, in terms of roles and beliefs, members of a given community will adopt some and reject others, positioning themselves sometimes conservatively, sometimes rebelliously. Certainly the *Autobiography* offers plenty of evidence that not all of Franklin's contemporaries react to the character of the times exactly as he does. "His own version of the age," Seavey notes, "was not the same Enlightenment as Voltaire's or Hume's or even Jefferson's."[52]

If it is useful and interesting to consider Franklin's conception of himself in relation to his age—and surely it is—it is equally useful and interesting to examine it in terms of human universals. The book's central character "sees … and fulfills natural, widely understandable desires."[53] Like every individual, Franklin finds himself situated in a particular cultural environment, an environment he must navigate successfully to achieve evolutionarily crucial objectives. His autobiography tells the story of his strivings as he wishes them to be perceived and understood. A literary artifact conveying its author's interpretations of the human condition, it attempts to render those interpretations plausible in light of readers' own observations of self and society.

---

52 Seavey, *Becoming*, 10.
53 Griffith, "Franklin's Sanity," 135.

CHAPTER 2

Nepotism in Hawthorne's "My Kinsman, Major Molineux"

As its title plainly announces, Hawthorne's 1832 short story, "My Kinsman, Major Molineux," concerns itself with the blood ties of family. The fact of kinship drives development of plot, setting, character, and theme; nepotism is the object of auctorial attention throughout. Hawthorne examines expectations for preferential treatment of relatives, along with the social context in which such favoritism manifests itself. Indeed, community reactions to the privileges and obligations of family relationship assume central importance in the protagonist's experience. Insights from evolutionary biology serve to illumine the workings of this much-admired text, usefully augmenting the already rich body of commentary it has generated over the past fifty years. Its central preoccupations are clearly rooted in principles of inclusive fitness and kin selection.

William Hamilton was among the first to recognize that individuals pass on genes indirectly as well as directly, that is, through the reproductive success of their relatives as well as by means of their own personal reproductive efforts.[1] Siblings and cousins, for example, who raise viable offspring contribute to the total number of an individual's genes represented in the next generation, that is, to that individual's *inclusive fitness*. Thus individuals without offspring (whose direct fitness is zero) nonetheless may leave a genetic legacy in ensuing generations through the reproductive efforts of kin. By the same token, those who do have offspring stand to raise their degree of fitness through the descendents of those to whom they are related.[2] The fitness benefits inherent in the reproductive success of kin help to explain nepotistic behavior, that is, altruism directed preferentially toward relatives.[3] Because of the potential genetic

---

1   Dawkins, *Selfish Gene*, 90; Eugene Burnstein, "Altruism and Genetic Relatedness," in *The Handbook of Evolutionary Psychology*, ed. David M. Buss (Hoboken, NJ: John Wiley and Sons, 2005), 528-29.
2   Dawkins, *Selfish Gene*, 91-95.
3   Martin Daly and Margot Wilson, *Sex, Evolution, and Behavior* (Belmont, CA: Wadsworth, 1983), 45.

payoff, individuals are apt to offer more substantial assistance to siblings and children, or to nieces and nephews, for example, than any they ordinarily provide to unrelated persons. The success in life even of collateral kin can enhance the altruist's inclusive fitness.[4] The closer the degree of relatedness, the more likely investment becomes: for instance, an individual's own children, who share half of each parent's genes, typically will be favored over a sibling's children, who share approximately one-quarter of an aunt's or uncle's genes.[5] The age, health, and socioeconomic circumstances of both helper and recipient also influence the likelihood of aid.[6] Investment in sickly, or post-reproductive, or physically unattractive, or socially discredited relatives, for example, is not likely to pay off in terms of realized fitness. Predictably, too, resources tend to flow from prosperous members of a family toward those less well off, since costs to the giver stand to be significantly outweighed by benefits to be enjoyed by a conspicuously more needy recipient.

Action in "My Kinsman, Major Molineux" is initiated by "hints" of benefits to be conferred by a wealthy, high-status individual upon a relative possessing far fewer resources (224).[7] Inclusive fitness theory explains the Major's motives: this "childless" man lacks direct descendents in whom to invest and, being "elderly," he evidently deems it unlikely now that he will sire offspring in the future (224, 228). Enjoying "inherited riches" and "acquired … rank," he acts to promote his indirect fitness by offering assistance to one member of the family constituting, readers must assume, his closest living kin (224). As "brothers' children," the protagonist's father and the Major are first cousins (224). Although there is reason to suppose that the Major's wealth and status are not altogether new, and that he has for some time enjoyed material well-being exceeding that of his cousin, he does not offer help until late in life when the probability that he will have children of his own has grown very low. The timing of his offer is significant because the assistance he gives to his first cousin's son is unlikely, at this point, to reduce any possible investment in offspring

---

4   Daly and Wilson, *Sex, Evolution*, 48.
5   Dawkins, *Selfish Gene*, 93-94.
6   Trivers, *Natural Selection*, 35; Dawkins, *Selfish Gene*, 95; Burnstein, "Altruism," 541-42.
7   This and all following parenthetical page references are to Nathaniel Hawthorne, "My Kinsman, Major Molineux," in *The Snow-Image and Uncollected Tales*, The Centenary Edition of the Works of Nathaniel Hawthorne, vol. 11, ed. William Charvat et al. (Columbus: Ohio State University Press, 1974), 208-31.

of his own.[8] He would have passed on to a child exactly one-half of his genes, but he shares only one-eighth, approximately, with his first cousin, and one-half of that amount (approximately one-sixteenth) with his cousin's son. Any genetic legacy is better than none, clearly, so that the Major's decision to underwrite "the future establishment ... in life" of a first cousin once removed represents the best he can do, reproductively speaking, at this moment in his life (224).

Arguably, too, the assistance he gives to one member of his cousin's family stands to benefit others indirectly. The Major's cousin has four children, evidently: remembering the home he has left, the protagonist, Robin, recalls an "elder brother" and two younger sisters (223). Now relieved of all need to help his second son find a place in life, Robin's father may be able to do more for his other three children. Robin himself, once established in an advantageous economic and social position in the larger arena of "town," very likely would offer various kinds of aid to his siblings, with each of whom he shares approximately one-half his genes—a much larger percentage than any of them shares with the Major. Robin might help with monetary support for the brother remaining on the family farm, perhaps, or marriage opportunities for his sisters. His generosity to siblings could well exercise a positive impact upon their reproductive success and, eventually, that of their children. Because the workings of nepotism incline an individual whose situation in life improves to pass on some of the benefits gained to close kin, enhanced status and resources tend to be distributed throughout a family in ever expanding circles. In short, an act of altruism directed toward a single related individual has the potential to enhance Major Molineux's inclusive fitness to a degree impossible to calculate precisely.

The Major's motives in choosing Robin as the recipient of his future favors fit well with the predictions of inclusive-fitness theory, as do Robin's family's motives in concurring with that choice. The selection of a male rather than a female no doubt reflects the historical period in which the story is set. Given the circumscribed vocational options for women in eighteenth-century America, Robin's sisters would be less able than their brothers to take advantage of many kinds of opportunities for professional advancement. Probably the most the Major could do for a niece would be to arrange an advantageous marriage. As an unmarried man himself, however, he would be poorly placed to take on guardianship of a young girl with a rural upbringing, to give her the social education and polish necessary to launch her effectively in high-status circles.

---

8   Dawkins, *Selfish Gene*, 89-90.

If she were to achieve prosperity and social prominence through marriage, furthermore, a woman would be less likely than her male counterpart to be able to increase that wealth or to extend the range of her family's dominance. It is not impossible that a particular individual woman might achieve such things better than a specific individual man, obviously; it is simply less probable, on average, that she could do so in the social setting Hawthorne defines.

Given the existence of high-quality male offspring in his cousin's family, therefore, Major Molineux presumably never considers the daughters as candidates for his assistance. Only in the absence of suitable male kin would he be predicted to choose a female beneficiary for his altruism. Of the two sons, the younger is preferred for a constellation of reasons. He is conspicuously available for outside investment because his family has no particular vocational goal marked out for him, nor is his father in an economic position to pay for educational or business opportunities. As a second son, traditionally a position that leaves young men at loose ends when inheritance favors primogeniture, Robin has nothing to lose by placing his destiny in the Major's hands. The elder of the two brothers, in contrast, has expectations: he is "destined to succeed to the farm" owned by his father (224). Although the farm appears to be modest in size and productivity, a well-defined future is secured to the eldest male through the inheritance of land in an agriculturally based economy.

By default, as it appears, the Major's choice falls upon Robin, a boy with no identified prospects in life. The narrator's descriptions of this physically robust and facially attractive young man indicate to readers, however, that the Major has good reason to regard Robin as a promising object of his "generous intentions" (225). With his "vigorous shoulders," "well-shaped limbs" and "well-shaped features," Robin displays the bodily strength and facial symmetry humans worldwide have been shown to prefer.[9] He is said to be "handsome" and "athletic" (209, 217, 218). His "bright, cheerful eyes" give evidence of energy and intelligence, as well as an agreeable disposition (205). In short, Robin's outward appearance signals traits associated cross-culturally with dominance and high mate value.[10] Commanding youth and vigor, good looks and a cheerful temperament, he is in a position to maximize his cousin's investment in him, that is, to become socially and materially successful, to marry well, and to enhance his benefactor's genetic legacy. It is reasonable to suppose that if

---

9 David M. Buss, *Evolutionary Psychology: The New Science of the Mind* (Boston: Pearson, 2007), 144.
10 Buss, *Evolution of Desire*, 38–41.

Robin had not possessed such promising personal traits, he would not have been designated as "rather the favorite" (225). Readers are told, after all, that Major Molineux "manifested much interest" in *both* brothers during his visit to their home (224, emphasis added). If, under such scrutiny, the second son had failed to evince the right kind of qualities, the Major perhaps would have bestowed his favor elsewhere in the family. There is evidence, too, that the Major may be influenced in his choice by some degree of physical resemblance between Robin and himself: phenotypic cues are an important factor in kin recognition, across species, and thus a powerful predictor of nepotistic altruism.[11] The "fair woman" who describes Robin as "the good old gentleman's very picture" may be mouthing empty flattery, to be sure, but the boy is quick to assume that an innkeeper's "superfluous civility" is motivated by detection of a "family likeness" (217, 213). Robin's thinking on this point suggests that similarities in appearance already have been noted (no doubt during the Major's visit to his country relatives) and have elicited comment.

Explanation of the Major's nepotistic motives and intentions occupies very little narrative space in Hawthorne's tale. One of the chief ironies in the final portion of the unfolding plot, of course, is that the projected benevolence never will be realized. Following Robin through a New England town on his frustrated quest to locate Major Molineux and "begin the world" with his kinsman's promised assistance, Hawthorne directs attention toward the social impact of nepotism (225): he foregrounds community reactions to kinship. As the tired and hungry young traveler makes his way through an unfamiliar community, larger and more populous than any he has known previously, he initiates a series of social exchanges that end, without exception, badly. He is thwarted repeatedly in his efforts to obtain directions to his kinsman's dwelling, and the individuals who refuse to answer his inquiries treat him with varying degrees of hostility and ridicule. Baffled by the rude responses his simple and seemingly harmless quest for information elicits, the youth grows increasingly agitated, even belligerent. His efforts to communicate are foiled, as he eventually discovers, by his insufficient knowledge of the community he has entered and his faulty assumptions about the position Major Molineux occupies in its status hierarchy.

Robin's behavior is colored throughout by his conviction that his kinsman is a politically and economically powerful person. He not only expects to find the Major residing in a "worthy" house located in the most prosperous part of

---

11 Daly and Wilson, *Sex, Evolution*, 51-55.

town, he assumes that everyone he meets will recognize the name of Molineux and accord it respect (210). He anticipates, in addition, that announcement of his familial connection to such a high-ranking individual will ensure him a gracious reception. Even though he makes an obviously countrified impression with his shabby, homemade clothing and oak cudgel, he does not imagine that his unprepossessing appearance could or "should outweigh the name of [his] kinsman, Major Molineux" (215). He is confident, rather, that community members' behavior will be guided by adaptations in human nature based on principles of kin selection. He knows, without consciously thinking about it, that people are inclined to guard the interests of those with whom they share genes and that, in consequence, they tend to resent and avenge insult or injury to relatives. He bases his own behavior, and his analysis of the behavior of others, on the corollary assumption that people refrain with particular care from antagonizing the kin of high-dominance individuals, since such individuals are especially well equipped to retaliate. Unarticulated and deep-seated awareness of the operations of nepotism in a social context explains Robin's certainty that even a redneck lad without resources will be treated respectfully if he is related to a person of recognized status.

When the first "citizen" he accosts dismisses him with "excessive anger and annoyance," Robin is nonplussed (211). Why would anyone risk antagonizing the relative of a powerful man like his cousin? Asking himself what could motivate this man, Robin concludes that only ignorance can explain such apparently self-destructive behavior. Because his tormentor seems unaware of the Major's high standing ("I know not the man you speak of," he declares), Robin decides he must be new in town, "some country representative" without knowledge of local personalities and status hierarchies (211). There is irony, clearly, in his assessment of the well dressed stranger (who even wears silk stockings) as a bumpkin who "lacks ... breeding" (211): it is Robin himself who is the rural newcomer and who is basing his behavior upon a profound misunderstanding of local political conditions. Despite further instances of bewildering disappointment, Robin remains supremely reliant upon his connection with the Major. He continues to assume that he will profit from the kinship he repeatedly emphasizes. He begins each social exchange in exactly the same manner, asking on six different occasions to be directed to the residence of *my kinsman, Major Molineux.*

Robin's certainty that the family tie he announces will guarantee him favorable treatment is so powerful that repeated disappointment serves to activate violent impulses in him. His irritable urge to reach for his cudgel (to "smite" an elderly man on the nose or break an innkeeper's head) helps to illustrate his conviction that the townsmen he meets deserve punishment (211). Their behavior violates established norms, in his view, for they are denying the social implications—and obligations—of nepotism. That is, to refuse courtesy to an important man's relative is to repudiate the importance of kinship. The unshakeability of Robin's expectations, even in the face of repeated rebuffs, helps to demonstrate that nepotistic behaviors represent much more than localized social custom; cross-culturally robust, they are rooted in evolutionary biological adaptations. To risk socially and economically damaging retaliation by derogating the relative of a highly placed individual must appear "strange" to Robin, for it defies cost-benefit analysis and contradicts self-interest (215). Meeting a succession of individuals who treat him with unvarnished incivility despite his kinsman's importance, Robin begins "desperately" to wonder if ordinary reality has been supernaturally suspended: he is "almost ready to believe that a spell was on him" (219). On this "evening of ambiguity," namely, some of his key ideas about human nature are confounded by events (222).

The physical environment effectively mirrors Robin's psychological disorientation. Arriving in "the little metropolis of a New England colony" at 9:00 o'clock in the evening, he finds himself literally in the dark (210). Quickly he becomes "entangled in a succession of crooked and narrow streets" which "crossed each other" and "meandered" in labyrinthine confusion (211). He is trapped in a place of baffling complexity, tantalizingly close to an objective he never reaches. Local inhabitants refuse him guidance and manifest unexplained antagonism. Unable to conclude his quest, he seems doomed to roam the streets of this "little metropolis" indefinitely, endlessly lost and confused (210). Skillfully Hawthorne utilizes these external features of Robin's journeying to underscore the youthful protagonist's feelings of helplessness and frustration, along with his social isolation. He suffers from profound dislocation—geographical, emotional, and intellectual. He does not understand where he is or what is happening; his experience in the environment he has entered strikes him as abnormal.[12] Confronted with an apparent dismantling of principles of nepotism, he has lost his bearings.

---

12 John N. Miller observes that Robin's "own conceptual ordering of experience" grows increasingly threatened as he finds himself unable to comprehend the behavior of the people he encounters. When his "rationalizing mind" no longer can cope with the interpretive dilemmas confronting him, his perception of his environment begins to assume "dreamlike" and "phantasmagorical" qualities. "The Pageantry of Revolt in 'My Kinsman, Major Molineux,'" *Studies in American Fiction* 17, no. 1 (1989): 53.

The climax of the story demonstrates that human nature has not changed; it is Major Molineux's status, rather, that is undergoing drastic alteration. Robin has been claiming kinship with a ruler about to be deposed, with a man suddenly bereft of power and influence. In the story's introductory paragraph, the narrator provides readers with a brief history of local resistance to colonial governors (who were, inevitably, appointees of the British Crown), thus preparing readers for the possibility of "a popular insurrection" at any moment (208). Robin's arrival in town on precisely the night when a *coup* is planned—that is, on the very night when his relative will be cast out of his high position—is a contrivance in plot readers accept because it has been foreshadowed adequately and supported with historical evidence. The secret plan to overthrow the Major explains at a stroke the negative response Robin's announcement of their cousinly relationship has provoked all evening long. The ill-natured treatment he has received from the town's inhabitants makes perfect sense to him once he sees his cousin tortured, humiliated, and expelled.

Just as there are benefits to be derived from kinship with prosperous, dominant individuals, kinship with social misfits or outcasts generally incurs costs. An individual's chances to marry well or to join elite groups can be hindered by family members who manifest signs of physical or mental ill-health, for example, or who experience catastrophic financial reverses, or who violate important cultural norms. Hawthorne comments on the potentially damaging effects of family connections in *The Scarlet Letter* when Roger Chillingworth declines to share in the "infamy babbling around [Hester] in the marketplace." Explaining Chillingworth's refusal "to be pilloried beside her on her pedestal of shame," the novel's narrator observes that "for her kindred ... there remained nothing but the contagion of her dishonor; which would not fail to be distributed in strict accordance and proportion with the intimacy and sacredness of the previous relationship."[13] Young Robin Molineux is similarly aware of the disadvantages his cousinship with the newly disgraced Major poses. He is the relative of a man who has lost all status, a man now wholly unable to assist him in any way. Instead of deference, consequently, Robin may expect to be ignored or taunted—as, in fact, he is. No matter how loyal Major Molineux might feel toward family members, he is at the moment incapable of promoting their welfare or avenging insults to them.

Robin's immediate response to the grisly spectacle of his relative "in tar-and-feathery dignity" is to distance himself from the latter's fate (228).

---

[13] Nathaniel Hawthorne, *The Scarlet Letter*, Centenary Edition, vol. 1, ed. William Charvat et al. (Columbus: Ohio State University Press, 1962), 118.

Despite feelings of horrified compassion for the Major ("a mixture of pity and terror"), he is frightened for himself ("Robin's knees shook"), and he allies himself with "the frenzied merriment" of the persecuting "multitude" (229, 230). Joining with the laughter of the mob, he plainly is deciding not to offer aid to a relative in distress. His earlier, barely controlled inclination to repay rudeness with physical violence does not translate into a willingness to engage in combat with a rioting "mass of people," nor does he attempt any verbal defense of the Major (228). Thus he is refusing assistance, as readers must notice, to the very person from whom he so recently anticipated receiving substantial benefits. Many readers are troubled by his passive collusion with the degradation of a kinsman.[14] It is true that the narrator's detailed descriptions of the "majestic" victim's sufferings at the hands of "fiends" seem calculated to evoke empathy for the Major and contempt for his tormentors (230). There is no hope that Robin could rescue the Major single-handedly from an enraged crowd, however, and his self-protective behavior makes good sense from an evolutionary biological perspective. As a nepotistic strategist, the boy undertakes an immediate (and unconscious) cost-benefit analysis, determining that there are no fitness benefits to be garnered from altruistic action in the present circumstances. All too obviously, the cost of any intervention on his kinsman's behalf is apt to be extremely high. At the same time, however, and this is a crucial point, Major

---

14 A large proportion of Hawthorne's readers condemns Robin's failure to assist his cousin as a moral fault, sometimes going on to identify it as a fall from innocence. See, discussions by Alexander W. Allison, "The Literary Contexts of 'My Kinsman, Major Molineux,'" *Nineteenth-Century Fiction* 3 (1968); Arthur T. Broes, "Journey into Moral Darkness: 'My Kinsman, Major Molineux' As Allegory," *Nineteenth-Century Fiction* 19, no. 2 (1964); Michael J. Colacurcio, "The Matter of America: 'My Kinsman, Major Molineux,'" in *Nathaniel Hawthorne: Modern Critical Views*, ed. Harold Bloom (New York: Chelsea House, 1986); Carl Dennis, "How to Live in Hell: The Bleak Vision of Hawthorne's 'My Kinsman, Major Molineux,'" *University Review* 37 (1971); Barbara Fass, "Rejection of Paternalism: Hawthorne's 'My Kinsman, Major Molineux' and Ellison's *Invisible Man*," *College Language Association Journal* 14 (1971); Rita K. Gollin, *Nathaniel Hawthorne and the Truth of Dreams* (Baton Rouge and London: Louisiana State University Press, 1979); Seymour L. Gross, "Hawthorne's 'My Kinsman, Major Molineux': History as Moral Adventure," *Nineteenth-Century Fiction* 12, no. 2 (1957); Marsha Smith Marzec, "'My Kinsman, Major Molineux' as Theo-Political Allegory," *American Transcendental Quarterly* 1, no. 4 (1987); Roy Harvey Pearce, "Hawthorne and the Sense of the Past or, the Immortality of Major Molineux," *English Literary History* 21, no. 4 (1954); Fred A. Rodewald and Neal B. Houston, "'My Kinsman, Major Molineux': A Re-Evaluation," *Real: A Journal of the Liberal Arts* 21, no. 1 (1996); Dwayne Thorpe, "'My Kinsman, Major Molineux': The Identity of the Kinsman," *Topic* 18 (1969); Hyatt H. Waggoner, *The Presence of Hawthorne* (Baton Rouge and London: Louisiana State University Press, 1979).

Molineux himself stands to benefit from his young relative's seemingly selfish calculations.

Just as an elderly, childless man's plan to invest resources in a promising young relative is predicable according to kin-selection theory, the decision of a young man with his whole reproductive future ahead of him to dissociate himself from an outcast and essentially post-reproductive kinsman is equally predicable. Instead of provoking the volatile crowd's wrath by a suicidal show of loyalty, Robin serves his and his cousin's genetic interests more effectively by preserving his own life and by doing his best to win acceptance from the Major's enemies—enemies who constitute a clear majority in the immediate social environment. If Robin lives to reproduce, which he is likely to do even without cousinly help, the Major's inclusive fitness will increase; and this is true even if the Major himself is no longer alive to notice or care. If Robin were to perish in a futile rescue effort, in contrast, his death would reduce the total number of Major Molineux's genes represented in the next generation. Criticism of Robin's acquiescence in the humiliation of his cousin loses much of its sting when considered in light of these evolutionary biological facts. Uncoupling nepotistic loyalty from moral principle, Hawthorne's story demonstrates emphatically that kin-directed altruism is situation-dependent. It shows, too, that the object of individual strategizing is to proliferate copies of genes—and only incidentally to protect the living bodies in which genes temporarily are housed. In this instance, a relative is sacrificed because the cost of helping stands to decrease the fitness of the potential helper. All of Robin's relatives stand to reap fitness benefits from his apparently disloyal conduct, furthermore, not excepting the sacrificed individual.

In addition to exploring the meaning of Robin's behavior toward his disgraced would-be benefactor, the story's climax suggests how powerfully the adaptations surrounding nepotism affect social custom and psychological well-being. The discourteous treatment he experiences all evening long serves, as already noted, to challenge Robin's understanding of familial entitlement. His inability to understand the animus directed toward him contributes in large measure to his discomfort and disorientation. Once he discovers that there is an excellent reason for behavior that earlier seemed inexplicable, he is greatly relieved. Uncomfortable as it is to be the target of second-hand hostility, it is still more disturbing to suspect that human nature itself has undergone some uncanny change. His kinsman's fall from power reassures Robin that the psychosocial implications of kin selection remain in effect. He begins to recognize in the crowd some of the townspeople who earlier mocked or scolded him, and he finds them laughing now at his "amazement" (229). They are curious to see how he responds to the one-hundred-and-eighty-degree shift in his conception of his kinsman's social stature. Under their scrutiny, Robin remembers and reinterprets the evening's adventures, realizing that all along he has been the butt of a terrible joke. The edge of ridicule and malice he felt in so many of his unhelpful encounters was rooted, evidently, in the secret knowledge possessed by his conversation partners: they were in possession of facts which rendered his behavior and his expectations absurd. As "the only person in the story who is not in on the plot," he has been isolated by his ignorance.[15] Recognizing, after the fact, that his hopes of profiting from his cousin's status were based on faulty premises, Robin joins in the general laughter at his own expense. His laughter is "the loudest there" because it is purgative: it expresses the enormous relief he feels at the restoration of normalcy in his perception of human motivation (230). The events of the night are vicious and cruel, to be sure, but unlike his earlier adventures in town they do not contradict his understanding of adaptive mechanisms.

    His relative's abrupt drop in status forces Robin to confront the dark side of nepotism.[16] He began his journey focused optimistically on the benefits to be obtained from kin, but circumstances confront him with potentially problematic, socially costly consequences of genetic ties. He learns how quickly advantageous connections may become liabilities, and how abruptly loyalties—including his own—can rupture.[17] In the space of a few hours, his views of kinship and its community context are decisively enlarged and corrected. Although he does not articulate any remorse for his betrayal of a family member, the hellish atmosphere of the climactic scene (complete with fire, fiends, and uproar) indicates his suffering, even as it demonstrates the overwhelming nature of the community forces marshaled against his cousin and, potentially, against Robin himself.[18] His hard-won realizations lend emphasis after the fact to his initial naiveté, moreover, demonstrating that his easy

---

15 Colacurcio, "Matter of America," 209.
16 Buss points to "the dark side of families," discussing "pervasive conflicts over resources" and other sources of diverging interests in kin groups. *Evolutionary Psychology*, 246.
17 See Burnstein, "Altruism," 529-30.
18 Readers have noted the resemblance of the story's climactic scene to hell, or Hades. See the following analyses for pertinent details: Dennis, "How to Live in Hell"; Alexander W. Allison, "Literary Contexts"; Max L. Autrey, "'My Kinsman, Major Molineux': Hawthorne's Allegory of the Urban Movement," *College Literature* 12, no. 3 (1985); Marzec, "Theo-Political Allegory."

confidence in his own powers of penetration was distinctly misplaced.[19] He is astute enough to recognize and evade advances from a prostitute, certainly, but not sufficiently discerning to suspect some change in the Major's status when mention of the latter's name elicits repeated rebuffs. Politically inexperienced, he appears oblivious to the precariousness of his kinsman's position in a hierarchy subject to frequent and tumultuous reorganization.

Robin fails to realize, initially, that nepotistic altruism functions in a social environment subject to many kinds of alteration, traumatic as well as gradual. Neither family nor community circumstances remain static over time; conditions influencing the wish and the ability to give help to relatives are subject to change. Examples, along with the economic and emotional havoc they wreak, are as common in literary plots as in life itself: people choose and discard partners; they acquire and lose wealth; they win and forfeit status. Alliances shift, and power changes hands. Every such occurrence affects the nature and kind of assistance a specific individual is likely to receive from particular kin. Like the "double-faced fellow" who frightens Robin with his painted visage, nepotism manifests "two complexions" (i.e., costs and benefits) and speaks with "several voices" (i.e., with competing interests) (228, 226). His new recognition of the complex, sometimes troubling interaction of nepotistic logic with environmental circumstance signals an important moment of maturation for Robin.[20]

In the story's aftermath, its young protagonist is helped to a further insight with the assistance of a kindly townsman who offers him companionship during the final events of the evening. This nameless "gentleman" intervenes when he learns that Robin intends to return immediately to his home (230). As his plan for departure demonstrates, Robin assumes that in the absence of help from a well-to-do and influential relative there is no chance for him to prosper in this unfamiliar place. His companion then suggests to him that it possible to "rise in the world" without the help of kin, an idea that appears to be new to the boy (231). Urging Robin to rely on his own efforts, rather than on the generosity of relatives, his informant implies that in this particular environment

---

19 Roger P. Wallins comments ably on the narrator's role in "mocking ... Robin's own view of himself." "Robin and the Narrator in 'My Kinsman, Major Molineux,'" *Studies in Short Fiction* 12 (1975): 175.

20 In addition to readers mentioned in note 14 above, who interpret Robin's experiences as a rite of passage into a fallen or sinful state, there are some who regard his coming-of-age in a more positive light. See, in particular, Charles Dodd White, "Hawthorne's 'My Kinsman, Major Molineux,'" *Explicator* 65, no. 4 (2007); Miller, "Pagentry of Revolt"; Terence Martin, *Nathaniel Hawthorne*, United States Authors Series, ed. Lewis Leary, rev. ed. (Boston: Twayne, 1983).

family connections are comparatively unimportant. As some readers have observed, the story's conclusion appears to valorize socioeconomic conditions existing in the American colonies.[21] In the mid-eighteenth-century, America was the home of countless new and recent immigrants, who generally had left the bulk of their kin behind in Europe. Without access to efficient methods of travel or communication, they were thrown upon their own resources: they survived, in many cases, without much material or emotional support from family. By the same token, they were unlikely to suffer liabilities from the malfeasance or misfortune of relatives living on the other side of the Atlantic Ocean.

When a population contains large numbers of individuals isolated from their kinship networks, networks that otherwise would play a significant role in their lives, the result is a social environment in which the effects of nepotism are to some degree diluted. This should be a source of solace to young Robin, as his new companion divines. A boy with no relatives to help him, even a boy connected to a person reviled and outcast, still may hope to thrive in such a place. This last piece of Robin's initiation into the complexities of intra-familial altruism offers a bit of relief from the painful knowledge earlier forced upon him. An inhabitant of a thinly settled colony, Robin is less dependent upon the wealth and status of his relatives than he would have been elsewhere—in mid-eighteenth-century Europe, for example. Thus the final twist in Hawthorne's narrative underlines the role played by environment in strategic decision-making: the adaptive logic of kin selection remains stable, but the expression of that logic is, within limits, culturally malleable.

Critical analysis of this much admired and often anthologized short story has by and large neglected the issues of kinship and nepotism its author clearly identifies as central to its workings. The story's literary and historical sources have been traced; its mythic, archetypal, Freudian, and political implications have been probed. It has been interpreted as an initiation into adulthood, as a fall from innocence, as a rebellion against Oedipal or governmental authority, and as political, historical, sociological, or moral allegory.[22] Historical context plays

---

21 Comments by Charles Dodd White and Robert C. Grayson are especially relevant to this point: see "Hawthorne's 'My Kinsman, Major Molineux'"; and "The New England Sources of 'My Kinsman, Major Molineux,'" *American Literature: A Journal of Literary History, Criticism, and Bibliography* 54, no. 4 (1982).

22 Roy Harvey Pearce, Peter Shaw, and Robert C. Grayson have undertaken detailed research into pertinent historical sources: see "Hawthorne and the Sense"; "Fathers, Sons, and the Ambiguities of Revolution in 'My Kinsman, Major Molineux,'" *New England Quarterly* 49, no. 4 (1976); "The New England Sources of 'My Kinsman, Major Molineux,'" *American Literature: A Journal of Literary History, Criticism, and Bibliography* 54, no. 4 (1982). Numerous other critics have commented on the historical context

an undoubted role in the story's setting and plot, and there is almost certainly political comment lurking behind its foregrounded themes. Allusion to a variety of sources undeniably enriches its statement and effect. It is suggestively symbolic in many of its features, and thus it points, potentially, to multiplicity of auctorial purpose. At bottom, however, it is exactly what its title promises—a story about claiming kinship. It scrutinizes nepotistic strategies, ruthlessly exposing the inclusive-fitness logic that drives them, along with the cost-benefit calculations that regulate them. Its youthful protagonist must confront the complex variables influencing kin-directed altruism, including the instability of status hierarchies and the terrors of collective violence. Finally, this disturbing narrative identifies what is at stake in nepotistic acts: not human beings but shared genes. Coming to grips with these harsh realities proves traumatic, nightmarishly so, for young Robin Molineux. The absence of auctorial judgment, explicit or implied, directed toward this nineteenth-century antihero underscores a confounding but incontrovertible truth: on some occasions, self-serving strategies may promote the evolutionary interest of a "kinsman"—namely, continuance of his lineage—more effectively than would altruism.

---

and political implications of Robin's experience, among them Broes, "Journey into Moral Darkness"; Joseph D. Adams, "The Societal Initiation and Hawthorne's 'My Kinsman, Major Molineux,'" *English Studies* 1, no. 1 (1976); Miller, "Pageantry of Revolt"; Joseph Alkana, "Disorderly History in 'My Kinsman, Major Molineux.'" *ESQ: A Journal of the American Renaissance* 53 (2007); Gollin, *Nathaniel Hawthorne and the Truth*; Paul Downes, "Democratic Terror in 'My Kinsman, Major Molineux' and 'The Man of the Crowd,'" *Poe Studies* 37 (2004); Peter J. Bellis, "Representing Dissent: Hawthorne and the Drama of Revolt," *ESQ: A Journal of the American Renaissance* 41, no. 2 (1995); Marzec, "Theo-Political Allegory"; John Russell, "Allegory and 'My Kinsman, Major Molineux,'" *New England Quarterly* 40, no. 3 (1967); Terence Martin, *Nathaniel Hawthorne*; Emily Miller Budick, "American Literature's Declaration of Independence: Stanley Cavell, Nathaniel Hawthorne, and the Covenant of Consent," in *Summoning: Ideas of the Covenant and Interpretive Theory*, ed. Ellen Spolsky (Albany: State University of New York Press, 1993), 211-27; and Colacurcio, "Matter of America". Autrey and Sydney H. Bremer discuss Robin's journey in terms of conflict between rural and urban values. "Hawthorne's Allegory"; "Exploding the Myth of Rural America and Urban Europe: 'My Kinsman, Major Molineux' and 'The Paradise of Bachelors and the Tartarus of Maids.'" *Studies in Short Fiction* 18, no. 1 (1981). Literary sources and allusions have been identified and discussed, most notably by Alexander W. Allison, "Literary Contexts"; Mario L. D'Avanzo, "The Literary Sources of 'My Kinsman, Major Molineux,'" *Studies in Short Fiction* 10 (1973); John C. Shields, "Hawthorne's 'Kinsman' and Vergil's *Aeneid*," *Classical and Modern Literature: A Quarterly* 19, no. 1 (1998); and Peter Shaw, "Fathers, Sons." Examples of Freudian analysis of Robin's experience as a search for a father figure or as rebellion against the father can be found in the work of Waggoner, *Presence of Hawthorne*; Simon O. Lesser, "The Image of the Father: A Reading of 'My Kinsman, Major Molineux' and 'I Want to Know Why,'" *Partisan Review* 22 (1955); Frederick C. Crews, *The Sins of the Fathers: Psychological Themes in Hawthorne* (New York: Oxford University Press, 1966); Colacurcio, "Matter of America"; and Fass, "Rejection of Paternalism."

CHAPTER 3

Biophilia in Thoreau's *Walden*

Thoreau's profound affinity with the natural world is central to his writing and has generated prolific comment. His simultaneously imaginative and investigative relationship to nature has been explored using a wide variety of interpretive paradigms, most recently that of ecocriticism, but it has yet to be seriously examined through the lens of evolutionary biology.[1] In particular, the concept of biophilia introduced by Edward O. Wilson promises to shed light on the intensely appreciative attentiveness Thoreau lavishes on the "living earth."[2] Studying the human propensity "to focus on life" and to affiliate with a wide variety of living organisms, Wilson and other scholars have amassed a considerable body of evidence suggesting that this tendency is innate, an evolved adaptation in Homo sapiens.[3] *Walden*, the book in which Thoreau describes his "life in the woods" and identifies nature as the irreplaceable source of human vitality, contentment, and purpose, speaks eloquently to the "biophilia hypothesis" now under study in fields ranging from biology and anthropology to psychology, cognition, and the arts. Recognizing Thoreau's multifaceted engagement with nature as the expression of a human universal enables readers to probe the adaptive significance of his radical reassessment of human purpose. His defiance of social norms, together with his affirmation of global kinship, reflects a coherent set of fitness-based choices.

Conditions prevailing in the ancestral environment served as the context in which biophilia could evolve. As foraging nomads, the earliest humans were fully integrated in the natural world: intimate familiarity with their physical

---

1 Lawrence Buell offers a detailed though "not exhaustive inventory of Thoreau's range of motives and analytical equipment in approaching nature." He notes the emergence of ecocritical and ecofeminist interest in Thoreau's work, making only brief mention of E.O. Wilson, biophilia, and "the evolutionary hypothesis." *The Environmental Imagination: Thoreau, Nature Writing, and the Formation of American Culture* (Cambridge, MA and London: Harvard University Press, 1995), 9, 134, 188, 215-18, 368.
2 Henry David Thoreau, *The Writings of Henry D. Thoreau: Walden,* ed. J. Lyndon Shanley (Princeton, NJ: Princeton University Press, 1971), 309. All citations refer to this edition.
3 Edward O. Wilson, *Biophilia* (Cambridge, MA and London: Harvard University Press, 1984), 1, 85.

environment (e.g., including flora, fauna, topography, and weather patterns) would have been essential to survival. Many cognitive paths, affective preferences, and psychological responses were shaped in the crucible of environmental necessity, and modern humans continue to inherit these adaptations, although opportunities for expressing them have undergone radical modification. Thoreau lived well before principles of genetic inheritance and behavioral evolution were formulated or understood, but he clearly begins with the assumption that "man's relation to nature has a permanent character"; he speaks "to our common … condition as human beings, a condition he viewed as universal."[4] His thinking, as naturalist, small-scale homesteader, proto-ecologist, and environmentalist, proves consistently congruent with the biophilic theory currently fueling research in many disciplines (e.g., biology, anthropology, philosophy, aesthetics), namely, that "the widest valuational affiliation" with nature "has conferred distinctive advantages in the human evolutionary struggle to adapt, persist, and thrive as individuals and as a species."[5]

Habitat Selection

"The crucial first step to survival in all organisms is habitat selection," as Wilson and others explain.[6] It is no accident that Thoreau describes at such length in *Walden* "where [he] lived" and what attracted him to his chosen site. He is interested in other people's choices as well: his curiosity concerning cultures worldwide, ancient and modern, reflects his "paramount interest in man's relation to nature," his eagerness to study humans "in one kind of natural setting after another."[7] Just as nonhuman animals follow "inborn rules of behavior" to get themselves into the precise environment "for which … their anatomy

---

4 William Drake, "Walden," in *Thoreau: A Collection of Critical Essays*, ed. Sherman Paul (Englewood Cliffs, NJ: Prentice-Hall, 1962), 73; François Specq and Laura Dassow Walls, "Introduction: The Manifold Modernity of Henry D. Thoreau," in *Thoreauvian Modernities: Transatlantic Conversations on an American Icon*, ed. François Specq, Laura Dassow Walls and Michel Granger (Athens and London: University of Georgia Press, 2013), 2.

5 Stephen R. Kellert, "The Biological Basis for Human Values of Nature," in *The Biophilia Hypothesis*, ed. Stephen R. Kellert and Edward O. Wilson (Washington, DC: Island Press, 1993), 42.

6 Wilson, *Biophilia*, 106; Michael E. Soulé, "Biophilia: Unanswered Questions," in *The Biophilia Hypothesis*, ed. Stephen R. Kellert and Edward O. Wilson (Washington, DC: Island Press, 1993), 443-44.

7 John Aldrich Christie, *Thoreau as World Traveler* (New York and London: Columbia University Press, 1965), 211.

and physiology is particularly well suited," there is evidence that humans, too, are guided by "a set of ingrained preferences," that in choosing living sites they are "responding to a deep genetic memory of mankind's optimal environment." Archaeological evidence indicates that "for most of two million years" the savannas of Africa served as the original human environment.[8] Its essential features are open space, abundant vegetation, well-distributed trees, water, and lookout points on near-by hills or ridges. To ancestral humans, such a site promised good hunting and foraging, together with water, fuel, and shelter; it included prospect points for descrying more distant game or approaching enemies.[9]

Thoreau offers numerous descriptions of the place he chooses for his "experiment of living," evidence that it contains critical elements of the optimal ancestral habitat (51). He builds his house "by the shore of a small pond" (86). The pond lies "in the midst of an extensive wood," but Thoreau makes clear that this is a reforested area, with smaller, second-growth trees and plenty of cleared ground: "From a hill top near by, where the wood had been recently cut off, there was a pleasing vista southward across the pond, through a wide indentation in the hills" (86). In some directions he is closed in by "the woods which surrounded" him, but in others he enjoys more extensive prospects "over the near green hills to some distant and higher ones … more distant mountain ranges in the north-west" (87). The house itself is located "on the side of a hill" and "on the edge of the larger wood"; a "narrow footpath" leads "down the hill" to the pond (113). There is "a narrow shelf-like path" completely "encircling the pond," as well (180, 179). Describing his daily walks, he indicates that numerous paths and routes connect his home-base to other places of interest to him. In sum, his chosen location corresponds quite faithfully to ancestral preferences. It abounds with animal and plant life, as well as with the critical resources of water and fuel. There are paths to facilitate movement to other places, as well as vantage points from which to survey more distant territory. Much of the open quality of Thoreau's home-site is provided by the body of water at its center: the views beyond and across the pond create important visual space.[10]

---

8   Wilson, *Biophilia*, 107, 109, 111–13.
9   Judith H. Heerwagen and Gordon H. Orians, "Humans, Habitats, and Aesthetics," in *The Biophilia Hypothesis*, ed. Stephen R. Kellert and Edward O. Wilson (Washington, DC: Island Press, 1993), 145-46; Roger S. Ulrich, "Biophilia, Biophobia, and Natural Landscapes," in *The Biophilia Hypothesis*, ed. Stephen R. Kellert and Edward O. Wilson (Washington, DC: Island Press, 1993), 81-82, 89-90.
10 Ulrich, "Biophilia, Biophobia," 82.

He notes with pleasure that in winter the frozen pond supplies him with "new ... routes to many points" and, just as important, with "new views ... of the familiar landscape" (271). In winter, his home looks more savanna-like than ever, with "snow lying deep on the earth dotted with young pines" and covering "the very slope of the hill on which my house is placed" (282).

Thoreau discusses the importance of habitat evaluation and selection at length in the second chapter of his book, "Where I Lived, and What I Lived For." Reporting briefly on his earlier attempt to purchase the Hollowell farm, he comments that people regularly make hypothetical decisions about suitable locations; they are ready "to consider every spot as the possible site of a house" (81). His insight points toward an adaptation that served humans well in the Environment of Evolutionary Adaptation (EEA): nomadic peoples needed to make habitat decisions repeatedly.[11] Thoreau's propensity to exalt the location he finally chooses lends biophilic energy to his discussion of his own selection process. He praises the site of his small homestead because it answers survival needs, enabling him to feed, shelter, clean, and warm himself, but at the same time he pays tribute to its intangible advantages. He demonstrates aesthetic appreciation of the site's features, large and small, pointing out that the natural resources he enjoys are beautiful as well as useful. The pond, for instance, serves him as a water supply, a mode of refrigeration, and a source of edible fish, but he also lauds Walden water for its "crystalline purity," its "remarkable transparency," its uniquely blue-green color, and the "rare beauty" of the "gold and emerald" pickerel that live in it (177, 178, 176, 285, 286).

Because water is such a critical element in human habitats, Roger S. Ulrich reports, "both modern children and adults evidence strong preferences for scenes with water and are sensitive to certain optical properties of water in landscapes, especially glossiness."[12] Singling out the pond for sustained attention—aesthetic and spiritual, as well as scientific—and attaching special importance to the qualities of purity and transparency he observes in it, Thoreau demonstrates precisely this kind of sensitivity. He further glorifies his home by associating it with paradisiacal places and times: the Golden Age, the Castalian Fountain, the Garden of Eden (179). By means of such comparisons he underlines the desirability of the site dramatically, confirming the foundational importance of habitat to the human animal.[13]

---

11 Heerwagen and Orians, "Humans, Habitats," 140.
12 Ulrich, "Biophilia, Biophobia," 90.
13 Sherman Paul discusses in detail Thoreau's use of paradisiacal allusions to invest Walden Pond with divine qualities. "A Fable of the Renewal of Life," in *Thoreau: A Collection of Critical Essays*, ed. Sherman Paul (Englewood Cliffs, NJ: Prentice-Hall, 1962), 109-10, 113-15.

Studying Nature

Wilson argues that we inherit the urge to study the living organisms around us—to learn as much as possible about their physiologies, life histories, and behaviors—from ancestors whose survival depended upon the acquisition of such knowledge. As amateur naturalist, Thoreau demonstrates this particular biophilic inclination straightforwardly. In his close examination of animal and plant life, seasonal cycles and elemental processes, we see at work the human propensity to understand "the natural world as illuminated by the scientific method."[14] A patient and curious observer, Thoreau salutes "the necessity of being forever on the alert," together with "the discipline of looking always at what is to be seen" (111). He reports on the appearance and behavior of wildlife in the area, including (among many others) mice, squirrels, ants, whippoorwills, jays, titmice, muskrats, ducks, and loons. He conducts experiments over time to discover how air bubbles become incorporated into ice; he keeps careful records of freezes and thaws, of high and low water-levels in near-by bodies of water: consistently he devotes attention to "sequence and verifiable patterns."[15] He goes to considerable trouble to refute the myth that Walden is a "bottomless" pond, fathoming its depths from a variety of positions ("more than a hundred" individual "soundings") in order to chart the conformation of its basin (289).

Frequently Thoreau suggests no immediate practical purpose to be served by the knowledge he acquires. He assumes that accumulating a store of information about the natural world, or at least the portion of it he inhabits, is interesting and valuable in and of itself. Such information may at some future time prove useful, as it does for the fisherman whose knowledge of insect life enables him to get good bait in winter. Even in the absence of pragmatic benefits, however, Thoreau communicates his conviction that studying the natural environment is fundamentally important and compelling, that "knowing [other living creatures] well elevates the very concept of life."[16] He shows that

---

14 Wilson, *Biophilia*, 81.
15 Joan Burbick, *Thoreau's Alternative History: Changing Perspectives on Nature, Culture, and Language* (Philadelphia: University of Pennsylvania Press, 1987), 71.
16 Wilson, *Biophilia*, 22. Reviewing Thoreau's revisions to the original draft of *Walden*, Buell indicates that these "show an irregular movement toward discovery, retrieval, and respect for the realm of physical nature whose substantial reality must be honored in the face of the desire to appropriate it for one's own use." "Thoreau and the Natural Environment," in *The Cambridge Companion to Henry David Thoreau*, ed. Joel Myerson. (Cambridge and New York: Cambridge University Press, 1995), 178. Commenting from a biographical perspective, Krutch similarly concludes that Thoreau moved "away from the transcendental

such study demands substantial investment of time and intellectual effort, and it is an investment he makes with unfailing enthusiasm.

The results of Thoreau's exuberant yet rigorous investigatory activities occupy a considerable portion of his book. Increasingly his work has been acknowledged "in mainstream scientific literature."[17] He provides, for instance, "a model of forest succession as an ongoing process with discernible rules upon which reliable predictions may be founded" and demonstrates "other properties of living communities [that] pointed straight toward the modern science of ecology."[18] Consistently he strives "to observe, order, and describe natural phenomena in temporal sequence" and thereby produce "a theory or law that explains a natural event."[19] "*Next* to us," he confidently asserts, "the grandest laws are continually being executed" (134, Thoreau's emphasis). His interest in discovering the principles governing natural growth and elemental processes sets him apart from numerous contemporaries who celebrated nature far less rigorously and systematically.[20] Acquainted with pre-Darwinian versions of evolutionary theory,[21] he demonstrated predictable "receptivity to Darwin's *Origin of Species*," reading it in 1860 and making "extracts from it."[22] "It seems clear," as David M. Robinson asserts, "that Darwin's depiction of the development of the forms of natural life tallied well with Thoreau's sense of nature's inexorable process of change, death, and renewal."[23]

---

assumption that the meaning of nature can be reached by intuition and toward ... scientific assumption." *Henry David Thoreau* (New York: William Sloan Associates, 1948), 175. Walls confirms and supports this assessment. *Seeing New Worlds: Henry David Thoreau and Nineteenth-Century Natural Science*, (Madison: University of Wisconsin Press, 1995), 115.

17 Buell, *Environmental Imagination*, 363.
18 Ronald Wesley Hoag, "Thoreau's Later Natural History Writings," in *The Cambridge Companion to Henry David Thoreau*, ed. Joel Myerson (Cambridge and New York: Cambridge University Press, 1995), 165; Edward O. Wilson, "Prologue: A Letter to Thoreau" in *The Future of Life* (New York: Vintage Books, 2002), xix.
19 Burbick, *Thoreau's Alternative History*, 71.
20 In his rejection of the notion of spontaneous generation, Thoreau distinguished himself from contemporaries such as Horace Greeley, Louis Agassiz, and Ralph Waldo Emerson. Robert Kuhn McGregor, *A Wider View of the Universe: Henry Thoreau's Study of Nature* (Urbana and Chicago: University of Illinois Press, 1997), 190.
21 Robert Sattelmeyer, *Thoreau's Reading: A Study in Intellectual History* (Princeton, NJ: Princeton University Press, 1988), 78-92.
22 Buell, *Environmental Imagination*, 363; Sattelmeyer, *Thoreau's Reading*, 89.
23 David M. Robinson, "Thoreau, Modernity, and Nature's Seasons," in *Thoreauvian Modernities: Transatlantic Conversations on an American Icon*, ed. François Specq, Laura Dassow Walls and Michel Granger (Athens and London: University of Georgia Press, 2013), 78.

Thoreau investigates a physical world largely tamed by human activity and thus radically unlike the EEA in many ways; his predominantly fearless attitude toward nature is keyed, realistically, to prevailing conditions. His exploration of nature includes appraisal, nevertheless, of its potentially deadly powers. Even in the settled countryside around Concord, long rid of bears and wolves, he reports struggles engendered by competition between and within species. He muses on the spectacle of "myriads" of creatures "suffered to prey on one another ... tender organizations ... serenely squashed out of existence" (318). The human race itself would be easily destroyed, he observes, by a small decrease in global temperatures: "a little sharper blast from the north ... would put a period to man's existence" (254). He acknowledges nature's destructive potential, balancing its "less peaceful" aspects against evidence of its "magnanimity" and "abundance" (228, 166). Interpreting natural processes of decay and death from a "comprehensive perspective," he emphasizes "the perpetual energy and dynamism of nature."[24]

Aesthetics and Cognition

Much research in the field of evolutionary psychology begins with the hypothesis that the ancestral environment exercised important influence on development of human cognitive powers, including development of the aesthetic sense. That hypothesis is generally consistent with Thoreau's understandings and assumptions. The exploration of the physical environment to which much of his activity at Walden is dedicated reflects his certainty that "the mind of man thinks and develops by meeting and coming to terms with the world he lives in," that human perceptions conform to evolved "cognitive frameworks."[25] Thoreau articulates such ideas most directly in connection with his appreciation of nature's beauty. Frequently he insists that the aesthetic pleasure conveyed by natural phenomena is as valuable as their practical utility. He gathers wild grapes "more precious for their beauty and fragrance than for food" and cherishes the "brilliant fruit" of the barberry even though it provides "food for [his] eyes merely" (238). He anticipates currently prevailing cognitive theory, namely, that "the mind is innately prepared to receive [the] symmetry and

---

24 Robinson, "Thoreau, Modernity," 74, 78.
25 Drake, "Walden," 90; H. Daniel Peck, *Thoreau's Morning Work: Meaning and Perception in "A Week on the Concord and Merrimack Rivers," the Journal, and "Walden"* (New Haven and London: Yale University Press, 1990), 82.

power" of natural phenomena[26]: admiring the "arching" grace of a local weed, wool-grass, he remarks that plant and animal life supplies "forms which art loves to copy" because of their "relation to types already in the mind" (310). He assumes that our capacity to respond to art is lodged "in our biology and in our relationship to other organisms."[27]

Linking the human aesthetic response to natural designs, Thoreau states unequivocally that "a taste for the beautiful is most cultivated out of doors" (38). Moving his small assortment of "household effects" outside whenever he scrubs his floor, he comments that these "familiar objects" look "much more interesting" in this outdoor setting (113). This leads him to speculate that "these forms" (vines, leaves, pine cones, and the like) "came to be transferred to our furniture" as cherished embellishment because once we lived "in their midst" (113). He argues that we choose natural shapes as ornaments because of our long history of dependence on nature for everyday subsistence, that our aesthetic preferences are shaped by our involvement, as a species, with nature. Such comments are congruent with the theory that immersion in the ancestral environment exercised important influence on development of human psychological responses.

Universal Kinship

Foundational to Thoreau's natural philosophy is the conviction that he is biologically connected to all life forms. He expresses in the language of his day the idea, soon to be articulated systematically by Darwin, that humans are neither central nor special as a species, but part of a vast, global network of kinship. Without knowing the precise mechanisms of inheritance and variation, or of evolution by natural selection over time, he insists that he is organically related to everything on earth. Geneticists in succeeding generations have proven the validity of that claim: all life on the planet is descended from single-celled ancestors, and a verifiable genetic relationship therefore links even seemingly distant species.[28] Thoreau rejoices in the fact of this profound and extensive connectedness, asking rhetorically, "am I not partly leaves and vegetable mould myself?" (138). Such declaration of kinship with the vegetable kingdom is not mere hyperbole, a pantheistically inspired figure of speech: throughout

---

26 Wilson, *Biophilia*, 61.
27 Ibid., 63.
28 Richard Dawkins, *River Out of Eden: A Darwinian View of Life* (New York: Harper Collins, 1995), 11-12.

Walden he points implicitly toward the biophysical basis of the interconnections he describes. Lawrence Stapleton distinguishes Thoreau from Emerson and other nineteenth-century transcendentalists in this respect, noting that while his contemporaries base their philosophy upon "the Platonizing idea of correspondences," Thoreau maintains a naturalist's focus on "the minute, the unseen or unnoticed resemblances or differences among concrete objects."[29] Consistently he establishes "a solid bottom," a physical basis, for the "cosmic empathy" he expresses (330).[30]

Thoreau's eccentric views on human agriculture can best be understood in the context of cross-species kinship. Instead of lamenting weather conditions unfavorable to farming, he takes an ecosystemic perspective, observing that if flooding rains should "cause the seeds to rot in the ground and destroy the potatoes in the low lands," there will be no cause to despair (131). Though destructive to potatoes, such rain "would still be good for the grass on the uplands, and, *being good for the grass, it would be good for me*" (138, emphasis added). He is convinced, clearly, that he has a stake in the survival of wild grasses: his well-being is bound up with theirs. Although he initially characterizes woodchucks as "enemies" and his efforts to eradicate weeds as "a long war," gradually he arrives at far less anthropocentric views (155, 161). The bean plants he has sown and hoed "grow for woodchucks partly," he concludes, and his labor as a gardener has "results which are not harvested by [him]" but, rather, by members of other species (166).[31] He similarly declines to value cultivated plants over wild ones. He regards the agricultural revolution with ambivalence for many reasons, not least because it is founded on the faulty premise of human supremacy. The fruits and vegetables tended so assiduously by farmers are not intrinsically more valuable than the indigenous plant life they replace, that "rich and various crop only unreaped by man" (158). Thoreau does not hesitate to assert that all life forms have equal claim on the elemental resources critical to plant growth, such as sun, rain, and nutrient-rich soil. "The sun looks on our cultivated fields and on the prairies and forests without distinction," he points

---

29 Lawrence Stapleton, "Introduction," in *Thoreau: A Collection of Critical Essays*, ed. Sherman Paul (Englewood Cliffs, NJ: Prentice-Hall, 1962), 167.
30 Christie, *Thoreau as World Traveler*, 201.
31 This recognition of kinship with woodchucks does not stop Thoreau from later announcing a desire to "seize and devour" one "raw" (210). He explains his urge as principally a symbolic one: he is "hungry" to assimilate the "wildness" the animal embodies (210). Examining some twenty references to woodchucks in *Walden*, John Bird concludes that "respect" for this animal predominates. "Gauging the Value of Nature: Thoreau and His Woodchucks," *The Concord Saunterer*, n.s., 2, no. 1 (1994), 141.

out; "in his view the earth is all equally cultivated like a garden" (166). If wild creatures eat his crops, or if his crops should die and be replaced by weeds, "whose seeds are the granary of the birds," his loss will be compensated by the sustenance gained by other, non-human, animals whose survival is as important as his own (166).

Thoreau is motivated, evidently, by the principle now defined as inclusive fitness. As W. D. Hamilton was the first to demonstrate, individual fitness cannot not be measured merely by personal, or direct, reproductive success (i.e., number of offspring); rather, it includes the reproductive success of all those sharing genes with the target individual.[32] The reproductive efforts of siblings, cousins, and collateral kin can raise appreciably the total number of genes an individual passes on to the next generation. Nepotistic behavior results from these facts: throughout the animal kingdom, individuals tend to help relatives, exhibiting a wide range of altruistic propensities, because assistance to relatives fosters the survival of shared genes. Thoreau communicates an evolutionarily expansive version of this principle when he identifies members of non-human species as kin: their fitness contributes to his. His conviction that "what is good for" other living things is also good for him demonstrates a highly developed sense of what Wilson refers to as "the phylogenetic continuity of life" and demonstrates allegiance to a central principle of biophilia, namely, that "we are literally kin to other organisms."[33] "From a molecular point of view," as Richard Dawkins emphasizes, "all animals are pretty close relatives of one another and even of plants."[34]

Since "the relation between man and nature is reciprocal," it follows that one need not rely solely on members of one's own species to enjoy nepotistic benefits of community and companionship.[35] As a naturalist, Thoreau investigates "interdependencies among species" and "mutual dependencies that made nature work."[36] As a writer, he employs a variety of rhetorical devices to lend vivid immediacy to an idea that would be articulated by later generations of ecologists, namely, "all of the environment is a social environment;" there is "continuous reciprocity between humans and nature."[37] Thoreau moves to the woods,

---

32 Daly and Wilson, *Sex, Evolution*, 28-32.
33 Wilson, *Biophilia*, 130.
34 Dawkins, *River*, 12.
35 Stapleton, "Introduction," 171.
36 McGregor, *A Wider View*, 4.
37 Aaron Katcher and Gregory Wilkins, "Dialogue with Animals: Its Nature and Culture," in *The Biophilia Hypothesis*, ed. Stephen R. Kellert and Edward O. Wilson (Washington, DC: Island Press, 1993), 187; Kellert, "The Biological Basis," 54.

he tells readers, because he is "better known" there (19). He develops an "intimate ... acquaintance" with the weeds he eradicates from his garden; he shares his habitat with "the squirrel tribe" (161, 65). He hikes many miles "to keep an appointment with a beech-tree," and pine needles "befriend" him (265, 132). He packs his book with instances of personification such as these, reporting on his daily involvement with nonhuman others and conveying a "sense of the neighborliness of nature."[38] As Thomas Pughe comments, such "anthropomorphic tropes ... may figure, even epitomize, our inevitably intermingled and interdependent relations" with nonhuman nature.[39]

Affiliating with life forms commonly regarded as insentient, like beech trees or pigweed, Thoreau indulges in humorous hyperbole to celebrate planet-wide familial ties, using metaphor "to relay not merely intellectual, but total experience," to combine "scientific interest, environmental care, and aesthetic appreciation."[40] He lends human traits to elemental forces and processes as well as to plants and animals, rejoicing in "the friendship of the seasons," or finding his loneliness assuaged by the other planets in the Milky Way (131, 133). At times he reverses his strategy, describing human nature or human occupations in terms of animal behavior, plant growth, or seasonal cycles. He compares the cellar of his house to the woodchuck den it replaces, for example, emphasizing common features in the shelters constructed by members of disparate species: "the house is still but a sort of porch at the entrance of a burrow" (45). He enjoys having time for his "thoughts ... to take root and unfold themselves" organically, like a sprouting seed (132). Metaphorically yoking human and nonhuman phenomena, he attempts to persuade readers that humans are neither unique nor isolated in the ecosystem. Even in apparently "wild" and "dreary" surroundings, he is supported by "the presence of something kindred" (13).

---

38 Buell, *Environmental Imagination*, 211.
39 Thomas Pughe, "Brute Neighbors: The Modernity of a Metaphor," in *Thoreauvian Modernities: Transatlantic Conversations on an American Icon*, ed. François Specq, Laura Dassow Walls and Michel Granger (Athens and London: University of Georgia Press, 2013), 256. Scott McVay defends the anthropomorphism often associated with biophilic discussion—and obviously inherent in many of the rhetorical devices Thoreau favors—as a legitimate component of "acceptable science." He contends that "any kind of deeper truth about the fellow organisms with whom we share space" requires some degree of "intimacy in observation and reporting." Prelude: "A Siamese Connexion with a Plurality of Other Mortals," in *The Biophilia Hypothesis*, ed. Stephen R. Kellert and Edward O. Wilson (Washington, DC: Island Press, 1993), 17.
40 Drake, "Walden," 78; Pughe, "Brute Neighbors," 254.

Walden Pond itself serves as the special focus of Thoreau's figurative language: persistently he invests the pond with human characteristics. It is his "neighbor" and "bed-fellow" (86, 272); he refers to its "face," "lips," "beard," "skin," "lashes," and "brows" (86, 311, 181, 294, 186). He likens the annual freezing and thawing of its waters to sleep or hibernation: in winter it "closes its eyes and becomes dormant," and in spring it "stretch[es] and yawn[s] like a waking man" (282, 301). It commands the power, Thoreau asserts, of expressive emotion ("glee," "joy and happiness") and of mental activity: "liquid thought is welling up to its surface" (311,193). He endows it, finally, with metaphysical awareness, describing the annual thawing of the pond's water in terms of spiritual regeneration: "Walden was dead and is alive again" (311). At the core of his book readers encounter "an almost animistic evocation of Walden as a living presence."[41] In portraying his central symbol, Thoreau persistently harnesses the force of metaphor to compel recognition of far-flung family, to insist upon equivalencies and commonalities linking the human animal with other portions of the biosphere.

The Ecosystem as Living Entity

Inclusive fitness theory typically predicts that affiliative and nepotistic tendencies will be correlated with genetic closeness: the more genes shared, the stronger the loyalties inspired. As discussion thus far has made clear, Thoreau operates according to a generous construction of kinship, egalitarian in spirit, one not regulated by mathematical calculations of relatedness. In Paleolithic populations, moreover, as researchers have noted, mortality rates would have left individuals, on average, with "many more distant kin than nuclear kin." This fact would have fostered "increased mutualism or strong reciprocity among distant kin," including an adaptive reliance on "the metaphor of kinship."[42] Humans regularly expand their perception of kinship networks, in fact, when they begin thinking of a coalition, tribe, or nation as a *fraternity* or *brotherhood*. A related phenomenon is that of fictional or ascribed kinship, which anthropologists encounter world-wide. It is necessary only to extend an appreciation of relatedness slowly farther, step by step, to acknowledge even distant life forms

---

41 Buell, *Environmental Imagination*, 208.
42 Jeffrey A. Kurland and Steven J. C. Gaulin, "Cooperation and Conflict Among Kin," in *The Handbook of Evolutionary Psychology*, ed. David M. Buss (Hoboken, NJ: John Wiley and Sons, 2005), 457.

as kin.[43] We may begin with "selfish genes," but we can utilize genetic 'selfishness' to widen rather than to narrow the range of our affiliations; we can extend our nepotistic loyalties "progressively outward until we end with the whole Earth."[44] From the perspective of evolutionary time, moreover, a narrow view of inclusive fitness makes little sense: "selves survive a little while; but all the while, really, the ecosystem in which the self lives is the fundamental unit of development."[45] Richard Dawkins describes "the river of DNA flowing down through the generations, only temporarily housed in particular bodies."[46] Taking the long view, "it seldom matters whether … genes are inside me, inside my cousin, or inside a chimpanzee. Indeed, it may not matter whether they are inside me or inside an oyster or an ant."[47] This is precisely Thoreau's point when he cheerfully relinquishes his crop to woodchucks, birds, or worms: "ecocentrism replaces egocentrism."[48] He subscribes to the notion that "selves have intertwined destinies with the landscapes they inhabit."[49] It was obvious to Thoreau, as Krutch maintains, "that man was a part of nature, not nature a part of man … so that the merely human was swallowed up in the natural."[50]

Thoreau's pronounced propensity to assign feeling and intention to inorganic phenomena—water, ice, soil, rain, sun, wind—helps to demonstrate the holistic quality of his thinking. One species "merges into another, groups melt into ecological groups until the time when what we know as life meets and enters what we think of as non-life: barnacle and rock … and rain and air."[51] His observations as a naturalist lead Thoreau to reflect upon resemblances he discovers across three seemingly disparate kingdoms. Waxing eloquent over the multitudinous shapes created in the flowing "sand and clay" of a thawing sandbank, he perceives essential commonalities in a wide variety of animal, vegetable, and mineral forms (304). He is struck in particular by the insight

---

43 For detailed discussion of the implications of planet-wide extended kinship, see Gordon M. Burghardt and Harold A. Herzog, Jr., "Beyond Conspecifics: Is Brer Rabbit Our Brother?" *BioScience* 30 (1980).
44 Holmes Rolston III, "Biophilia, Selfish Genes, Shared Values," in *The Biophilia Hypothesis*, ed. Stephen R. Kellert and Edward O. Wilson (Washington, DC: Island Press, 1993), 381.
45 Rolston, "Biophilia, Selfish Genes," 394; "Across a thousand years, the approximate threshold interval of *evolutionary time*," Wilson points out, "individuals lose most of their relevance as biological units." *Biophilia* 43-44, Wilson's emphasis.
46 Dawkins, *River*, 28.
47 Rolston, "Biophilia, Selfish Genes," 407.
48 Buell, *Environmental Imagination*, 155.
49 Rolston, "Biophilia, Selfish Genes," 407.
50 Krutch, *Henry David Thoreau*, 186.
51 Kellert, "The Biological Basis," 55.

that a single "principle," or design, appears to serve as the basis for thousands of structures, animate and inanimate. "Citing foliation in all its forms as the essential type of natural growth," he exults to witness how the "idea" of the leaf repeats itself with variations in a bird's wing, a coral plant, a leopard's paw, a bird's foot, and an ice crystal, as well as in a human hand, ear, or lung (306).[52] "Lava-like," representations of all these forms are "bursting out" in ever shifting patterns of sand and clay: the base plan of all organic design seems vitally manifest in the soil itself (305). He puts forward a proposition resembling the Gaia hypothesis now garnering attention from ecologists: "all living beings together (the biota) behave as a single integrated system with properties more akin to systems of physiology than those of physics."[53]

Engaging in linguistic playfulness and baroque elaboration throughout his much-admired encomium to the sandbank, Thoreau grounds his conceit, like his insights, in observed physical similarities.[54] "While he does not speak the emerging language of natural selection or the modern language of biocentrism," Robinson comments, "he is clearly beginning to conceptualize both these perspectives and consider their implications."[55] Saluting the

---

52   Hoag, "Thoreau's Later Natural History," 157.
53   Dorion Sagan and Lynn Margulis, "God, Gaia, and Biophilia," in *The Biophilia Hypothesis*, ed. Stephen R. Kellert and Edward O. Wilson (Washington, DC: Island Press, 1993), 352. The idea of Gaia was initially put forward by James Lovelock in *Gaia: A New Look at Life on Earth* (1979). Rpt. with new Preface, (New York: Oxford University Press, 1987). Leonard M. Scigaj and Nancy Craig Simmons point out that Thoreau's insistence on "the biocentric value of all life" proves "surprisingly congruent with the central tenets of ecofeminism" as well. "Ecofeminist Cosmology in Thoreau's *Walden*." *Interdisciplinary Studies in Literature and Environment* 1, no. 1 (1993): 121, 124.
54   This rich passage has generated comment from a variety of perspectives—psychological, historical, literary, linguistic, scientific, and religious; Gordon V. Boudreau ably summarizes and categorizes many of these in *The Roots of "Walden" and the Tree of Life* (Nashville, TN: Vanderbilt University Press, 1990), see 125-31. Andrew McMurry addresses the passage at some length, emphasizing that "for Thoreau, what counts is the *aliveness* of the whole planet." *Environmental Renaissance: Emerson, Thoreau, and the Systems of Nature* (Athens and London: University of Georgia Press, 2003), 135-40. According to Max Oelschlager, the passage illustrates Thoreau's intuitive grasp of "fundamental evolutionary principles," namely, that "complex forms evolve from simpler ones." *The Idea of Wilderness* (New Haven: Yale University Press, 198), 164. Leo Marx discusses Thoreau's "endless creation of new forms" here in the context of pastoral defiance of the machine age. *The Machine in the Garden: Technology and the Pastoral Ideal in America* (London and Oxford: Oxford University Press, 1964), 262. Most intriguingly of all, perhaps, Boudreau points out that the passage seems to anticipate the final paragraph in *The Origin of Species*, where Darwin examines the teeming life represented on a single overgrown bank, noting the different yet interdependent "forms" it assumes. *Roots of "Walden,"* 127-28.
55   Robinson, "Thoreau, Modernity," 74.

diversity emerging from underlying unity, he goes on to personify "the earth": "inwardly" it "labors with the central "idea" of leaf (306). Taking a panoramic view, as if he were looking down at the planet's surface, he concludes that such a perspective would reveal "still vaster leaves," with rivers forming the veins (307). The planet as a whole appears to be a macroscopic version of the shape that is everywhere manifest in individual earthly phenomena: "Gaia is simply symbiosis seen from space," the "global life and environment, the planetary surface seen as body rather than place," Sagan and Margulis similarly contend.[56] Thoreau regards the planet itself as a living entity: "the earth is all alive and covered with papillae" (302). He presents a modern view of the ecosystem, which is "as real, as ultimate, as any genetic self."[57]

Arguing decisively against an anthropocentric approach to existence, Thoreau reminds readers that "the universe is wider than our views of it" (320). Even the planet we inhabit is but one in "a system of earths" (10). From first to last he urges us to make peace with our personal insignificance, to recognize the "somewhat inconsequential roles" humans play "in the larger drama of which they are a part."[58] Asking us to hoe our beans in the "light" of cosmic vastness (10), he demonstrates a "philosophical humility largely absent from the predominant religions and philosophies of the day."[59] "All life, he feels, is one, and it is to the All, not merely the small human segment, that he wishes to belong."[60] The recognition of universal interconnectedness can prove liberating, furthermore, because it reduces the importance of direct fitness. Since so much of the DNA in any one individual, even that in members of now extinct species, is passed on collaterally by all manner of distant relatives, the earth's inhabitants, past, present, and future, in effect belong to a single, enormous gene pool.[61] Regarded as a multifaceted yet coherent whole, nature manifests an "unequalled fertility," Thoreau avers, and thus "is likely to outlive all her children" (137, 138). He rejoices in the reproductive success of his multitudinous kin, expressing implicit contentment with the high degree of inclusive fitness that he, like every organism on earth, inevitably enjoys.

---

56 Sagan and Margulis, "God, Gaia," 352.
57 Rolston "Biophilia, Selfish Genes," 396.
58 Robinson, "Thoreau, Modernity," 80. In her analysis of Thoreau's response to emerging evolutionary science, Nina Baym comes to different conclusions, arguing that Thoreau discerned and repudiated the negative implications of Darwin's work: he refused to accept "the irrelevance of man in the universe." "Thoreau's View of Science," *Journal of the History of Ideas* 26, no. 2(1965), 234.
59 Robinson, "Thoreau, Modernity," 80.
60 Krutch, *Henry David Thoreau*, 188.
61 Dawkins, *River*, 27-29; Wilson, *Biophilia* 43-44.

Taking this "wider ... view" of lineage enables Thoreau to assume a nonchalant attitude toward personal fitness and, significantly, toward ensuing competition in the social arena (320). Struggles to accumulate resources and achieve status may be motivated by proximate goals of various kinds, but the ultimate goals such struggles serve are those of direct fitness: mating and reproduction. Individuals who succeed in building wealth and reputation enjoy enhanced mating opportunities and command means to rear offspring successfully.[62] Thoreau's indifference to individual reproductive success, which reflects his perception of the extensive kinship network linking all organic life, permits him to reject "the kind of life men praise and regard as successful" (19). He need not seek to acquire elite employment, prestigious alliances, luxurious furniture, imported foods, or fashionable apparel. From the perspective of "ecological and then evolutionary change," as Wilson observes, moment-by-moment concerns of "biography and political events ... shrink steadily in proportion."[63] The sources of Thoreau's disaffection with the materialism, technophilia, and professionalism dominating mid-nineteenth-century America are many-stranded, inevitably, but his biocentric analysis of the human condition provides a firm foundation for his stalwart rejection of social rewards and encumbrances.[64]

Inevitably, his disparagement of community values includes unstated defiance of typical life-history assumptions: he pays scant attention in *Walden* to mating and parenthood, issues generally regarded as central to human endeavor. In his encounter with John Field's large and hungry family, he indicates that his principles for living might well be consistent with providing for dependents, but he does not tackle the question directly.[65] Biographers have sought to account for his silence on this topic, speculating that romantic disappointment, homoerotic yearnings, or sexual squeamishness, for instance, might account for it.[66] Such explanations, whether true or not, fail to place Thoreau's

---

62 Buss, *Evolution of Desire*: 22-27, 46-48, 59, 285-86.
63 Wilson, *Biophilia*, 144.
64 See discussions of Thoreau's economic philosophy by Leo Stoller and Michael T. Gilmore. Leo Stoller, *After "Walden": Thoreau's Changing Views on Economic Man* (Stanford, CA: Stanford University Press, 1957); Michael T. Gilmore, "*Walden* and the 'Curse of Trade,'" in *Critical Essays on Henry David Thoreau's Walden*, ed. Joel Myerson (Boston: G.K. Hall, 1988).
65 Krutch notes that "there is no evidence to suggest that Thoreau ... advocated universal celibacy." Thoreau acknowledges that a person with dependents "would need more than he did ... but such a man would also ... need less than he thought." *Henry David Thoreau*, 88.
66 Llewelyn Powys, for one, suggests that Ellen Sewell's rejection of Thoreau's marriage proposal "helped to dry up his already somewhat sapless nature." "Thoreau: A Disparagement," in *Critical Essays on Henry David Thoreau's "Walden,"* ed. Joel Myerson (Boston: G.K. Hall, 1988), 55. Richard Bridgman also comments on Thoreau's possible sexual timidity, "his

attitude toward marriage and children in the larger context of the "kindred-ship ... in Nature" he consistently celebrates (159). As Joseph Wood Krutch justly remarks, "Thoreau himself would have been astonished at the suggestion that a passion for nature was inexplicable except on the theory that it substituted for some other passion which had been frustrated."[67] He constructs no argument against individual reproductive efforts; he adopts a perspective, rather, from which these may come to seem relatively unimportant. Given the universal relatedness everywhere manifest in the natural world, genetic continuity is inevitable. It is planetary life as whole that is valuable, Thoreau suggests, rather than the continued existence of any one individual or species. The task of eco-proliferation is so broadly shared that the contribution of any one organism is miniscule. Affiliating with the "great central life" of the planet, he construes family and, by extension, fitness, in the widest possible sense (309).

In considering whether such insistence on universal kinship and corresponding disinterest in personal fitness might prove to be adaptive, prevailing environmental conditions must be taken into account. During the nineteenth century, the human population was experiencing such unprecedented growth that the species, together with its technological modifications of habitat, was beginning to threaten the well-being of the planet. Thoreau lived and wrote at a moment when it became possible for persons with scientific knowledge and imaginative sensibilities to realize the threat humans posed to the natural world and, concomitantly, to their self-interest as a species.[68] In the decades since his death, human activity has precipitated wide-scale extinctions, polluted groundwater, lakes, and oceans, and punctured the protective layer of ozone. Meanwhile human population growth has continued to accelerate. Modern environmentalists consequently support principles that elevate planetary fitness above personal fitness, emphatically endorsing the point of view Thoreau adopted on the basis of evidence available in his day.[69] Rolston, for one, argues that our species needs to be "released from an ethics that is nothing but selection for maximum

---

inability to come to terms with the quite powerful feelings that were tormenting him." *Dark Thoreau* (Lincoln and London: University of Nebraska Press, 1982), 119. Walter Harding points out that Thoreau "delighted in jibing at women and at marriage," speculating that he "was able to sublimate his love for the opposite sex in a worship of the world of nature." *The Days of Henry Thoreau*, rev. ed. (Princeton, NJ: Princeton University Press, 1982), 110, 104.

67 Krutch, *Henry David Thoreau*, 33.
68 See Walls, *Seeing New Worlds*, 187-88.
69 Edward O. Wilson, "Biophilia and the Conservationist Ethic," in *The Biophilia Hypothesis*, ed. Stephen R. Kellert and Edward O. Wilson (Washington, DC: Island Press, 1993), 39-40; Kellert, "The Biological Basis," 65.

production of human offspring" in order to affirm "biophilia and concern for environmental integrity."[70] From the perspective of twenty-first-century readers, a nepotism divorced from egocentric weighting looks more adaptive than "fanciful."[71] Determined to "live deliberately," Thoreau in effect proposes a conscious reconfiguring of evolved mechanisms for kin selection (90).

Competition and Conservation

A sense of cosmic kinship tends to reduce the intensity of competition between individuals and between species, at the same time fostering a conservationist spirit.[72] Thoreau clearly is committed to biodiversity, a crucial component of twenty-first-century environmentalism, and he manifests a concomitantly respectful and protective attitude toward all life forms. His appreciation of the intrinsic, intangible value in every insect, shrub, rodent, and pebble dovetails as well with emerging awareness of the "nonmonetary ... value" of natural resources.[73] Refusing to "carry the landscape ... to market," he valorizes the non-commercial benefits it yields (196). Wilson credits Thoreau with having articulated "the first elements" of "a global land ethic."[74] Thoreau insists, moreover, that "nature is not elsewhere, but everywhere, and all the land holy, not just a few last, best places."[75]

His noncompetitive philosophy is further buttressed by his often expressed confidence that nature's plenty is inexhaustible, more than sufficient for the needs of all the earth's diverse inhabitants. He tells his readers that it costs "incredibly little trouble to obtain one's necessary food," even in a New England climate, if one adopts "as simple a diet as the animals" (61). If one aspires only to self-sufficiency, losses sustained to other creatures during the growth or storage of crops become manageable. The individual who can "do with less" is "richer" indeed, better equipped for survival in a world of volatile natural forces, than one who requires more (23). Biophilic philosophy accounts in large measure for Thoreau's conviction that the quest to accumulate resources

---

70 Rolston, "Biophilia, Selfish Genes," 412.
71 Buell, *Environmental Imagination*, 128.
72 Wilson, *Biophilia*, 131-32; Rolston, "Biophilia, Selfish Genes," 410-13.
73 Ulrich, "Biophilia, Biophobia," 115.
74 Wilson, "Prologue: A Letter," xxiv, xxiii.
75 Laura Dassow Walls, "Believing in Nature: Wilderness and Wildness in Thoreauvian Science," in *Thoreau's Sense of Place: Essays in American Environmental Writing*, ed. Richard J. Schneider (Iowa City: University of Iowa Press, 2000), 24.

in excess of need ("more warmth ... richer food, larger and more splendid houses") is unnatural and unsatisfying (15). Information he obtained through his reading about diverse human cultures, ancient and modern, further convinced him that "the basic necessities of man's physical life had not changed much over the long course of the centuries; even the means of acquiring them had changed less than might be supposed."[76] In his discussions of railroad workers or displaced aboriginal populations, he offers evidence that the human animal's pursuit of material luxury has led to the many miseries associated with social and economic stratification, "the luxury of one class ... counterbalanced by the indigence of another" (34).

Advocating a cross-species sharing of planetary resources, Thoreau clearly is convinced that he will not lose everything to weevils or woodchucks: he can afford to share because there always will be enough left for him. A committed locovore before his time, he advises readers to minimize the effort needed to sustain themselves by relying on locally available foods rather than "depend on distant and fluctuating markets" (63). He points out that it is cheapest and most efficient to plant those crops already adapted to regional growing conditions. Hence, grains like rye and corn contribute significantly to his diet, and he proves by experimentation that he can make or obtain, on the spot, a number of foods that his neighbors import at considerable cost and inconvenience. He can make sweeteners from home-grown "pumpkins or beets," for instance, or tap local maple trees for syrup (64); he notes that he could get his own salt without traveling far. Repeatedly he identifies unutilized local resources.

He also makes use of wild foods, sustaining himself in part with nuts, berries and wild apples he collects in the vicinity of his Walden home; during his first year there he also eats fresh-caught fish. He is a knowledgeable gatherer, utilizing his familiarity with his habitat to exploit its resources effectively. Instead of regarding squirrels solely as competitors, for example, he respects them as allies in the quest for food and profits from their instinctive knowledge: he gleans their "half-consumed nuts" because "the burrs they had selected were sure to contain sound [centers]" (238). He locates groundnuts and acorns in the vicinity, preparing sample batches in Native American fashion. He does not adopt either as a staple in his diet, but he is glad to discover that such food sources, currently unexploited, are readily available. His goal is to make plain the many unused or under-utilized food sources all around us in the natural

---

76 Christie, *Thoreau as World Traveler*, 215.

world, to recognize the "promise of Nature to rear her own children and feed them simply" (239).

He goes on to remind us that cultivated crops are far more vulnerable to ecological disasters than are wild-growing plants. If "wild Nature" were to "reign" again, he warns, "the tender and luxurious English grains will probably disappear before a myriad of foes … but the now almost exterminated groundnut will perhaps revive and flourish … and resume its ancient importance and dignity as the diet of the hunter tribe" (239). His cautions sound eerily like those E. O. Wilson would make in the 1980's: "we have come to depend completely on less than 1 percent of living species for our existence, with the remaining waiting untested and fallow."[77] Thoreau is determined to undertake such neglected testing, to explore the extent of nature's bounty. He would be unsurprised by the statistics biologists currently have amassed: they estimate the existence of "at least 75,000" sources of unutilized but edible vegetation, "and many of these are superior to the crop plants in use."[78] For readers living in a natural world largely "cut to pieces, mowed down, plowed under, gobbled up," his experiment in simplicity, with its emphasis on appreciative investigation of local resources, appears ever more prescient, an adaptive response to environmental deterioration.[79]

Nature's Mysteries

Despite the constant quest to investigate nature that has characterized humans since hunter-gathering days, our species is dismayed by the prospect of knowing or taming the natural world completely. This is an intriguing aspect of the biophilia hypothesis, one Wilson considers at some length. "The greater the knowledge" we acquire about the natural world, he muses, "the deeper the mystery" that remains—and we would have it no other way: "Nature is to be mastered, but (we hope) never completely."[80] Thoreau's views on this point mirror Wilson's: "At the same time that we are earnest to explore and learn all things, we require that all things be mysterious and unexplorable, that land and sea be infinitely wild, unsurveyed and unfathomed by us because unfathomable" (317-18). We require contact with "the vastness and strangeness of nature," he maintains (171). Life in towns and cities is tenable only because the world of

---

77 Wilson, *Biophilia*, 132.
78 Ibid., 132.
79 Wilson, "Prologue: A Letter," xxii.
80 Wilson, *Biophilia*, 10.

nature remains accessible. "Our village life would stagnate if it were not for the unexplored forests and meadows which surround it," Thoreau declares: "we need the tonic of wildness" (317).

Even the spectacle of violent interspecies competition assures us of nature's "inexhaustible vigor" (318). Luckily, Thoreau reminds his readers, they need not go far from settled communities to find hidden pockets of "strangeness": "It is remarkable how many creatures live wild and free though secret in the woods, and still sustain themselves in the neighborhood of towns, suspected by hunters only" (227). Only our own apathy can prevent us from investigating and enjoying nature's rich variety: "there is an incessant influx of novelty into the world, and yet we tolerate incredible dulness" (332). Thoreau anticipates Wilson's contention that "our intrinsic emotions drive us to search for fresh habitats, to cross unexplored terrain," asserting that "we still crave the sense of a mysterious world stretching infinitely beyond."[81]

Nature as Restorative

Biophilia theory culminates in the proposition that humans need to foster a relationship with nature in order to enjoy full psychological and emotional health. "There can be no very black melancholy," Thoreau asserts, "to him who lives in the midst of Nature and has his senses still" (131). Although we live daily lives that are very disconnected, for the most part, from the natural world, Wilson reminds us that "the brain evolved into its present form over a period of about two million years … during which people existed in hunter-gatherer bands in intimate contact with the natural environment."[82] From these ancestors we inherit an inclination to involve ourselves with the natural world, to learn about it, to grapple with its dangers, beauties, and mysteries. Examining the adaptive value of close contact with the natural environment from a "functional-evolutionary perspective," Ulrich concludes that such contact fosters a "recharging of energy" and thus may "enhance survival chances."[83] Even simple enjoyment of "the quiet motion of pond life," research suggests, may promote "physiological relaxation" or "better problem solving."[84] Some of the most compelling research supporting the biophilia hypothesis explores the psychological and physiological damage caused by humans' increasing disconnection

---

81 Ibid., 76.
82 Ibid., 101.
83 Ulrich, "Biophilia, Biophobia," 98, 99.
84 Katcher and Wilkins, "Dialogue with Animals," 177.

from nature, together with the manifold benefits to be obtained by deliberate acts of reconnection.[85]

Predisposed to associate nature with vital, even curative, energies, humans invest it with significance: "we are in the fullest sense a biological species," Wilson explains, "and will find little ultimate meaning apart from the remainder of life."[86] One of Thoreau's chief purposes is to communicate exactly this conviction. Persistently he compares natural phenomena to celestial ones, investing nature with transcendent significance by means of metaphor and analogy. Declaring that "Olympus is but the outside of the earth every where," he assures us that the natural world we live in is, in very fact, supernaturally wondrous (85). "Reflecting the sky," Walden Pond is "a lower heaven" (86). Its water is comparable to "the sacred water of the Ganges," endowed by implication with holy and healing effects (298). Associating a humble New England pond with regenerative potency, Thoreau demands awe and reverence for the natural world in its most commonplace manifestations. His strategy is to insist that the ordinary *is* extraordinary: the ponds near his home are "great crystals on the surface of the earth, Lakes of Light," more valuable than "the diamond of Kohinoor" (199). The common trees in his neighborhood, whether pine, or black-birch, or dogwood, are "temples" or "shrines," inspiring "worship" (201, 202).

Involving himself in natural cycles of regeneration, he, the human is reinvigorated: like the thawing pond, he finds that he is "alive again." Likening the "coming in of spring" to "the creation of Cosmos out of Chaos and the realization of the Golden Age," he places the re-making of the natural world, which occurs each year, in a profound context (313).[87] Marveling at nature's energies, Thoreau expresses "the cathedral feeling" Darwin described in response to seeing the results of nature's prolixy in a tropical forest: "wonder, astonishment, and sublime devotion, fill & elevate the mind."[88] Readers of *Walden* encounter the same expression of reverence and awe in Thoreau's evocations of the

---

85   Some of this research is presented and discussed in *The Biophilia Hypothesis*; see essays by Katcher and Wilkins, by Ulrich, by Orr, and by Kellert.
86   Wilson, *Biophilia*, 81.
87   Many readers have discussed the centrality of the theme of rebirth in *Walden*, analyzing the analogies, and metaphors Thoreau invokes in this context. See commentary by Paul, "A Fable of the Renewal of Life"; Lauriat Lane Jr., "On the Organic Structure of *Walden*," in *Critical Essays on Henry David Thoreau's "Walden,"* ed. Joel Myerson (Boston: G. K. Hall, 1988), 74-76; Stanley Edgar Hyman, "Henry Thoreau in Our Time," in *Thoreau: A Collection of Critical Essays*, ed. Sherman Paul (Englewood Cliffs, New Jersey: Prentice-Hall, 1962), 28-29; Drake, "Walden," 72-74.
88   Quoted in Wilson, *Biophilia* 27.

natural environment in Concord, Massachusetts. Nineteenth-century versions of pantheism provide him with a vehicle to exalt the regenerative organic interconnectedness he discovers everywhere around him.[89]

Biophilia and *Walden*

Point for point, Thoreau articulates in his book ideas and values compatible with those Edward O. Wilson would gather together under the concept of "biophilia" more than a hundred years later. He expresses the foundational biophilic conviction that every individual needs a close relationship with nature, in all its wildness and variety, in order to thrive, and he further implies that this need is an inherent part of human nature. He argues in passionate detail that "improved means" of agriculture, industry, and technology have disrupted the original relationship between the human species and the natural world (52). As corrective, he undertakes an experimental re-immersion in nature, demonstrating how the experience contributes to increased emotional health, mental alertness, aesthetic pleasure, and psychic renewal. Investigating his immediate environment closely, he offers evidence that all living organisms and elemental phenomena are kin; he comes to appreciate his position as an individually insignificant member of a coherent ecological whole. He acts on these perceptions by extending nepotistic affiliations and loyalties beyond himself and even beyond his species, concluding that all life forms have equal claim on planetary resources. Thus he rejects anthropocentrism. Instead he highlights conservationist principles, particularly that of biodiversity; he models living simply and without waste, relying on local resources. At the same time, he promotes the idea of interaction and sharing across species.

Adopting "wider ... views" of fitness, he celebrates a planet-wide network of ancestry and descent; in this larger context, he implies, personal

---

89 There is a discernible line of causal connection between Romantic philosophy, particularly its idealization of nature, and the changes precipitated in Europe and America by rapid growth in industry and technology. Emerging just as natural environments were undergoing radical degradation, Romanticism expresses a collective response to thwarted biophilia. It forms a critical part of the biocultural framework in which Thoreau's views take shape. Robert Sattelmeyer justly observes that "a thoroughgoing Transcendentalist naturalist would find it easier to accept organic evolution than special creation," including a "dynamic" rather than a hierarchical conception of nature. *Thoreau's Reading*, 88. "Holism ... pervaded romantic science," moreover, as William Rossi emphasizes. "Thoreau's Transcendental Ecocentrism," in *Thoreau's Sense of Place: Essays in American Environmental Writing*, ed. Richard J. Schneider (Iowa City: University of Iowa Press, 2000), 32.

reproduction is an irrelevant goal. The individual organism is merely "a sojourner in nature" (37). Thoreau's evolutionarily expansive understanding of inclusive fitness not only supports ecosystemic health, it frees him from competition for status and wealth in the social environment. Ignoring or rejecting the personal reproductive goals motivating so much human behavior, he extricates himself from a host of societal constraints and directives.[90] Biophilia provides the logical launching-ground for his socioeconomic philosophy, rendering explicable, in fitness terms, behavior that otherwise might be labeled maladaptive. Indeed, his powerful identification with the well-being and continuity of the biosphere as a whole serves as necessary context for his most controversial social criticisms and personal abnegations.

---

90 Readers long have tended to dichotomize Thoreau's ideas, attempting to explain the "distance between the social and the natural" in his thinking: Sharon Cameron, *Writing Nature: Henry Thoreau's "Journal"* (New York and Oxford: Oxford University Press, 1985), 24. He enjoys "two separate reputations," as social critic on the one hand, and as nature writer on the other: Krutch, *Henry David Thoreau*, 287. Exploring the supposed "nature/culture opposition" in his thinking, readers wonder whether his work "is meant as an appeal from culture *for* nature, or as a reproach from nature *against* culture": McMurry, *Environmental Renaissance*, 121, 131. Viewed through the lens of biophilia, the relationship between these two thematic strains in *Walden* becomes much clearer. Thoreau "subordinates human presence" to an all-encompassing affiliation with the natural world: Cameron, *Writing Nature*, 154.

CHAPTER 4

Bateman's Principle in "Song of Myself": Whitman Celebrates Male Ardency

From an adaptationist perspective, one of the most conspicuous themes in Walt Whitman's "Song of Myself" is its ebullient celebration of key male sexual strategies. Universally regarded as Whitman's finest poem,[1] this "supreme lyric" creates a persona who revels in his own ardency and makes high claims for it.[2] Throughout the poem, the speaking "I" describes, indulges, and ratifies an erotic agenda emphasizing frequency and variety. Infusing his enthusiastic promiscuity with spiritual significance and political purpose, he frames the sexual psychology of the human male as idealistically as possible. He inhabits a wish-fulfilling environment that favors the expression of reproductive strategies evolutionarily advantageous to men. Competitive counter-strategies and social norms that ordinarily limit full expression of male sexuality have been eliminated from the imaginary realm of "Song," leaving its Singer free—as no man in the real world ever has been or could be—to pursue proximate satisfactions with joyous abandon.

Sexuality emerges most frequently in the poem as part of a recurrent metaphor designed to describe its pantheist-protagonist's spiritual questing. Keen to make contact with the divine energies inherent in every phenomenon in the material world, sentient and insentient, the persona of "Song" draws on the vocabulary of sexual congress to lend vivid intensity to spiritual conjunction. Like many writers before him, notably St. Theresa and John Donne, Whitman repeatedly borrows the language of physical passion to communicate the non-corporeal ecstasy of transcendent experience.[3] Consistently he

---

1 Edwin Haviland Miller, *Walt Whitman's "Song of Myself": A Mosaic of Interpretations* (Iowa City: University of Iowa Press, 1989), xiii-xiv.
2 Gay Wilson Allen, *A Reader's Guide to Walt Whitman* (New York: Farrar, Straus and Giroux, 1970), 126.
3 James E. Miller, Jr, discusses the transcendent implications of Whitman's metaphors of "union," placing him squarely in the mystic tradition. *A Critical Guide to "Leaves of Grass"* (Chicago and London: University of Chicago Press, 1957), 30.

portrays the "merge" he seeks "with all" in sensual terms, presenting himself as spokesman for "passionate love."[4] He extends his metaphor to the political arena as well, using physical touch and sexual contact to describe the bonding force of democracy. He praises the United States as an experiment in which many thousands of disparate individuals have been knit together, becoming part of an immense economic, social, and ideological network of inter-relationships. To illustrate the intangible ties joining people of mountainous, desert, or coastal regions, people of different races, religions, ethnicities, and vocations, he will "embrace" and "possess" each in turn (line 1019). Determined to join with even the lowliest, he infuses the notion of egalitarian belonging with erotic fervor; he becomes the spokesman for a "democratic sexual politics."[5]

Throughout the poem, consequently, sexuality serves Whitman as a source of vivid figuration. The patterns of erotic behavior he highlights in his metaphoric comparisons are distinctly *male* patterns, furthermore, as evolutionary biological analysis clearly demonstrates. The masculine drives depicted in the poem can be traced to fundamental facts of human reproduction. The strategic differences in male and female sexual behaviors begin with differences in the size of their sex cells. Eggs are larger and costlier to make than sperms, so that a female must from the outset invest more significantly in the reproductive enterprises than does the male.[6] In addition to her large egg, the human female contributes, at a bare minimum, nine months of pregnancy and a period of lactation. "Female reproductive capacity is limited by the energy and time demands of parental nurture," consequently, "whereas no comparable ceiling exists for the males."[7] Among men, indeed, a conspicuously wide differential in reproductive success prevails; the outermost limits have been tested by some harem-holders, who have sired many hundreds of children.[8] Reproductive success is limited not by a man's sperm supply, but by the supply of women with

---

4 Walt Whitman, "Song of Myself," in *Leaves of Grass*, ed. Sculley Bradley and Harold W. Blodgett (New York and London: Norton, 1973), lines 381, 373, 447. Citations refer to this edition, a reprint of the 1891-1892 edition. Readers interested in the history of the changes Whitman made in the text, title, and structure of the poem between its first publication in 1855 and the 1891-1892 version will find useful material in Miller Jr.'s *Critical Guide*, 6.
5 M. Jimmie Killingsworth, "Whitman and the Gay American Ethos," in *A Historical Guide to Walt Whitman*, ed. David S. Reynolds (Oxford and New York: Oxford University Press, 2000), 125.
6 Dawkins, *Selfish Gene*, 145-46; Daly and Wilson, *Sex, Evolution*, 78-79.
7 Daly and Wilson, *Sex, Evolution*, 79.
8 Buss, *Evolution of Desire*, 63.

whom he can mate. Since each woman can bear him a strictly limited number of offspring, to sire more children he must mate with more women. "The greater the number of sexual partners," as Donald Symons points out, "the greater the benefit."[9] Men who gain sexual access to large numbers of fertile women tend to leave more descendents than do rival males with fewer mating options.

Given the clear fitness payoffs for men who actively seek out sexual opportunities with numerous partners, it follows that "adaptive benefits" typically accrue to those who reduce pair-bond commitment and paternal investment in order to pursue casual, extra-pair copulations.[10] "Because of a fundamental difference between the size and numbers of sperms and eggs," Dawkins sums up, "males are in general likely to be biased towards promiscuity and lack of paternal care." Able to produce "millions of sperms every day," a man "has everything to gain from as many promiscuous matings as he can snatch."[11] In short, the evolutionary basis of Bateman's Principle is well established: males are ardent and females are choosy for biologically comprehensible reasons. Because the total number of offspring she can produce is so strictly limited, the human female has much to lose from a mating mistake: it follows that she will evaluate potential partners carefully and be slow to commit her reproductive resources. A man's situation is dramatically different: it pays him to seek partners energetically and indiscriminately. The negative effects on his reproductive success of any low-quality partners will be outweighed by sheer volume. Whereas female choosiness manifests itself in high standards, protracted courtship, and long-term commitment, male ardency expresses itself in rapid arousal, abbreviated foreplay, and transient encounters, with an emphasis on frequency and variety.[12] It is precisely this set of male strategies that Whitman delineates so rhapsodically in "Song of Myself."

Sexual energy is the cornerstone of ardency, and the "hankering" persona of "Song" delights in his unbounded lustiness (line 389). He describes his personal reserves of sperm as oceanic in vastness: "dash me with amorous wet," he playfully tells the seawater: "I can repay you" (line 453). Indeed, his ejaculatory power is sufficient to "moisten the roots of all that has grown" (line 467). Unabashedly "fleshy," "sensual," and "breeding," he revels in the sheer intensity of his physical receptiveness (line 498): "to touch my person to some one else's

---

9   Donald Symons, *The Evolution of Sexuality* (Oxford: Oxford University Press, 1979), 208.
10 Buss, *Evolution of Desire*, 76.
11 Dawkins, *Selfish Gene*, 161, 164.
12 Buss, *Evolution of Desire*, 47-48; Daly and Wilson, *Sex, Evolution*, 280-81.

is about as much as I can stand" (line 618). The whole of Section 28 is devoted to the topic of the speaker's exquisite and unfailing responsiveness. He portrays an environment full "on all sides" of "prurient provokers"—exciting sources of tactile stimulation (line 623). Time after time, his "flesh and blood" respond with "lightening" to "a touch" (lines 622, 619). Scarcely disguised references to phallus, erection, and climax demonstrate the swiftness and completeness of his capacity for arousal.

He embellishes his portrait of the erotically eager male with detailed description of his "luscious" body (line 544). From the very beginning of the poem, he exhibits his body unabashedly, presenting himself to readers "undisguised and naked" (line 19). Cataloguing his physical attributes in Section 2 and again in Section 24, he presents himself as brawny, sweaty, and muscular—characteristics signaling masculinity.[13] In clear violation of nineteenth-century readers' expectations, furthermore, he includes affectionate mention of his phallus ("love-root"), pubic hair ("silk-thread" or "fibre of manly wheat"), testes ("nest of guarded duplicate eggs") and ejaculatory fluid ("trickling sap of maple") (lines 22, 537, 535). Comparing his intimate body parts to animal and vegetative growth (roots, eggs, wheat, sap), he indirectly argues that human sexual activity serves natural purposes. He makes a case, in effect, for his own erotic impulses by embedding them in the larger framework of nature's fertility. His forthright descriptions of his genitalia contribute, very obviously, to the impression he wishes to create of a sensually vital, highly sexed man. He is making a masculine display before readers, highlighting his sexual capacity and suggesting availability: "I have stores plenty and to spare" (line 999).

Throughout the poem, sexual eagerness is closely allied to a promiscuous welcoming of all possible partners. Whitman's easily aroused persona announces himself as the "mate and companion of all people" and, indeed, "the caresser of life wherever moving" (lines 137, 232). "Many seek me," he boasts, "and I do not fail them" (line 1262). He claims as partners the whole array of human types, acknowledging no boundaries of gender, age, or situation: "those that have been boys and that love women," "the man that is proud," "the sweetheart and the old maid," "mothers and the mothers of mothers," "children and the begetters of children" (lines 140-44). Cataloguing his lovers, he typically devotes only a brief mention to each, a single line of verse: "the young mechanic … knows me well"; "the soldier … is mine"; "my face rubs to the hunter's face" (lines 1257, 1261, 1264). He delights in momentary acts of joining ("I anchor my ship for a little while only"), and he is always in search of new

---

13 Buss, *Evolution of Desire*, 48.

opportunities: "my messengers continually cruise away or bring their returns to me" (lines 804, 805).

He broadens the range of his courtship beyond the human, approaching vast, elemental encounters with confidence and poise. "Press close bare-bosom'd night," he urges; "smile O voluptuous cool-breath'd earth!" (lines 435, 438). Even as they illustrate a pantheistic union between self and nature, such passages cannot help but draw attention to the immense erotic appetite of Whitman's persona. With this "eroticization of the universe," William H. Shurr points out, "the whole of the physical world has now become related to him sexually, the object of his desire."[14] Taking pride in the all-inclusiveness of his desire, he makes himself available to "the first that will take" him: "What is commonest, cheapest, nearest, easiest, is Me" (lines 261, 259). He lavishes his attentions even on those with low status, poor health, physical imperfections, or moral failings—the "stale" and the "discarded"—proudly announcing his lack of exclusiveness (145): "I do not ask who you are, that is not important to me, / You can do nothing and be nothing but what I will infold you" (lines 1001-1002). This emphasis on a perpetually eager, nondiscriminatory lust provides clear illustration of Bateman's Principle at work. "If the effort and risk are low enough," Symons observes, "it is adaptive for a man to experience lust ... without respect to ... physical attractions or other personal attributes."[15]

The extravagant ardor of Whitman's persona manifests itself in voyeuristic activity as well. Presenting himself with hyperbolic assurance as a kind of Transcendental Peeping Tom, he asserts his ability to discern nude bodies beneath the garments of the clothed individuals all around him: "I see through the broadcloth and gingham whether or no" (line 146). As he performs acts of imaginative disrobing on everyone he meets, he illustrates men's sexual responsiveness to visual stimuli.[16] At the same time he exploits the Transcendentalists' often reiterated metaphor of seeing or piercing *through* material phenomena in order to appreciate their spiritual essence. Emerson frequently praises this kind of optical acuteness, arguing that the poet, in particular, possesses a "very high sort of seeing" with which he "turns the world to glass."[17] Thomas Carlyle links such visual metaphors specifically

---

14 William H. Shurr, "Whitman's Omnisexual Sensibility," *Soundings: An Interdisciplinary Journal* 74, no. 1-2 (1991): 113.
15 Symons, *Evolution of Sexuality*, 212.
16 Buss, *Evolution of Desire*, 82.
17 Ralph Waldo Emerson, "The Poet," in *The Collected Works of Ralph Waldo Emerson*, vol. 3, Essays: Second Series, ed. Joseph Slater, Alfred R. Ferguson and Jean Ferguson Carr (Cambridge, MA and London: Harvard University Press, 1983), 12.

to apparel in *Sartor Resartus* with Diogenes Teufelsdröckh's "Philosophy of Clothes": "the thing *Visible* ... what is it but a *Garment*, a Clothing of the higher, celestial Invisible?" "The beginning of all Wisdom," therefore, "is to look fixedly on Clothes ... till they become *transparent*."[18] Shifting attention away from the spiritual discoveries awaiting those who see through the mundane surfaces of things, Whitman's protagonist points out the obvious, namely, that in looking through clothing, one is bound to discover a naked body.[19] He claims significance and value for that body; it is a fact equal in importance to other, more intangible truths lurking beneath social conventions. Peering here, there, and everywhere as he zooms across the American continent, he utilizes Transcendentalist ideas and imagery as the basis for a "rhetoric of interpenetration."[20] In this way, he demonstrates the glorious ubiquity of male ardor, as well as its responsiveness to the unclad human form.

Enthusiastically seeking the widest possible variety of mating options, Whitman's "caresser of life" eschews commitment to any particular union. "Appearing and disappearing" very much on his own terms, he declares himself to be "a free companion": "I make appointments with all" (lines 796, 817, 373). Simultaneously "regardless of others" and "ever regardful" of them, he speaks tenderly of each partner but lingers with none (line 331). In the real-world environment of human relationships, male ardency is constrained by female goals and strategies. For evolutionary biological reasons already discussed, women are highly selective in choosing mates; they seek men who offer the resources and commitment necessary to see the reproductive enterprise through to a successful conclusion.[21] Their mating preferences interfere strategically with men's tendency to seek frequent, no-strings-attached sex with a wide variety of partners. Men who refuse to make any long-term commitment risk the loss of sexual opportunities to more reliably committing rivals. Depending upon environmental conditions, they may incur additional fitness costs: reduced survival prospects for offspring raised without a contributing male parent. Confronted

---

18 Thomas Carlyle, *Sartor Resartus*, in *"Sartor Resartus" and "On Heroes and Hero Worship"* (New York: E. P. Dutton, 1959), 49, 50.

19 Robert K. Martin makes the case for even more radical reading of Whitman's language in this context, arguing that the poet calls, implicitly, for an undraping of the male genitalia, e.g., "the penis beneath the foreskin." *The Homosexual Tradition in American Poetry* (Austin and London: University of Texas Press, 1979), 18.

20 M. Jimmie Killingsworth, "Whitman's Physical Eloquence," in *Walt Whitman: The Centennial Essays*, ed. Ed Folsom (Iowa City: University of Iowa Press, 1994), 68.

21 Buss, *Evolution of Desire*, 20-21; Daly and Wilson, *Sex, Evolution*, 301.

with these realities, men frequently pursue a mixed reproductive strategy. That is, they make a primary commitment to one woman and her offspring, while taking advantage of opportunities for casual, low-investment sex with extra-pair partners.[22] In Whitman's poem, however, there is no need for such compromise because there is no conflict between the wooing male's desires and those of his partners. There are no requests for resources, no demands for fidelity, no accusations of abandonment. There are, conveniently, no children. The speaker-protagonist pursues an exclusively short-term strategy, rejoicing in his insatiability and singling out no one partner for even the most limited commitment.

Although the idea of "inception," or "increase," is treated with reverence, no actual offspring result from the many couplings recorded in "Song," and there is no mention of paternal care (lines 40, 46). Saluting "the procreant urge of the world," or the unending "breed of life," the poem's speaker emphasizes the drive that leads to conception rather than its consequences, identifying sexual impulses as the animating force of the natural world (lines 44, 46). As Gay Wilson Allen observes, Whitman lays emphasis throughout "Song" on "the generative power and fecundity underlying and permeating the universe," at the same time creating a persona "acutely sensitive to sexual touch."[23] The parallel the poet draws between cosmic creative force (sometimes defined as "supernatural") and the ardent male's capacity to become an earthly "creator" (thanks to his "life-lumps") highlights virility, not paternity (lines 1050, 1052). The nearest Whitman's "free companion" comes to the idea of fatherhood is an assertion of his own genetic quality: "on women fit for conception I start bigger and nimbler babes" (line 1006). This confident prediction cannot be interpreted as a declaration of paternal commitment, any more than it is the expression of discriminative mate choice. He is boasting, simply, that he does not require exceptional partners to sire exceptional offspring: he claims the ability to conceive a physically and mentally high quality child ("bigger" and "nimbler") with *any* fertile woman (one minimally "fit for conception").[24] The emphasis falls on his ability to impregnate: no fatherly duties are anticipated, here or elsewhere in the poem. There is no reckoning up of the large number

---

22 Daly and Wilson, *Sex, Evolution*, 281.
23 Gay Wilson Allen, "Mutations in Whitman's Art," in *Walt Whitman: A Collection of Criticism*, ed. Arthur Golden (New York: McGraw-Hill, 1974), 40.
24 "The new eugenics" of the times contributed, Harold Aspiz argues, to Whitman's presentation of himself as "the champion American breeder to be matched with prize female stock." "Sexuality and the Language of Transcendence," *Walt Whitman Review* 5, no. 2 (1987): 2.

of children likely to be "start[ed]" by the self-acknowledged "mate ... of all people" (line 137). No demand for long-term investment is anticipated, no curtailment of sexual liberty. The poem celebrates proximate goals (achieving sexual pleasure) rather than ultimate ones (passing on genes via offspring).[25]

Outside the fantasyland of "Song," a man with the sexual history reported by Whitman's exuberantly promiscuous persona would leave behind him a trail of abandoned children (children with sub-optimal survival potential) and an equally long trail of accusatory mothers, some of whom would be accompanied by irate male relatives wielding weapons. In real-world human communities, certainly, no man could obtain access to such a vast supply of willing female partners. In the absence of committed resources and the related qualities women demand, no man—no matter how potent and attractive—could entice so many into such breathtakingly brief affairs. In "Song of Myself" Whitman has constructed a world ideally suited to male mating behavior, a world in which there are neither tedious hindrances nor burdensome consequences to copulation. An important corollary is that there are no unwilling partners. He endows a larger-than-life male figure with persistent sexual appetite, "tenacious" and "tireless," then places him in an environment packed with potential short-term partners who are unable to resist him (line 147).[26] He "cannot be shaken away" and is "not to be denied" (lines 147, 999). Indeed, he is besieged by a host of eager suitors: "my lovers suffocate me," he exclaims in mock complaint (line 1172). They are "crowding" and "jostling" him, "coming naked" to him "at night," "calling [his] name from flower-beds, vines, tangled underbrush"; they cover his body with kisses and offer him "handfuls out of their hearts" (lines 1173-79). Even elemental forces desire him. The "crooked inviting fingers" of the incoming tide "refuse to go back without feeling" him (lines 449, 450).

Readers must notice yet another unrealistic component to the world Whitman presents in "Song": there is no competition for mating opportunities.

---

25 Martin places the "nonprocreative sexual behavior" featured throughout *Leaves of Grass* in a sociopolitical context, arguing that the poet's homoerotic vision offers an important challenge to capitalistic productivity, competitive aggressiveness, and power-hungry progress. *Homosexual Tradition*, 21-22, 69-70.

26 James E. Miller, Jr. discusses the "gigantic" features of Whitman's protagonist, pointing to descriptions emphasizing literal hugeness, e.g., "my elbows rest in sea-gaps, / I skirt sierras, my palms cover continents" (715-16). Miller argues that these "superhuman proportions" help to delineate an "archetypal New World personality." *Critical Guide*, 199. Given the persistent celebration in "Song" of male genitalia, male arousal, and male promiscuity, however, it seems important to supplement this reading. Whatever else they may signal, the "superhuman proportions" of the persona in "Song" represent Whitman's homage to a larger-than-life masculinity.

In the context of ordinary life, ardent males must contend with equally ardent rivals. To be chosen as a woman's partner, even temporarily, a man must offer more—in terms of personal attributes, material resources, or social benefits, for instance—than his competitors can provide.[27] Frequently he must overcome resistance from men defending exclusive sexual access. Amazingly, however, Whitman's amorous protagonist encounters neither rivals nor prior claims. Even when he decides to displace a young husband from his conjugal pleasures, that is, to "turn the bridegroom out of bed and stay with the bride ... / ... tighten her all night to [his] thighs and lips," he does so with impunity (lines 818-19). Here he depicts a new husband on his wedding night, about to reap the rewards of courtship, mate guarding, and commitment—a man who has worked to ensure paternity and is now engaged in the critical process of insemination. The bridegroom's direct fitness is threatened by a sexual interloper, a circumstance in which men often resort to "lethal violence," yet he registers no objection and offers no resistance.[28] In this scene, biological adaptations are absurdly suspended. Social and legal forces that support the sexually exclusive privileges of long-term mating similarly fail to become operational. Whitman's lusty persona enjoys inexplicably universal access to a seemingly endless series of temporary partners. He inhabits a utopian environment that permits uninhibited expression of his erotic desires. Those he woos never measure his attractions against those of other suitors or resent the brevity of his attentions, and he need never defeat or outwit challengers. He is the only sexual aggressor in the universe of the poem.

There is no denying that the fantasy-driven environment of "Song," like the prototypically ardent behavior of its persona, is admirably suited to transmit Whitman's spiritual and political themes. The pursuit of pantheistic and national connectedness demands an all-inclusive approach. Naturally, the individual soul wishes to achieve a simultaneously material and immaterial oneness with as many phenomena in the cosmos as possible. Naturally, the individual citizen wants to unite with a large and diverse group of compatriots. Equally obviously, those with whom the soul or citizen desires to join will not resist: universal connectedness is, and must be, the highest goal for all. Neither competition nor choosiness would make sense in the spiritual and political realms Whitman presents, since the absolute value of each individual point in the vaster network—whether of divinity or democracy—is beyond question, and

---

27 Buss, *Evolution of Desire*, 47.
28 Ibid., 129.

the number of potential connections—all equally desirable—is unlimited. In both these contexts, the male sexual strategies exhibited throughout the poem are ideally illustrative. Spiritually and politically, there are no costs to the unrestrained and promiscuous pursuit of oneness.

Confronted with so much sexual activity and masculine posturing, however, readers may have difficulty remembering that all this male ardor serves as the vehicle in Whitman's double-hinged central metaphor. Sensual and erotic images occupy so much space in the poem that they tend to crowd out the more intangible ideas they ostensibly represent. Consequently, readers confront "sets of interacting and interchangeable constructs."[29] Like a reversible jacket, each set of comparisons can be turned inside out. "It is unclear," as Betsy Erkkila observes, "whether Whitman is describing sexuality in the language of spiritual ecstasy or a mystical experience in the language of sexual ecstasy, for he seems to be doing both at once."[30] Sexual imagery invests pantheistic and democratic ideals with vital urgency and, simultaneously, erotic activity assumes noble purpose. With dazzling effrontery, Whitman transforms male ardency into a metaphysical and patriotic imperative. To a great extent, readers in his own and subsequent generations have cooperated with his program: they have been only too willing to interpret the sexual activities described in his poetry as "rituals of transcendence," "the dramatic representation of a mystical experience" or "mystical visions."[31] They have been far less ready to notice how Whitman's abstractly conceived agenda—to participate in a cosmic or national web of interconnectedness by joining with a plethora of others—obliquely ratifies his sexual agenda. And that agenda is unquestionably masculine.

Composed by a poet with a reputation as "probably the most ... relentlessly phallic writer in the annals of literature," "Song" concentrates overwhelmingly on male bodies, male urges, and male satisfactions.[32] Female bodies and desires are not denigrated, but they are largely ignored. Nowhere in the poem are women singled out as special, let alone exclusive, objects of male desire, nor are their physical attributes described with amorous attentiveness. The absence of any prurient interest in women's bodies may contribute, in fact, to readers' willingness to interpret the poet-speaker's ardor in spiritual and

---

29 Aspiz, "Sexuality and the Language," 1.
30 Betsy Erkkila, "Whitman and the Homosexual Republic," in *Walt Whitman: The Centennial Essays*, ed. Ed Folsom (Iowa City: University of Iowa Press, 1994), 158.
31 Aspiz, "Sexuality and the Language," 3; Miller, Jr., *Critical Guide*, 6; Geoffrey Dutton, *Whitman* (New York: Grove, 1961), 66.
32 Gary Schmidgall, *Walt Whitman: A Gay Life* (New York: Dutton, 1997), 77.

political terms. Just as Whitman's poem fails to link women specifically with male lust, it all but eliminates women's own erotic feelings from consideration. Women's maternal function is occasionally mentioned, but the mate-selection strategies that serve female reproductive interests garner almost no mention in "Song." Only in Section 11 does "womanly" desire emerge as a topic (line 201). The "twenty-ninth bather" sees a gaggle of handsome young men, all naked, and she imagines frolicking with them in the surf, passing her hand "tremblingly" over their bare bodies (208, 212). This portrait of female sexual yearning presents a woman thinking in terms of short-term mating strategies: it emphasizes a typically male responsiveness to visual stimulus, along with a typically male interest in many partners. Thus it focuses precisely on an aspect of female sexuality that overlaps closely with masculine adaptations. Since this is the only description of female desire presented in "Song," readers are left with a very limited picture of women's erotic experience. It has been suggested that Whitman is using the female perspective here as a convenient device, retaining his focus on male experience while pretending to broaden his scope.[33] At the same time, as readers concede, he is taking a liberating stance on female sexuality, underlining its many modes of expression. Demanding recognition of female assertiveness, along with the very real existence of female short-term sexual strategies, the twenty-ninth bather highlights "the repressed sexuality of Victorian women."[34]

Sexuality per se contributes to the foregrounded subject matter of the poem insofar as the poet's openly avowed purposes include an assault on nineteenth-century sexual prudery. *Leaves of Grass* communicates "a radical reformist

---

33 A number of scholars discuss Whitman's identification with the feminine perspective in Section 11, identifying the twenty-ninth bather as a disguised portrait of the watching male persona. See, e.g., Frederik Schyberg, *Walt Whitman*, trans. Evie Alison Allen (New York: Columbia University Press, 1951), 119-20; Edwin Haviland Miller, *Walt Whitman's Poetry: A Psychological Journey* (Boston: Houghton Mifflin, 1968), 94; Roy Harvey Pearce, *The Continuity of American Poetry* (Princeton, NJ: Princeton University Press, 1961), 78; Shurr, "Whitman's Omnisexual," 106; Martin, *Homosexual Tradition*, 20. There is disagreement among Whitman's biographers concerning the extent and authenticity of his feminist commitment and, indeed, about his attitude toward women per se. Schmidgall points to "hints of gender bias ... small but telling" in the life and work. Emphasizing the "masculinist purport of *Leaves*," he labels Whitman an "elaborately misogynist poet." *Walt Whitman: A Gay Life*, 159, 169. David S. Reynolds presents Whitman's attitude toward women and women's rights in a much more positive light, tracing his "sympathy for the social and economic plight of women" in early newspaper pieces, 220. *Walt Whitman's America: A Cultural Biography* (New York: Alfred A. Knopf, 1995), 213-22.
34 Martin, *Homosexual Tradition*, 20.

approach to sexuality."[35] Declaring that no part of the body is shameful or unmentionable, Whitman takes pantheism to its logical conclusion: the divine energy permeating the material universe manifests itself in the human body—genitals and all. Sensual and erotic experiences achieve new validation in this interpretation of Transcendentalism because spiritual and corporeal health are inextricably intertwined. Like the soul, the body is "clear and sweet" (line 52). "Every organ and attribute" of that body is made "welcome," for "not an inch nor a particle of an inch is vile" (lines 57, 58). Passages extolling nudity or naming taboo body parts support the poet's demand for definitive change in mid-nineteenth-century social norms: he aspires to nothing less than full acceptance of all bodily functions and sensual pleasures.[36] Evidently, too, he means to include women in his revolutionary reappraisal of human sexuality. He proclaims that he is "the poet of the woman the same as the man," adding an emphatic affirmation of gender-based equality: "And I say it is as great to be a woman as to be a man" (lines 425-26). Although the reiterated parallel construction of his phrasing ("man or woman," "my brother, my sister," "male and female," "maternal as well as paternal," "all men and women," "each man and woman") begins to sound formulaic, even mechanical, he commits himself in theory, at least, to an all-inclusive program of sexual liberation (lines 989, 1144, 139, 333, 1136, 1037).

Because sexuality serves a dual function in "Song," emerging both as a topic in its own right and as a metaphoric vehicle for the presentation of other topics, it dominates the text. In section after section, readers are confronted with a highly sexed male self, who exhibits and admires his naked body, who seeks and finds partners, and who engages in acts of amorous joining. The text thus tempts readers to discover sexual suggestiveness in language that in other contexts might not be erotically interpreted. Recurring images of absorption, swallowing, and incorporation, for example, or of appetite and hunger, invite

---

35 Harold Aspiz, "Walt Whitman: The Spermatic Imagination," *American Literature* 54, no. 2 (1987): 379.

36 Aspiz traces the sources of Whitman's campaign for sensual and sexual liberation to the "new eugenics" (the "ideological mainstay of phrenology") propounded in the mid-nineteenth century by "an array of American reformers and scientists." The poet draws on "the ideology and language of sexual reform" current at the time, giving lyrical expression to "reformists' notion that sexual ecstasy is eugenically desirable and, ultimately spiritual." "Sexuality and the Language," 2. A number of scholars have discussed the clearly significant contribution of phrenological theory to Whitman's ideas about friendship, love, and eros. See, e.g., Edward Hungerford, "Walt Whitman and his Chart of Bumps," *American Literature* 2, no. 4 (1931); Reynolds, *Walt Whitman's America*; Peter Coviello, "Intimate Nationality: Anonymity and Attachment in Whitman," *American Literature* 73, no. 1 (2001).

more salacious interpretation in "Song" than they elsewhere might. Readers have been primed to view the action of the poem through the lens of eros, to picture amorous rather than spiritual activity when confronted with a phrase like "the thoughtful merge of myself, and the outlet again" (line 381). The poet-speaker's parting announcement that he will be "somewhere waiting" for readers who may "want" him similarly carries seductive implications (lines 1346, 1340). In addition to offering philosophical, political, and literary camaraderie, he appears to be envisioning a posthumous continuation of the sexual paradise in "Song" and enumerating generations of future readers among his potential partners. Even when Whitman's persona is not invoking sexual images or topics, the language of the poem is loaded with subtle and not-so-subtle sexual connotation: "his language of sexuality becomes involved in his language of transcendence."[37] Some of Whitman's most devoted critics nonetheless overlook or downplay this aspect of the poem: "out of embarrassment or ignorance, they have moved quickly to a symbolic interpretation" of the text.[38]

Without doubt, Whitman has created in "Song of Myself" a male sexual paradise. Easily aroused and superbly robust, its protagonist displays unfailing potency in an environment brimming with available partners. A universal receptiveness to his advances confirms his desirability, even as it guarantees him speedy access to new and novel mating opportunities. Never frustrated or rejected, he joins with innumerable short-term partners, enjoying a high degree of variety. At the same time, all sources of inter- and intra-sexual competition have been eliminated from this Never-Never-Land. There is no competition from rival males to reduce his mating options or complicate his pursuit of them. There are no demands from potential partners (for courtship, commitment, or investment) to interfere with his short-term, promiscuous strategy. No societal regulations limit his activities. In sum, he exercises preferred male strategies unconstrained by the forces that men inevitably encounter in ordinary human settings. The unrealistic environment of the poem, with its many gender-specific biases, accurately reflects the contents of men's fantasies worldwide: "numbers and novelty are the key ingredients for men's fantasy lives," Buss reports; men imagine having sex with "strangers, multiple partners, or anonymous partners."[39] Just as important, they enjoy picturing sexual activity stripped of "encumbering relationships, emotional elaboration, complicated

---

37 Aspiz, "Sexuality and the Language," 2.
38 Martin, *Homosexual Tradition*, 21.
39 Buss, *Evolution of Desire*, 82.

plot lines, flirtation, courtship, and extended foreplay."[40] "Virtually every strand of Whitman's utopian thought," Peter Coviello asserts, reflects an "unwavering belief in the capacity of strangers to recognize, desire, and be intimate with one another."[41] In Whitman's poem, the self-interested desires propelling men's fantasies not only prevail, they are invested with higher meaning. Thus the poet offers "clear defense" for anonymous sexual encounters.[42] Promoted as a value on several levels of statement, the union of self with the widest possible variety of others is the most significant motivating force in "Song."

Whitman's exultant emphasis of male sexuality reflects biases embedded in his culture, as Aspiz points out in his useful summary of nineteenth-century sexual theory.[43] The primal significance of male potency, including "emphasis on the well-sexed male" and "the sanctity of sperm," was emphasized in phrenological and medical communities, as well as in the popular imagination. Belief in "the vital linkage between the brain and the sexual organs" furthermore encouraged artists and philosophers to regard semen as a vital source of intellectual achievement and imaginative creativity.[44] This cultural context helps to explain Whitman's eagerness to claim extraordinary virility and fecundity on behalf of his "hypermasculine persona."[45] Seeking validation for the uninhibited expression of male ardor, moreover, he rejects that part of popular medical theory which recommended "conservation of energy" through "the withholding of sperm": instead "Whitman proposes a radical redistribution of that energy through the release of sperm."[46] Aspiz and others have argued that Whitman consciously associates poetic speech with orgasmic release: in his "spermatic utterances," consequently, "the orgasm ... is the poem and ... the poem is the orgasm."[47] This connection is less insistent, less well developed, in "Song of Myself" than in other portions of *Leaves of Grass*, but it is nonetheless recognizable. Readers will learn "the origin of all poems," the persona of "Song" promises at the outset (line 33). Immediately thereafter he emphasizes "the procreant urge of the world," offering his enthusiastic "welcome" to "every organ and attribute" of the male

---

40 Bruce J. Ellis and Donald Symons, "Sex Differences in Sexual Fantasy: An Evolutionary Psychological Approach," *Journal of Sex Research* 27 (1990): 544.
41 Coviello, "Intimate Nationality," 85.
42 Martin, *Homosexual Tradition*, 19.
43 Aspiz, "Walt Whitman: The Spermatic Imagination," 380-82.
44 Ibid., 381.
45 Reynolds, *Walt Whitman's America*, 103.
46 Martin, *Homosexual Tradition*, 21.
47 Aspiz, "Walt Whitman: The Spermatic Imagination," 379, 395.

body (lines 45, 57). In this way he sets up an implied comparison, extending throughout the poem, between sex and art. Indubitably "procreant" and creative, sexual and artistic activities are driven by the same "original" and originating energies (lines 45, 13). Like his use of sexual metaphor in the realms of politics and metaphysics, this linking of the aesthetic with the erotic has the effect of ennobling Whitman's preoccupation with male physiology and masculine drives. "Giving tongue is associated at once with sexuality, including sexuality between men, democracy, spiritual vision, and poetic utterance."[48] Even as he invests poetry with potent intensity and pleasure, he associates male sexual strategies with aesthetic meaning and design.

The poem speaks to all men, recasting the world to fit and to flatter evolved patterns of male sexual behavior. If the promiscuous, male-centric environment of "Song" appears more homosexual than heterosexual in its workings, this is because it promotes the fulfillment of male preferences so completely. As social researchers and theorists have observed, gay men are free to exercise the strategies that straight men also would employ if women would cooperate. "When men are unconstrained by the courtship and commitment requirements typically imposed by women," as they are when pursuing same-sex liaisons, "they freely satisfy their desires for casual sex with a variety of partners."[49] Thus it has been argued that the behavior of homosexuals "provides a window for viewing the nature of men's ... sexual desires, unclouded by the compromises imposed by the sexual strategies of the opposite sex."[50] As public acceptance of homosexuality has grown in recent decades, literary scholars have addressed this aspect of Whitman's life and work with increasing frequency and candor. New biographical studies, coupled with detailed new analyses of internal evidence in the poetry itself, offer persuasive proof of Whitman's homoerotic preference. Recent commentary on the "Live Oak, with Moss" sequence, in particular, buttresses this understanding.[51] Spurred, at least in part, by the evidence in this recovered text, Whitman scholars have paid increased attention to direct and indirect homosexual content throughout the poet's oeuvre. Erkkila is among those decrying "a critical tradition that has insisted on silencing, spiritualizing,

---

48 Erkkila, "Whitman and the Homosexual," 154.
49 Buss, *Evolution of Desire*, 84.
50 Ibid., 84. Symons discusses the point in useful detail in *Evolution of Sexuality*, 292-305.
51 See Hershel Parker, "The Real 'Live Oak, with Moss': Straight Talk about Whitman's 'Gay Manifesto,'" *Nineteenth-Century Literature* 51, no. 2 (1996) and Alan Helms, "Whitman's 'Live Oak, with Moss,'" in *The Continuing Presence of Walt Whitman: The Life after the Life*, ed. Robert K. Martin (Iowa City: University of Iowa Press, 1992).

heterosexualizing or marginalizing Whitman's sexual feelings for men," even in the face of "widespread if covert agreement" that such feelings were a crucially important motivating force in both his life and his art."[52] As already noted, moreover, the homoerotic suggestiveness of Whitman's vision—almost certainly forged with deliberate, if unacknowledged, intent—works to reinforce the incontrovertible masculinity of the assumptions supporting that vision. The omnivorous ardor exhibited by the persona of "Song" is fully congruent with adaptationist understanding of sexual strategies favored by human males cross-culturally and worldwide. The poem appeals to adaptive preferences of all men, regardless of sexual preference.

Outside the artificially constructed world of "Song," societal and biological forces of many kinds limit men's ability to act freely and fully on their evolved preferences: male ardency does not operate in a vacuum. Men frequently restrain the expression of their proximate desires by undertaking long-term mating commitments, for example, or by providing paternal care, but the forces motivating them to do these things are not the ones described and celebrated in "Song of Myself." (Readers must go to poems in "Live Oak, with Moss" to observe the poet yearning for the satisfactions of long-term sexual and emotional partnership.) In "Song," Whitman creates an idyllic setting in which male sexual eagerness prevails unchallenged. Nature itself—from the "inviting fingers" of the sea to the ejaculatory "bright juice" of sunrise—echoes, promotes, and responds to it (lines 449, 556). "The urge toward tumescence" and "the imagery of arousal ... are ubiquitous."[53] This alternative version of reality very obviously addresses universal masculine self-interest, which in any "even remotely natural human environment" is well served by the "desire for variety."[54] "Copiously and elaborately male-centered," the poem responds to male sexual frustrations by eliminating their sources.[55] The thwarting effects of impotence, rejection, and competition are absent; issues of courtship and commitment, or paternal certainty and investment, do not arise. A host of related interpersonal issues, all aggravatingly complex, are eliminated at a stroke. The

---

[52] Erkkila, "Whitman and the Homosexual," 153, 154. For discussion of this topic see Killingsworth, "Walt Whitman and the Gay American Ethos"; Louis Simpson, "Strategies of Sex in Whitman's Poetry," in *Walt Whitman of Mickle Street: A Centennial Collection of Essays*, ed. Geoffrey M. Sill (Knoxville: University of Tennessee Press, 1994); Martin, *Homosexual Tradition*; Schmidgall, *Whitman: A Gay Life*.
[53] Schmidgall, *Whitman: A Gay Life*, 77.
[54] Symons, *Evolution of Sexuality*, 250.
[55] Schmidgall, *Whitman: A Gay Life*, 156.

persona of "Song" inhabits a blissfully simplified world, one in which a critical cluster of male sexual impulses may be expressed "without check" and "with original energy" (line 13). Opportunities for ardent behavior (which may occur "only rarely" in real-life environments, as Symon notes) are delightfully maximized and gloriously validated.[56]

Like all fantasies, and like much human art, the imaginatively conceived realm of "Song" is based upon exaggeration. The vision its author presents is dramatically oversimplified in terms of both individual psychology and social dynamics. An exuberant, often witty hyperbole, one of the chief stylistic hallmarks of the poet-speaker, indicates that the extravagant lopsidedness of its representation—of human nature and of human community—is intentional. Whitman is consciously engaged in an act of wish-fulfillment, imagining an idyll surpassing the possible. He dazzles, shocks, and titillates, loading his poem with extreme instances and extravagantly conceived illustrations. His Song of Himself is a paean to masculine ardor, writ large. The Darwinian premise underlying the utopian appeal of the poem is simple: individuals experience the satisfaction of their proximate desires not only as pleasurable, but as inherently valuable and meaningful. Appealing to significant features of evolved human psychology, "Whitman's triumphant and sexually charged persona shows that the universe is not purposeless."[57] "Song of Myself" reassures men of any sexual orientation that their desires are wholesome and even admirable. Their erotic make-up is fully in tune with natural process and cosmic design: within the framework of Whitman's poem, male ardency enjoys political, aesthetic, and transcendent validation.

---

56   Symons, *Evolution of Sexuality*, 208.
57   Aspiz, "Sexuality and the Language," 6.

CHAPTER 5

Maladaptive Behavior and Auctorial Design: Huck Finn's Pap

In a novel replete with characters inviting strongly negative judgments from readers, Huck Finn's Pap elicits a larger share of hostility and blame than any of the others: he is the single most unsympathetic, most repellant major figure in Twain's *Adventures of Huckleberry Finn* (1884). Twain withholds all redeeming qualities from the father of his fourteen-year-old protagonist. With his filthy personal habits and alcoholic excesses, his aggressive bullying, his self-pitying hypocrisies, conscienceless greed, and self-centered social philosophy, Pap seems to have been created with the deliberate intention of evoking condemnation. Much narrative attention is devoted to his faults as a parent, which emerge with especial flagrance. He does not merely neglect his son, withholding parental care; he is selfishly coercive and capriciously cruel. Such behavior flies in the face of evolutionary self-interest: it is biologically maladaptive. Finding Pap's actions as a father inexplicable and unnatural, readers judge them all the more harshly. Twain deliberately courts this reaction, creating a despicable character in order to reinforce his central thematic concerns. This bad, unnatural father is associated, necessarily, with bad, unnatural values. Whatever Pap finds good and right, readers will be disposed to reject and condemn. It is not accidental that Pap is the most outspoken and self-aggrandizing racist in the novel. Twain effectively strengthens the case he makes against racial bigotry by linking it with violations of fitness, violations calculated to trigger particularly intense emotional outrage.

From an evolutionary biological point of view, parental care serves an ultimately selfish purpose: it helps copies of the parent's genes to survive and make more copies, increasing the incidence of parental DNA in the gene pool.[1] Since a child shares exactly half of each parent's genes, mother and father both stand

---

1   Dawkins, *Selfish Gene*, 88. The whole of chapter Six, "Genesmanship," (88-108) is relevant here.

to benefit from providing care to every little "gene-machine" they produce.[2] By assisting a child to survive infancy and then to thrive—physically, socially, and reproductively—parents seek to increase their own fitness. People often help relatives other than children, since such nepotistic assistance potentially increases the indirect fitness of all those with whom the recipients share genes.[3] "The closer the relationship," however, "the stronger the selection" for altruistic investment.[4] For obvious reasons, parental care presents the most significant instance of nepotistic investment in humans.[5] The long period of juvenile dependency in our species, together with the complexity of human social structures, renders such care essential. Young children require provisioning and personal attendance, at a minimum; parents position older children for survival advantage and optimal reproductive success by providing vocational and social training. The percentage of genes shared by parent and child is much higher than the percentage shared by any other relatives except for full siblings, furthermore, so that the payoff for care given to offspring is maximal. The relative ages of parent and child also influence the flow of benefits: if a grown child gives help to an elderly, post-reproductive parent, that help will garner no increase in direct fitness, shared genes notwithstanding. Benefits travel more reliably from parent to child than the other way around, not only because the adult parent more often is in a position to provide them, but because the child's procreative potential is nearly always greater than the parent's.[6]

The necessity and value of parental care are consciously acknowledged in human communities; parental sacrifice is praised in art and religion, sentimentalized in popular fiction. Framing parental investment in highly laudatory terms, humans recognize the immense cost—in terms of material resources, personal labor, and long-term commitment—of rearing a child to reproductive age. Stories of extraordinary parental sacrifice and filial gratitude provide cultural encouragement to individuals struggling with the demands

---

2   Ibid., 46-47.
3   As Dawkins states, "a gene might be able to assist *replicas* of itself that are sitting in other bodies. ... This would appear as individual altruism but it would be brought about by gene selfishness." Ibid., 88.
4   Ibid., 94.
5   Trivers defines parental investment as "*any investment by the parent in an individual offspring that increases the offspring's chance of surviving (and hence reproductive success) at the cost of the parent's ability to invest in other offspring.*" "Parental Investment and Reproductive Success," in *Natural Selection and Social Theory: Selected Papers of Robert Trivers* (Oxford: Oxford University Press, 2002), 67.
6   Dawkins, *Selfish Gene*, 95-96.

of parenthood, augmenting biological benefits that may be less consciously perceived. The motivation for providing energy-sapping, long-term care to offspring, at the expense of other personal projects, typically is described as parental "love," an emotion extolled in literature, painting, folk songs, and tabloid articles. The mother who invokes superhuman strength to lift an automobile off her child, like the starving father who gives his last crust of bread to his children, illustrates with enthusiastic hyperbole the potency of maternal and paternal affection. Parental love is an emotion, an unforced upwelling of feeling that functions as a proximate mechanism to enforce adaptive, or evolutionarily advantageous, behavior. It is adaptive, from the perspective of parental DNA, for the parent to invest in offspring, clearly, but a parent need not consciously think, *rearing this child is my best hope of getting my genes into the next generation,* in order to provide the years of altruistic care and attention needed to achieve that end. The parent need only feel *I love this child* and act accordingly.

Failures of parental love and, consequently, of parental investment, usually exact a biological penalty. Children who die young from neglect, malnutrition, or abuse do not pass on the parents' genes at all. Children forced to marry people they dislike tend to have low reproductive success, passing on fewer genes than they might have with a more compatible mate. Children with personality defects or social handicaps caused by poor parenting experience difficulty finding and keeping mates (as well as jobs and friends); if they do have families they often perpetuate poor parental care, thereby imperiling the reproductive success of the next generation. One way or another, people who fail to nurture their offspring adequately tend to leave small, if any, genetic legacies. The built-in biological cost of insufficient parental investment explains why extremely deficient parents are observed relatively infrequently: the genes of individuals who do not feel and act upon the emotion of parental love are not well represented in successive generations. Insofar as there is a heritable component to their maladaptive behavior, the frequency of its occurrence in the human gene pool tends to be reduced.

The behavior (parental care) and the proximate motivation (parental love) are species-typical, universally regarded as natural and necessary. Their absence, consequently, is noticed and condemned. At the same time that outstanding examples of parental sacrifice are highlighted for attention and praise, markedly sub-optimal parenting earns community disapproval. In art, as in life, failures of parental love and care are strongly reprobated. Literary examples suggest, moreover, that poor parents tend to be flawed in other respects as well. Thackeray's Becky Sharp, Butler's Theobald Pontifex, Wharton's Undine

Spragg, Dickens's Mrs. Jellyby, and James's Gilbert Osmond, to name a few well-known instances, are bad parents who violate social and ethical norms unconnected to their faults as mothers and fathers. Even in this infamous line-up, Huck Finn's Pap stands out, "one of the most memorable bad fathers in literature."[7]

A parent can accrue fitness benefits by withholding investment from a child only in unusual circumstances. Unfavorable environmental conditions might dictate allocation of limited resources to a limited number of offspring (whether living or unborn), those with best long-term prospects for survival and reproduction.[8] However reluctantly, when parents have reason to think not *all* their children can survive, they make strategic decisions to ensure survival of *some*, overriding parental "love" selectively in order to secure the highest possible direct fitness for themselves. Nothing resembling this kind of *Sophie's-Choice* parental dilemma explains the failure of Huck's father to care for his son. There is no evidence that Pap has any living children except Huck, and no evidence that he currently seeks—or could attract—sexual partners with whom he might hope to sire children in the future. His disinterest in personal grooming, for instance, suggests that courtship is far from his mind. It seems likely that his addiction to liquor has suppressed or replaced sexual ardor as a motivating force in his existence. At the age of "most fifty" and apparently in sub-optimal health (e.g., with a "fish-belly white" complexion), Pap is unlikely now to father additional children (23). Thus his failure to nurture Huck, his sole hope for achieving some degree of direct fitness, cannot be explained as differential parental investment based on cost-benefit calculations.

Because Twain does not provide a detailed back-story for his narrator-protagonist, readers know almost nothing about Huck's infancy and early childhood. Approximately fourteen years old when the novel opens, he has been sheltering until the recent past in a "sugar-hogshead" and dressing in "old rags," apparently securing food by means of odd jobs, scavenging, and "borrowing" (2, 80).[9] No information is provided concerning his mother's role in his life. When, exactly, did she die? Did she look after Huck during his infancy and early childhood? If not, who did? These are questions the text does not answer.

---

7   Jeanne Campbell Reesman, "Bad Fathering in *Adventures of Huckleberry Finn*," in *The Turn Around Religion in America: Literature, Culture, and the Work of Saven Bercovitch*, ed. Nan Goodman and Michael P. Kramer (Surrey, England: Ashgate Publishing, 2011), 157.
8   See Trivers, "Parental Investment and Reproductive Success," 67-68.
9   Mark Twain, *Adventures of Huckleberry Finn*, in *The Works of Mark Twain*, vol. 8, ed. Walter Blair and Victor Fischer (Berkeley: University of California Press, 1988), 1, 80. All citations refer to this edition.

As the sole remaining parent, and with no other kin in evidence (e.g., uncles, aunts, or grandparents), Huck's father normally would be motivated to provide parental care sufficient to ensure his child's survival. The death of a mother counteracts the species-typical tendency for a mother's parental investment to exceed the father's. If the surviving parent does not provide adequate care, after all, the child may well die or fail to thrive, with consequent loss of fitness benefits.[10] Obviously, the behavior of Huck's father does not match predictions for adaptive adjustment of parental investment.

All readers know for sure about Huck's recent caregivers is that when the Widow Douglas takes him "for her son," offering him a home and intending to "sivilize" him, Huck's father has "not been seen in these parts for a year or more" (1, 10). This means that Pap left a boy of twelve, possibly thirteen, to fend for himself. Very likely Huck was essentially on his own even before that age, given his father's shiftless, alcoholic lifestyle: "he used to lay drunk with the hogs in the tanyard" (10). Some allowance must be made for the relatively greater independence granted to children, particularly boys, in the relevant time period: approximately 1835-1845, according to Twain's prefatory note. In the absence of child labor laws and child welfare programs, young teens could find employment and earn wages, conducting themselves more like junior adults than like members of a group entitled to special protection. Huck's status as an abandoned child scraping together a livelihood would not have attracted the kind of attention and interference, in his day, that it would have from the mid-twentieth century on.

There are indications, nevertheless, that even in Huck's environment an unsupervised, homeless boy is a somewhat disquieting phenomenon. In all of Huck's tales of origin, invented chiefly to disarm suspicion and elude danger during the journey down the river, he is careful to assign himself a background of family and adult protectors. These protectors generally are victims of illness or misfortune, as described in Huck's woeful tales, and usually deceased, but he is concerned to present himself as an orphan only recently deprived of credible kinship networks. He is trying to avoid trouble for Jim and himself, of course, but some of the trouble he anticipates may be the well-meaning intervention of would-be benefactors. The fact that he receives at least two offers of permanent homes—from the Grangerford and the Phelps families—indicates that an orphaned boy evokes an actively sympathetic response: people judge

---

10 Dawkins, *Selfish Gene*, 154-56; Trivers, "Parental Investment and Reproductive Success," 68-76, 100-01.

that a child of Huck's age still needs adult sponsors, together with some degree of care and support.

An "orphan alternately bullied and deserted by his father," Huck does appear perfectly willing to assume responsibility for himself.[11] He expresses neither resentment nor self-pity when describing his way of life prior to his adoption by the Widow Douglas. He relishes the freedom his sugar-hogshead affords him and runs away almost immediately, though briefly, from "the dismal regular and decent" lifestyle at the widow's, preferring independence to the restrictions of proper clothing, regular hours, middle-class etiquette, school lessons, and Bible study (1). Readers familiar with *The Adventures of Tom Sawyer* may remember that in the earlier book boys like Tom, with families, and consequently subject to discipline, schooling, and scheduling, envy Huck Finn precisely because of what is missing from his life: responsible adult supervision. As the "son of the town drunkard," he is perceived as "idle and lawless, and vulgar, and bad."[12] Lacking adult caregivers, he has been liberated from middle-class rules and expectations, freed from education for adult community membership. Consequently "every harassed, respectable boy in St. Petersburg" marvels at his autonomy and "wished they dared be like him" (74, 73). Like most people in their age group, Tom and his friends do not foresee or appreciate the benefits to be garnered from the social training they find gratuitously oppressive.

In *Adventures of Huckleberry Finn*, in contrast to the more lighthearted narrative focusing on Tom Sawyer, Huck's premature independence is not romanticized. He is no longer presented as a "gaudy outcast," an object of envy and emulation, but as a slightly disreputable social outsider (74). His "happy truancy" is recognized for what it is, "a struggle for survival."[13] This more realistic depiction reflects increased seriousness of auctorial purpose. The disadvantages of his situation, as the deserted child of a social pariah, receive more attention. He is allowed to join the boys' gang, for instance, only if he returns

---

11 Robert Sattelmeyer, "'Interesting, but Tough': *Huckleberry Finn* and the Problem of Tradition," in *One Hundred Years of "Huckleberry Finn": The Boy, His Book, and American Culture*, ed. Robert Sattelmeyer and J. Donald Crowley (Columbia: University of Missouri Press, 1985), 354.
12 Mark Twain, *The Adventures of Tom Sawyer*, in *The Works of Mark Twain*, vol. 4, ed. John C. Gerber, Paul Baender, and Terry Firkin, 31-237 (Berkeley: University of California Press, 1980), 73. All citations are to this edition.
13 Bruce Michelson, "Huck and the Games of the World," in *Huck Finn among the Critics: A Centennial Selection*, ed. M. Thomas Inge (Frederick, MD: University Publications of America, 1985), 214.

to the Widow Douglas and agrees to "be respectable" (2). By conforming to this demand, he proves that "his social desires are stronger" than his discomfort with bourgeois convention.[14] He almost fails to qualify for membership, even so, because he "hain't got no family" (10). The proposal to kill "the *families* of boys that told the secrets" calls negative attention to Huck's place in St. Petersburg's social hierarchy (10, Twain's emphasis). A boy whose sole parent is a notorious drunkard, long gone missing, is perhaps unfit to associate with boys whose place in the community is securely established by family connections. His father's absenteeism has put Huck at risk of ostracism by age-mates. The fact that "you can't never find" Pap, or that Huck is the victim of parental abandonment, seems more socially condemnable even than Pap's habit of lying "drunk with the hogs" (10).

When Huck offers a way around the problem of "no family" by suggesting that Miss Watson serve as stand-in ("they could kill her"), readers laugh at this violation of nepotistic logic (10). Miss Watson is scarcely the equivalent of a valued family member, yet the boys accept her as such: "She'll do. That's all right" (10). The whole point of the threat of killing family members, clearly, is to enforce loyalty by evoking family feeling. Because members of the gang love their relatives—or wish, at any rate, to protect them from harm—they will obey gang policy rather than endanger them. A source of daily aggravation to Huck, Miss Watson has inspired no personal affection in him; more important, she is not related to him. The absurdity of accepting her as a locus for nepotistic feeling is compounded by the fact that she is not even Huck's current guardian. It is the Widow Douglas, not Miss Watson, who has taken Huck into her home as "her son," yet neither he nor his companions suggest that the widow more plausibly might be regarded as his "family." Substitution of Miss Watson suits Twain's comic purposes better, obviously, because it directs mockery toward the boys' failure to understand the principles they pretend to espouse and the practices they pretend to imitate. A sobering afterthought may occur to readers, moreover, as they learn just how much Huck fears and despises his one remaining parent. "Miss Watson is a nuisance, Pap is a threat," as Alan Trachtenberg notes.[15] Given the dread with which he anticipates Pap's re-emergence into his life (a dread soon to be triggered by discovery of his father's footprints), it is fair

---

14 Catherine H. Zuckert, "Law and Nature in the *Adventures of Huckleberry Finn*," in *Huck Finn among the Critics: A Centennial Selection*, ed. M. Thomas Inge (Frederick, MD: University Publications of America, 1985), 233.
15 Alan Trachtenberg, "The Form of Freedom in *Huckleberry Finn*," in *Huck Finn: Major Literary Characters*, ed. Harold Bloom (New York: Chelsea House 1990), 56.

to conclude that he would feel worse about even the annoying Miss Watson's death than about his father's. The ironic impact of this realization would be diminished if the more kindly widow had been selected as Huck's substitute family for purposes of gang reprisals.

Readers witness the full extent of Pap's paternal flaws first-hand when he takes center-stage in Chapters 5, 6, and 7. His abdication of paternal care (the desertion already described) appears benign in comparison with his brutal in-person parenting. He re-enters Huck's life not as a nurturer but as a thief, with the sole purpose of appropriating Huck's material resources. Later he will seize Huck himself, "whom he considers as property suddenly become valuable."[16] Pap has heard rumors about the robbers' loot Huck and Tom have found, and he intends to walk off with the whole six thousand dollars: "that's why I come" (25). He does not propose to share any of the money with Huck and in no way acknowledges that Huck has any claim to it. He rants self-righteously about "all the trouble and all the anxiety and all the expense of raising" a child, arguing that grown children owe their parents compensation for having reared them (33). Coming from a man who has gone to absolutely no "trouble" or "expense" on his son's behalf, who has abandoned that son in violation of the most minimal standards of parental responsibility, Pap's self-justifying arguments inspire ridicule as well as contempt. His suddenly emergent concern with parental rights and responsibilities is self-evidently "a ploy to get for himself Huck's fortune."[17] Efforts instigated by Judge Thatcher and the Widow Douglas to remove Huck from Pap's guardianship disturb him chiefly because this step would block his access to Huck's property.

If Pap had succeeded in getting his hands on the six thousand dollars, there is no reason to predict that he would have used any part of it to shelter, feed, or educate his son. He would have disappeared with the money, in all probability, and continued to withhold paternal care. His strenuous efforts to lay hands on money belonging to his son constitute a spectacular reversal of ordinary parent-child relations: instead of providing material support to his minor child, he proposes to take possession of resources the child has acquired on his own account. Children who accumulate resources are susceptible, of course,

---

16 James M. Cox, "Remarks on the Sad Initiation of Huckleberry Finn," in *Huck Finn among the Critics: A Centennial Selection*, ed. M. Thomas Inge (Frederick, MD: University Publications of America, 1985), 146.

17 William E. Lenz, "Confidence and Convention in *Huckleberry Finn*," in *One Hundred Years of "Huckleberry Finn": The Boy, His Book, and American Culture*, ed. Robert Sattelmeyer and J. Donald Crowley (Columbia: University of Missouri Press, 1985), 189.

to exploitation by parents and other kin: their inexperience and powerlessness render them helpless in the face of financial turpitude or mismanagement on the part of adult relatives (the sometimes misappropriated wages of successful child actors and athletes come to mind). Pap's style of parental exploitation is characteristically crude. He does not pretend to be acting in Huck's best interest; he feigns no fondness. He proposes to leave his son destitute, and he manifests no concern for any hardship Huck might suffer in consequence.

In addition to his complete disinterest in the physical survival of his offspring, Pap flouts parental self-interest by preventing Huck from enjoying social and economic benefits provided by the Widow Douglas. Instead of rejoicing that his son is being clothed, fed, and educated at someone else's expense, Pap resents and rejects these advantages. An alloparent with no ties of kinship to the Finn family, the Widow Douglas is altruistically promoting Pap's fitness by caring for his child, yet he repudiates the cost-free benefits she is providing. He sneers at Huck's "starchy clothes" and pours scorn on the teachings of school and church as "highfalut'n foolishness" (23, 24). His anger is rooted in fear that Huck will think he is "better" than his father (24). He tells Huck that "none of the family" could read or write, specifically naming Huck's mother and himself, and insists that Huck not surpass his progenitors in acquired accomplishments. Huck is a bad son, according to Pap, because he is "putting on frills" and trying to "put on airs over his own father" (24). Once again, this is a reversal of adaptive parental strategy. Since a child's chances for reproductive success are enhanced by training, vocational or social, that can increase future income and status, parents typically seek out precisely such opportunities for their offspring. They work "to confer on their children advantages similar to those they enjoy themselves" and, if possible, more.[18] Such advantages are likely to increase the parents' genetic legacy. The more social and vocational success children achieve, clearly, the more likely they are to acquire high-quality mates and thus provide their parents with healthy, prosperous, and socially dominant grandchildren.

Pap's rejection of materially and socially advantageous opportunities for Huck thus is evolutionarily misguided. Ensuring his son's continued low status, keeping him at the very bottom of the local social hierarchy, Pap will pass on fewer genes, almost certainly, than if he helped to conserve Huck's wealth and encouraged Huck's participation in status-raising educational activities—school and church, to name obvious examples. Sponsored by the Widow Douglas, a

---

18 Dawkins, *Selfish Gene*, 6.

prominent member of the St. Petersburg community, and commanding with his robbers' loot "more money than a body could tell what to do with," Huck could anticipate considerable success in adulthood despite his lowly beginnings (1). Susan K. Harris suggests that Huck's decision to attend school "to spite Pap" might mean he "realizes that education will make him different from Pap," that is, he appreciates the chance to escape classification as social "dregs."[19] By insisting that Huck remain as poverty-stricken, ignorant, and uncultured as his father, Pap self-destructively undermines his own fitness prospects.

To make sure Huck does not continue to improve his future opportunities under the widow's influence and also, no doubt, to retain ready access to Huck's property, Pap snatches him from her supervision, forcibly isolating him in a small cabin in the woods. The kidnapping constitutes an act of retributive defiance, aimed against Huck and his current protectors, to "show who was Huck Finn's boss" (29). It is emphatically not a sign of nurturing intent. He keeps Huck captive not only to prevent him from profiting from advantages non-kin are offering, but to assert possession: Huck is chattel, and Pap will demonstrate that he can do with Huck as he likes. Typically, parental rights are asserted in order to prevent harm to children. Pap reverses socially normative and biologically adaptive behavior once again by exploiting parental privilege for negative purposes: to deny his child access to survival- and fitness-enhancing benefits.

Huck takes the abduction in stride, noting that the release from etiquette, hygiene, and school renders his existence "kind of lazy and jolly"; he goes so far as to say, even that he doesn't "want to go back" to the widow's (30). Away from the social pressure exerted by "respectable" adults and age-mates, he is "comfortable" living in "rags and dirt" (24). Evidently his father's lifestyle is not notably different from the one he forged for himself in his sugar-hogshead days, and he is unable to recognize the long-term disadvantages of embracing Pap's way of life (24).[20] Readers are likely to be more distressed than Huck by the

---

19 Susan K. Harris, "Huck Finn," in *Huck Finn: Major Literary Characters*, ed. Harold Bloom (New York: Chelsea House, 1990), 74.
20 Readers have observed commonalities between Huck and Pap—in taste, assumptions, and superstitions, for example—sometimes with unease. Harold Beaver points out that Pap's lifestyle is the one his son knows best; thus he imitates Pap's slatternly housekeeping, vulgar language, and habit of "borrowing." For representative discussion of the father-son resemblance and influence, see the following: Harold Beaver, "Huck and Pap," in *Huck Finn: Major Literary Characters*, ed. Harold Bloom (New York: Chelsea House, 1990); Stanley Brodwin, "Mark Twain in the Pulpit: The Theological Comedy of *Huckleberry Finn*," in *One Hundred Years of "Huckleberry Finn": The Boy, His Book, and American Culture*, ed. Robert Sattelmeyer and J. Donald Crowley (Columbia: University of Missouri Press, 1985); Michelson, "Huck and the Games."

primitive and prison-like conditions in which his father keeps him. He gives no sign that he takes any pleasure in his father's companionship, tellingly; his contentment with their laid-back routine, "smoking and fishing," includes no hint of filial affection (30). Quite quickly, Pap's physical cruelty and callous disregard for his safety motivate Huck to plan an escape from paternal abuse, an escape he intends to be permanent.

He decides to leave, he states, because of the beatings Pap administers with increasing regularity ("I was all over welts") and because he fears being left to die a slow death, "locked ... in," if his father should fail to return from one of his frequent trips to town (30, 31). Physical violence is a leitmotif in Huck's relations with his father: "he used to always whale me when he was sober and could get his hands on me"; "I used to be scared of him all the time, he tanned me so much"; "he said he'd cowhide me till I was black and blue"; "Pap got too handy with his hick'ry, and I couldn't stand it" (14, 23, 26, 30). In addition to his faults of omission as a parent—failure to provide shelter, food, clothing, and education—Huck's father regularly commits acts of physical aggression against his son, employing for this purpose sticks, belts, and whips. The beatings do not represent responsible parental chastisement for misbehavior, moreover, as the thrashings he gives Huck "for not stopping school" ironically demonstrate (29). A notoriously bad-tempered man, drunk or sober, Pap evidently uses his child as an all-purpose outlet for frustration, and clearly he feels entitled to do so. Even allowing for nineteenth-century tolerance of corporal punishment for children, Pap's violence as a father appears excessive, one more proof of deficient paternal investment. He beats his boy with apparent relish, to suit his temper or his whim, simply because he can "get his hands on" this smaller and weaker creature who belongs to him and who commands no means of resistance (14).

In every way imaginable, Pap inverts adaptive principles of parenting. He replaces investment with exploitation, care with abuse, affection with bullying; instead of providing social advantages, he forbids them. His paternal failings loom large in readers' perception of his character and in their memory of the novel. It is important, consequently, to consider what purposes—structural and thematic—his bad parenting serves in the narrative. Its contribution to plot is immediately discernible. Despite the relatively small amount of textual space devoted to Pap, his role as instigator is critical.[21] He does not figure directly in the action after Chapter 8, earning

---

21 "It is amazing how few pages of type [Pap] occupies; the effect is as of a prolonged, minute analysis," Bernard DeVoto observes. "The Artist as American," in *Twentieth Century*

only brief and scattered mention in the rest of the book, but he supplies the impetus for Huck's trip down the Mississippi. The need to free himself from "a dangerous, indeed murderous father" sets Huck's escape plan in motion.[22]

Pap's role as provocateur is somewhat blurred by Huck's assertion that he also is running away from the Widow Douglas, "a much less understandable" and less urgently motivated course of action.[23] Readers must suspect that survival-oriented considerations, as much as youthful resistance to being "sivilized," cause Huck to evade her fostering. The Widow Douglas and Judge Thatcher have shown themselves to be powerless against Pap's aggressively enforced paternal claims. They have been unable to wrest Huck from his rapacious parent by legal means, with their "lawsuit" to transfer guardianship, and equally unable to succor the boy through pragmatic intervention: Pap drives off "with the gun" a would-be rescuer sent by the widow after the abduction (31, 30).[24] The law is intended to provide "a source of protection ... of both person and property," as Catherine H. Zuckert points out, but here it proves "too weak ... to protect people from violence."[25] Pap's use of brute force has intimidated Judge Thatcher and the Widow Douglas, stymieing their rescue efforts. Having escaped captivity entirely by his own efforts, Huck has no reason to trust himself to the care of these well-meaning but ineffectual protectors. If he were to seek shelter again with the widow, Pap would simply recapture him and "stow" him, as threatened, in an even more remote place of confinement (32). It is clear that Huck is fleeing

---

Interpretations of "Adventures of Huckleberry Finn", ed. Claude M. Simpson (Englewood Cliffs, NJ: Prentice-Hall, 1968), 10.

22 Harold Bloom, Introduction to *Huck Finn: Major Literary Characters*, ed. Harold Bloom (New York: Chelsea House, 1990), 2. Bloom points out that the freedom Huck seeks "in the first place must mean freedom from such a deathly father," 1. Nancy Walker notes that Miss Watson's "decision to sell Jim down the river" provides parallel impetus for Jim's flight. "Reformers and Young Maidens: Women and Virtue," in *Mark Twain's "Huckleberry Finn": Modern Critical Interpretations*, ed. Harold Bloom (New York: Chelsea House, 1986), 70.

23 Kenneth S. Lynn, "Critical Extracts," in *Huck Finn: Major Literary Characters*, ed. Harold Bloom (New York: Chelsea House, 1990), 25-26.

24 Beaver argues that Pap's illiteracy renders him unable "to defend his legal and financial and civil rights": "what make him rage and roar is his complete helplessness." "Huck and Pap," 177. Such assertion is largely contradicted by the text, however: Pap is initially successful, rather than helpless, in upsetting plans to interfere with his parental rights, and after Huck's supposed death he is expected to "walk into Huck's money as easy as nothing" (70). Pap's very brutishness enables him to intimidate and resist his genteel antagonists in the St. Petersburg community.

25 Zuckert, "Law and Nature," 233.

the danger Pap represents; that danger is so acute, moreover, that he must run from other adults whose inadequate resistance to Pap's perceived parental rights would leave him at his father's mercy.

Having initiated action by precipitating Huck's flight from St. Petersburg, Pap's bad parenting also contributes significantly to the two-part resolution of the novel's plot. His death removes all threats to Huck's security, enabling him to return to the place he calls "home" (361). Huck is assured the use of his six thousand dollars, which Pap has not, after all, "got ... away from Judge Thatcher and drunk ... up" (361). More important, Huck can rest "comfortable" in the certainty that Pap will never again reappear to batter and "boss" him (14, 29). The wish the boy expresses near the beginning of the book—"I didn't want to see him no more"—is realized: Pap "ain't a comin' back no mo'" (14, 316). Pap is such a terrible parent that only his death can provide a happy ending for his son: this is a highly unusual fictional circumstance. Although he is "almost infinitely good-natured and accommodating,"[26] Huck has not a single word of grief or pity for his murdered father. Even the King and the Duke, identified and condemned as Pap's "kind of people," elicit a softened response from Huck when he sees them tarred and feathered: he "couldn't ever feel any hardness against them any more" (165, 290). The King and the Duke have treated Huck coercively and exploitatively, but they are not his parents, a critical ameliorating factor in the judgment he renders on them. Precisely because of the parent-child relationship, Pap's death is a necessary condition of Huck's safety and freedom, just as Miss Watson's death, together with her manumitting testamentary bequest, is the necessary condition of Jim's safety and freedom.[27] In each case, biology—either kinship or race—is used to support claims of ownership, with attendant rights to control, exploit, confine, and abuse. Although their situations clearly are not equally perilous or soul-searing, Twain has strengthened the parallel between Huck and Jim as much as possible with his dramatically negative portrait of Pap.[28]

---

26 Richard P. Adams, "The Unity and Coherence of *Huckleberry Finn*," in *Twentieth Century Interpretations of "Adventures of Huckleberry Finn"*, ed. Claude M. Simpson (Englewood Cliffs, NJ: Prentice-Hall, 1968), 49.

27 Michael Egan explores parallels between Huck's circumstances and Jim's in some detail. He notes, for instance, that both "are incarcerated" (Huck by his father and Jim by the Phelps family) "because they represent a potential pecuniary profit." *Mark Twain's Huckleberry Finn: Race, Class and Society* (London: Sussex University Press, 1977), 37.

28 Henry Nash Smith speaks for most readers when he notes that "Jim's freedom has been brought about by an implausible device" (as has Huck's), reflecting Twain's "need to resolve his plot." "A Sound Heart and a Deformed Conscience," in *Twentieth Century Interpretations*

Once Pap is dead, Huck's safety and prosperity are assured. Nothing in the text encourages readers to speculate about the long-term psychosocial consequences of the deficient parenting he has received. The narrative concludes with Huck ready to join Tom Sawyer for a new round of boyishly conceived games: "a couple of weeks or two" of "howling adventures" (361). Far from seeking shelter and nurture from an alloparent, Huck plans to "light out ... ahead" of his companions, as eager as any normal preadolescent to evade the rules and regimens imposed by adults upon the minors in their care (362). Thus the benefits of adoption by Aunt Sally are outweighed in his estimation by the costs of conforming to her authority, however kind. In contrast to the physically dangerous incarceration and battering he suffered at his father's hands, obviously, supervision by a well-meaning adult determined to "sivilize" him triggers no alarm in readers' minds. Whether or not Aunt Sally should succeed in her scheme to "adopt" him, readers are given no cause to worry any longer about Huck (361). He endures in their memories as a perpetual boy, lingering forever in prepubescent naiveté, now chiefly concerned to resist the proprieties and posturings imposed by the adult world.

Since it closes before its protagonist has grown up, *Adventures of Huckleberry Finn* cannot be regarded as a bildungsroman or coming-of-age story. Narrative action in the novel comprises only a few months: when the plot winds up, Huck is the same fourteen-year-old boy he was at the outset. He undergoes no mental or emotional maturation.[29] Significantly, he is no more able to formulate moral or philosophical challenges to the ideas about race prevailing in his social community than he was before his trip down the Mississippi with Jim. He has come to a fuller appreciation of Jim's humanity, certainly, but his identification with Jim's escape plans remains vacillating and ambivalent. There is incontrovertible evidence, moreover, that increased personal loyalty and empathy do not lead him to larger sociopolitical realizations. Despite his concern for Jim's welfare (consistently keener than that expressed by most of those around him), he continues to accept the institution of slavery as morally right and divinely ordained. Most conspicuously, he is convinced that he will

---

of *"Adventures of Huckleberry Finn"*, ed. Claude M. Simpson (Englewood Cliffs, NJ: Prentice-Hall, 1968), 73.

29 Richard Poirier points out that Huck's "acceptance of Tom's leadership in the mock freeing of Jim" necessarily involves "a sacrifice" of the nascent "emotional growth" readers observe in the scene when Huck humbles himself 'to a nigger.'" "Huck Finn and the Metaphors of Society," in *Twentieth Century Interpretations of "Adventures of Huckleberry Finn"*, ed. Claude M. Simpson (Englewood Cliffs, NJ: Prentice-Hall, 1968), 100.

be damned to hell for helping a run-away slave. At the same time that readers applaud his decision to choose loyalty to Jim over personal salvation (in the famous "all right, then, I'll *go* to hell" moment), they must notice that he never entertains the possibility that the systematic exploitation and dehumanization of African Americans might be wrong (271). In the conflict between "generous impulse" and "perverted moral code of a society built on slavery," as Henry Nash Smith states, the impulses of the "uncoerced self" continue to yield to "social conformity."[30] Walter Blair provides evidence from Twain's notebooks in support of this point, showing that, in Twain's view, "moral standards ... made by society" shape "conscience" and thus exert a monitoring effect on behavior.[31] As R. J. Fertel and others have pointed out, readers recoil at "the horror" of Huck's acquiescence to Tom Sawyer's leadership in the final portion of the book: "his tacit participation in the belittlement of Jim in the Evasion sequence."[32] To the very end, Huck takes for granted the doctrine of racial inequality: Jim's self-sacrificing behavior when Tom Sawyer is wounded offers proof, Huck shockingly concludes, that Jim is "white inside" (341). The continued rebelliousness Huck expresses with respect to *sivilization* clearly does not encompass culturally constructed obstacles to freedom confronting the African American population in 1835-1845.

Huck's unchanged acceptance of these large-scale social evils—evils the novel's author condemns—is necessary to preserve consistency in his role as narrator. Huck's obliviousness to racial injustice is strategically designed to rouse in readers the very recognitions and reactions eluding the boy himself. Huck's unreliability as narrator (in that his views about race contradict Twain's) is a device that "elicits the reader's participation" in Huck's crisis of conscience.[33] Actively arguing against Huck's unexamined, conformist values, readers are shouting from the margins, as it were: *No, no! You won't go to hell for helping Jim escape! This is a good deed, not a wicked one!* Having chosen to employ his boy narrator's naïve acceptance of the status quo as part of his persuasive strategy, Twain cannot permit him to reach adulthood and assess his social environment with mature wisdom. A grown-up Huck either would

---

30 Smith, "A Sound Heart," 80.
31 Walter Blair, "'So Noble ... and So Beautiful a Book,'" in *Twentieth Century Interpretations of "Adventures of Huckleberry Finn"*, ed. Claude M. Simpson (Englewood Cliffs, NJ: Prentice-Hall, 1968), 66, 70.
32 R. J. Fertel, "Spontaneity and the Quest for Maturity in *Huckleberry Finn*," in *Huck Finn: Major Literary Characters*, ed. Harold Bloom (New York: Chelsea House, 1990), 91.
33 Harris, "Huck Finn," 76.

remain susceptible to what Leo Marx dubs "the crippling power ... of social morality,"[34] thereby undermining the author's purposes, or he would become an outspoken proponent of abolition, giving direct voice to ideas Twain wished to convey with the subtle force of irony and satire. Huck's "paradoxical situation, as teller and as character," Trachtenberg asserts, ensures that despite "the self-consciousness and process of self-discovery implicit in many scenes," he must forfeit "his chance to grow up."[35] For good reasons, Huck's character shows none of the development readers would expect in a coming-of-age story. The potentially damaging long-term effects of bad parenting on Huck's adult self-image, community reputation, or reproductive success are irrelevant, since the narrative does not extend that far into his future. Outrage triggered by Pap's paternal flaws, an outrage that might have been expended in mourning his child's blasted future, is conserved for other purposes, lending fuel to condemnation of Pap's White Supremacist ideology.

Thematically, Twain's characterization of Pap as a vicious and unnatural father supports the argument he is making throughout the novel against racial bigotry. Situating his tale in the American South, fifteen to twenty-five years before the Civil War, Twain depicts his fictional characters realistically, that is, committed to the institution of slavery and convinced of white superiority. All the novel's characters, virtuous or villainous, share the prejudices typical of the time and place: not a single "low down Ablitionist" takes part in the action (52). The often quoted exchange between Huck and Aunt Sally Phelps perfectly illustrates the deeply embedded racist assumptions of even the more likeable characters. Aunt Sally wants to know if "anybody" was hurt in a steamboat accident. "No'm," Huck tells her, adding, "killed a nigger." She responds with relief: this outcome is "lucky" because "sometimes people do get hurt" (279). In the course of the next few chapters, readers learn that Aunt Sally, like Huck, is basically a good-hearted person, yet their words betray their shared conviction that "niggers" are not "people." Mrs. Phelps's "notorious one-liner" demonstrates that "Twain's indictment of bigotry is all-encompassing."[36] The more ethically minded characters generally treat slaves better than others

---

34 Leo Marx, "Mr. Eliot, Mr. Trilling, and *Huckleberry Finn*, in *Twentieth Century Interpretations of "Adventures of Huckleberry Finn"*, ed. Claude M. Simpson (Englewood Cliffs, NJ: Prentice-Hall, 1968), 36.
35 Trachtenberg, "Form of Freedom," 58, 60. Trachtenberg discusses the problem of Huck's incomplete—or failed—moral development in considerable detail.
36 Alex Pitofsky, "Pap Finn's Overture: Fatherhood, Identity, and Southwestern Culture in *Adventures of Huckleberry Finn*," *Mark Twain Annual* 4, no. 1 (2006): 62.

do—refraining from selling them "down to Orleans" for example, and avoiding separation of families—but none of them talk of abolishing slavery or consider blacks the equals of whites (53). Clearly unable to employ any of his historically realistic characters to voice and promote his views, Twain must convey his most important social and moral comment indirectly.

Characterization of Pap, the protagonist's unnaturally bad father, proves to be a key factor in the alignment of reader sympathies against racism. Pap's "toxic mix of racism, alcoholism, and child abuse functions as the novel's overture," Alex Pitofsky observes.[37] Despising Pap, readers necessarily despise Pap's opinions, and he quickly emerges as "the arch-racist in the novel."[38] He is the only character who articulates a philosophy of white entitlement and superiority. The behavior of other characters demonstrates their allegiance to such a philosophy, but Pap puts it into words—crassly, vulgarly, unforgettably. He is, as Millicent Bell points out, "a subscriber to society's formulas, for all his seeming unregeneracy"; he is the "wicked soul of conventionality."[39] Inhabitants of the antebellum South "share (and have codified) his racial intolerance."[40] David L. Smith similarly stresses that "Pap's views correspond very closely to those of most of his white Southern contemporaries, in substance if not in manner of expression." Pap gives voice to opinions "held not only by poor whites but by all 'right-thinking' Southerners, regardless of their social class."[41]

Ranting drunkenly at the cabin where he has hidden Huck, Pap shifts from the topic of parental entitlement to that of racial entitlement. The "govment" thwarting his efforts to take possession of his son's money is the same "govment" that supports the right of a "free nigger" to acquire resources, education, status, and suffrage (33, 34). Pap is outraged that "a mulatter" should show signs of prosperity ("fine clothes," "a gold watch and chain") and achieve vocational status (that of "a p'fessor in a college") (33, 34). Resenting the accomplishments of this man who "could talk all kinds of languages, and

---

37 Ibid., 55. Reesman argues that Pap's alcoholism is a key factor in his failure as a father in "Bad Fathering," 177, 171. She also explores the theme of fatherhood from the perspective of Twain's harsh criticisms of orthodox Christianity, interpreting Pap as Twain's contemptuous portrait of a "God figure." "Bad Fathering," 170.
38 Egan, *Mark Twain's Huckleberry Finn*, 74.
39 Millicent Bell, "*Huckleberry Finn* and the Sleights of the Imagination," in *Huck Finn: Major Literary Characters*, ed. Harold Bloom (New York: Chelsea House, 1990), 115.
40 Pitofsky, "Pap Finn's Overture," 61.
41 David L. Smith, "Huck, Jim, and American Racial Discourse," in *Huck Finn among the Critics: A Centennial Selection*, ed. M. Thomas Inge (Frederick, MD: University Publications of American, 1985), 251.

knowed everything" (34), Pap is "incensed "by what appears to him as a crime against natural laws."[42] It is wrong, in Pap's view, that a member of the African American race—a race defined in his social environment as inferior—should have more, more of anything, than Pap himself has. The "cool" assurance of this "free nigger" distresses him most of all: "why, he couldn't a give me the road if I hadn't shoved him out o the way" (34). The picture of Pap, with his ratty clothes, greasy hair, and boorish manners, shouldering the "p'fessor" aside with deliberate insolence, burns itself odiously into the reader's imagination.

Pap ends his tirade by expressing indignation that this man "from Ohio" enjoys governmentally supported rights that render him, legally, Pap's equal (33). The appearance of a wealthy and educated black *citizen* angers and appalls him because it defies all his assumptions about their relative places in the social, political, and economic universe of the Old South. Despite temporary residence in Illinois, the visitor cannot be "put up at auction and sold," and this fact contradicts Pap's conviction that, by virtue of racial inheritance, this "free nigger" is property (33). When Pap learns that "at home" this man can vote, he declares that he will no longer participate in "govment": "I says I'll never vote agin" (34). It is ludicrous, of course, to hear Pap talk as if the country would be a worse place without his vote ("the country may rot for all me"), but the comedic touches in the scene are harsh—and all at Pap's expense.[43] They highlight his unshakeable belief that his human worth is greater than any black person's. In the judgment of readers who have witnessed his vicious greed, drunken rampages, hypocritical posturing, and paternal failures, Pap's human worth is close to nothing. When he lays claim to intrinsically higher human value than an entire population, based on race, the doctrine of white superiority appears acutely untenable.

To achieve maximum reader support for his denunciation of institutionalized slavery and racial bigotry, Twain invests Pap, "the most viciously articulate exponent of Southern racism," with other traits calculated to evoke outrage and contempt.[44] Readers have noted, of course, that Pap is guilty of both

---

42 Ibid., 250.
43 James M. Cox argues that Pap is intentionally humorous, but readers are more likely to be laughing at Pap than with him. Pap actually believes, for instance, that his vote is worth something; he sees no irony in his threat to force the country to get along without his civic participation. Thus he becomes the butt of reader's mockery. "A Hard Book to Take," in *Mark Twain's "Adventures of Huckleberry Finn"*, ed. Harold Bloom (New York: Chelsea House, 1986), 90.
44 Egan, *Mark Twain's Huckleberry Finn*, 74.

child abuse and racial bigotry.[45] United in a single character, this particular combination of behaviors strengthens mightily the case against racial injustice. By accentuating Pap's paternal deficiencies so monstrously, Twain ensures that readers will condemn everything Pap stands for. There is shock value in the spectacle of excessively bad parenting, and fitness-based analysis of parental investment explains how and why this is so. The *unnaturalness* of Pap's actions as a father is a crucial factor: his behavior defies and denies universals of human nature, together with cultural ideals that validate and support those universals. "In the swamp of Pap's life," as Robert Shulman puts it, all positive "ties of family" and kinship have been lost: nepotistic adaptations, which form a "basic force of human cohesion," fail to function.[46] Consequently, Pap inspires reactions tinged with primal horror and revulsion. Identifying him as a deviant father from an evolutionary as well as from a societal perspective, Twain effectively indicates that the racist doctrine Pap espouses is as unnatural as his parenting.

---

45 Cox points out that "these two forms of behavior" mark Pap as "a reprobate," for instance, without further exploration of the relationship between them. "A Hard Book," 90.

46 Robert Shulman, "Fathers, Brothers, and 'the Diseased': The Family, Individualism, and American Society in *Huck Finn*," in *One Hundred Years of "Huckleberry Finn": The Boy, His Book, and American Culture*, ed. Robert Sattelmeyer and J. Donald Crowley (Columbia: University of Missouri Press, 1985), 329.

CHAPTER 6

Hell's Fury: Female Mate-Retention Strategies in "Pomegranate Seed" and *Ethan Frome*

A recurrent predicament in Edith Wharton's fiction is that of the woman whose hold on a long-term mate is threatened by an interloper. Devoting persistent attention to female-female competition, Wharton focuses with special intensity on the married or affianced woman who takes action to avoid displacement by a mate-poaching rival. Memorably successful defenses are mounted, for example, by Bertha Dorset in *The House of Mirth*, by May Welland in *The Age of Innocence*, and by Alida Slade in "Roman Fever." These characters concoct elaborate and underhanded plots to thwart competitors. The ruthlessness of their mate-retention strategies effectively highlights the evolutionarily critical stakes in such competition. In "Pomegranate Seed" (1936) and *Ethan Frome* (1911), Wharton portrays female possessiveness in a particularly sinister light, associating it with supernatural forces. Identifying it as a significant locus of power, she pays backhanded tribute to women's ability to protect their self-interest. By casting a demonic light on female mate-guarding behavior, moreover, she directs readers' sympathies decisively away from idealized standards of spousal commitment, directing it instead toward disloyal husbands and potential new partners. In these tales, consequently, she invites readers to consider the topic of marital loyalty from an unexpected ethical and emotional perspective.

Mate Guarding: Background

Mate guarding is an important adaptive strategy: individuals of both sexes attempt to protect their reproductive success by preventing rivals from gaining intimate access to their partners. Historically, mate-guarding strategies practiced by men have garnered more attention than those employed by women.

From sequestration to foot-binding, men have resorted to notoriously extreme measures to enforce female fidelity. The coerciveness and brutality sometimes employed reflect the gravity of the loss men fear to sustain if their partners are unfaithful: they risk making substantial paternal investment in children fathered by other men. The potential fitness costs are high—hence the strenuous efforts of human males to ensure their exclusive rights of access to long-term mates.[1] Wharton manifests small interest in male mate-guarding efforts, however; throughout her career she focuses chiefly on female versions of this behavioral strategy.

Although they run no risk of misplaced parental investment, women stand to lose reproductively vital resources if they fail to guard their relationships against encroachment. If a man channels material and emotional resources to an extra-pair woman and her children, his primary mate and *her* children will have to make do with less. Depending upon environmental circumstances, such diluted male investment can threaten the well-being and even the survival of offspring from the original union.[2] The social status and social opportunities of both mother and children are apt to decline, too, when the primary provider strays; the perceived mate value of a betrayed wife is typically reduced. Just as a cuckolded man tends to become an object of ridicule and suffer reputational damage, a deceived wife is likely to incur social costs.[3] It benefits women as well as men, therefore, to take decisive measures, both preemptive and reactive, to foil rivals. Physically and legally, women seldom have been in a position to guard their mates as thoroughly, or as cruelly, as have men: harem-style imprisonment and bodily mutilation of men by women, for example, do not appear in the anthropological record. In place of physical intervention, women typically choose indirect tactics. Exercise of vigilance tends to be their "first line of defense," supported by strategic spying and interrogation, intervention by family members, appeals to social norms, and a variety of related guilt-inducing strategies.[4] In addition to "emotional manipulation" of various kinds, women

---

[1] Buss, *Evolution of Desire*: 66-67.

[2] David M. Buss, *The Dangerous Passion: Why Jealousy Is as Necessary as Love and Sex* (New York: Free Press / Simon and Schuster, 2000), 53. Anne Campbell's analysis of women's reasons for engaging in mate-guarding behavior, an analysis consciously concerned to exclude potential male bias, supports that offered by Buss. *A Mind of Her Own: The Evolutionary Psychology of Women* (Oxford: Oxford University Press, 2002), 255-58.

[3] Buss, *Dangerous Passion*, 40.

[4] Ibid., 42.

may seek to instill "psychological fear" with displays of righteous wrath.[5] Wharton reminds readers that women can and do go to extraordinary lengths to retain their hold on desirable mates: in her fiction she portrays numerous female characters who initiate notably creative and "ferocious" action to thwart interlopers.[6]

"Pomegranate Seed"

To maximize the impact of her portraits, Wharton sometimes draws upon the "primal" evocative power of the horror story, a genre rooted in "the earliest folklore of all races."[7] In the preface to her collected ghost stories, she explains that spectral phenomena inspire dread and thus heighten emotional engagement with a tale. Readers sense a "strange something" at work behind unfolding events, "something" beyond the familiar boundaries of reality.[8] We are deeply disturbed, Wharton contends, by what H. P. Lovecraft describes as the "malign and particular suspension or defeat of those fixed laws of Nature which are our only safeguard against the assaults of chaos."[9] In "Pomegranate Seed" she incorporates the dislocating strangeness of the supernatural to lend dramatic and emotional intensity to the phenomenon of female mate guarding. The occult activities of a possessive wife prove central to the story's action, triggering the initial conflict and leading relentlessly to its spine-chilling climax. A deceased woman exercises such irresistible influence over her husband that she is able to reach out from beyond the grave to separate him from his new wife, finally drawing him to join her in the realm of the dead. The central plot device—a series of letters seemingly sent from a dead woman—defies the limits of ordinary reality, as does the spooky disappearance of the husband at the story's conclusion.

---

5   Buss, *Evolution of Desire*, 140.
6   Edith Wharton, "Roman Fever," in *Collected Stories, 1911-1937*, ed. Maureen Howard (New York: Library of America, 2001), 761.
7   H. P. Lovecraft, *Supernatural Horror in Literature* (New York: Dover, 1973), 17. For further discussion of the origins of "belief in supernatural agents," including the adaptive value of horror stories, see Mathias Clasen, "'Can't Sleep, Clowns Will Eat Me': Telling Scary Stories," in *Telling Stories / Geschichten Erzählen: Literature and Evolution*, ed. Carsten Gansel and Dirk Vanderbeke (Berlin: De Gruyter, 2012).
8   Edith Wharton, "Preface," *The Ghost Stories of Edith Wharton* (New York: Scribner/Macmillan, Hudson River Ed., 1986), 4.
9   H. P. Lovecraft, *Supernatural Horror*, 15.

The series of "mysterious letters" sent to Kenneth Ashby assume a supernatural aura only gradually.[10] The untraceable gray envelopes, with their faint, almost inkless writing, might well originate from a disembodied realm like the underworld described in Homer's *Odyssey*. The handwriting itself manifests a contrasting "strength and assurance"; the impression created is paradoxically "bold but faint" (55). The fact that the letters have not been sent by post and arrive without observable means of delivery ("always in the evening, after dark") adds to the unease they provoke (56). It is their effect on the recipient that proves most disturbing: each time Kenneth Ashby receives one of the strange gray missives, he complains of a headache, he looks "years older," and he withdraws from his wife (57). He rejoins her only to indulge in unaccustomed "faultfinding," with either her housekeeping or her treatment of his children (59). Curiously, however, these criticisms appear "to be uttered against his will" and he looks as if has been "far away from ordinary events" (59).

Following up on the strong hint provided by the story's title, evidence mounts that the letters emanate from the underworld, penned by the ghostly spirit of Kenneth's dead wife. Much critical commentary addresses the cryptic allusion in Wharton's title.[11] No one-to-one parallels can be clearly established between Wharton's characters and those in the myth. The chief effect of the allusion is to suggest, at the outset, that the mysterious letters come from Hades: the region of the dead. Choosing the pomegranate seed for her title, rather than some other phrase or name that would recall the myth, Wharton draws attention to the power of the food to enforce spousal obligation. In the myth, Persephone (a bride-by-capture) must remain with Pluto because she has partaken of his food; hence the one-month-per-seed resolution. That is, Persephone is said to owe Pluto her wifely presence because of, and in proportion to, the nourishment she has accepted from him. In Wharton's tale, the "seed" points in similar fashion toward the reproductive benefits Kenneth

---

10 Edith Wharton, "Pomegranate Seed," in *The World Over* (New York and London: Appleton-Century, 1936), 59. All citations refer to this edition.

11 R.W. B. Lewis, for example, discusses Wharton's "lifelong obsession" with "Persephone and her sojourn in the underworld" in *Edith Wharton: A Biography* (New York: Harper Row, 1975), 495. Judith Fryer and Josephine Donovan explore Wharton's use of the myth in a number of novels, novellas, short stories, and poems in *Felicitous Space: The Imaginative Structures of Edith Wharton and Willa Cather* (Chapel Hill: University of North Carolina Press, 1986) and in *After the Fall: The Demeter-Persephone Myth in Wharton, Cather, and Glasgow* (University Park: Pennsylvania State University Press, 1989), 43-83. See also Carol J. Singley and Susan Elizabeth Sweeney, "Forbidden Reading and Ghostly Power in Wharton's 'Pomegranate Seed,'" *Women's Studies* 20 (1991).

has received from his deceased wife. Having enjoyed access to her fertility, or "seed," he is expected (and spectrally commanded) to maintain his marital commitment to her. Since he has "already eaten the pomegranate seeds (his first marriage and allegiance to Elsie)," as Kathy Justice Gentile notes, "Charlotte's struggle to keep him is doomed from the start."[12] His loyalty is enforced by supernatural agencies, which support his wife's efforts to ensure that his devotion remains everlasting, even if for him this means, literally, going to hell.

Kenneth's behavior upon receiving the missives makes their content easy to infer: she rebukes him for remarrying; she denigrates the domestic and maternal capabilities of his new wife; she urges him to return to her.[13] This is exactly the kind of thing deserted wives say and have said, from time immemorial. Such letters and such sentiments would be merely trite, and would cause no dread, if they were written by a woman cast off or divorced in ordinary, real-life fashion. It is the implicitly supernatural origin of the letters that renders them frightening. The writing on the ninth and last letter in the sequence, opened by Charlotte and Kenneth's mother after he has failed to come home at the usual time, is so faint as to be entirely unreadable except for two words: "mine" and "come" (105). In fact, no other words are necessary, since these express the writer's message unambiguously: she is laying claim to her husband, insisting even after death on his prior commitment to her.

It would have been easy and natural, readers might suppose, for Wharton to evoke sympathy for the displaced first wife. How sad it is, after all, for Elsie to die at a relatively young age, while her husband lives on to love again and find happiness with someone else. Wharton encourages readers to identify with the second wife instead, however; the third-person-limited perspective employed throughout the narrative is hers. Experiencing everything from Charlotte's point of view, readers share her horrified response to the letters threatening her marital happiness. The first wife, Elsie, is presented as a strong-willed woman who throughout her twelve-year marriage held her husband in psychological subjugation: "she absolutely dominated him" (58). Her "firm handwriting," full of "strength and assurance," evidently reflects her unyielding character (55).

---

12 Kathy Justice Gentile, "Supernatural Transmissions: Turn-of-the-Century Ghosts in American Women's Fiction: Jewett, Freeman, Wharton, and Gilman," in *Approaches to Teaching Gothic Fiction*, ed. Diane Long Hoeveler and Tamar Heller (New York: Modern Language Association, 2003), 213.

13 Clasen explains that such reproachful messages are typical of ghosts, who often "seek revenge" or "seek to right a wrong" perpetrated against them. Tellingly, ghosts also "may wish to consume your soul." "'Can't Sleep'" 331.

Kenneth seems certainly to have been the more submissive, more insecure partner in their union, compelled to strive continually for an exacting wife's approval. As acquaintances observe, "during all the years of their marriage he was more like an unhappy lover than a comfortably contented husband" (60). Elsie's hold on him, during her lifetime and afterward, manifests itself in an emotional subservience on her husband's part. His admiration and "great love" for her take the form of almost obsequious devotion.[14] He feels "despair" when she dies (61); friends predict that he will "mentally compare" other women to Elsie forever, and always to their disadvantage (60); he presses his lips to one of the letters she sends him; he tells Charlotte he has "never forgotten Elsie" (76).

Even during her lifetime, nonetheless, Kenneth chafed under his first wife's markedly controlling personality. There is evidence, in his improved spirits and appearance, that he is thriving in his new relationship with Charlotte, a relationship that allows him "a little liberty for a change" (58). The second marriage visibly rejuvenates him. At the same time, however, he seeks from Charlotte protection from some indefinite, threatening influence: at times he is "too eagerly dependent on her, too searchingly close" (78). The cause of his forebodings is soon revealed, and he responds to the arrival of each successive gray envelope with symptoms of physical and emotional distress. Charlotte does not hesitate to interpret the letter campaign as "a secret persecution before which he quailed, yet from which he could not free himself" (79). Regarded through the eyes of his second wife, Elsie is a relentlessly jealous wife who begrudges her husband any happiness that does not include her. Withholding direct access to Elsie's side of the story, Wharton encourages readers to condemn the "conscious, malevolent" tenacity with which she clings, in death as in life, to her husband (79).

From a Darwinian perspective, Elsie's posthumous activities make sense—up to a point. It is potentially adaptive to prevent a former spouse from taking a new wife and fathering more children. Elsie leaves him alone during the first two years of his bereavement and mourning, consequently, and begins to haunt him by letter only when he remarries. As long as Kenneth remained an inconsolable widower, there was no danger that Elsie's children would have to share his attention and his resources with stepsiblings or suffer from a stepmother's preferential regard for her

---

14 Buss states that despite the "common stereotype that women are more submissive than men," studies of mate-keeping tactics demonstrate something quite different. Interestingly, "men submit to and abase themselves before their mates roughly 25 percent more than women in order to keep their mates." *Evolution of Desire*, 34.

own children's interests. Such dangers are real, as much twentieth-century research has demonstrated. The presence of a stepparent and half-siblings often leads to unequal apportionment of attention and education, as well as money and property, with the second family taking a larger share. Statistically, too, stepchildren experience heightened risk of physical and emotional abuse.[15] Insofar as Elsie Ashby's goal is to protect the children who survive her—and who represent, we must suppose, her chief genetic legacy—from such potential dangers, her campaign to "separate" and "estrange" Kenneth from a new mate is recognizably adaptive. Her ghostly haunting is calculated to promote her children's fitness and thereby her own (77, 72). Moving the emotions and behavior of the displaced wife into a supernatural realm, Wharton heightens their impact even as she renders it impossible to subject them to fully realistic analysis.

The timing of the letters supports the hypothesis that Elsie's principal objective is, in fact, to prevent the birth of children in the new marriage. The first letter is delivered when the new couple returns from a leisurely honeymoon, and thereafter the square gray envelopes arrive with special persistence directly "after ... holidays," that is, after Charlotte and Kenneth have spent leisure time together (63). Freeing a couple from domestic routines and business cares, "holidays" offer special opportunities for intensified emotional and sexual intimacy; chances of impregnation increase accordingly. Attempting to hinder the couple's reproductive success, Elsie uses her letters to punish Kenneth for spending special time alone with his new wife, thereby discouraging future trips featuring intimacy-inducing relaxation. Her punitively reproachful messages constitute one of the "destructive" mate-retention tactics described by Buss.[16] As her ghostly influence over Kenneth increases, she manages to interfere with the new couple's journeying even before it takes place: Letter Number Seven appears to contain an explicit warning against further travel. When Charlotte suggests that the two of them take "a long holiday" because he looks so ill and over-worked, Kenneth responds with "apprehension," telling her that he "can't ... can't possibly go away," "no matter how much I might want to" (82, 83, 84). At this point, approximately one year into the new marriage, Elsie appears to have achieved her goal: Kenneth is too cowed by her ominous communications

---

15 Martin Daly and Margo Wilson, "Evolutionary Psychology and Marital Conflict: The Relevance of Stepchildren," in *Sex, Power, Conflict: Evolutionary and Feminist Perspectives*, ed. David M. Buss and Neil M. Malamuth (New York and Oxford: Oxford University Press, 1996), 16-17.

16 Buss, *Evolution of Desire*, 137.

to undertake any more intimate get-aways with Charlotte. Before her death, Elsie's mate-retention efforts had successfully prevented extramarital dalliance ("Kenneth's never looked at another woman since he first saw Elsie"), and her posthumous mate-guarding activities promise to be similarly effective (60).

As part of her spectral efforts to retain her hold on Kenneth, Elsie exploits his natural inclination to protect his investment in the children already in existence: she attempts to instill dissatisfaction with the new wife by inspiring "mistrust" about the latter's effectiveness in her role as stepmother (61). Causing Kenneth to question Charlotte's "ability to manage the children," Elsie temporarily deflects his interest in new reproductive ventures (61). When it looks as though Kenneth is yielding to his second wife's wish for an intimate holiday, however—leaving Charlotte a message that they will set sail together "tomorrow"—Elsie reacts decisively (90). Readers are led to infer that she entices or compels him to take a very different kind of journey, that is, to join her in the shady realm her spirit presently inhabits. From a realistic perspective, this final step seems to contradict the best interests of Elsie's children, who now will be left with no living biological parent. Certainly, there is plenty of research indicating that orphaned children are likely to pay high costs.[17] Elsie's mate-retention efforts would appear more evolutionarily sound, indubitably, if she were not dead. A deserted wife has much to gain if she can induce her defecting husband to return by reminding him of his prior commitments, for instance, inducing guilt, and activating his concern for offspring: if successful, she will reroute the flow of resources back to herself and her children. Reconciliation and continuation of the marriage also may produce more children, with consequent increased fitness for both spouses. A dead woman can bear no more children, however, so that Elsie will realize no additional fitness benefits by insisting that Kenneth join her in death. Her action leaves her surviving children in the care of a grandmother, who may well not live long enough to finish raising them, and at the mercy of the very stepmother she sought to eliminate from their lives. If Charlotte were to take another husband after Kenneth's spooky departure, her children from that union would be no kin to Elsie's and thus not motivated by the nepotistic loyalty of the half-siblings Charlotte might have given them while married to their father.

It is difficult not to conclude that Elsie's children are likely to suffer more harm from their father's death than from his second marriage. Their situation as the children of a first marriage (unprotected by their biological mother) is

---

17 Buss, *Evolutionary Psychology*, 202.

somewhat precarious, to be sure, but their prospects as orphans (wholly bereft of parental protection) surely would be worse still. Wharton's purpose, evidently, is to portray the pathological extremes to which a jealous wife may go. Female jealousy, a proximate mechanism designed to serve adaptive functions, has gone into overdrive in this instance, with potentially maladaptive consequences. The desperate intensity of Elsie's rivalry causes her to take high-risk measures, endangering her children and her fitness. It appears, however, that Elsie calls her husband to join her in Hades only as a last resort. The initial purpose of the letters is to separate him from Charlotte; if they had achieved that end, Elsie presumably would have permitted Kenneth to continue living. But because her final action—the spectral murder of her husband—seems so perversely damaging, emotionally and biologically, the negative judgment she inspires in readers escalates dramatically.

As Elsie's behavior clearly illustrates, mate guarding is a simultaneously intra- and intersexual form of competition. Defending her position as long-term partner, Elsie thwarts the interests of a female rival who seeks genes, resources and commitment from the man in question and, simultaneously, she foils the interests of the man himself, who stands to increase his reproductive success by obtaining sexual access to a second female. It would be in Charlotte's interest, obviously, to procreate—to achieve some degree of direct fitness by having children. Her interests overlap with Kenneth's, whose direct fitness will increase with every child Charlotte bears him. He will share just as many genes with a child of Charlotte's, obviously, as he does with a child of Elsie's. In sending letters intended to estrange Kenneth from Charlotte, Elsie intervenes to protect her own fitness at the expense of theirs. Except for the supernatural features of the situation, there is nothing unusual—or unusually selfish—about Elsie's motives or actions.

Like Elsie, the other two characters in the triangle seek to enhance their personal fitness. By the act of remarrying, Kenneth Ashby indicates that he is ready to father more children by a second mate and thus to increase his direct fitness. In her efforts to free her husband from the dead wife's influence, that is, to obtain his undivided romantic and domestic commitment, Charlotte, too, acts to protect her own reproductive interests. Her "passionate need to feel herself the sovereign even of his past," to believe that Kenneth enjoys a different and better kind of happiness with her than with his first wife, is further manifestation of her wish to assure herself of his exclusive devotion (62). Her impulse to rescue him by taking him off for a long, intimate holiday similarly serves her own genetic interests: her avowed goal is to remove Kenneth from Elsie's influence and secure his affections irrevocably for herself. Such intervention, although she makes no direct reference to her own reproductive future, is nicely calculated to foster her chances of becoming pregnant. Because Elsie's interests run counter to Kenneth's and Charlotte's, conflict ensues. The defensive tactics Elsie employs constitute a form of strategic interference.[18]

Each of the three characters has scripted a personal narrative in which his or her individual interests assume highest value. Kenneth's narrative, readers infer, runs like this: *I was devoted to my first wife, and I have mourned her sincerely; now, two years after her death, it is acceptable for me to seek "new gifts" from life* (61). Whether or not Kenneth consciously thinks in such terms, the "new gifts" he anticipates encompass more, potentially, than the emotional satisfactions of a new romance and marriage; they point logically toward the possibility of offspring born to a second wife and a correspondingly enhanced genetic legacy. Elsie's narrative also is plainly decipherable: *I must protect my children's interests by ensuring that my husband's commitment and devotion remain focused on me—and therefore on them. Since half-siblings and a stepmother might pose threats to my children, I will do everything in my power to ensure that my husband does not procreate with a new long-term mate.* Charlotte's narrative is presented most directly, most centrally in the story, and it is the one readers are encouraged to validate, morally as well as emotionally: *I have a right to supplant a deceased wife and to enjoy my husband's undivided devotion, to be the object of his exclusive domestic, emotional, and sexual attention. I am correct, furthermore, in concluding from indirect evidence that I make him happier than did his first wife: my love is more generous and less controlling, less restrictive of his personal autonomy, than was hers.* Dispassionately examined, Elsie's motives are not intrinsically more self-serving than those of the two individuals with whom she is contending. Only the fact that she is dead might suggest that she should quit the arena and allow the living to pursue their ends unhindered. If dead wives *were* able to intervene in the affairs of survivors, however, they would be motivated by precisely the kind of gene-guarding impulses that fuel Elsie's ghostly machinations. For reasons already explained, a deceased wife typically has more to lose than to gain if her surviving husband remarries and sires more offspring.

Wharton does not encourage readers to engage in dispassionate assessment of her characters, obviously. The point of the story, the reason for its existence, is to provoke readers' outrage against Wife Number One. Every aspect of the story, from narrative perspective to plot, is carefully calculated

---

18 Whenever tactics employed by one sex interfere with those employed by the other, so-called "strategic interference" occurs. Buss, *Evolution of Desire*, 13.

to support Charlotte's view of the inter- and intrasexual competition taking place. The presence of a fourth character, who stands just outside the struggles preoccupying those in the central triangle, further assists in steering readers' sympathies in the chosen direction. Kenneth's mother, who serves in the role of mother-in-law to both wives, sides clearly with Charlotte. Voicing vigorous approval when Elsie's portrait is relegated to the nursery, she subtly offers support for her son's new marriage, asserting the couple's right to a special bond that excludes Charlotte's predecessor. She hints that she shares the general perception that her first daughter-in-law was a formidably strong-willed and domineering woman, thus encouraging readers to accept Charlotte's view of herself as a more desirable partner for Kenneth. The elder Mrs. Ashby's efforts to help this second marriage thrive make evolutionary sense: by taking a new wife, her son may provide her with additional grandchildren and a correspondingly increased genetic legacy. Her interests are aligned with her son's and, by extension, with Charlotte's. In terms of numbers of genes passed on to another generation, all three stand to gain if the new union is reproductively successful. Since a man's relatives are always alert to signs of undesirable traits in a wife or fiancée (potential infertility or infidelity, most obviously, along with related physical or social liabilities), the approbation expressed for Charlotte by her mother-in-law makes an especially strong impact on readers.[19]

In addition to encouraging readers to favor Charlotte's interests over Elsie's, Mrs. Ashby Senior plays a particularly important role in the concluding portion of the story's plot. Standing by her daughter-in-law with advice and sympathy when Kenneth goes missing, she joins Charlotte in opening the final letter, concurring in the assignment of supernatural origin to the whole letter sequence. Because this sensible, down-to-earth character interprets the mysterious letters as commands emanating from Elsie's ghost, readers cannot dismiss Charlotte's response to them as the mad ravings of a jealous wife. Kenneth's own mother, who obviously had opportunity to observe her son's first marriage at close quarters, assumes that the deceased Elsie is fully capable of haunting her husband and using uncanny means to impose her will: readers are bound to take her opinion seriously. The corroborating testimony of Mrs. Ashby Senior compels readers to accept as incontrovertible the unrealistic, or "ghostly," elements in the narrative action; the hair-raising central premise of the plot

---

19   Buss explains how paternal uncertainty tends to promote wariness in a husband's kin, along with diluted investment. *Evolutionary Psychology*, 236, 249. In this context, as Singley and Sweeney aptly point out, support from a mother-in-law enables Charlotte to "gain power," precisely because such support is not automatic or typical. "Forbidden Reading," 193.

cannot be explained away as a figment of Charlotte's emotionally overcharged imagination.

In plot and in characterization, Wharton integrates the realistic with the uncanny to validate Charlotte's views of the other two main characters. Reports of Elsie's domineering personality are reinforced by spectral effects that invest her mate-retention behavior with sinister potency. It is impossible not to sympathize with a man subject to possessiveness so extreme, so weird, in its tenacity. Alive, Elsie dominated her husband and limited his "liberty" (58); dead, she continues to thwart and subjugate him. Observing a wife who avails herself of occult means to enforce marital commitment, readers respond, like Charlotte, with a mixture of condemnation and dread. The impact of the uncanny in this situation emerges with especial clarity in comparison with a well-known incident from George Elliot's *Middlemarch*. In that novel the deceased Edward Casaubon attempts to control his widow's mate choice and reproductive future, but he does so via testamentary bequest. His behavior is arrogant, coercive, and despicable, but it is not *eerie*. Mean-spirited legal documents are far less frightening than letters from the dead. In the event, as readers will recall, Casaubon's efforts also prove ineffectual: his widow contravenes his wishes in her choice of a second husband. The supernatural means employed by Wharton's character are successful, contrastingly, in thwarting the procreative agenda of a surviving spouse.

Commentary on "Pomegranate Seed" in recent decades sometimes tends to downplay or ignore the themes of sexual jealousy and female-female competition. Judy Hale Young joins Carol J. Singley and Susan Elizabeth Sweeney, for example, in considering it "as a story about writing and reading," emphasizing "Wharton's ambivalence toward female art."[20] Moving the acts of letter-writing and letter-reading to the forefront of the story's concerns compels readers to ponder a number of socio-cultural and vocational issues: Wharton's discomfort as a woman writer entering a traditionally masculine field, for instance, or her ambiguous attitude toward female readers. Exploration of such topics proves historically and biographically thought-provoking, but it leaves the main matter of the story unaddressed. Overlooking the malevolent jealousy inspiring the main action, such critical emphasis renders the story bland, draining it of passion, dread, and terror. An adaptationist focus redirects attention to the obvious thematic and emotional center of the narrative: a jealous wife's

---

20 Judy Hale Young, "The Repudiation of Sisterhood in Edith Wharton's 'Pomegranate Seed,'" *Studies in Short Fiction* 33 (1996): 2; Singley and Sweeney, "Forbidden Reading," 196.

demonically possessive behavior. Wharton portrays a supplanted wife ruthlessly protecting her own fitness at the expense of her husband's.

Ethan Frome

In *Ethan Frome*, a work often admired for its local color and regional realism,[21] Wharton incorporates supernatural features more inconspicuously than in "Pomegranate Seed" but for similar purposes, to present a mate-guarding wife's behavior in an ominous light. In the romantic triangle dominating this novel, Wharton again relies heavily on point-of-view to direct reader sympathy definitively away from the wife, presenting the situation from the husband's perspective. The selective omniscience that prevails in the bulk of the tale concentrates exclusively on Ethan's thoughts and feelings; except for dialogue, no direct access is provided to the interior world of either his wife, Zeena, or his potential new partner, Mattie. Encountering Zeena through Ethan's eyes, readers obtain a harshly negative impression. She is prematurely aged: wrinkled and "angular," devoid of womanly curves.[22] Her attention is narrowly focused on her perceived poor health and consequent need for medical attention, household assistance, and husbandly sympathy: "when she spoke it was only to complain" (78).

Whether she suffers chiefly from chronic illness or chronic hypochondria is never conclusively demonstrated, but in either case her invalidism reduces her mate value significantly.[23] She uses sickness, real or feigned, to control her husband and to extract resources from him. She spends on doctors and patent medicines money she could not have demanded for more frivolous purposes, and her chief goal, a paid servant to do her housework, represents a luxury that only the most serious of conditions could justify. Her exploitation of illness to commandeer resources and attention is as unattractive as her whining self-absorption. Considering herself socially superior to her husband, she communicates her belief that she is entitled to a better life than he can offer her; she regards his poverty and low-status occupation as on-going sources of grievance. Beyond all this, Zeena is maliciously cruel: she takes pleasure in tormenting those around her and making them suffer. "The one pleasure left her was

---

21   Blake Nevius, for example, identifies the novella "as a picture of new England life." "On *Ethan Frome*," in *Edith Wharton: A Collection of Critical Essays*, ed. Irving Howe (Englewood Cliffs, NJ: Prentice-Hall, 1962), 130.
22   Edith Wharton, *Ethan Frome* (New York: Charles Scribner's Sons, 1911), 58. All citations refer to this edition.
23   Buss, *Evolution of Desire*, 53, 97.

to inflict pain" (142). She is delighted, for instance, to have in Mattie a servant to whom she need not show even minimal courtesy or consideration; that is, she enjoys "the freedom to find fault without much risk of losing her" (65). Her bullying, unkind disposition lowers Zeena's value as a long-term mate still further. "Worldwide," as Buss explains, "one of the most highly valued characteristics in a committed mate is kindness, because it signals a willingness to engage in a cooperative alliance." Individuals saddled with disagreeable, annoying, or abusive partners incur "severe costs psychologically, socially, and physically."[24] Ethan has strong motivation, clearly, to escape such disadvantageous circumstances.

It is not surprising that the Fromes' seven-year marriage is barren. Physically, Zeena already makes a postmenopausal impression, and clearly her relationship with Ethan lacks emotional intensity and erotic energy. Buss points out that infertility, that is, failure "to deliver the reproductive resources that provide the evolutionary raison d'être for long-term mating," represents one of the "most prevalent causes of divorce worldwide."[25] Having languished for seven years in a marriage that shows every sign of remaining reproductively unsuccessful, Ethan predictably finds the attractions of Mattie Silver irresistible: young and lively, she radiates a vitality that contrasts conspicuously with Zeena's sickliness. "Womanly in shape and motion," cheerful and docile in temperament, Mattie is everything Zeena is not (88). In addition to offering far more pleasant companionship, she seems to possess the crucial attribute of fertility.

Mattie's appearance, which receives considerable textual attention, reflects the traits men most value when seeking long-term mates: youth (promising high residual reproductive value), facial symmetry and beauty (suggestive of high genetic quality), good waist-hip ratio (indicative of fertility), and such universally appreciated personality traits as intelligence, kindness, and good humor.[26] The only shadow on her mate value is her slightly reduced social status, a consequence of her father's financial misdeeds (which include exploitation and betrayal of relatives, friends, and neighbors). Her tendency to exhibit helpless submissiveness is appealing to Ethan, inevitably, because it contrasts so delightfully with Zeena's domineering personality. Mattie's readiness to rely on Ethan demonstrates an appreciation of his qualities that enhances her attraction for him; he feels more effectually manly in her presence. When he

---

24 Ibid., 179-180.
25 Ibid., 176.
26 Ibid., 34, 35, 51-57.

soothes her distress over the broken pickle-dish, for instance, her willingness to accept his assurances evokes a quasi-erotic response in him: "Except when he was steering a big log down the mountain to his mill he had never known such a thrilling sense of mastery" (94).

The strongest hint that Ethan consciously thinks of future children in connection with Mattie emerges when he contemplates the possibility of running off with her, leaving the farm and mill to Zeena. For a brief interval he fantasizes an outcome in which all three members of the triangle might live happily ever after, and what triggers that idealized fantasy is his memory of "a case" much like his own (142). A young man "over the mountain" had "escaped ... a life of misery" by marrying the girl he loved, while the "deserted wife," financially able to open a business, at the same time "bloomed into activity and importance" (142-43). Crowning this tale in which everyone ends up better off (and the deserting husband therefore need feel no guilt), the young pair brings back "a little girl with fair curls, who wore a gold locket and was dressed like a princess" (143). This image conveys a doubly successful outcome for the defecting husband: not only has his new marriage proven reproductively successful, he has grown sufficiently prosperous to lavish luxuries on his child.

Indirect but unmistakable further hints that Ethan associates Mattie with reproductive opportunity are evident in the metaphoric representations attributed to him when he thinks of her. Persistently he links her with spring and summer, with the warmth of the growing season: "spring rills in a thaw" or "a wheat-field under a summer breeze" (49, 98). In a landscape dominated by cold and snow, she fills his imagination with images of organic growth and ripening. He longs to preserve the feeling of her hair under his stroking hand "like a seed in winter" (180). The idea of mating and procreation is especially strong in a comparison that emerges during their one evening alone, when Mattie's hands move over her sewing work like "a pair of birds ... over a nest they were building" (101). The fragility of the hope she represents for a fertile future is captured aptly in a description of their fugitive moments of mutual happiness, feeling "as if they had surprised a butterfly in the winter woods" (167). Trapped in the endless winter of a barren marriage, Ethan sees in Mattie the lovely but improbable hope of spring: fertility and new life.

Like the major characters in "Pomegranate Seed," those in this novel all are pursuing individual fitness interests. Ethan's original estimation of Zeena as a capable, efficient, and "smart" wife (and "the very genius of health") has declined drastically over the seven years of their marriage (76, 77). Such change in one partner's mate value can lead to conflict and infidelity, frequently ending a marriage, as Buss explains.[27] In comparison with the powerfully attractive new mating option suddenly within his reach, Zeena's value to him has evaporated. Ethan desperately wishes to replace an aging, sickly, disagreeable, and barren wife with an attractive, youthful woman who is offering him affectionate appreciation and, potentially, erotic fulfillment. At this point, clearly, switching mates is Ethan's best hope for achieving some degree of direct fitness. He constructs a personal narrative justifying such a course of action, doing his best to assuage his guilt at breaking a long-term commitment, abandoning a sick dependent, and violating community standards of probity. He tells himself that he has "done all [he] could" for Zeena, but to no avail, that he is "too young" to submit to the "destruction of his hopes" and the "waste" of his youth (144, 142). He lacks the financial resources to leave even minimal provision for the wife he would like to abandon, moreover, or to finance a journey of escape for Mattie and himself. Economic and moral considerations combine to create an overpowering sense of entrapment, and he tells Mattie he is "tied hand and foot" (172). His dilemma shows Wharton's awareness that competing fitness interests create more problems and misery in an environment devoid of material resources.[28]

Mattie is motivated by the desire to secure a high-quality mate for herself in a social environment too small to afford her much choice. In choosing to love Ethan—the husband of the woman who is her cousin and employer-hostess—as opposed to the wealthy and womanizing Denis Eady, for example, she demonstrates a preference that may be discerning but is, at the same time, fraught with social peril. Propinquity no doubt plays a role in her attachment to Ethan, but his attentive and affectionate behavior is irresistible to a once well-protected girl cast unexpectedly into a friendless world. In addition to displaying delight in her company, Ethan has assisted Mattie with the heavier household tasks and encouraged her in the face of Zeena's criticisms. Such signs of kindness and commitment, always attractive in a potential mate, are especially valuable to Mattie, whose passive personality reflects her

---

27 Ibid., 170, 188–99.
28 Jennifer Travers argues that the ultimate locus of pain in the novel is "the suffocation of the small farmer," including "tension between agrarian and industrial America." "Pain and Recompense: The Trouble with *Ethan Frome*," *Arizona Quarterly* 54, no. 3 (1997), 53. Elizabeth Ammons supports this view, underlining "the fear and hopelessness many New England inhabitants experienced as industrialization ... undermined the area's economy." "The Myth of Imperiled Whiteness in *Ethan Frome*," *New England Quarterly* 81, no. 1 (2008), 6.

upbringing as an only child who clearly was not expected to fend for herself in life. Subtly encouraging Ethan's growing inclination, she is engaging in high-risk mate-poaching behavior. Consciously or unconsciously, she decides the fitness payoffs in this instance are potentially high, particularly given the paucity of alternatives. Her personal narrative, probably not fully articulated even in her own mind, runs something like this: *Ethan's wife does not appreciate him properly, but I do. He also appreciates me; we are compatible. Our union, unlike his marriage to Zeena, could be companionable, fulfilling, fruitful. I need a husband badly, furthermore, as I cannot subsist on my own, and I see no equally attractive mating options.*

Zeena's vigorous efforts to fend off an interloper likewise represent the pursuit of self-interest. Although Ethan stands to benefit enormously from switching mates, Zeena does not. Her marriage has been reproductively unsuccessful, true, but her poor physical condition means that mate switching is very unlikely to increase her chances of becoming pregnant. Not being young, attractive, personable, or prosperous, moreover, Zeena is unlikely to attract a new husband of any kind if she loses Ethan, let alone one of equal or better quality. Since she has no children to suffer from reduced paternal investment, her direct fitness cannot decrease if Ethan deserts her. In this respect, obviously, her situation differs substantially from Elsie Ashby's. What is likely to be damaged, should Ethan discard her for Mattie, is her reputation. In a small, conservative community, Zeena's pride and social standing will suffer if she is known as a wife whose husband abandoned her for another woman. The case of the man "over the mountain" stands as evidence that desertion and divorce are not entirely unknown in Berkshire villages in the 1880s. Instances would be rare, however, and almost certainly would occasion stigma. Zeena's sense of personal entitlement and social superiority would make her especially sensitive to such social penalty. Readers know, too, that Zeena has collateral kin in nearby villages, relatives whose social and mating opportunities might be reduced if Zeena were to experience a drop in status. Zeena's indirect fitness (i.e., the reproductive success of relatives who share some of her genes) might decrease, if only slightly, if she fails to enforce her husband's fidelity. Above all, the poverty serving as a constant backdrop in the novel strongly indicates that Zeena's economic survival would be threatened if her husband deserted her. That consideration would, necessarily, contribute importantly to her efforts to retain Ethan's marital commitment.

Like those constructed by Ethan and Mattie, Zeena's personal narrative is easy to decipher. In order to sustain belief in her own high mate value, she must convince herself that, since she comes from a slightly larger village, her family and social connections more than compensate for the disadvantages of her illness and consequent physical deterioration. *I am socially superior to Ethan, and he is lucky to have me as a wife. I deserve to be supported in more luxury than he provides. Indeed, by keeping me in such poverty, Ethan has caused my health to break down. It is his fault that I am sick, and he owes me attention and consideration.* Zeena manages to preserve a belief in her own high mate value and consequent entitlement to the utmost in care and resources.

Since the woman seeking to displace Zeena is her relative as well as her rival, yielding to her in the hope of increasing her inclusive fitness through the offspring of the new pairing might appear to be adaptive. The result of Zeena's cost-benefit analysis, however, is that the threats to her survival (through financial hardship) and to her indirect fitness (through reputational damage) would exceed the potential gain from any genes shared with Mattie's future children. The financial and social costs are inevitable, moreover, whereas Mattie's future reproductive success is less certain. Since Mattie is youthful and attractive, Zeena may with justice deem her rival's chances of finding a husband to be fairly high: surely Mattie can find a long-term mate without divesting a cousin of hers.

As in "Pomegranate Seed," readers must acknowledge that the mate-guarding wife's behavior is not activated by motives any more inherently selfish than those of the husband and the female rival. Mattie's interests are largely congruent with Ethan's: both stand to increase their reproductive success if Ethan deserts Zeena and replaces her with Mattie. Since the mate switching so tempting to the two younger characters would prove economically and socially disadvantageous to the wife-in-residence, she undertakes decisive maneuvers to foil it. The manner in which she proposes to eject Mattie from the household is abrupt and cruel, without doubt, but her decision to rid herself of this threat to her marriage easily might have been presented sympathetically. She emerges instead as a villainous, venomous personality with no redeeming features whatsoever. Her disposition is as unattractive and off-putting as her appearance. There is a fundamental contrariness in the make-up of her character: she does not merely suffer ill-health; she exploits and enjoys it. She does not act in simple self-defense, protecting her claim to a long-term mate; she delights, rather, in thwarting the would-be lovers and in observing the excruciating penalties they pay for their dreams of escape. Again, as in "Pomegranate Seed," readers observe Wharton shaping her fictional materials to garner empathy for a straying husband and his potential new partner rather than for the wife successfully defending a legitimate prior claim.

Zeena's attitude toward her husband, an unattractive combination of condescension and complaint, condemns her in readers' eyes from the outset. She guards her marriage the same way she guards the red glass dish that so obviously symbolizes it: it is the thing she "set[s] most store by of anything," yet it remains unused (138). Exercising this same perverse logic, she wants to keep Ethan, but she seems determined to take no pleasure in being married to him. There is evidence in Wharton's autobiographical essay, "A Little Girl's New York," that Zeena's attitude toward the pickle dish is intended to elicit decisively negative reactions. Describing how ladies of her mother's generation preserved quantities of "fine lace" for permanent display, pinned to "indigo-blue paper," she announces her own "conviction that what was made to be used should be used." She underlines this statement by declaring that she has never regretted "having worn out what was meant to be worn out."[29] Zeena, contrastingly, guards but does not *use* her marriage. She takes no pleasure in Ethan's company. Instead of making "displays of kindness" and concern that typically signal long-term investment, she disparages her husband.[30] She insists that he maintain his commitment to her, yet she withholds all emotional and erotic proofs of reciprocal loyalty. In no way does she attempt to nurture the union or profit from its potential benefits. Her childlessness is the most glaring indicator of those unrealized benefits. She is a wife who holds her husband at a distance, holds her husband in contempt—but hold him she does. Much as she denigrates Ethan as a provider and social inferior, she values the external benefits, social and financial, of being married, and she intends to retain them. Her marriage is something she possesses, like the pickle dish; it is an important status-marker and therefore must be preserved intact. In both instances, however, her refusal to utilize what she has—to use either marriage or dish for its intended purpose—reveals the negativism that renders her personality so repellent.

Ethan Frome: Supernatural Elements

Zeena's all-encompassing refusal of the gifts of life, though off-putting, is insufficient to explain the unmitigated dislike readers are encouraged to feel for her. To complete the negative picture of this wife clinging contrarily to a marriage and a husband she does not appreciate, Wharton endows Zeena Frome with

---
29 Edith Wharton, "A Little Girl's New York," in *Edith Wharton: The Uncollected Critical Writings*, ed. Frederick Wegener (Princeton, NJ: Princeton University Press, 1996), 277, 278.
30 Buss, *Evolution of Desire*, 103, 102.

witchlike qualities. Although no direct comparison is offered, readers must notice that Zeena corresponds physically to the stereotypical witch: gaunt, wrinkled, toothless, and supremely ugly.[31] Her malicious nature is equally stereotypical, particularly when considered in tandem with her ascendancy over Ethan. In an era when husbands assumed legal and social authority over their wives, Zeena wields a remarkable degree of power in her marriage. Her radical departure from the gentle, compliant, and nurturing behavior associated with womanliness contributes to the impression that she, like Elsie Ashby, has inverted traditional, or socially idealized, husband-wife relationships—another demonic attribute.[32] To Ethan, Zeena's possessive and commanding presence constitutes "an oppressive reality" (43). His sense of entrapment, reinforced by the harsh climate of Starkfield and by inescapable poverty, is exacerbated by her possessiveness. Secretiveness serves to magnify her manipulative and controlling nature, rendering her mysterious and unknowable: "nobody can tell with Zeena"; "nobody knows Zeena's thoughts" (102, 193). She has a "way of letting things happen without seeming to remark them, and then, weeks afterward, in a casual phrase, revealing that she had all along taken her notes and drawn her inferences" (43). Her silence is more menacing than her nagging, for it appears "deliberately assumed to conceal far-reaching intentions, mysterious conclusions" (78).

Zeena also keeps a cat, and this pet animal functions very much like a witch's familiar. During her overnight absence from the farm, when Ethan

---

31 Ammons was among the first to observe that Zeena is "the perfect witch of nursery lore," complete with "stealthy, destructive" pet cat. *Edith Wharton's Argument with America* (Athens: University of Georgia Press, 1980), 64. Benjamin K. Fisher similarly points out that Zeena's "physique" and "psychological make-up" suggest those of a witch or vampire. "Transitions from Victorian to Modern: The Supernatural Stories of Mary Wilkins Freeman and Edith Wharton," in *American Supernatural Fiction: From Edith Wharton to the "Weird Tales" Writers*, ed. Douglas Robillard (New York: Garland, 1996), 28.

32 See Singley and Sweeny's discussion of Elsie's "oddly masculine traits." "Forbidden Reading," 183. Young offers similar comments on Elsie's "gender-neutrality" and "androgynous" characters in "Repudiation of Sisterhood," 7. Stuart Clark notes that both "scholarly demonology" and "romantic fiction" emphasize that witches do "everything backwards." Such "reversal of customary priories" frequently includes an "exchange of sex roles." "Inversion, Misrule and the Meaning of Witchcraft," in *The Witchcraft Reader*, 2nd ed., ed. Darren Oldridge (London and New York: Routledge, 2008), 121. Elaborating on this point, Louise Jackson describes historical examples of women accused of witchcraft for "failure to conform to the accepted norms of female behavior." The witch was "the stereotypical opposite of the good wife ... asserting her own powers ... to gain financial reward or carry out revenge." "Witches, Wives and Mothers," in *The Witchcraft Reader*, 2nd ed., ed. Darren Oldridge (London and New York: Routledge, 2008), 311, 314.

dreams of enjoying a peaceful and potentially romantic evening alone with Mattie, Zeena's pet persistently reminds the would-be lovers of its missing mistress, apparently exercising watchfulness on her behalf: "the cat, unbidden, jumped *between them* into Zeena's empty chair" (90, emphasis added). Later in the evening, when "a counter-current" of erotic tension begins to grow between Ethan and Mattie, the cat again interrupts them by leaping precipitously from Zeena's chair: "as a result of the sudden movement the empty chair had set up a spectral rocking" (103). Ghostlike, the spirit of the absent wife seems to enter the room, forbidding illicit intimacy: "she'll be rocking in it herself this time to-morrow," Ethan reminds himself (103). Repeatedly, the cat demonstrates an ability to conjure Zeena's presence, effectively restraining the young people's ardency. The animal's intervention is particularly important because this unchaperoned evening offers Ethan and Mattie an unprecedented opportunity to avow and consummate their love. It is in Zeena's interest to prevent such consummation and its potential long-term consequences, most obviously conception and subsequent parental investment from Ethan. Her vigorous efforts to prevent Ethan from driving Mattie to the train station, two days later, similarly evince her concern that privacy may foster intimacy. Her willingness to leave the two young people alone together on this occasion, aware though she is of their mutual attraction, is explained and justified by her pet cat's uncanny power to intervene for her. With its help, she effectively haunts her husband, projecting her forbidding presence into the home they share.[33]

The spectral features of Zeena's intrusion unnerve Ethan and Mattie even more than do the social strictures her ghostly appearance summons up, repeatedly draining a sexually charged evening of energy and momentum. Narrative details emphasize that both Ethan and Mattie have made lover-like preparations for their evening together, investing anticipatory emotion in this singular opportunity. Ethan acknowledges that he and Mattie had experienced "a thirst for each other in their hearts" on the preceding night, walking home from the village (84). Now "for the first time they would be alone together indoors ... like a married couple." He revels in "the sweetness of the picture," which focuses on domestic companionability but also includes lustful components (73). He is surprised and "ashamed," tellingly, when he experiences a "storm of jealousy" at the suspicion that Denis Eady may be visiting Mattie that afternoon (83). For her part, Mattie goes to extra trouble with her appearance, calling

---

33 As Ammons notes, Zeena is "almost a sorceress in her ability to control the fates of others, possessed of the power, seemingly, to communicate with or through her cat." "Myth of Imperiled Whiteness," 24.

attention to her luxuriant, dark hair with a band of "crimson ribbon" (88). Such ornamentation is a typical courtship display; she wants Ethan to find her desirable. He interprets her "transformed" appearance as a "tribute" to the occasion, a sign that she reciprocates his desire (88).

Her romantic interest in Ethan is supported by proofs that she wishes to please him and attend to his comfort, all calculated to highlight her desirability as a long-term mate: the table is "carefully laid"; the doughnuts are "fresh"; his "favourite" foodstuffs are prominently displayed (88). The "dish of gay red glass" that she has taken down without permission "to make the supper-table pretty" highlights her unarticulated admission that the occasion is not only special but tinged with forbidden possibilities (88, 138). In defying Zeena's clearly expressed wish that the pickle dish not be used, Mattie indicates that she is willing to pursue her own interests at the expense of Ethan's wife's. It is the cat, significantly, that knocks the pickle-dish from the table, this time disrupting a moment in which Ethan's and Mattie's hands meet "on the handle of the jug" (91). The "crash" of dish on floor not only puts a quick end to this accidental but lingering touch, it disturbs the mood of happy harmony that has prevailed at the supper table. Causing the dish to break, the cat lays the groundwork for an accusatory confrontation between Zeena and the usurper who has dared to take and use this scupulously guarded and symbolically evocative possession. As other readers have pointed out, the red color of the dish underlines the passionate meaning with which it becomes associated, in Mattie's mind as well as Zeena's.[34] Zeena is not wrong to equate her cousin's willingness to appropriate her dishware with a willingness to appropriate her husband.

Against this backdrop of barely suppressed sexual excitement, the prospect of a whole night alone for the two young people leads readers to expect a scene of intense emotional and physical intimacy. That the scene unfolds very differently might be ascribed to Ethan's and Mattie's reluctance to violate convention with overtly adulterous activity. Both are individuals with high levels of self-control, who ordinarily comply with social norms. They are aware, necessarily, of likely negative consequences should they embark upon a tempting but

---

[34] Jennifer Travis associates the broken dish with Ethan's and Mattie's "secret desires." "Pain and Recompense: The Trouble with *Ethan Frome*," *Arizona Quarterly* 53, no. 3 (1997): 50. Ammons similarly observes that eating from the "precious, sexy, never-used, red, glass pickle dish" represents "erotic intimacy." "Myth of Imperiled Whiteness," 27. Joseph X. Brennan points out that the dish is the most important in a series of red objects associated with Mattie (e.g., a cherry-colored scarf, a crimson hair ribbon), all of which serve to emphasize the potential "pleasure and passion" she represents to Ethan. "*Ethan Frome*: Structure and Metaphor," *Modern Fiction Studies* 7, no. 4 (1961): 352.

high-risk sexual affair. Instead of attributing their reticent behavior wholly to internalized values and respect for social sanctions, however, Wharton's narrator depicts an additional, externally inhibiting force: the cat and its apparently omnipresent mistress. Zeena is presented as an ever watchful, ever jealous wife, whose ability to monitor her husband's fidelity is supranormal.

There is other evidence, beyond the spooky role assigned to her cat, that Zeena commands supernatural powers. During her evening alone with Ethan, Mattie seats herself at his request in Zeena's chair, so he can enjoy looking at her while she sews and talks. Immediately Ethan is confronted with a vision of his wife's "gaunt countenance," which seems to be superimposed on Mattie's "young brown head." "It was almost as if the other face, the face of the superseded woman, had obliterated that of the intruder" (96). Seemingly "affected by the same sense of constraint" that has given Ethan a "shock," Mattie immediately quits Zeena's chair (96). Like Elsie Ashby, who sends letters from the grave to instill guilt and foil mate poaching, Zeena Frome demonstrates an ability to intrude herself into Ethan's and Mattie's consciousness even when she is physically elsewhere. "The supernatural typically takes the shape of occult agency or disembodied minds," as Clasen reminds us.[35] The restraining influence of this absent yet determinedly clinging wife manifests itself most horrifying in the story's climax, when Ethan and Mattie have determined to escape their miseries by sledding deliberately into "the big elm" (176). That they are crippled instead of killed in this "smash-up" is due more than anything else to a last-minute swerve that reduces the momentum of the crash (4). It is caused in large measure by a hallucinatory vision of Zeena's face which superimposes itself, like an ectoplasmic image, between Ethan and the tree: "suddenly his wife's face, with twisted monstrous lineaments, thrust itself between him and his goal, and he made an instinctive movement to brush it aside" (184). "The apparition," as Candace Waid points out, "thwarts the suicide."[36] The wife who is unwilling to let him abandon her for a new wife is equally unwilling to allow him to escape her through death. Once again, her intervening agency takes occult form.

Though Wharton offers only the barest of information about the lives of the three members of this "eternal, infernal triangle" after the accident, readers can infer details too dreadful to be made explicit.[37] Chief among the unstated

---

35 Clasen, "'Can't Sleep,'" 331.
36 Candace Waid, *Edith Wharton's Letters from the Underworld: Fictions of Women and Writing* (Chapel Hill: University of North Carolina Press, 1991), 72.
37 Cynthia Griffen Wolff, *A Feast of Words: The Triumph of Edith Wharton* (New York: Oxford University Press, 1977), 162.

horrors is the fact that Zeena is giving all personal care to the now paralyzed Mattie: feeding, bathing, toileting, dressing and undressing the girl who once threatened her marriage. Readers are sufficiently aware of Zeena's malicious pleasure in the suffering of others to imagine that she silently gloats in having her rival delivered thus helpless into her hands. The markedly perverse streak in her personality suggests that this outcome, though devoid of positive fitness benefits for her, nonetheless pleases Zeena very well; indeed, it endows her with a "morbid strength."[38] Unable to increase her own reproductive success, she has at least prevented rivals from increasing theirs.[39] There is evidence, too, in the testimony of Mrs. Hale, that Zeena wins social approbation for her seemingly altruistic behavior in undertaking Mattie's care and enduring the financial hardships imposed by Ethan's physical disabilities. Such reputational gain would support her inflated calculation of her own mate value and community standing.

Zeena's victory over her female rival is psychologically and physically complete. Readers are left to imagine how she has watched the gradual deterioration of Mattie's once lovely, healthy body, along with the corresponding deterioration of the girl's cheerful disposition. As the ghostly agent of the sledding accident, Zeena has transformed Mattie into a querulous and barren duplicate of herself. Not only has Ethan failed to escape his domineering and possessive wife, he now finds himself burdened with yet another needy and disagreeable female dependent. Mattie's transformation from lovely maiden to whining invalid, arguably the single most horrific feature of the plot, is carefully placed in the tale's conclusion so as to achieve maximum shock value. There is awful irony inherent in her metamorphosis from a girl Ethan is sure, at first sight, "ain't a fretter" into a whining nag (36). She has been carefully presented in polar opposition to Zeena in order to highlight the grotesque similarity that finally prevails. Zeena has effected an unnatural cloning, malignly subverting Ethan's procreative hopes for himself and Mattie.[40] Despite her "witch-like stare," however, the paralyzed Mattie clearly does not share Zeena's power (188).

---

38 Brennan, "*Ethan Frome*," 354.

39 Buss explains that reproductive success always is relative; that is, an individual is more or less successful in comparison with others in a given population. In addition to undertaking positive action to enhance their fitness, individuals sometimes may find it advantageous to thwart the reproductive efforts of those with whom they are in competition. *Dangerous Passion*, 123.

40 Mattie's dreadful metamorphosis has elicited much critical notice. Ammons usefully traces textual details that foreshadow and render plausible Mattie's emergence as a "replicate image." *Edith Wharton's Argument*, 67. Mary V. Marchand discusses the doubling of identity

Auctorial Purpose, Judgment, Sympathy

Forced to observe at close hand, for years on end, the degrading physical intimacy between his victorious wife and her totally subdued rival, Ethan looks, all too understandably, like a man "dead and in hell" already (6). The conclusion of the novella thus reverses that of "Pomegranate Seed." Like Elsie Ashby, Zeena Frome refuses to allow their husband to escape her domination: Elsie compels her husband to die, while Zeena forces hers to live. Employing ghostly means, Zeena dooms her husband to a hellish existence on earth that proves far worse than death. Some readers have questioned whether the agonies visited upon the story's characters fulfill any coherent thematic purpose. Irving Howe, for example, characterizes the suffering of Wharton's fictional characters as "gratuitous," and Lionel Trilling notoriously condemns that suffering for failing to communicate "some meaning, some show of rationality"; the final, terrible fate of the central characters he dubs "accidental."[41] To regard the awful destinies of Ethan and Mattie as accidental or meaningless, however, is to minimize Zeena's role in the outcome of events. A jealous wife intent upon keeping her husband at any cost, Zeena is the principal author of the suffering readers are compelled to witness. With excruciating vividness, Wharton illustrates female mate-retention strategies in action. She highlights the anguish of potential defectors and interlopers, who are subjected to immoderate spousal vigilance, jealousy, and rage. Thus she draws attention to the ferocity of competition, between and within the sexes, for critical fitness-enhancing resources. Those thwarted in their reproductive efforts by strategic interference from jealous wives experience the frustration of their desires as intolerably oppressive. The more acute their frustration (i.e., the more effectual the spousal constraints prove to be), the more inclined the victims are to ascribe supernatural power and intent to the woman obstructing their desires.

Readers are strongly inclined to condemn these particular wives because their goals are negatively framed: they are struggling to retain reproductive

---

as a sociological statement, a reflection of Wharton's "insistence on projecting the rural matriarchite as a menacing community of women." "Cross Talk: Edith Wharton and the New England Women Regionalists," *Women's Studies* 30 (2001): 379. Fisher points to an intriguing parallel with vampire legends, in which "victims frequently take on a resemblance to their oppressors." "Transitions from Victorian," 30.

41 Irving Howe, "Introduction: The Achievement of Edith Wharton," in *Edith Wharton: A Collection of Critical Essays*, ed. Irving Howe (Englewood Cliffs, NJ: Prentice-Hall, 1962), 5; Lionel Trilling, "The Morality of Inertia," in *Edith Wharton: A Collection of Critical Essays*, ed. Irving Howe (Englewood Cliffs, NJ: Prentice-Hall, 1962), 141, 145.

resources they themselves cannot use. Elsie Ashby is dead, and Zeena Frome (barren, sickly, and prematurely aged) is reproductively nonviable. With perverse energy, each seeks to prevent others from reaping benefits she herself is unable to enjoy. They act on the *if-I-can't-have-it-why-should-you* principle. Regarded in largest terms, their destructive motivation illustrates an unpleasant truth about human competition. Since success in life—reproductive, financial, reputational—necessarily is relative, it can be increased by negative as well as positive means: setbacks experienced by one individual necessarily boost the relative standing of close competitors. There is a universal human tendency, consequently, to contemplate the failure of rivals (a colleague denied a promotion, a neighbor's child losing a contest, a brother disappointing parental hopes) with secret relief and even pleasure.[42] Actively intervening to reduce the fitness of poaching rivals and defecting mates, that is, engineering competitors' losses rather than simply rejoicing in them, Elsie and Zeena display an exaggerated version of the competitive schadenfreude to which all humans are susceptible. Unable to increase their fitness through positive endeavor, these two characters can improve their relative success in life only by obstructing the success of rivals. Preventing their husbands from reproducing with new partners, they ensure that those husbands will not leave genetic legacies greater than their own. At the same time, of course, they deprive both husbands and female rivals of other benefits (social, psychological, emotional, and sexual) associated with long-term mating. Readers recoil from the malignant ambition motivating Elsie and Zeena: it is a harsh reminder of threats facing every social animal. Because one person's loss is another's gain, human communities are populated with individuals surreptitiously wishing harm on one another and, not infrequently, instigating it.[43]

Some of the most recent critical commentary has examined *Ethan Frome* for additional sources of meaning. Biographical implications of Wharton's choice of topic have been, explored, with focus on possible resemblances between Zeena Frome and Wharton's husband Teddy, or between Zeena and one or both of Wharton's parents.[44] Such interpretive frameworks provoke

---

42 Symons, *Evolution of Sexuality*, 125.
43 Analyzing "ruthless competitive struggle" with specific reference to evolved adaptations for homicide, Buss explains how a "victim's costs become his rival's benefits." *The Murderer Next Door: Why the Mind Is Designed to Kill* (New York: Penguin, 2005), 28.
44 See R.W.B. Lewis, *Edith Wharton*, 309; Susan Goodman, *Edith Wharton's Women: Friends and Rivals* (Hanover, NH: University Press of New England, 1997), 74; Carol J. Singley, "Calvinist Tortures in Edith Wharton's *Ethan Frome*," in *The Calvinist Roots of the Modern*

intriguing speculation about the relationship between personal experience and literary representation. Environmentally grounded comment, understandably, has pointed to compelling connections between physical setting and evolutionary concerns. Ethan's personal reproductive failure, or "dead-end fate," is framed in the larger context of a barren environment; harsh climatic and economic circumstances contribute to the suffocating sense of suffering and hopelessness the novel communicates.[45] "Images of stasis and death crowd this novel," as Carol Wershoven states, making Starkfield "a place of desolation, of living death."[46] This larger picture of a deadened and deadening world serves admirably to underline the fundamental importance of biological continuity. As a direct consequence of strategic interference by Zeena, Ethan's and Mattie's proximate impulses are thwarted. Those impulses are, as noted, reproductively oriented. Foiled in one of life's central activities, the quest for direct fitness, they experience desperation, despair, and depression. Mattie's and Ethan's final fates, clearly more terrible than death itself, encompass their personal genetic extinction: their DNA has been effectively eliminated from the human gene pool. Whatever else the bleak landscape of Wharton's Starkfield conveys, it effectively communicates the crucial importance of procreative effort in human life history. Projecting her protagonist's sterile destiny and futile striving onto the landscape he inhabits, Wharton utilizes setting to intensify readers' pity and outrage.

Elsie Ashby and Zeena Frome are forceful, domineering women whose strength elicits dismay and disapproval rather than admiration. They are not lauded as loyal wives by either fictional protagonists or implied author but excoriated, rather, as "monstrous entities" who exercise selfish "dominance" in the tales they inhabit: like all literary and folk monsters, they are depicted as "horrible, odious, or unnatural."[47] Their power over their husbands is implacable, inspiring unearthly dread. From a Darwinian perspective, these

---

Era, ed. Aliki Barnstone, Michael Tomasek Manson, and Carol J. Singley (Hanover, NH: University Press of New England, 1997), 168, 173, Wolff, *Feast of Words*, 183; Ferda Asya, "Edith Wharton's Dream of Incest: *Ethan Frome*," *Studies in Short Fiction* 35, no. 1: (1998):28.

45 Ammons, "Myth of Imperiled Whiteness," 32.
46 Carol Wershoven, *The Female Intruder in the Novels of Edith Wharton* (Rutherford, NJ and London: Associated University Presses, 1982), 20. Fisher points out that Wharton makes use of "snowscapes" as setting in at least two stories ("The Ladies Maid's Bell" and "Mr. Jones") in addition to *Ethan Frome*. In these frozen environments, "emotional isolation is enhanced by the natural surroundings." "Transitions from Victorian," 21; see also 27, 31.
47 Clasen, "'Can't Sleep,'" 331.

highly negative qualities may be attributed to a proximate mechanism: untrammeled female jealousy. In these two otherwise realistically rendered tales, the uncanny emerges exclusively in the service of wives whose eerie mate-retention tactics produce in readers the "cold shiver" Wharton deems essential in supernatural fiction.[48] Engaged in competition for resources associated with long-term mating, Elsie's and Zeena's victims are "identifying and negotiating monstrous threats."[49] Suggesting that the female mate-guarding propensity can be stronger than life itself, Wharton attributes terrifying power to this competitive strategy. A ghost or witch "is an entity that defies death," Jeffrey Andrew Weinberg points out. Consequently, spectral phenomena are endowed with "the capacity to inspire fear and awe and to intervene in the course of events."[50] The possessiveness driving Elsie Ashby and Zeena Frome is an extreme manifestation of a familiar constellation of human emotions, invested in Wharton's narratives with supranormal potency.

With her "emotionally saturated images," Wharton inspires extraordinary revulsion for jealous wives, at the same time inviting reader sympathy for behaviors that typically elicit social disapproval, such as infidelity, desertion, or mate poaching.[51] All the major characters are pursuing individual fitness benefits, demonstrably, and all create self-justifying personal narratives to legitimize their goals, yet only the behavior of the mate-guarding wives is demonized. Wharton aims to leave readers aghast at the unrelenting persistence and ominous success with which wives struggle to retain long-term mates, not to mention the vengeful fury they wreak upon antagonists, male and female, who dare to pursue self-interest at their expense. She highlights the claustrophobic, paralytic, even deadly effects of female mate-retention tactics, which undermine the emotional, physical, and mental well-being of husbands and rivals and, above all else, inhibit reproductive success. Thus she directs empathy toward those whose fitness efforts the strategy is designed to frustrate, rather than toward those whose fitness it is designed to protect. In "Pomegranate Seed" and *Ethan Frome*, strategic interference with the interests of the Kenneth-Charlotte and the Ethan-Mattie dyads is allied with what Ethan calls "evil energy," and readers

---

48 Wharton, "Preface," 4.
49 Clasen, "'Can't Sleep,'" 326.
50 Jeffrey Andrew Weinstock, *Scare Tactics: Supernatural Fiction by American Women* (New York: Fordham University Press, 2008), 17.
51 Carroll makes the case that literature provides emotionally saturated images for a psyche designed to ... use them for evaluative, affective, and ultimately behavioral orientation." "An Evolutionary Paradigm for Literary Study," 49.

are encouraged to condemn it accordingly (128). They are urged to interpret wives' mate-retention behavior not only as a moral evil but as a violation of the natural order of things. The unrealistic, ghostly elements in these narratives prove critically important in guiding readers to allocate sympathy and render judgment as the author intends.

CHAPTER 7

Male Reproductive Strategies in Sherwood Anderson's "The Untold Lie"

Singled out repeatedly as one of the finest stories in Sherwood Anderson's *Winesburg, Ohio*, "The Untold Lie" (1919) has attracted surprisingly little sustained critical comment.[1] Like all the stories in the *Winesburg* cycle, this one delineates a revelatory moment of inner turmoil. There is little outward action; conflict and suspense are generated chiefly in the interior of the protagonist's psyche, focusing on his ambivalence as husband and father. Readers become privy to "the buried life" of unacknowledged impulses and the "hidden truth" of repressed resentments,[2] as Anderson's characters struggle with the varied, sometimes mutually exclusive "choices available to the individual as biology works its will."[3] A portrait of the male mind deliberating the relative advantages of alternative reproductive strategies, the story features themes with obvious evolutionary implications. It illustrates with particular poignancy how proximate mechanisms (such as male ardency) serve ultimate goals (reproduction and fitness): goals neither consciously perceived nor deliberately chosen. The psychological disjunction between

---

1. The story is singled out for special praise by Malcolm Cowley, "Introduction to *Winesburg, Ohio*," in *"Winesburg, Ohio": Text and Criticism,* ed. John H. Ferres (New York: Viking Press, 1966), 362; by Waldo Frank, "*Winesburg, Ohio* After Twenty Years," in *The Achievement of Sherwood Anderson: Essays in Criticism,* ed. Ray Lewis White (Chapel Hill: University of North Carolina Press, 1966), 119; and by Irving Howe, "The Book of the Grotesque," in *"Winesburg, Ohio": Text and Criticism,* ed. John H. Ferres (New York: Viking Press, 1966), 418. Dieter Schulz notes the paucity of critical comment on the story in "Sherwood Anderson: The 'Untold Lie,'" in *Amerikanische Short Stories des 20. Jahrhunderts,* ed. Michael Hanke (Stuttgart: Reclam, 1998), 18.
2. Charles Child Walcutt, "Sherwood Anderson: Impressionism and the Buried Life," in *The Achievement of Sherwood Anderson: Essays in Criticism,* ed. Ray Lewis White (Chapel Hill: University of North Carolina Press, 1966), 161; Edwin Fussell, "*Winesburg, Ohio*: Art and Isolation," in *The Achievement of Sherwood Anderson: Essays in Criticism,* ed. Ray Lewis White (Chapel Hill: University of North Carolina Press, 1966), 104.
3. Ray Lewis White, *"Winesburg, Ohio": An Exploration* (Boston: Twayne Publishers, 1990), 88.

proximate and ultimate causes of behavior takes center stage, as the story's protagonist recognizes how the urgencies of sexual desire have "tricked" him into paternity.[4]

Anderson concentrates on the interactions between two men at different stages in life, one middle-aged, "perhaps fifty," and one youthful, "only twenty-two" (202, 204). The older man, Ray Pearson, has made his most important reproductive decisions well before the story begins: he has been married for many years and fathered "half a dozen" children (203). He works as a farm hand, eking out a meager living for his family by means of hard physical labor. A few details are sufficient to suggest his poverty: his house is "tumble-down," his children "thin-legged," his coat "torn" and "shiny" with age (202, 206). Ray's wife, "sharp" in both features and voice, appears to be a perpetually anxious scold, concerned with fundamental problems of family subsistence (202). Ray's direct fitness (as measured by reproductive success) promises to be respectable, but the task of rearing his numerous offspring to adulthood has required and will continue to require his utmost effort and full-time commitment. He is just barely able to support his family (food is being purchased on a day-by-day basis), and there is little margin of safety in his situation.

As foil to Ray, Anderson presents Hal Winters, a man not only younger but different in physique, in temperament, and in social class. Hal is big, tall, and "broad-shouldered"; by way of contrast, Ray's shoulders are described as "rounded by too much and too hard labor," and he is "almost a foot shorter" than the robust Hal (203, 202, 205). Inclined to prototypical masculine display, Hal is observed "roistering" about the town at night, dressing in "cheap, flashy clothes" (206, 203). He challenges his own father in a fistfight, and as a result he is arrested and jailed. His brash and often reckless behavior is very unlike that of the "quiet, nervous," and "altogether serious" Ray (203). In the community Hal has the reputation of "a bad one" (203). A fighter, a drinker, and a womanizer, he is "always up to some devilment" (203). Unsurprisingly, Hal's family background is said not to be particularly "respectable" (203). The fathers of both Hal and Ray are small-business owners: the Winters operate a sawmill, the Pearsons a bakery. (The narrator never explains why Ray did not join or succeed his father in the bakery business, which presumably would have offered him a better income and a physically less onerous profession.)

---

4   Sherwood Anderson, "The Untold Lie," *"Winesburg, Ohio": Text and Criticism*, ed. John H. Ferres (New York: Viking Press, 1966), 204. All citations refer to this edition.

The stated difference in social standing appears to derive from the two families' differing records of conduct.

Hal's aggressive propensities seem to be at least in part hereditary. He is "the worst" of three notoriously "bad" brothers, all sired by "a confirmed old reprobate" (203, 202). The father, old Windpeter Winters, is remembered best for the gratuitous violence of his death. Drunk, he drove his team of horses along the railroad tracks straight into the path of an oncoming train, having slashed with his whip at a neighbor who tried to deter him from his suicidal course. His death is described as an act of senseless bravado. Like an Ahab without a cause, he pits himself against a gargantuan opponent, refusing to yield: "They said that old Windpeter stood up on the seat of his wagon, raving and swearing at the onrushing locomotive, and that he fairly screamed with delight when the team, maddened by his incessant slashing at them, rushed straight ahead to certain death" (203). There is no purpose to this insane contest between man and machine, but as a display of male competitive drive it wins old Windpeter a considerable degree of local fame. "Although everyone … said that the old man would go straight to hell and that the community was better off without him, they had a secret conviction that he knew what he was doing and admired his foolish courage" (203). Anderson points out that young men, especially, tend to value the raw, risk-taking aggression inspiring an act like Windpeter's: "Most boys have seasons of wishing they could die gloriously instead of just being grocery clerks and going on with their humdrum lives" (203). Grotesque, bloody, and pointless, the image of a man going head-to-head with a smoke-belching monster lives as a magnetic moment in the community's history.

The behavioral tendencies prompting Windpeter's final deed clearly did not profit him much during a lifetime spent in a twentieth-century American small town, but his recklessly combative pursuit of dominance might have paid off hugely in the ancestral environment. The secret admiration posthumously accorded him demonstrates residual respect felt by contemporary humans for qualities that once could have won access to resources, status, and women. The lingering hero-worship surrounding Windpeter Winters's "unusual and tragic death" furthermore helps to explain why his son Hal, well on his way to establishing a reputation much like his father's, has been successful in attracting female attention (202). When the story begins, the notoriously ardent Hal has "already been in two or three of what were spoken of in Winesburg as 'women scrapes'" (204). Young as he is, evidently he has fathered several children, but he has chosen not to invest in them. Instead he has taken advantage of a series of short-term mating opportunities, leaving the resulting offspring to the sole care of their mothers. Appropriately, readers do not learn the fate of the pregnancies for which Hal is said to be responsible; he himself presumably does not know for sure the results of his seduce-and-abandon reproductive strategy. With luck, however, he may at the age of twenty-two already have achieved nearly half the reproductive success of his faithfully investing counterpart, the fifty-year-old Ray. Ray's current fitness (expressed numerically as the number of copies of his genes he has managed to get into the next generation) may be calculated as 3.0, and Hal's—with somewhat less certainty—as between 1.0 and 1.5. "As long as his deserted [mates] have any chance of bringing up some of the children," Dawkins points out in *The Selfish Gene*, "the philanderer stands to pass on more genes than a rival male who is an honest husband and father."[5]

Even in the face of widespread gossip condemning behavior the community perceives as outrageous, Hal continues to enjoy intimacies with Winesburg women, including some whose social rank is much more "respectable" than his own. When the story begins, he has taken work at the farm employing Ray Pearson simply to be in convenient proximity to a schoolteacher who has "taken his fancy" (204). Already the locals predict Nell Gunther's probable fate: "He'll only get her into trouble, you'll see, was the word that went around" (204). Like the other young women who have accepted Hal's attentions despite clear risk of abandonment, Nell evidently is willing to sacrifice parental investment for genetic quality.[6] She appears to be exercising what Dawkins calls the "he-man strategy," rather than the "domestic-bliss strategy" in mate selection.[7] Possessing many "predictors of competitive success,"[8] Hal appeals to women in part due to the very traits that foster his "bad" reputation. Bold and swaggering, large and tough, he is careless of rules and unintimidated by authority. His attributes correspond well to those that research has identified as attractive to potential mates: "larger, more muscular and more athletic than ... peers, and more dominant in personality."[9] Getting involved with Hal

---

5   Dawkins, *Selfish Gene*, 154.
6   David. M. Buss and David. P. Schmitt, "Sexual Strategies Theory: An Evolutionary Perspective on Human Mating," *Psychological Review* 100 (1993): 214, 224.
7   Dawkins, *Selfish Gene*, 149.
8   Daly and Wilson, *Sex, Evolution*, 303.
9   Geoffrey Cowley, "The Biology of Beauty," *Newsweek*, June 3, 1996, 64.

might not contribute to a young woman's happiness, but very possibly could result in the birth of a high-quality child—perhaps a "sexy son" capable of reaping success in his turn as an irresistible philanderer.[10]

Anderson's story highlights male characters' choices and decisions, providing considerable direct insight into their conscious thought processes. The main action of the plot is triggered when Hal confides to Ray that he has, predictably, "got Nell Gunther in trouble" and asks the older man for advice (205). Customary reserve between the two men momentarily breaks down, as the younger man asks the elder whether "marriage and all that" are worth the price they exact (206). Hal knows, he tells Ray, "what everyone would say is the right thing to do," but he is wary of dedicating so much of his life's energy to a family (206). "Shall I marry and settle down? Shall I put myself into the harness to be worn out like an old horse?" he asks a man whose prematurely bent frame provides vivid testimony to the cost of male parental investment (206). Neither Nell herself, nor the power of public opinion, can compel him to commit himself to this unborn child, Hal boasts, but he can impose the obligation on himself if he so chooses. "Come on, you tell me," he urges; "shall I do it or shall I tell Nell to go to the devil?" (206).

Within the space of a few hours, before Ray has had the opportunity to articulate any counsel, Hal informs him that he has come to a decision on his own: "I want to marry. ... I want to settle down and have kids," he announces (208). He offers no reasons for this dramatic change in his reproductive strategy, but from a Darwinian point of view such a shift in his behavior might well prove adaptive. The "optimal male course" is to invest heavily in some offspring, meanwhile exploiting opportunities for short-term matings if these do not detract too much from the time and resources required for the principal paternal investment.[11] Pursued over a lifetime, such a "mixed strategy" is likely to result in maximum fitness.[12] Hal will safeguard the survival of some offspring by offering high M.P.I. (male parental investment) to Nell's children; meanwhile, those he has already fathered and abandoned may thrive even without his assistance, possibly eliciting investment from other men. In future, furthermore, his strategy may continue to be mixed. His past history leads

---

10 Robert Wright, *The Moral Animal: Evolutionary Biology and Everyday Life* (New York: Vintage Books, 1994), 81.
11 Robert Trivers, "Parental Investment and Sexual Selection," in *Sexual Selection and the Descent of Man 1871-1971*, ed. B. G. Campbell (Chicago, IL: Aldine Books, 1972), quoted in Wright, *Moral Animal*, 61.
12 Wright, *Moral Animal*, 61.

readers to predict occasional extramarital matings, as does his behavior after he announces to Ray that he has decided to "settle down" with Nell. Instead of visiting her to give her the glad news and arrange their nuptials, Hal dresses up and sets off for "a roistering night in town"—hardly the behavior of a man whose future fidelity is likely to prove flawless (206).

Seeking to optimize his fitness by investing selectively in some offspring, Hal also is showing good evolutionary judgment in choosing Nell as a long-term mate. Although readers lack detailed information about his former partners, it is reasonable to infer than none were of higher socioeconomic standing than Nell. As a schoolteacher, she is well educated and occupies a position of respect in the community. There is evidence, obviously, that she is intelligent. Thus she offers Hal an attractive package of high status and good genes, not to mention immediate resources in the shape of her salary. He is unlikely ever to be able to obtain a substantially more desirable long-term mate. His sudden urge to "settle down" therefore may be attributed to two factors working in congruence: his unconscious impulse (as a member of a high-M.P.I. species) to begin making an investment, rather than continuing to leave child after child to take its chances, peaks at the precise moment when he encounters an extremely suitable candidate for long-term partnership. Nell's pregnancy makes her all the more desirable to Hal: it confirms her fertility, and his summer-long, on-the-spot courtship gives him high paternal confidence.

Readers may credit Nell with having weighed some of these factors (unconsciously, of course) before beginning her affair with Hal. It would not have been unrealistic for her to gamble that she offers the hitherto profligate Hal a sufficiently attractive opportunity for investment. If their affair resulted in no pregnancy and no proposal, she would lose only her time (depending on community mores, she might also suffer some reputational damage). If she became pregnant and Hal deserted her—the worst case—she still would have the expectation of a high quality child. In her handling of the situation, moreover, she demonstrates excellent interpersonal skill, or social intelligence. Although her behavior with Hal certainly has not been very reserved from one point of view, she does manifest coyness by refraining from demanding a commitment from him once she discovers her pregnancy. "Nell ain't no fool," Hal tells Ray; "she didn't ask me to marry her" (208). Psychologically, she leaves him in control: commitment remains his option rather than her command. Despite her willingness to engage in a short-term affair, significantly, she has succeeded in instilling some doubt in her lover as to whether she will accept him on a long-term basis (thus establishing her choosiness), and Hal responds favorably to her restrained behavior, concluding, "I *want* to marry her" (208, emphasis added).

Hal's decision to marry the pregnant Nell resolves his dilemma and provides closure to the story's plot, in terms of outward action, but the real drama of the tale centers on Ray Pearson. Hal's request for advice precipitates an inner crisis for Ray, causing him to reflect upon his own past choices and current situation. Like Hal, we learn, Ray married a girl he accidentally had made pregnant. Unlike Hal, the "sensitive" Ray seems not to have considered deserting his partner, although he does not indicate that he felt any particular affection for her (205). Confronted with Hal's predicament, essentially parallel to his own, he finds himself filled with resentment at the way paternal investment has consumed his life. Nostalgically, he recalls the freedom he enjoyed as "a young fellow" simply "to loaf about," to spend long days roaming aimlessly in the woods, hunting and nutting (204). He had entertained vague plans "to go west," he remembers nostalgically, and there take up a vocation far more exciting than that of a farm hand: "he would go to sea and be a sailor or get a job on a ranch and ride a horse into western towns, shouting and laughing and waking the people in the houses with his wild cries" (207). He is mourning the road not taken, reproductively speaking, imagining a roving lifestyle obviously compatible with short-term mating opportunities, even if he does not mention these explicitly. His imaginary self-portrait—in which he sits astride a horse, impressing all and sundry with his "wild," boisterous personality—reads like a toned-down version of the "gloriously" violent last ride of Windpeter Winters. Ray takes pleasure in envisioning a rowdy version of himself, a self more like the "bad" young Hal Winters, in fact. Having tamed, or "harnessed" himself to domestic responsibilities early in life, he has never permitted that potentially wilder self to govern his behavior. Now, suddenly, he regrets lost opportunities: in his mind, his children are "clutching at him," holding him captive (208).

His commitment to supporting a wife and children has "worn out" Ray prematurely, just as the prospect of such commitment inspires Hal's repeated urge to desert the women he impregnates (207). The obvious differences between the two men offer proof of widespread male ambivalence toward long-term investment in offspring. The carefully depicted moment when Ray and Hal stand staring into each other's eyes, the taller man's hands on the other's shoulders, is one of great intensity: the two "become all alive to each other" (205).

They are nearly diametric opposites, the narrator emphasizes, "as unlike as … two men can be," yet they bond profoundly as together they contemplate the burdens of acknowledged fatherhood (203). The story thus confirms that humans are not a species in which paternal investment is automatic. As Dawkins points out, "males are in general likely to be biased towards promiscuity and lack of parental care."[13] Such care is not always congruent with even the high M.P.I. human's best genetic interests, nor does it necessarily coincide with personal contentment. In men of widely divergent phenotypes, Anderson's story demonstrates, decisions surrounding paternal investment stimulate painful internal conflict.

It is perhaps not accidental that this inner debate occurs in "late October," at harvest-time (204). "Throughout *Winesburg*," as Epifanio San Juan Jr. points out, "Anderson exploits natural scenery as an objective fact whose emotive charge or connotativeness may act as an index or correlative key to the affective or psychic situation of the characters."[14] In "The Untold Lie" readers observe men engaged in tasks that characterize the end of the growing season, gathering crops and "husking corn" (204). The narrator emphasizes the effect of the autumnal atmosphere on Ray Pearson in particular. The landscape seems to be "alive with beauty" and color, "splashed with yellows and reds" (207, 204). The middle-aged Ray finds himself "sad" and "distracted," for this final flaring of beauty at summer's end is, necessarily, poignant (204). The gorgeous colors and ripened grains mark the apex of nature's fertility and, simultaneously, notice of its imminent decline. A pivotal moment in the annual cycle, the advent of autumn suggests powerfully the brevity of all organic life, as well as its preciousness. Subconsciously, Anderson's characters read human meaning into the season and identify with it, as if foreseeing the end of their own opportunities to sow and reap, reproductively speaking. They are moved to take stock of their own fruitfulness—or fitness—recognizing the necessity to maximize reproductive opportunities before it is too late.

Against his own expectations, Ray finds himself unwilling to advise Hal to marry Nell. He experiences one of the "sudden realizations" that form the crux of nearly all the tales in *Winesburg*,[15] apprehending all at once an

---

13 Dawkins, *Selfish Gene*, 161.
14 Epifanio San Juan, Jr., "Vision and Reality: A Reconsideration of Sherwood Anderson's *Winesburg, Ohio*," in *"Winesburg, Ohio": Text and Criticism*, ed. John H. Ferres (New York: Viking Press, 1966), 476.
15 Alfred Kazin, "The New Realism: Sherwood Anderson," in *"Winesburg, Ohio": Text and Criticism*, ed. John H. Ferres (New York: Viking Press, 1966), 327.

"inward reality" that runs counter to "established social and moral orders."[16] Identifying powerfully with the younger man, Ray is overcome by "a spirit of protest" (204). He wishes, he decides, to spare Hal the heavy cost of male parental investment that he himself has experienced: "I don't want Hal to become old and worn out" (207). The fact that Ray seems to have assessed his own qualities realistically and selected fidelity, appropriately, as the best strategy for maximizing his fitness does not alter his regrets. Given his physical and psychological make-up, short-term exploitation of a series of mates would seem to have been a doubtfully successful and therefore less adaptive strategy for Ray. He is not focusing on the positive results of his choices, however, but on opportunities those choices have precluded. Like Hal, he is drawn to reproductive options he has not yet exercised, but unlike the younger man he is not in a position to modify his decisions. At this point in his life, certainly, he lacks the resources and energy to pursue extramarital matings.

There is unmistakable bias, as well as self-deception, in the argument Ray Pearson rapidly constructs against paternal investment. First he divorces himself from agency: pregnancy is "something" that "happened," rather than the result of voluntary behavior, he tells himself, and children merely "the accidents of life" (204, 208). Next he denies that any commitment has been tendered in advance. "I didn't promise my Minnie anything and Hal hasn't made any promise to Nell," he maintains; "I know he hasn't" (207). Anderson's narrator effectively undercuts this claim, however, by reporting that Ray "induced" Minnie to allow him sexual favors, indicating that persuasion of some sort was necessary to obtain the girl's cooperation (204). Ray has become a strict constructionist after the fact, insisting that in the absence of a marriage contract he can ignore any implicit assurances he may have offered his partner. Neither Minnie nor Nell is described as promiscuous, so it is probable that both Ray and Hal hinted at commitment, even if they did not explicitly "promise" it. Robert Wright observes that an unmarried man is, in any case, more likely than an unmarried woman "to exaggerate emotional commitment (consciously or unconsciously) and obtain sex under these false pretenses." Given that "his warmth is then more likely than hers to fade" immediately afterward, the man very easily may deceive himself by underestimating the degree of commitment he has intimated.[17]

---

16 Walcutt, "Impressionism and the Buried Life," 166.
17 Wright, *Moral Animal*, 147.

In the most intriguing portion of Ray's internal dialogue he addresses the issue of reciprocal exchange. Wright argues that the human mind is programmed to regard "symmetry of exchange" as essential. In asymmetrical transactions, consequently, the party enjoying an advantage makes great efforts to "concoct reasons" defending the imbalance.[18] Ray Pearson indeed tries hard to present the sexual exchange between himself and Minnie (and that between Hal and Nell) as symmetrical: "She went into the woods with him because she wanted to go. What he wanted, she wanted" (208). The behavior of the two individuals is motivated by the same proximate drive (erotic passion), he reasons, and both have obtained the desired fulfillment. Therefore, he concludes, the transaction can be closed: no imbalance exists. "Why should I pay? Why should Hal pay? Why should any one pay?" (208) The disingenuous assertion of symmetry belies biological facts which are well known to both Ray and Hal. Once conception has occurred, the female partner in the enterprise is going to "pay." She is committed, willy-nilly, to gestation, labor, lactation, and whatever more it takes in the way of time and resources to rear a child to the point of self-sufficiency. It is too late to insist that no one should have to invest in a reproductive project that is already underway and to which one party's investment is irretrievably committed. In his effort to avoid the guilt attached to lopsided exchange, Ray resorts to biased thinking, and he convinces himself momentarily with his self-serving logic.

In the event, of course, Ray never reveals the socially deviant (and probably maladaptive) advice he had planned to offer Hal Winters. Having steeled himself to voice harsh truths about male parental investment, moreover, he discovers to his surprise that his feelings on the topic are more mixed than he thought. He finds himself recollecting, unbidden, more positive aspects of fatherhood, "some memory of pleasant evenings spent with the thin-legged children in the tumble-down house" (208-209). The story ends with his realization that any counsel he might have given Hal would have reflected one side only of a complex issue: "whatever I told him would have been a lie" (209). Anderson deliberately gives extra emphasis to this insight by using Ray's phrasing in the story's title. Ray has grasped that none of the reproductive strategies available to human males is ideal. Each offers benefits, but each in turn exacts costs. For this reason it is impossible to advise absolutely for or against any one strategy. The inner struggles of Anderson's fictional characters show that no

---

18 Ibid., 273, 274.

matter what choices he makes, the individual human male is bound to spend time second-guessing his investment decisions and regretting reproductive opportunities foregone.

If Ray Pearson commands reader sympathy, it is because his predicament is so clearly universal: the seeds of human unhappiness lie in "the stratagems of the genes."[19] When Ray denies responsibility for children he knows full well are his ("They are not mine," he cries; "I had nothing to do with them"), he is mustering as defense the obvious point that procreation was not his goal; rather, sexual gratification was his goal (208). Since "lust and other such feelings are natural selection's way of getting us to act as if we wanted lots of offspring," Ray is now stuck with unintended byproducts of his proximal drives.[20] His agonized ruminations represent an outcry against adaptive mechanisms designed to pass on genes. These mechanisms may have ensured him descendents, but they have not necessarily promoted his happiness. As Dawkins comments, "so long as DNA is passed on, it does not matter who or what gets hurt in the process. ... Genes don't care about suffering, because they don't care about anything."[21] Ray claims he has been "tricked" by forces larger than himself, accusing "life" of having "made a fool" of him (204). He senses, moreover, that these treacherous forces work from within. For one luminous moment, he recognizes himself for the "gene machine" he is and longs to detach himself from its designs[22]: "he shouted a protest against his life, against all life" (207).

Neither valedictory nor judgmental, Anderson provides remorselessly honest insight into a crucial component of male psychology. He shows men of different types and at different life stages wracked with ambivalence about paternal commitment. In place of a direct attack on misogyny,[23] he exposes its origins in evolved tendencies: exploitation of sexual partners to maximize personal fitness, for example, and biased moral accounting. Thus his depiction of Ray Pearson strikes an admirable balance between compassion and irony, "acuity and charity."[24] Ray's plight, like that of many twentieth-century anti-heroes, is the stuff of tragicomedy. In thrall to adaptive mechanisms,

---

19 Ibid., 88.
20 Ibid., 44.
21 Dawkins, *River*, 131.
22 Wright, *Moral Animal*, 36.
23 For comment on Anderson's treatment of the theme of misogyny in the story, see Schulz, "Sherwood Anderson," 21.
24 Fussell, "*Winesburg, Ohio*: Art and Isolation," 107.

adept at self-justification, this mild-mannered and apparently ordinary individual nonetheless commands the capacity (uniquely human, so far as we know) to recognize and question the forces driving his own behavior. In addition to its contribution to the understanding of evolutionary psychology, therefore, "The Untold Lie" demonstrates with special clarity some of the principal uses of literary art: it provides an arena in which to rehearse competing strategies, to explore diverging courses of action, and to imagine varying outcomes. "Due to many often incompatible forces which pull on us," as Brett Cooke explains, "our art, like our behavior, sometimes takes the character of a tug-of-war."[25] A literary work such as Anderson's engages us, above all else, because it carves a space in which rebellion against the biological conditions of human existence may be sounded.

---

25 Brett Cooke, "Biopoetics: The New Synthesis," in *Biopoetics: Evolutionary Exploration in the Arts*, ed. Brett Cooke and Frederick Turner (Lexington, KY: International Conference on the Unity of Science, 1999), 20.

CHAPTER 8

The Great Gatsby: An Unusual Case of Mate Poaching

F. Scott Fitzgerald's 1925 novel, *The Great Gatsby*, features mating problems with obvious bearing on fitness. Characters wrestle with issues ranging from mate selection and retention to infidelity and desertion. Competition among men for women's sexual attention and loyalty—and among women for men's—occupies much narrative space: it plays a critical role in events and provokes violence, including fatalities. Impetus for the main action is provided by the unusual and elaborate mate-poaching scheme devised by the title character. Jay Gatsby's protracted pursuit of an unavailable woman, a wife and mother who has been married to someone else for three years before the story opens, serves as raison d'être for the whole. The far more ordinary adultery dominating the secondary action provides necessary backdrop for Gatsby's "long secret extravaganza," designed to entice another man's wife into an act of permanent mate switching.[1] There is evolutionary logic to his stunning display of fidelity and bold plan for reappropriation, moreover, even though his fixation on a woman he already has lost proves biologically counterproductive. From a Darwinian point of view, the self-deceptive mechanisms that enable him to overlook or deny the negative implications of his quest are fascinating. His long-term mating plan is based on creative falsification of social and temporal reality.

Tom and Daisy

Gatsby's program for reclaiming his lost love entails disruption of her marriage to Tom Buchanan. That marriage represents mate choices following predictable patterns. The two come from comparable backgrounds in terms of status, wealth, and social milieu: prosperous families at the top of the social

---

1   F. Scott Fitzgerald, *The Great Gatsby* (New York: Charles Scribner's Sons, 1925), ed. and rpt. Matthew J. Bruccoli (Cambridge and New York: Cambridge University Press, 1991), 115–16. All citations refer to the 1991 edition.

hierarchy. Similarities in their "values and interests," together with shared "race, ethnicity, and religion," reflect "the tendency for like people to mate."[2] Tom's family's wealth is vaster than Daisy's: his affluence is conspicuous even among the wealthy. Consequently he exercises great appeal in terms of women's evolved preference for "resource-laden" men.[3] Daisy's physical beauty and social gifts are as striking as Tom's wealth, ensuring her social success: she is "by far the most popular of all the young girls" in town; hordes of "excited young officers" find her desirable and seek her attention (59). With her youth and beauty (indicators of fertility), her resources, status, and popularity, she represents an extremely appealing package to men seeking a long-term mate.[4] Tom represents an equally attractive package from the female perspective: in addition to great wealth, he possesses a muscular build and a dominant personality, buttressed by an aggressively masculine glamour lingering from his college football days.[5] Tom's and Daisy's mate value, in sum, is similarly high: each has acquired a much sought-after, top-value spouse "of roughly equivalent desirability."[6]

The shared interests of this couple appear to revolve around spending and displaying their great wealth: horses and stables, manorial estates, expensive automobiles, European journeys. Since Tom has—and needs—no regular employment, no identifiable objective or necessity dictates their activities. There is no apparent reason for their various comings and goings or their changes of residency: no discoverable cause, for instance, for their decision to leave Chicago for East Egg or, indeed, for having gone there in the first place, and nothing to keep them in the East. Nick observes that the Buchanans "spent a year in France, for no particular reason, and then drifted here and there, unrestfully" (9). Terms like *drift* and *unrestful* indicate that their existence is neither purposeful nor contented. During the Chicago period, according to Jordan Baker, they put in time partying with "hard drinking people," "a fast crowd, all of them young and rich and wild" (61). The Buchanans congregate with idle people like themselves who "played polo and were rich together" (9). *Being rich* is, in effect, their vocation. Nick's final pronouncement on Tom and Daisy is that they are "careless people" whose wealth has allowed them to cultivate a profound obliviousness to interests other than their own: "They smashed

---

2   Buss, *Evolution of Desire* 36.
3   Ibid., 27.
4   Ibid., 51-60.
5   Ibid., 25, 39-40.
6   Ibid., 125.

up things and creatures and then retreated back into their money or their vast carelessness" (139). Thus he associates the Buchanans' extreme wealth with a grotesquely inflated sense of entitlement, suggesting that a shared assumption of special privilege is what "kept them together" (139).

The Buchanans' marriage has been troubled by adultery, readers discover, long before Gatsby appears on the scene. Tom's apparently unlimited financial resources confer social privileges of many kinds, including easy access to short-term sexual partners. Readers learn from Jordan that Tom was caught in an extramarital fling with a hotel chambermaid just three months after he married Daisy. He had concealed the affair successfully from his wife, apparently, until he "ran into a wagon" by driving aggressively and "ripped a front wheel off his car." Because "the girl who was with him" was injured, the accident was reported in a local newspaper (61). In addition to foreshadowing the violent role to be played by automobiles later in the story, this incident shows that from the very beginning of his marriage Tom is implementing a mixed reproductive strategy. That is, he combines long-term investment in a high-quality, long-term partner—and the children of that partnership—with opportunistic short-term affairs. When feasible, this is the optimal male strategy: it enables a man to dedicate paternal care and resources to the children of the best long-term mate he can acquire, maximizing their chances to survive and thrive; at the same time, he takes advantage of other mating opportunities, offering limited resources to his secondary partners. Typically he provides less support and care (in some cases none) to any offspring resulting from his peripheral, usually furtive, relationships. Since such offspring may survive even under less than ideal conditions, the extramarital dalliances tend to secure him a more substantial genetic legacy than would unwavering fidelity to one long-term mate, no matter how high her quality.[7]

Even after he acquires Myrtle Wilson as a steady mistress, Tom remains an avid womanizer: he continues to seek out new fitness-enhancing sexual opportunities. At one of Gatsby's parties, for instance, he picks up a girl more or less under his wife's nose: Daisy observes that she is "common but pretty" (83). The small sample provided to readers of Tom's choice in extramarital partners—a hotel chambermaid, a garage owner's wife, a "common" girl—illustrates the "relaxed standards" men typically apply in short-term involvements.[8] Since they are making no enduring commitment and no major investment in

---

[7] Ibid., 80-81; Dawkins, *Selfish Gene* 154.
[8] Buss, *Evolution of Desire*, 78.

their temporary partners, they need not make high demands for sexual fidelity, genetic quality, or social status. As Buss observes, "men's standards for sexual affairs reveal a precise strategy to gain sexual access to a variety of partners."[9] In contrast to their preference in wives—who must demonstrate sexual reserve and fidelity—men seek short-term partners with sexual experience and high sex drive.[10] Myrtle Wilson meets these specifications in all particulars. As a married woman, she is experienced. Her libido is notably active, and she gives off distinct indicators of sexual availability. Seething with "immediately perceptible vitality," she is "sensuously" fleshy, "smouldering" (23). She responds to Tom Buchanan at their first meeting, strangers on a train, with physical arousal: "I was so excited" (31). She violates etiquette by sitting on Tom's lap in front of Nick, and when Nick goes out for cigarettes she retreats to the bedroom with Tom—behavior clearly signaling ardency.

In addition to offering sexual favors, Myrtle makes a desirable mistress because of the very qualities rendering her unsuitable as a wife for a man like Tom. The social disparity between them enables Tom to please her with a relatively small financial investment. A mistress whose status and background were closer to Tom's would be hard to come by, and if he did succeed in enticing a social equal into an affair he would be confronted with expensive tastes and high-class expectations. Myrtle's distinctly lower socioeconomic position, contrastingly, induces her to admire Tom's status and resources. She is delighted with the magazines, perfumes, face creams, and clothing he purchases for her, pleased with the apartment he has rented for their use. Proud of the tasteless furnishings he has permitted her to select, she feels "regal" when she enters their small love-nest (25). Given his wealth, Tom is easily able to afford the resources he chooses to spend on Myrtle. Her married state, and consequent need to conceal their affair from her husband, constitutes yet another advantage for Tom: he can count on her discretion because she is anxious to keep their relationship hidden from her spouse. Her limited education and experience render her naively vulnerable, in addition, to Tom's two-faced evasion of future commitment: he keeps Myrtle happy by implying that he would like to marry her at some future date, even as he explains that his wife's religion forbids divorce. Someone more nearly Tom's social equal, a woman with worldly knowledge and fact-checking facility, would not be so easily put off.

---

9 Ibid., 79.
10 Ibid., 79.

Myrtle Wilson's selection of Tom as an extramarital affair partner, like his selection of her, is strategically sound. Access to otherwise unobtainable material resources is "a key adaptive benefit" women stand to gain from casual liaisons.[11] Research in evolutionary psychology indicates that women prefer temporary partners who lead "an extravagant lifestyle," who "spend a lot of money on them," proving "generous with their resources."[12] A man like Tom Buchanan, who belongs to an extremely small pool of the super-rich, finds it easy to exploit these preferences. He moves with assurance in privileged, upper class circles; Myrtle's husband, in contrast, is the owner of a garage, a distinctly unprepossessing and "unprosperous" business (22). As his wife, Myrtle is forced to help out by pumping gas (22). Her stolen days with Tom in New York City offer temporary elevation from dirt and poverty into wealth and ease. Their relationship provides Myrtle with access, however limited, to Buchanan money, which procures goods and services she otherwise could not afford, and she clearly revels in this opportunity. Greedily she enumerates her plans for self-indulgent spending (a new dress, a wave, a massage); she makes impulse purchases (a puppy); she indulges her whims (riding in a lavender-colored taxicab).

A collateral benefit for Myrtle is the boost in self-esteem a woman typically enjoys when a man with "better financial prospects" and "more successful than her current partner" takes an interest in her.[13] Dressed in one of the "elaborate" gowns Tom's money has supplied, Myrtle assumes an air of "hauteur" (26). In her mind, her relationship with Tom has raised her social standing, and she enjoys playing the lady, mimicking the "high mincing" speech she associates with refinement and speaking contemptuously of service staff, people she now can imagine belong to "lower orders" than her own (26, 27). Being chosen by Tom, savoring a lifestyle far more luxurious than she has known before, increases her sense of self-worth: she is convinced, consequently, that her husband is socially beneath her (not "fit to lick my shoe"), not really "a gentleman" (30). Because a man with far more claim than her husband to the title of *gentleman* has offered her attention and gifts, she feels classy and important.

Myrtle also obtains from Tom "one of the most important benefits of an extramarital affair," namely, sexual gratification.[14] An obviously sensual woman, she finds Tom physically attractive, and she evidently carries on an active sex life with him. Descriptions of George Wilson as "spiritless" and

---

11 Ibid., 87.
12 Ibid., 86.
13 Buss, *Dangerous Passion*, 168.
14 Ibid., 170.

"anaemic" hint that his lack of vitality may extend into the bedroom; the childlessness of the Wilsons' longstanding marriage (about eleven years) corroborates such speculation (22). Thus Myrtle may obtain direct reproductive benefits, consciously desired or not, from Tom. She is a woman "in the middle thirties" whose procreative potential is waning (23). Since her husband has failed "to deliver the reproductive resources that provide the raison d'être for long-term mating," she has nothing to lose and much to gain—in terms of fitness—by testing her fertility with a different man.[15] If pregnancy should ensue, she has options for obtaining paternal support from two men. One possibility is that George Wilson would accept the child as his. Another possibility is that pregnancy would bring the infidelity to light and break up the Wilsons' marriage, in which case Tom Buchanan might provide Myrtle and the child with private financial support. Myrtle also may imagine that the prospect of a child would provide Tom with inducement to abandon his current wife and marry her.

Quite apart from the possibility of pregnancy, Myrtle harbors hopes, if not strong expectations, that her affair with Tom may lead to marriage. The opportunity to "trade up" for a higher-quality husband would vastly improve her socioeconomic circumstances and fitness prospects: the hope of realizing such benefits motivates much female infidelity.[16] Unlike men, who lower their selection criteria when choosing short-term partners, women choose affair-partners using the same standards of evaluation they apply to potential husbands.[17] Like many women involved with men of higher mate value than their current long-term partners, Myrtle would like to convert her lover into a husband. The dishonest explanation Tom gives for failing to divorce his current wife indicates that he is deceiving Myrtle "by feigning long-term intentions," a tactic men often utilize when seeking short-term sexual partners.[18] The true nature of his commitment is made plain in the violent quarrel that ends the party in the New York apartment, a quarrel triggered by Myrtle's jealous resentment of Tom's wife. When he forbids Myrtle to mention his wife's name, striking her brutally after she fails to comply with his order, she surely knows that he places higher value on Daisy than on her. Tom has shown Myrtle, forcibly, that he does not consider her to be marriage material; indeed, she is so obviously inferior in

---

15 Buss, *Evolution of Desire*, 176.
16 Buss, *Dangerous Passion*, 166-69.
17 Buss, *Evolution of Desire*, 88.
18 "Men are aware that simulating commitment is an effective tactic for gaining access to short-term sex, and they admit to deceiving women by this means." Ibid., 105.

his view that for her to utter Daisy's name would constitute contamination. Confronted with these insulting realities, tellingly, Myrtle does not threaten to walk out; the other benefits Tom provides (i.e., other than long-term commitment) are sufficiently valuable to keep her in the relationship. Instead of protesting that she will not remain with a man who uses violence against her, she makes "despairing" efforts to shield her cherished upholstery, bought with Tom's money, from the blood streaming copiously out of her broken nose (32). Clearly she intends to continue the affair along whatever lines Tom dictates, showing off her fancy furniture and clothing, playing Lady of the Manor in a tiny apartment.

The partners in this doubly adulterous relationship are motivated to carry on with it indefinitely (long enough, in any event, to make semi-permanent arrangements for their meetings), a clear indication that both are satisfied with the benefits it brings. They take some care to minimize potential costs, in particular by concealing Myrtle's infidelity from her husband. Having used his wealth to attract a short-term partner, Tom also wields it effectively to deceive her husband. Offering to sell Wilson a nice car, presumably for eventual re-sale at a profit, he has a fine excuse for dropping in at the garage to arrange his meetings with Myrtle. There is distinct meanness in his proceedings, since he never does produce the promised vehicle. He keeps Wilson vacillating uncomfortably between anticipation and disappointment, overriding the latter's feeble protests with bullying displays of social dominance. He takes advantage of Wilson's poverty for his own ends, though he obviously could afford to invest the price of a car (or two or three) in order to lull husbandly suspicion. He seems to enjoy perpetrating a double deception, cheating Wilson financially as well as sexually. Derogating the rival he has duped so successfully ("he's so dumb he doesn't know he's alive"), Tom expresses the contempt universally directed at a cuckolded husband (22).[19]

Tom takes less trouble to conceal his relationship with Myrtle from his wife, in part, perhaps, because women's reaction to a partner's infidelity tends to be less dramatic than men's. For evolutionarily understandable reasons, women are less likely to respond with violence to infidelity and also are less likely to leave an unfaithful spouse. Reluctance to lose a husband's support for herself and her offspring may motivate a woman to tolerate sexual straying,

---

19 "Cuckolds are universally ridiculed." A husband is disgraced by a wife's sexual disloyalty; he suffers reputational damage and is considered "unmanly," weak, and inadequate. Buss, *Dangerous Passion*, 52.

particularly if resources are not noticeably depleted and long-term commitment is not undermined.[20] Women are not troubled, furthermore, by anything equivalent to the threats to paternal confidence men suffer when their wives betray them sexually. These realities notwithstanding, it is emphatically in a woman's best interest to prevent her husband from cheating if she can. It is adaptive to avert possible loss of paternal care and resources, as well as potential damage to social reputation and self-esteem.[21] The most significant danger of extramarital affairs, from a wife's point of view, is the eventuality that a relationship intended to be casual may assume emotional importance, precipitating a husband's defection from the marriage.[22] Wives are likely, therefore, to use surveillance, recrimination, and a variety of guilt-inducing tactics to discourage and punish a husband's infidelity. To avoid these unpleasant consequences, men engaging in extramarital escapades generally try to avoid detection.

Tom Buchanan's attempts to deceive his wife are somewhat halfhearted and therefore only partly successful. He does not tell his wife about his relationship with Myrtle, certainly, nor does he mention the apartment he has rented in the city for purposes of adulterous dalliance. When Myrtle telephones his home, triggering Daisy's suspicions and "impassioned" interrogation, he attempts, albeit futilely, to soothe her (15). His efforts to hide the existence of his "girl" from his wife prove inadequate principally because of his indiscreet public behavior: he has broadcast the affair by escorting Myrtle to "popular restaurants," where he inevitably encounters people who know him (21). Instead of retreating in embarrassment from acquaintances, furthermore, he initiates "chatting" interaction (21). Although he stops short of introducing Myrtle, he is very evidently showing her off or, more accurately, showing off the fact that he has a mistress. The fact that "Tom's got some woman in New York" is an open secret, a secret that no doubt has been relayed to his wife by acquaintances said to have "resented" Tom's tasteless display of his extramarital conquest (15, 21). Despite the attendant costs (in the shape of wifely reproaches), he cannot resist demonstrating publicly that he possesses the power and resources to "gain access to the mates of lower status men."[23] As the anthropological record shows, men worldwide have competed to monopolize

---

20 Buss, *Evolution of Desire*, 266-67.
21 Buss, *Dangerous Passion*, 40.
22 Buss, *Evolution of Desire*, 266.
23 Barbara Smuts, "Male Aggression Against Women: An Evolutionary Perspective," in *Sex, Power, Conflict: Evolutionary and Feminist Perspectives*, ed. David M. Buss and Neil M. Malamuth (New York and Oxford: Oxford University Press, 1996), 248.

women's reproductive potential, and Tom delights in presenting himself as a winner in that age-old competition.[24] He is convinced, with some justification, that the ability to attract and maintain two women simultaneously provides evidence of his material resources, social dominance, and masculine appeal. Advertising his sexual success, Tom intends to excite the envy and admiration of other men. His behavior indicates that he regards the consequences of his all-but-proclaimed infidelity as low-cost.

The most significant cost Tom could incur would be loss of his high-quality mate, and clearly he does not fear this. The fact that he has indulged in short-term affairs throughout their marriage no doubt bolsters Tom's assumption that Daisy is willing, however reluctantly, to tolerate his sexual wandering. Having learned of Tom's affair with a hotel chambermaid almost before the honeymoon was over, Daisy has had several years to come to terms with her husband's persistent infidelity. Her behavior when Tom leaves her at supper, during Gatsby's party, to pick up a girl at another table shows that she has hardened herself to his womanizing. "Genially" she tells her husband to "go ahead," adding sarcastically that she will lend him her "little gold pencil" if he wants to "take down any addresses" of potential affair partners (82-83). In this exchange, both parties demonstrate a mixture of self-assertion and accommodation. He picks up a girl while attending a social event with his wife but shows a modicum of respect for her by creating a veneer of excuse and concealment, pretending he wants to listen to "a fellow's ... funny stuff" rather than crudely announcing that he is off to conduct a short-term seduction (82). Daisy refrains from outright condemnation or threat but conveys displeasure, obliquely, with sarcastic needling. The double-edged offer to loan Tom her "little gold pencil," though superficially pleasant and forthcoming, proclaims aloud her awareness of Tom's extramarital activities, letting him know that she is not a pitiful dupe. There is a *here we go again* tone to her sarcasm, however, that tells listeners she is not contemplating radical action in response to Tom's dalliances.

Daisy remains a worthy antagonist in their ongoing marital dueling, for she commands impressive verbal weapons. In the embarrassment caused by Myrtle's disruptive telephone call, earlier that summer, Daisy torments Tom in the presence of guests with ironic praise of the "romantic" evening, extolling with mocking warmth the inspiring "home influence" she and Tom

---

[24] Felicia Pratto, "Sexual Politics: The Gender Gap in the Bedroom, the Cupboard, and the Cabinet," in *Sex, Power, Conflict: Evolutionary and Feminist Perspectives*, ed. David M. Buss and Neil M. Malamuth (New York and Oxford: Oxford University Press, 1996), 206-207.

can provide for Jordan (16, 18). The "tense gayety" with which she couches her obliquely accusatory comments renders them especially effective (16). They are also unanswerable: Tom is forced "miserably" into a corner by Daisy's aggressive baiting (16). Punishing her husband with barbed wit rather than tearful pleading, Daisy asserts confidence in her own desirability and worth—confidence a husband's disloyalty often undermines.[25] To counter behavior she cannot prevent, she demeans her husband in front of an audience with her witty put-downs. Because he never acknowledges his affairs to his wife or in her presence, he is unable to make any rebuttal to her derogatory innuendos. In this way, she enforces a cost: she compels him to pay for the advantages he derives from his adultery with psychological discomfort and social humiliation. The couple has reached a stand-off. He exercises sexual freedom, which she tolerates but resents; she retaliates with punitive verbal assaults, souring as much as she can the pride and pleasure he takes in his extramarital escapades.

Gatsby and Daisy: Phase I

With its classic patterns of mate choice and mutual accommodation, including successful implementation of a mixed sexual strategy on the part of the husband, the Buchanan marriage aptly illustrates a number of Darwinian principles. Indeed, the evolutionarily predictable features of Tom and Daisy's relationship may help to explain why there is little about it to rivet readers' attention. As Brian Boyd points out, "no one savors stories confined to the banal and expected": audiences respond, rather, to "the striking," that is, to "unusual characters or events" (115).[26] Readers' interest also can be sparked by identification with characters or their predicaments, but Fitzgerald's presentation of the "dully simple" partners in the Buchanan marriage is not calculated to evoke empathy.[27] Their shared interests and values are ignoble; Tom's adulteries and Daisy's "sophisticated" tolerance of them put neither spouse in an admirable light; as the Other Woman, Myrtle Wilson is too coarse and acquisitive to garner sympathy (17). Nobody in this sexual triangle exhibits a trace of appealing eccentricity. The situation is unhappy without arousing pity, sordid without compensatory titillation. It takes the intrusion of an

---

25 Buss, *Dangerous Passion*, 40.
26 Boyd, *On the Origin of Stories*, 115.
27 Robert Ian Scott, "Entropy vs. Ecology in *The Great Gatsby*," in *Gatsby: Major Literary Characters*, ed. Harold Bloom (New York: Chelsea House: 1991), 90.

outsider to render this particular constellation of intra- and intersexual conflict interesting. That outsider, the mysterious Jay Gatsby, proves sufficiently unusual in his motives, goals, and methods to serve as a magnet for readers' curiosity. In his pursuit of Daisy Buchanan, Gatsby transforms ordinary adaptive strategies into a fascinating quest.

The first phase of Gatsby's romance with Daisy Fay, in the summer of 1917, clearly indicates how and why this particular woman comes to exercise such a powerful hold on him. Emerging from a distinctly lower-middle-class milieu, "a penniless young man without a past," the twenty-five-year-old Gatsby is enchanted by the physical beauty, social poise, high status, and material prosperity of eighteen-year-old Daisy (116). The only term he finds adequate to explain the impression she makes of upper-class untouchability is *nice*: she is "the first 'nice' girl he had ever known" (116). Intangible but unassailable class lines—"indiscernible barbed wire"—normally would have prevented their acquaintance, but wartime military service provides him with the "invisible cloak of his uniform" (116). Exploiting the anonymity it provides, he woos a girl whose mate value exceeds his own astronomically. It is this vast disparity in their relative mate value that renders her "excitingly desirable" to him, sealing his fixation (116). Given his unprepossessing upbringing, the trappings of Daisy's prosperous life seem almost magical: her "beautiful house" exudes "ripe mystery," promising "gay and radiant activities" (116). The fact that "many men had already loved Daisy" further ratifies her worth.[28] "Daisy embodies the idea of perfection for Gatsby, an almost unapproachable ideal of social success and self-realization," as Peter L. Hays observes.[29] To win her would be the stuff of fairy tales, with Gatsby playing the role of a peasant chosen by a princess. Their romance illustrates, as Bert Bender states, "the female's power to select the superior male and the male's struggle to be selected."[30] To marry Daisy would prove fitness-enhancing for the young Gatsby in every possible way. In addition to the promise of fertility and good genes, she would bring him status and prosperity: his children would be born into upper-class privilege and enjoy the advantages of elite social networks. Gatsby is not concentrating overtly on these fitness benefits,

---

28 Individuals manifesting highly valued traits "are in great demand" as mates, Buss points out. Inevitably, they attract numerous suitors, who compete actively for their attention. *Evolution of Desire*, 8.

29 Peter L. Hays, "Oxymoron in *The Great Gatsby*," *Papers on Language and Literature* 47, no. 3 (2011): 320.

30 Bender, *Evolution and "the Sex Problem,"* 232.

obviously, nor is it necessary that he do so: "the Darwinian evaluation of a mate needn't be *consciously* Darwinian."[31] The operation of proximate mechanisms serves to excite his desires and cement his devotion.

Initially, Gatsby's objective is short-term, "to take what he could and go," but the benefits of temporary sexual access are limited compared with those he stands to gain from long-term commitment (116). Daisy—marriage to Daisy—becomes a "grail," a goal to which he dedicates himself with unwavering, quasi-religious fervor (117). The implied comparison of Daisy's reproductive potential to the golden chalice of ancient legends, imbued with mystically restorative powers, highlights the evolutionary basis of her "gleaming" significance to Gatsby (117). Her mate value so far exceeds his that obtaining her as a wife would represent fulfillment of all but impossible dreams. It is not inexperience with women or an inability to attract them, as Nick explains, that causes Gatsby to devote all energies to the exclusive pursuit of Daisy: "he knew women early and since they spoiled him he became contemptuous of them" (77). It is her difference from all the others, her incomparably "golden" worth, that renders her irresistible (94). Discovering to his surprise that he "loved" this uniquely desirable girl, and without conscious intention has "committed himself" to her, Gatsby illustrates the critical role of emotions as "evolution's executioners" (117, 116).[32]

His courtship of Daisy during their first "month of love" seems to be moving toward a successful outcome: she yields to him sexually and emotionally, declaring that she is "in love" with him (117). To win her regard, however, he has relied on deception: he has "taken her under false pretences," allowing "her to believe that he was a person from much the same strata as herself … fully able to take care of her" (116). Had war service not intervened, readers must surmise, his hopes would have been crushed when Daisy's family began looking into his antecedents and asking how he planned to support a wife. He assumes, using evolutionarily sound reasoning, that revelation of his origins and circumstances would extinguish her dawning attachment to him. Being called to duty abroad rescues him from damaging disclosures. He does not appear to appreciate this escape for what it is, however, and he continues to engage in significant self-deception as he corresponds with Daisy and encourages her to count on their eventual marriage. Even if he had returned to Louisville sooner, in time to head off her marriage

---

31 Wright, *Moral Animal*, 95.
32 Ibid., 88.

to another man, he could not have carried out the intentions he has confided to her. He has won promotion in the military but has had no opportunity to improve his financial situation; thus he still is in no position to conduct an open courtship. He is not planning an elopement, after all: he wants to marry with all attendant ceremony and full backing from her family. This could not have occurred: investigation and unmasking would have been inevitable. Gatsby seems not to have faced these discouraging facts, deceiving himself, in fact, almost as much as he deceives Daisy.

Because she breaks faith with him by marrying another man before his return from Europe, Gatsby's deceptive self-presentation is not challenged: humiliating revelations are averted. There are evolutionarily plausible explanations for Daisy's failure to wait for the lover to whom she evidently has made private promises. According the somewhat vague timetable provided by Jordan, Daisy waits about a year after Gatsby's departure before resuming an active social life, a substantial time period in the life of a vivacious eighteen-year-old.[33] There are additional signs that she has made a serious emotional investment in the relationship with Gatsby, including an abortive attempt to travel East to see him off to France. Her last-minute, drunken insistence that she has changed her mind about marrying Tom ("tell 'em all Daisy's change' her mine") provides more proof of attachment, even though she allows herself to be dissuaded from jilting Tom at the altar (61). Her commitment to Gatsby seems genuine, though wavering; she fails to sustain it over time not so much because she lacks strength of purpose as because there are so many factors operating to undermine her loyalty.

The first undermining factor is secrecy: apparently the couple has confided the seriousness of their intentions to no one. This secrecy is doubtless a byproduct of Gatsby's dissimulation: he would not want to expose himself to scrutiny by Daisy's family in his present "penniless" state. Daisy's parents sponsor her début the year following his departure, a social launching that would be pointless if she already were affianced: clearly her parents do not so regard her. She is subject, accordingly, to "the pressure of the world outside" (i.e., the world outside her unacknowledged relationship with Jay Gatsby) to conduct herself like a typical debutante. As an eligible young woman awaiting proposals, she is expected to remain active in the courtship arena (118). She is approximately nineteen years

---

33 Gatsby leaves Louisville in October of 1917, and "by the next autumn" (1918) Daisy is "as gay as ever." In June 1919, approximately a year and a half after the romance with Gatsby, she marries Tom Buchanan. Fitzgerald, *The Great Gatsby*, 60.

old at the time of her début: reproductively considered, she has reached the height of her mate value. Friends and relations expect her to take advantage of present opportunities, which are unlikely to increase with the passage of time. Daisy herself appears to be motivated by both biological and social pressures: "Something within her was crying for a decision. She wanted her life shaped now, immediately" (118). From an evolutionary psychological perspective, Daisy's unease may be explained at least in part as reproductive anxiety: she wonders if she is wasting her prime fertile years waiting for a man whose continued absence may cause her to miss out on optimal mating options. When the immensely rich, socially dominant Tom Buchanan appears on the scene, she chooses not to pass up the "wholesome bulkiness" of "his person and his position" (118). Ending any possible worry about decreasing mating options and declining mate value, the decision to accept Tom brings "a certain relief" even if it also triggers "a certain struggle" with lingering tenderness for her absent lover (118).

Thus Tom's obvious desirability as a husband is the final factor in Daisy's decision to wait no longer for Gatsby. Despite justifiable confidence in her own high value, she is "flattered" by the attentions of this extraordinarily well qualified suitor (118). She is beautiful, personable, and prosperous, to be sure, but Tom's family is far richer than hers and his social position accordingly more powerful. His courtship gratifies her, a clear indication that she judges his mate value to be at least as high as hers. This equivalency not only explains her reasons for choosing Tom, as discussed earlier, it provides significant motivation for withdrawal from a prior commitment. Although Gatsby has given her a false "sense of security" by persuading her that his background is "much the same" as hers, he has provided no evidence that he commands resources or status markedly better than her own (116). Taking for granted that her future husband will come from an elite socioeconomic milieu, Daisy is not unduly excited by the prospect of a husband "fully able to take care of her": this would be her minimal expectation (116). Unlike Gatsby, whose long-continuing commitment is fueled by the prospect of winning a woman whose mate value far exceeds his own, Daisy believes Gatsby's mate value approximates hers; so far as she knows, his social and financial circumstances are no different from those of her many other suitors. Consequently her ideas about a shared future with Gatsby lack the element of magical promise that so enthralls him.

Daisy is not dazzled by Tom's desirable qualities as Gatsby is by hers, but she is impressed by what Tom has to offer, sufficiently so, given the other pressures she is experiencing, to make an immediate mating decision. She decides to take the bird in hand. If Gatsby had managed to make a timely reappearance, "his presence beside her" might have influenced her to reject the rival candidate, but the problem of Gatsby's falsified background must still have prevented their marriage (118). Daisy cannot know that, of course, but viewed from any angle her decision to break her commitment to him is self-protective; it may not strike observers as particularly admirable, but it is strategically sensible. By accepting Tom instead of waiting for Gatsby, Daisy locks in very real benefits. In addition to securing financially and socially superior resources for herself and potential offspring, she avoids the risks inherent in postponing long-term mating and reproduction.

Error management theory helps to show the evolutionary logic that guides her: based on mostly unconscious calculations, she has identified "the less costly error."[34] She has more to lose, potentially, by waiting for Gatsby than she does by marrying Tom. The potential cost to marrying Tom is loss of a perhaps more faithful, more agreeable partner—a loss likely to affect her personal happiness more than her direct fitness. (Natural selection serves "genetic proliferation," alas, not happiness, as evolutionary research repeatedly demonstrates.[35]) A decision to refuse Tom and await Gatsby's return, contrastingly, might for a variety of reasons constitute a more costly error. Gatsby's absence might be indefinitely prolonged, or he might not reappear at all. While waiting for him, she might pass up never-to-be-repeated mating opportunities, that is, she might not be wooed again by a man offering as many matrimonial advantages as Tom Buchanan. As a result of waiting, she might delay having children longer than she otherwise would, possibly imperiling or reducing her lifetime reproductive success. Gatsby, once returned, might prove to be a less desirable long-term mate than she imagines. This last consideration, as readers know, is not a risk but a certainty: if Gatsby had arrived in Louisville on schedule and proceeded with his courtship, Daisy necessarily would have discovered his social and financial liabilities. The investigative process and consequent termination of the relationship likely would have proven socially disadvantageous as well as emotionally painful: costs she would have paid by maintaining her commitment to Gatsby.

Gatsby and Daisy: Phase II

Once Daisy has married Tom, the result of mating decisions influenced for better or for worse by evolved adaptations, Gatsby's courtship of her might

---

34 Buss, *Dangerous Passion*, 76.
35 Wright, *Moral Animal*, 211.

be supposed to be finished. Instead of moving on to new romantic options, however, he defies ordinary expectations by continuing to pursue the woman who has thrown him over. Gatsby's long, secret campaign to repossess the woman he has lost constitutes the heart of the novel, captivating readers with its boldness and creativity. The strangeness of his project, together with the unlikelihood of its success, proves irresistibly intriguing. The first unusual feature of his three-year courtship is the decision to disappear from Daisy's life. Unlike many other men in similar circumstances, in life or in literature (e.g., Goethe's Werther), he does not seek meetings or correspondence with her. This is a clever tactic. He avoids presenting himself in the guise of cringing hanger-on or emasculated loser—male types women reject as mates.[36] He does risk being forgotten (a risk he probably does not consider substantial, given the intensity of their 1917 affair), but by withdrawing entirely from her attention he prepares the way for surprise. Once his elaborate preparations are complete, he can re-enter Daisy's life with flair. He can hope to exert a doubly potent appeal, combining the allure of novelty with the comfort of the familiar. He will burst into her life with glorious suddenness, an ideally re-invented version of a man she already has found worthy of love. Wizard-like, he plans to create a richly "magical world" in which, temporarily at least, "appearance becomes social reality."[37]

The most important element in Gatsby's self-transformation is the acquisition of material resources. To meet Daisy's upper-class expectations and to compete effectively with her enormously rich husband, he rightly judges that he needs to amass extraordinary wealth. During the three post-military years of separation from Daisy, his energies are directed toward this end. He judges, in addition, that his newly acquired resources must be conspicuously displayed. Since Daisy rejected him to marry a man whose expensive lifestyle, in Nick's words, "rather took your breath away," Gatsby assumes that to win her attention he must flaunt his prosperity, proving to Daisy and to the world that he has outdone all possible rivals (8). With his European-style mansion, special-order automobile, and fancy parties featuring "celebrated people," he is targeting the universal female concern with resources and utilizing typically masculine show-and-tell tactics (71). Men "go to great lengths to display their resources to attract mates," Buss points out, and Gatsby is determined to make a lavish

---

36   Buss discusses women's preference in potential mates for traits indicating dominance and confidence, *Evolution of Desire*, 107-109.
37   Jeffrey Hart, "Anything Can Happen: Magical Transformation in *The Great Gatsby*," *South Carolina Review* 25, no. 2 (1993): 39, 40.

statement with the fortune he has accrued in his protracted mating effort.[38] Discussing this aspect of Gatsby's courtship, Philip McGowan argues that Gatsby underlines his financial metamorphosis by exploiting the transformative power of money, creating "spectacles and entertainments," a "lifestyle of illusion." As "the circus master" and the "carnivaliser of reality," he attempts to infuse his newly acquired wealth with magical potential and thus render it even more attractive.[39]

Gatsby plans his reunion with Daisy carefully, ensuring that she will see his "enormous" dwelling, and thus grasp the extent of his wealth, at their first meeting (69). Taking her on a tour of his "Marie Antoinette music rooms and restoration salons," the "period bedrooms" and "sunken baths," he shows off his exquisite possessions in loving detail (71). Moving deliberately from public to private portions of his home, he ends the tour in his bedroom, tacitly inviting Daisy to associate his riches with sexuality and mating opportunities. He shows her his "toilet set of pure dull gold" and is delighted when she immediately begins to smooth her hair with his brush, a subtle sign that she is responding positively to this spectacular show of resources (72). The scene reaches its well-known climax when he piles his high-priced British shirts before her in "many-colored disarray" (72). There is sound calculation (conscious or not) behind this display of luxurious garments. Evolutionary anthropologists have observed that women are attracted, across cultures, to "costly" apparel: they are sensitive to "the expense and high status of clothing."[40] Intimate and extravagant, the "soft rich heap" of Gatsby's "beautiful shirts" moves Daisy to stormy tears (72). In a "symbolic sexual act," he spreads out for her admiration the magnificent apparel that has clothed his own body, triggering an emotionally intense reaction that promises to lead, as in fact it does, to a romantically charged sexual affair.[41]

Showing off the splendid things his money has bought, Gatsby overwhelms Daisy with the resources he has acquired: he has acquired them, indeed, with the intention of creating precisely this reaction. He also hopes to impress her with the tenacity of his devotion. Women seeking long-term mates value commitment almost as much as resources: a man must demonstrate

---

38 Buss, *Evolution of Desire*, 99.
39 Philip McGowan, "The American Carnival of *The Great Gatsby*," *Connotations* 13, no. 1-2 (2003/2004): 147.
40 Buss, *Evolution of Desire*, 101.
41 Ross Posnock, "'A New World, Material Without Being Real': Fitzgerald's Critique of Capitalism in *The Great Gatsby*", in *Critical Essays on F. Scott Fitzgerald's "The Great Gatsby,"* ed. Scott Donaldson (Boston: G. K. Hall, 1984), 208. Posnock accurately describes Daisy's sobbing response to Gatsby's shirts as essentially "orgasmic," 208.

willingness to invest his money, time, and energy reliably in his chosen mate and their common offspring. Displays of generosity and kindness typically are interpreted as signs of commitment, for example, as is emotional supportiveness.[42] "Persistence in courtship," above all, tends to persuade a woman that her suitor is "interested in more than casual sex" and envisions a shared long-term future.[43] While guiding Daisy on the long anticipated tour through his home, consequently, Gatsby provides evidence of his long-term fidelity as well as of his astounding wealth. He makes a point of showing her his collection of newspaper stories featuring her name and picture: "a lot of clippings—about you" (73). Gatsby's surprising re-emergence and renewed courtship prove initially successful: Daisy responds positively to discovery of his secret, unwavering devotion. He offers a combination of loyalty and riches sufficient to lure her into an extramarital romance of some intensity: she visits Gatsby "quite often—in the afternoons" through what remains of the summer (88).

Gatsby and Daisy: Phase III

Although he gains Daisy's sexual attention, Gatsby fails to achieve his long-range purpose, which is to convert their affair into marriage. There are two important reasons for his failure: the strength of the Buchanans' marital bond is one; his confusion of wealth with status is the other. As noted earlier, Daisy's marriage to Tom is based on important commonalities. Their shared socioeconomic background and upper-class concerns have lent stability to the union despite the friction caused by Tom's infidelities; shared parental commitment to their child provides another stabilizing element. When Daisy confides to Nick, early on, that she's had a "very bad time" being married to Tom and has grown "pretty cynical about everything," Nick is struck by "the basic insincerity" of her complaints (17). Instead of taking action to change her situation, she appears to derive smug enjoyment from her "sophisticated" disillusionment with marriage and "everything" (17). Paradoxically, as Nick suggests, Daisy's dissatisfactions seem to solidify her bond with Tom. Their jaded, been-there-done-that sense of superiority qualifies them for membership in "a rather distinguished secret society," a small circle composed, presumably, of wealthy and "cynical" social peers (17). Much later in the novel, Nick attests again to the robustness of the Buchanan's marital tie when he describes the scene he observes in their

---

42 Buss, *Evolution of Desire*, 102-104.
43 Ibid., 102.

kitchen (following the dramatic face-off between Gatsby and Tom and the fatal accident to Myrtle). It is a quiet tableau. Tom is "talking intently," covering Daisy's hand with his in a gesture that seems half-affectionate, half-possessive (113). Not only do the two of them radiate a "natural intimacy," they look as if they are "conspiring together" (113). The image of Daisy and Tom as co-conspirators supports Nick's understanding of their marriage as a durable alliance created to serve overlapping self-interests and protect elitist privilege.

Given this marital background, it is not surprising that Daisy crumbles quickly during the showdown between her lover and her husband: she refuses to commit herself to the new man in her life. Jolted out of her everyday boredom by Gatsby's spectacular reappearance in her life, she evidently has accepted his vision of permanent togetherness as a titillating fantasy rather than as a serious plan. More bluntly put, she views him as an affair-partner rather than as a potential husband. She is satisfied with the short-term benefits their romance supplies. In addition to sexual pleasure, she obtains a terrific boost to her self-esteem. Gatsby's five years of devotion validate, in the most flattering fashion, her desirability. She may view his besotted devotion as gratifying payback for Tom's many infidelities, but she is not prepared to abandon the security of her marriage. Nick's interpretation of her behavior during the confrontation between her husband and her lover is that "she realized at last what she was doing—and as though she had never, all along, intended doing anything at all" (103).

Tom's response to the threat Gatsby poses is calculated to make Daisy understand the full implications of the mate switch Gatsby is proposing: he tells her just how risky life with "Mr. Nobody from Nowhere" would be (101). He concentrates his mate-retention efforts on derogating his rival, a tactic commonly employed by members of both sexes against competitors.[44] Tom exposes Gatsby's lack of social status and upper-class connections, making Daisy realize that her lover is not *her kind*. He offers information about Gatsby's shady business dealings, discreditable associates, and possibly criminal enterprises. Daisy's upstart suitor is "a bootlegger" and "a common swindler," Tom sneeringly asserts; Gatsby belongs to the class of people who deliver "the groceries to the back door" (104, 102). Daisy is "staring terrified," Nick observes, as Tom makes these damning accusations (105). Not only is her image of Gatsby irretrievably damaged, she recognizes that marriage to him would take her out of the privileged socioeconomic milieu in which she has always lived. The safety

---

[44] Ibid., 97-98.

net provided by high status, social influence, and prestigious connections would be lost to her if she left Tom for this "Mr. Nobody."

Listening to Tom's angry denunciations with increasing "panic," Gatsby does not fully realize why he is losing Daisy (104). From the beginning he recognized the vast difference in class between Daisy and himself (that difference was, indeed, an important component in her appeal for him), but "now foolishly he believes that the money he has earned erases much of that social gap."[45] He has planned to win her back with a splendid show of wealth, but from the very beginning, unbeknownst to him, his plan had a fatal flaw: wealth alone does not guarantee entrée into elite social circles. It is true that material resources almost always are associated with social prestige, but in the highest echelons of society it takes more than one generation, typically, for the nouveau riche to win upper-class status. Nick's description of differences between the "raw" splendor of West Egg, where Gatsby has taken up residence, and the more sedately "fashionable" East Egg, where the Buchanans have bought property, points to the class barriers Gatsby must encounter in his pursuit of a Daisy Buchanan (8).[46] Notable dissimilarities in their social training and acquired tastes signal a host of more profound dissimilarities in behavior, motivation, association, and assumption. By East Egg standards, Gatsby's display of wealth is garish. His home, an imitation of a European hotel, is pretentious; his pink suit is noxiously flashy; his parties are spectacles of "many-keyed commotion" (81). Tom Buchanan, a representative of Old Money, drives an expensive but conservative vehicle (a blue coupé), while the newly rich Gatsby takes pride in his ostentatiously designed nickel-and-cream car, "swollen" with "triumphant hatboxes and supper-boxes and tool-boxes, and terraced with a labyrinth of wind-shields" (51). Its rococo embellishments and "monstrous" size clearly indicate that it is the property of a man untutored in upper-class understatement: Tom contemptuously labels it a "circus wagon" (51, 94). Since Gatsby never recognizes the imperfect overlap between wealth and status, he does not understand that his social origins present an insurmountable obstacle to fulfillment of his dreams. Tom's disclosures only confirm Daisy's increasingly negative response to the "raw vigor" of Gatsby's West Egg style: during the one party she attends at his home, her upper-class sensibilities are "offended" and "appalled" (84).

---

45 Hays, "Oxymoron in *The Great Gatsby*," 319.
46 W. T. Lhamon, Jr. discusses Fitzgerald's presentation of class in relation to money, identifying *Gatsby* as a novel "clearly establishing profoundly different groups of people in America, characterized by their relative access to a broad notion of power." "The Essential Houses of *The Great Gatsby*," in *Critical Essays on F. Scott Fitzgerald's "The Great Gatsby*," ed. Scott Donaldson (Boston: G. K. Hall, 1984), 175.

Derogation is not the only tactic Tom employs during the confrontation scene; he also attempts to reactivate his wife's loyalty by presenting himself and their marriage in the most favorable possible light. Despite evidence that she has become emotionally and sexually involved with another man, his jealousy does not take the form of aggression against her. He concentrates on driving away the interloper rather than on punishing Daisy for her infidelity. His goal, clearly, is to retain her as his wife, which indicates his awareness of her high mate value. He is unlikely to be able to replace her with a long-term mate of equivalent value—or, at any rate, not easily. Readers can only speculate about his probable response if Daisy had become pregnant in late summer or early autumn. Nick runs into Tom in late October and there is no mention then of a pregnancy: thus Tom's wish to keep his wife is not tested by any question of paternal confidence. The only threat he makes against Daisy is a warning, couched in pseudo-loving terms, that in future her activities will be more strictly monitored and, perhaps, limited. "I'm going to take better care of you from now on," he tells her, implying more attention and nurturing on his part but also more rigorous mate guarding (104).

In a compelling show of masculine self-confidence, Tom goes on to assure everyone present that he and Daisy love each other.[47] He reaffirms his enduring commitment to her ("in my heart I love her all the time"), reminding her that he has always "come back" to her after "a spree" of casual infidelity (103). He attempts to rekindle warmth by reminding her of tender moments in their shared past. He tries hard, in sum, to capitalize on women's adaptive preference for men who offer them attention and caring as well as resources. Buss observes that potentially defecting partners often respond favorably to "displays of love."[48] Shrewdly, too, Tom indicates that he is willing to excuse her affair with Gatsby as a temporary lapse in judgment instead of condemning it as culpable disloyalty: "sometimes she gets foolish ideas in her head and doesn't know what she's doing" (102). Finally, he dismisses Gatsby's five-year devotion to Daisy as a "presumptuous little flirtation" (105). He belittles Gatsby's dedication, at the same time reiterating his own marital commitment. Astutely employing a combination of defensive and offensive tactics, he wards off a serious mate-poaching attempt.

Charged though it is with emotions inspired by sexual competition and conflict, the scene in the hotel room remains relatively pacific: all the aggression

---

47 Buss explains that men often make displays of bravado and self-confidence in order to attract mates. Among other things, such displays signal "status and resources," criteria of obvious importance in the showdown taking place between the high-status Tom Buchanan and his social-upstart rival. *Evolution of Desire*, 107-108.

48 Ibid., 191, 192.

is verbal. Escalation of jealousy into violence is provoked by events occurring in the sexual triangle dominating the secondary action: George-Myrtle-Tom. Coincidentally, George Wilson has "gotten wised up" to his wife's infidelity around the same time Tom Buchanan begins to suspect Daisy's interest in Gatsby (96). Unlike Tom, George doesn't know the identity of his wife's paramour. Since he, too, is determined to retain his mate, Wilson plans to "get her away" from the unknown man's vicinity by taking her permanently to a distant state, "whether she wants to or not" (96). Until he can make arrangements for this move, he has locked her up. This is a much more physically coercive form of mate guarding than the supervision with which Tom threatens Daisy: Wilson has forcibly imprisoned his wife.[49] He engages in punitive shaming, additionally, telling her that "God knows" what she's done and implying that she will suffer otherworldly retribution for her adultery (124). When Myrtle is fatally struck by the conspicuous yellow car, Wilson assumes that she has been purposely run down by its driver; he further concludes that the driver is Myrtle's lover, who now deliberately has murdered her. In Wilson's view, this man has deprived him of his wife twice over: first he enticed her into sexual infidelity and "then he killed her" (123). Rendered almost "incoherent" with grief and rage, Wilson can think only of finding and slaying the man who has committed this assault on his fitness: a sexual interloper who first appropriated and then destroyed reproductive resources in which Wilson has proprietary interest.

Wilson's vengefulness exemplifies the "jealous violence," up to and including homicide, frequently "directed toward same-sex rivals."[50] He can act on his murderous impulse only with Tom Buchanan's cooperation, in this instance, and he gets it. Following up on Tom's connection with the yellow car, Wilson learns Gatsby's name and duly kills him. Using Wilson as a tool to kill the man who sought to usurp his own wife, Tom achieves a more violent, more risk-laden vengeance than he himself was willing to undertake. Without realizing that he is acting on Tom's account as well as his own, Wilson permanently removes a contender for Daisy's affection. Thus Tom benefits from his tacit complicity in murder. Had he not been killed, Gatsby doubtless would have continued his intrusion into the Buchanan marriage, an ongoing source of aggravation, if not serious worry, to Tom. (Gatsby's all-night vigil outside the Buchanan home, together with his comments to Nick about a probable call from Daisy, suggests

---

49 Buss discusses the prevalence of "dramatic" mate-guarding tactics historically and cross-culturally, noting that women have been concealed and confined in many societies in order to "prevent their contact with potential sexual partners." Ibid., 136.
50 Buss, *Dangerous Passion*, 111, 119.

that he still has not given up all hope of winning her back.) Tom has yet another motive for helping Wilson: because he believes Gatsby was the driver of the car that killed Myrtle, he blames Gatsby for the death of his mistress. His reasons for homicidal hatred of Gatsby are even stronger, therefore, than Wilson's. Having made a serious attempt to poach Tom's wife, Gatsby has deprived him (as Tom mistakenly assumes) of his extra-pair partner. Tom views Gatsby as a sexual trespasser and conscienceless killer ("he ran over Myrtle like you'd run over a dog") who clearly deserves to die (239).

Like her husband, Daisy plays an instrumental role in disposing of an important sexual rival. Although Daisy does not know the identity of her hit-and-run victim, she has succeeded in eliminating the hated "woman in New York." As a driver, she is of course criminally culpable; having failed, through cowardice, to take evasive action to avoid hitting a pedestrian, she compounds her guilt by refusing to stop to offer assistance and admit responsibility.[51] Her behavior represents fundamental "carelessness" rather than calculated murder, but she has inadvertently achieved fitness-enhancing results: she has rid herself of a competitor vying for her husband's time, attention, and wealth. Without conscious awareness or deliberate intent, she has acted as if inspired by sexual jealousy, committing an act of violence that protects her long-term reproductive interests.

Because loss of resources and desertion represent the most significant evolutionary threats to women in long-term partnerships, female jealousy is more easily provoked by signs of a husband's emotional investment in another woman than by signs of sexual disloyalty.[52] Daisy is right to think Myrtle represents a greater danger to her marriage than Tom's other casual partners. He has, after all, made provision for an indefinitely protracted involvement, even setting up an apartment. He is tolerating Myrtle's intrusion, via the telephone, into the Buchanan home—behavior he certainly could forbid. In Tom's last conversation with Nick, significantly, he confides that in his grief for Myrtle he "cried like a baby" (119). For evolutionarily sound reasons, any wife would feel jealous of a rival who had insinuated herself this deeply into her husband's affections. Even though, as already discussed, Myrtle poses only the smallest of long-term threats to the Buchanan marriage, her presence in Tom's life is an ongoing source of aggravation and unease to Daisy. Thus Daisy benefits from Myrtle's death in the same

---

51 Barry Edward Gross accurately points out that by the time this accident occurs, pervasive references to automobiles and driving styles have "established reckless driving as indicative of some fatal inner ... dishonesty." *Critical Extracts*, in *Gatsby: Major Literary Characters*, ed. Harold Bloom (New York: Chelsea House, 1991), 25.
52 Buss, *Dangerous Passion*, 52-62.

way, if not to the same degree, that Tom does from Gatsby's. Conscious intention aside, her vehicular homicide creates a perversely appropriate symmetry in her marriage. She and Tom are quits: he has killed her lover, and she has killed his. There is indirection, and thus deniability, in both homicides: Tom does not pick up a gun and shoot Gatsby, any more than Daisy knowingly targets Myrtle for slaughter. Since neither knows what the other has done, moreover, their relationship can continue undisturbed by any after-the-fact suspicion or rebuke.

The jealous violence erupting at the end of the novel sheds unsparing light on the fitness-based emotions seething beneath the glittering surface of the principal settings. The ferocity of inter-and intrasexual competition emerges with especial clarity. Not only do characters take radical steps to guard and retain their mates, they wreak vengeance, sometimes fatal, on rivals seeking to displace them. In addition to showing the intensity of mating conflicts, the killing of Gatsby and Myrtle encourages readers to judge the Buchanan couple harshly. Tom and Daisy appear untouched by the deaths they have caused, unabashed by what Nick dubs their "vast carelessness"; they regard their actions as either unavoidable or "entirely justified" (139). They fortify the stability of their union by eliminating sexual rivals, and they do so with a callousness that underlines their essential compatibility. Their hasty departure following the deaths of Myrtle and Gatsby smacks of unspoken collusion: on some level they may intuit that they are assisting each other to cover up crimes. Their "banal and shabby intimacy" provides foundation for a marriage that is, in Brian Way's summation, "a realistic, if worthless, practical arrangement that suits their shallow personalities."[53] There is no reason to suppose that either partner will change as a result of the homicidal events in which they have participated, or that the intersexual conflict coloring their interactions will cease: Tom will continue womanizing, and Daisy will continue sniping.

Gatsby: Misconceptions and Delusions

Gatsby's identification of wealth with status is not the only mistaken idea shaping his career. Another misconception he harbors is that ambition can be severed from procreative concerns. Because material resources and social reputation play such a decisive role in female mate selection, it is adaptive for men to work strenuously to acquire them. More than anything else, the hope of attracting

---

53 Brian Way, "*The Great Gatsby*," in *F. Scott Fitzgerald's "The Great Gatsby*," ed. Harold Bloom (New York: Chelsea House, 1986), 99.

women—who are, after all, the limiting factor in male reproductive potential—spurs men's striving. Men need not be aware of the procreative purpose fueling their quests for fame and fortune. Gatsby, for example, tells Nick that falling in love with Daisy has prevented him from "doing great things," derailed his plans: "there I was, way off my ambitions" (117). Before meeting her, he has cherished ill-defined but "ineffable" fantasies about his "future glory" (77). Setting forth at the age of seventeen for profitable adventures, he is not consciously thinking that shedding his "shiftless and unsuccessful" farming background is the first step to improved mating opportunities (76). "Extravagantly ambitious," he is attracted to "beauty and glamour" in and of themselves—or so he thinks (78). With the confidence of youth, he is convinced that he could reach "incomparable" heights "if he climbed alone," but to "wed his unutterable visions" to a "perishable" girl will keep him earthbound (86).

Reduced to its essence, Gatsby's thinking on this point resembles the last-minute reservations expressed by many bridegrooms: marital commitment ties a man down, imposes obligations, limits future options. A wife is a living being, "perishable," who must be supported with material resources rather than with "unutterable visions." Thinking that now "his mind would never romp again like the mind of God," Gatsby contemplates in advance the disadvantages of the reproductive strategy to which, emotionally at least, he has just committed or "wed" himself (86). Long-term responsibilities largely will replace the unattached man's "god"-like sense of infinite potential. Because humans are intelligent and complex creatures who command an array of behavioral strategies, mating behavior included, they are able to entertain a multiplicity of options, exercising a high degree of conscious choice. Here the young and unencumbered Gatsby engages in anticipatory nostalgia, mourning strategic alternatives he has decided to forego. In terms of fitness, of course, reproductive success trumps reproductive potential. By *wedding* his ambitions to a potential mate, Gatsby is behaving adaptively, a fact he never recognizes.

His incomprehension is not unusual. Men frequently speak of wives and offspring as if they were obstacles to success rather than proof of it. Riches and fame often are praised as if they constituted ultimate goals. Once a particular pattern of behavior becomes adaptive, it can take on a momentum of its own (as happens, for instance, in run-away sexual selection). People value money and prestige for sound evolutionary reasons, but in contemporary environments these can be sought and often obtained in much larger quantities than reproductive needs dictate. The agricultural revolution, which first enabled humans to create permanent settlements, also enabled them to amass far more property than a nomadic, hunter-gatherer lifestyle will permit. Increased wealth, coupled with unequal distribution, leads inevitably to greater socioeconomic stratification: the struggle for advantageous hierarchical placement grows more difficult. Given conditions of excess and extremes, an adaptive trait or tendency may become detached, in terms of conscious intention, from the reproductive purposes it is designed to serve. Maladaptive accumulation of resources in a modern environment is, of course, a principal thematic concern in *The Great Gatsby*. Much secondary commentary focuses accordingly on the corrupting effect of wealth, including Fitzgerald's presentation and critique of the rags-to-riches "American Dream."[54]

The novel's narrator demonstrates that he does not share Gatsby's misconceptions about the purpose of material resources. It is only when Nick discovers that Gatsby's fantastical show of wealth is a courtship tactic, designed to attract the attention of a woman he has pursued devotedly for five years, that he finds him intriguing: "He came alive to me, delivered suddenly from the womb of his purposeless splendor" (62). The metaphoric use of procreative vocabulary ("deliver," "womb") helps to emphasize Nick's insight: a magnificent display of material assets is pointless unless it promotes fitness. As a mating effort, Gatsby's "career as Trimalchio" is dedicated to reproductive ends and thus makes evolutionary sense (88). No frivolous exhibitionist, as Nick initially assumed, Gatsby is the "high-bouncing" lover described in the poem serving as the novel's epigraph: he dons a "gold hat" chiefly in order to "move" the girl of his dreams (epigraph, lines 3, 1).[55]

---

54 For representative analyses of Fitzgerald's presentation of the American Dream in the novel, see Marius Bewley, "Scott Fitzgerald's Criticism of America," in *Twentieth Century Interpretations of "The Great Gatsby,"* ed. Ernest Lockridge (Englewood Cliffs, NJ: Prentice-Hall, 1968); Edwin S. Fussell, "Fitzgerald's Brave New World," *English Literary History* 19, no. 4 (1952); David Stouck, "*The Great Gatsby* as Pastoral," in *Gatsby: Major Literary Characters*, ed. Harold Bloom (New York: Chelsea House, 1991); James E. Miller, Jr., "Fitzgerald's *Gatsby*: The World as Ash Heap," in *Critical Essays on F. Scott Fitzgerald's "The Great Gatsby,"* ed. Scott Donaldson (Boston: G. K. Hall, 1984); Neila Seshachari, "*The Great Gatsby*: Apogee of Fitzgerald's Mythopoeia," in *Gatsby: Major Literary Characters*, ed. Harold Bloom (New York: Chelsea House, 1991); Posnock, "'A New World, Material Without Being Real': Fitzgerald's Critique of Capitalism"; Hugh Kenner, "The Promised Land," in *Gatsby: Major Literary Characters*, ed. Harold Bloom (New York: Chelsea House, 1991).

55 Attributed to "Thomas Parke D'Invilliers," a character from Fitzgerald's 1920 novel, *This Side of Paradise*, the poem was written by Fitzgerald himself, as Matthew J. Bruccoli points out. "Explanatory Notes," in *The Great Gatsby*, ed. and rpt. by Matthew J. Bruccoli (Cambridge and New York: Cambridge University Press, 1991), 180.

Gatsby's conviction that pursuit of women interferes with the real business of men's lives ("doing great things") is further explored in the novel by the association of Daisy with the sirens of classical mythology. The seductive power of those monstrous females figures, most familiar to Fitzgerald and his readers from the famous anecdote in Homer's *Odyssey*, is concentrated in the irresistible sweetness of their singing. Exercising a supernatural capacity to bewitch and beguile, they use their beautiful voices to lure men to destruction. Persistent references to the "inexhaustible charm" of Daisy Buchanan's voice subtly compare her to Homer's sirens, attributing to her a similarly dire erotic power (94). On at least eight different occasions, Nick draws attention to the unique quality and effect of Daisy's voice. The "principle instrument with which she casts her spell over Gatsby," as Bender points out, it communicates "excitement"; it exercises "a singing compulsion" that "men" find "difficult to forget" (11).[56] The "exhilarating ripple of her voice" acts like "a wild tonic," simultaneously seductive and entrancing (67). Nick speculates that Gatsby's spellbound fascination with Daisy is inspired chiefly by the "feverish warmth" of her voice, which "couldn't be over-dreamed—that voice was a deathless song" (75). Presentation of Daisy as a siren-figure emphasizes the almost mystical strength of her hold on Gatsby.

The siren allusion also calls attention to Gatsby's evolutionarily unsound notion that wooing Daisy prevents achievement of important masculine ambitions. Like Homer's mariners, he was going about his business when a voice of incomparable sweetness called to him, luring him to his doom. Such negative presentation of women's attractiveness to men is, of course, an important purpose of siren mythology and related legends, as Barbara Smuts points out. In many societies, historically and cross-culturally, women have been "portrayed as dangerous and polluting, and it is their sexuality that makes them so."[57] With tales of fatally alluring females, men attempt to blame women for male behavior—male sexual behavior, in particular. It comforts men to think that Helen's beauty or Circe's magic, rather than masculine ardor and male-male competition, caused the Trojan War or turned men into swine. Daisy's siren-like effect on Gatsby accordingly evokes sympathy for the male victim and

---

56 Bender, *Evolution and "the Sex Problem,"* 238.
57 Smuts, "Male Aggression," 252. Sarah Blaffer Hrdy similarly notes that in ancient Greece female sexuality was associated with the uninhibited, insatiable ardency of lionesses and female bears. The legend of the maenads, to name an obvious example, illustrates the danger such women's eroticism allegedly poses to men. *Mother Nature: A History of Mothers, Infants, and Natural Selection* (New York: Pantheon Books, 1999), 262.

his obsessive devotion, even as it censures the woman's indifference to her destructive attractions. Daisy drives Gatsby's life off-course twice by choosing Tom Buchanan over him: his inextinguishable yearning to possess her ends in his destruction. The comparison between Daisy and mythological monsters thus supports auctorial judgments on the novel's characters.

At the same time that they represent deadly danger, paradoxically, sirens embody female preciousness. Calling from a distance, they rely on their singing to telegraph their beauty and so to stimulate male desire. Physical beauty, of course—displaced in the sirens' case from facial and bodily features to vocal qualities—provides the single most important cue to female reproductive capacity: this is why it triggers an ardent response in men.[58] Men labor and compete to gain access to beautiful (i.e., fertile) women. They will dash themselves upon the rocks, figuratively speaking, in pursuit of the youthful, healthy, facially symmetrical, small-waisted, and wide-hipped females who hold the key to their fitness. Fertile women are dangerous precisely *because* they are so valuable: the desire to possess them moves men, willy-nilly, to engage in energy-sapping and high-risk behavior.

Like the singing of Homeric sirens, the unusually desirable Daisy's "deathless song" tantalizes suitors seeking immortality for their DNA (75). Gatsby describes her great worth metaphorically—and aptly, given the centrality of wealth to the novel's setting and plot—when he tells Nick that "her voice is full of money" (94). The many references to the "magic" of Daisy's voice culminate in this statement, which Nick greets as a revelatory insight: "that was it" (84, 94). The "jingle" of coins men hear when she speaks, the "cymbals' song" of "a white palace" and a "king's daughter," signal wealth and status (94). These augment and underline, via metaphor, the sexual benefits simultaneously conveyed by her voice: that "feverish warmth" and promise of "amour" (94, 61). She is, as Gatsby recognizes from the start, a doubly worthy object of desire. Her biologically attractive qualities (youth, health, beauty) are accompanied by socially attractive ones (material possessions, high status, elite networks, community regard). She offers an ideal combination of intrinsic and extrinsic worth. Gatsby's fixation on her, which continues even after he becomes well able to woo other, more available and more amenable partners, is grounded in his initial, overwhelming impression of Daisy as "the golden girl," a top prize in the stakes for fitness (94). For reproductively explicable reasons, she exercises siren-like appeal for him; her very voice spills over with confirmation of her high value.

---

58   Buss, *Evolution of Desire*, 52-58.

The most unusual feature, by far, of Gatsby's pursuit of Daisy Buchanan is the self-deception driving it. Having formulated a three-year plan to seduce another man's wife, he never admits that he is engaged in an act of mate poaching. Such poaching is, as Buss explains, "a common mating strategy." "Glamorous, interesting, attractive, socially skilled people" are in short supply, inevitably, because they are identified, courted, and removed from "the marriage market" with great rapidity.[59] Those who fail to secure high-value mates on the first go-round, consequently, often tempt the already-married to make new choices. Gatsby does not admit that his goal is so ordinary, that is, to persuade an especially desirable woman to abandon her marriage in order to form a new bond with him. Instead he explains his goal to himself, to Daisy, and to onlookers in terms of time-travel. Turning back the clock, he and Daisy will find themselves at "the starting place" in 1917, about to begin their life together as a couple (86). They will "be married from her house" in Louisville "just as if it were five years ago" (86). Gatsby intends to "fix everything just the way it was before" (86). His goal is nothing less than to revise history by wiping out a selected piece of the past. His conviction that this is possible, that he actually can undo temporal progression, illustrates with astounding clarity the self-deceiving powers of the human mind. Except with regard to his relationship with Daisy, moreover, Gatsby's conception of time is rational and undistorted. He does not assume, for instance, that his hard-won wealth will disappear when he and Daisy start afresh. His false ideation is caused by selective self-deception rather than by pervasive mental derangement. Evolutionary psychology helps to explain the origin and function of his deluded thinking.

Robert Trivers neatly sums up self-deception as "the active misrepresentation of reality to the conscious mind."[60] The principal "reality" Gatsby seeks to misrepresent is Daisy Fay's marriage to Tom Buchanan. The imaginary do-over, once the clock has been set back, will expunge that union from Daisy's personal history. Obliterating the Buchanan marriage is vitally important to Gatsby because he views Daisy as belonging to him, in all but the legal sense, by virtue of prior claim. Emotionally "he felt married to her" after their mutual declarations of love and future intent: he "had committed himself" and has reason to think she has done the same (117, 116). This conviction is the foundation of the "fictitious narratives of intention" he thereafter constructs.[61]

---

59 Ibid., 265, 264.
60 Robert Trivers, "Self-Deception in Service of Deceit," in *Natural Selection and Social Theory: Selected Papers of Robert Trivers* (Oxford: Oxford University Press, 2002), 277.
61 Trivers, "Self-Deception," 276.

If Daisy and Gatsby are joined in mutual commitment, it is Tom Buchanan who is the mate-poaching interloper. Such reasoning is counterfactual, of course: Gatsby is not and never has been Daisy's husband. He has employed "denial and projection," rather, "to create a self-serving world."[62] The illusion that he is virtually "married" to Daisy enables Gatsby to see and present himself in the most favorable possible light. So long as he considers himself a devoted long-term partner rather than a wife-stealing seducer, he can maintain a positive self-image.

What is far more important to him, however, is seeing Daisy in a favorable light, and here his reconstruction of reality does not serve him well. According to Gatsby's interpretation of the past, he and Daisy have made a mutual long-term commitment. It must follow, then, that in marrying Tom she is guilty of infidelity and desertion: she is a defecting spouse. This is, very obviously, not how Gatsby wishes to view her. For evolutionarily excellent reasons, men expect to enjoy exclusive sexual access to their long-term partners. They demand sexual fidelity, if only to ensure that they do not waste paternal investment in offspring sired by a wife's lovers. An unfaithful wife not only squanders her reproductive resources outside the marriage, she introduces the possibility of cuckoos in the nest, threatening her husband's fitness.[63] Female infidelity is a critical source of male sexual jealousy and, depending on prevailing norms, also may incur social penalties. Gatsby's reverence for Daisy, the grail-like girl whose mate value so blindingly exceeds his own, would be severely challenged if he were compelled to regard her as sexually disloyal. Her "gleaming" image would be tarnished, her mate value diminished (117).

His misrepresentation of reality has led him into an apparently insurmountable difficulty. On the one hand, the illusion that Gatsby and Daisy are united by a bond equivalent to marriage serves his interest because it renders Tom's claim to her illegitimate. On the other hand, that very illusion makes Daisy guilty of infidelity, a fault that renders her less desirable as a mate and less worthy of Gatsby's extraordinary devotion. Unlike Tom Buchanan, Gatsby thinks in terms of ideals and absolutes: he could never imitate Tom's sophisticated management or thick-skinned tolerance of Daisy's involvement with another man (105). Gatsby long ago placed Daisy on a pedestal: she is the Madonna-like, ever loyal partner, and his elaborate plan to repossess her would lose its significance if she ceased to be worthy of his bedazzled homage. This

---

62 Ibid., 271.
63 Smuts, "Male Aggression," 246; Buss, *Evolution of Desire*, 66-72.

problem explains why he must convince himself that he and Daisy can "repeat the past" (86). Once her marriage to Tom is "obliterated," there will be no question of her having been unfaithful to Gatsby (85). There will be no cause for sexual jealousy on his part, no decrease in her mate value. All he has to do to achieve these evolutionarily beneficial results is take the two of them back to "the way it was before" she met Tom (86).[64]

Thus Gatsby's doubly distorted vision of reality supports evolutionarily sound goals: acquisition of a high-value mate, nonviolent elimination of a rival, prevention of a mate's infidelity and defection. Those goals remain unobtainable, however, because the methods and assumptions he relies upon to achieve them are delusional: reality keeps interfering with his program. He conveniently forgets, for instance, that Daisy has borne Tom a child, a child who is not going to vanish obligingly when the marriage that produced her has been wiped from the slate of her mother's past. Nick observes that when Gatsby finally sees the child he stares "with surprise," never having "really believed in its existence before" (91). He has not thought about the child because to do so would interfere with his fantasy of turning back the clock. The child is living proof that Daisy has not remained sexually faithful to him; instead she has entered into a reproductive enterprise with his sexual rival. Daisy's and Tom's genes are traveling toward the future in the shared vehicle of Pammy. Offspring tend to strengthen a marital bond for this very reason: parents have equal genetic interest in the jointly created beings who represent both parties' hopes for biological continuity.[65] These facts threaten the pattern of denial shaping Gatsby's behavior. There is no place for Daisy and Tom's child, ineradicable evidence of her reproductive betrayal, in his projected return to an idyllic "starting place."

Tom Buchanan contradicts Gatsby's "false narratives" with additional unwelcome facts when he boasts of the three years of shared intimacy he has enjoyed with Daisy. "There're things between Daisy and me that you'll never know," he justly states, "things that neither of us can ever forget" (103). Even if she should choose to leave Tom, Daisy's memory never can be wiped clean of those recollections. Her three-year union with Tom, which is social and emotional as well as reproductive, now forms an inextricable part of her present identity, which is different in some ways from the eighteen-year-old self who inspired Gatsby's worshipful commitment. His dreams require her to remain

---

64 David Stouck suggests that it is because Gatsby's initial possession of Daisy is "incomplete that his imaginative vision of her remains so "vibrantly alive." He "is obsessed … with that moment back in time when she 'will become' his bride." "*The Great Gatsby* as Pastoral," 69.
65 Wright, *Moral Animal*, 125.

unchanged, however; she must come to him just as she was in summer 1917, with her loyalty to Gatsby intact. By insisting that neither the Buchanan marriage nor Daisy's memory of it can be erased, Tom confronts Gatsby with facts inimical to his illusions. Gatsby's dismaying experience in the course of a single afternoon illustrates what Trivers identifies as the most significant cost of self-deception, namely, "misapprehension of reality," especially "social" reality.[66]

Daisy, too, confronts Gatsby with unpalatable psychological truths by failing to understand and comply with his project for defying temporal reality. He plans to assert his exclusive rights to Daisy on terms to be dictated by him, terms corresponding to his counterfactual assumptions. Since he cannot bear to think that he has been dispossessed of his treasured woman by a rival, he denies that this has happened. Such denial requires that the Buchanan marriage be rendered null and void. "Only in this way," as Robert Ornstein accurately observes, "can the sacrament of Gatsby's 'marriage'—his prior claim—be recognized."[67] To achieve the self-interested goal of erasing Daisy's relationship with Tom from her sexual history, Gatsby relies on magical thinking. He persuades himself that if Daisy retracts her "love" for Tom, telling him that she "never" cared for him, she will, in effect, annul her marriage (85). Gatsby invests the words he requires Daisy to say to Tom with transformative power; like a magical incantation, the phrase "I never loved you" will alter reality (85). Bibbidi-Bobbidi-Boo: the marriage is eradicated and Daisy's fidelity restored. Here Gatsby's powers of self-deception assume fairy-tale proportions. Unsurprisingly, Daisy does not understand the significance of the repudiation he demands: "I love you now—isn't that enough?" she asks; "I can't help what's past" (103). This is the crux of the matter: moving forward on the basis of a fully acknowledged past will not solve the problem of Gatsby's sexual jealousy and proprietary demands. The only way he can achieve his projected future with Daisy is by revising their personal histories: canceling—and then reliving—selected events from the previous five years. The typical announcement of a defecting mate, 'I don't love you any more,' is inadequate for his purposes because it would constitute admission of a commitment—legal, social, and sexual—existing between Daisy and Tom.

---

66 Trivers, "Self-Deception," 276.
67 Robert Ornstein, "Scott Fitzgerald's Fable of East and West," in *Twentieth Century Interpretations of "The Great Gatsby,"* ed. Ernest Lockridge (Englewood Cliffs, NJ: Prentice-Hall, 1968), 59. Neila Seshachari characterizes Gatsby's reverential, quasi-religious understanding of his and Daisy's mutual commitment in similar terms: Gatsby regards them as "eternally wedded … in mystical rites." "*The Great Gatsby*: Apogee," 100.

Commentary on the novel often describes Gatsby's character and aims in mythic terms.[68] He appears heroic, larger than life, because he commits himself to an imaginatively conceived, unachievable goal. From an evolutionary perspective, his obsessive pursuit of Daisy appears less than glorious in that it signally fails to secure fitness benefits: he dies, so far as readers know, without issue. His life history underlines the fact that adaptations are not algorithms that guarantee reproductive success. As Robert Wright points out, "the best that natural selection can do is give us adaptations ... that play the odds."[69] Gatsby sets his sights on a high-quality mate (*adaptive*); he demands sexual fidelity in his chosen long-term partner (*adaptive*). Yet his dedication to indubitably fitness-enhancing principles (*get the best mate possible and enforce her fidelity*) garners fewer benefits, in this instance, than more flexible strategizing might have obtained for him. The obvious step for a man in his position to take would be to select a different, even if less attractive, mate once Daisy became unavailable. A second, more time-consuming and more risk-laden option would be to implement his mate-poaching scheme with full awareness of its implications. This would mean that in persuading Daisy to abandon her marriage for him, Gatsby would acknowledge her sexual history, recognizing her less-than-sterling record for fidelity (she has deserted Gatsby for another man once already, and in leaving Tom she would further demonstrate that she is poachable). Either of these alternative mating strategies would have strengthened Gatsby's chances to achieve a genetic legacy. Both are unacceptable to him, very evidently, because they would require him to modify his image of Daisy—to view her as something less than the ultimately precious and perfect woman—and to revise his goals accordingly.

Refusing to lower his expectations for his chosen mate or to replace her with a second choice, Gatsby turns to the realm of illusion: fantasy, make-believe, dream, myth. These terms, so often used by readers and sometimes by Fitzgerald's narrator to describe Gatsby's thinking and aims, are exalted descriptions of his counterfactual ideation. In William Troy's view, for instance,

---

68 For representative discussion of mythic elements in Gatsby's quest and personality, see Kennth Eble, "*The Great Gatsby*," *College Literature* 1, no. 1 (1974); Miller, Jr., "Fitzgerald's *Gatsby*"; Scott, "Entropy vs. Ecology"; Seshachari, "*The Great Gatsby*: Apogee"; Arnold Weinstein, "Fiction as Greatness: The Case of Gatsby," in *Gatsby: Major Literary Characters*, ed. Harold Bloom (New York: Chelsea House, 1991); Marius Bewley, "Scott Fitzgerald's Criticism of America"; Giles F. Gunn, "F. Scott Fitzgerald's *Gatsby* and the Imagination of Wonder," in *Critical Essays on F. Scott Fitzgerald's "The Great Gatsby,"* ed. Scott Donaldson (Boston: G. K. Hall, 1984).

69 Wright, *Moral Animal*, 106.

Gatsby is a "mythological creation" who illustrates the "projected wish fulfillment carried out on a larger scale and by the whole consciousness of a race."[70] Gatsby revises the truth about Daisy's life history in order to preserve her goddess-like image and so to his sustain his reverence for her. The mythic ideal to which he commits himself is that of the infinitely beautiful, infinitely faithful woman.[71] The archetypal attributes of beauty (*fertility*) and fidelity (*exclusive sexual privilege*) very obviously serve men's reproductive interests.[72] Judith Fetterley speaks to this point in her feminist analysis of the novel, noting that the ideals portrayed are masculine: "the imaginative structures to which the book gives such brilliant expression are merely those of all *men*."[73] Gatsby's idealized vision of Daisy represents clearly male-centered wish-fulfillment.

Her failure to live up to Gatsby's image of her calls attention to the self-deceiving, myth-making power of the human mind. His false beliefs about her are juxtaposed to her glaring inadequacies: what she is proves incommensurate to what he imagines.[74] Way rightly observes that this disparity between Daisy-the-person and Daisy-the-dream excites readers' interest and empathy: "Fitzgerald has completed his immensely difficult task of convincing us that Gatsby's capacity for illusion is poignant and heroic, in spite of the banality of his aspirations and the worthlessness of the objects of his dreams."[75] To laud Gatsby's commitment to false narrative as "poignant and heroic," however, is to valorize mental operations of seemingly dubious worth. There is nothing inherently noble about a capacity for self-interested denial and projection, yet readers marvel at Gatsby's creative manipulation of reality, even if they also shake their heads. Fitzgerald's protagonist provides an extreme example of the human tendency to subscribe to self-made truths.

---

70 William Troy, "Scott Fitzgerald—the Authority of Failure," in *F. Scott Fitzgerald: A Collection of Critical Essays*, ed. Arthur Mizener (Englewood Cliffs, NJ: Prentice-Hall, 1963), 21.
71 Seshachari points out that the object of Gatsby's "personal quest" is "woman" per se, woman as "mythic ideal," rather than Daisy herself. "*The Great Gatsby*: Apogee," 94.
72 Seshachari frames the situation from an evolutionarily understandable perspective when she observes that the projected union between questing hero and "woman, in her mythic concept," is designed to achieve "fulfillment of the purpose of life." Ibid., 94, 95.
73 Judith Fetterley, "*The Great Gatsby*: Fitzgerald's *droit de seigneur*," in *The Resisting Reader: A Feminist Approach to American Fiction* (Bloomington and London: University of Indiana Press, 1978), 98.
74 As "actual correlative," W. J. Harvey notes, Daisy cannot satisfy "the hunger of his aspiring imagination." "Theme and Texture in *The Great Gatsby*," in *Critical Essays on F. Scott Fitzgerald's "The Great Gatsby*," ed. Scott Donaldson (Boston: G. K. Hall, 1984), 83.
75 Way, "*The Great Gatsby*," 99.

Invoking powers of memory, anticipation, and imagination, the human animal mentally replays and revises social history on a daily basis, subverting What-Is and What-Was in satisfying fashion with What-If and What-Might-Have-Been. Joseph Carroll, Brian Boyd, Blakey Vermeule, and other Darwinian literary theorists point out that human art—particularly literary art in the form of fictional narrative—exploits, exercises, and hones these species-typical behavioral tendencies.[76] When real-world circumstances fail to match our imaginings, we endow our disappointment with exalted significance: we create myths, symbols, and tales to preserve and extol our commitment to unrealizable visions. Instead of bemoaning our inability to live fully in the moment as other animals do, we value our "ghostly" dreaming more highly than we do the "fire and freshness" of the phenomenal world (75). Gatsby's life history demonstrates that mental images, no matter how self-deceiving, can become more compelling than obtainable, real-world satisfactions: "Daisy is the 'still unravished bride' of Keats' urn."[77] Obsessed with a version of reality he does not consciously recognize as his own invention, Gatsby "incarnates the power of dream and illusion."[78] "The kernel of his experience," Roger Lewis astutely observes, "is safely embedded in a previous time." Because "his love became most intense" during the five years of their separation, "it is largely a function of his imagination."[79] Readers are impressed by "the power of belief" he demonstrates as he transforms ordinary things into "enchanted objects."[80] Fitzgerald encourages a positive response to his protagonist, furthermore, by stacking the deck against reality: that "foul dust" defiling Gatsby's "dreams" (6). The unedifying spectacle of the Buchanans and the Wilsons, with their ordinary mate choices, rivalries, and jealousies, their banal fidelities and tawdry infidelities, renders Gatsby's deluded quest appealing by force of contrast.

It is not coincidental that his falsifying of social and temporal facts serves his efforts to acquire and retain an ideal mate. The novel's final passage, much admired and much discussed, dramatically expands the connection between

---

[76] Carroll, "An Evolutionary Paradigm for Literary Study," see especially 23-25; Carroll, "Wilson's *Consilience* and Literary Study," 81-82; Boyd, *On the Origin of Stories*, see especially "Fiction as Adaptation," 188-208. Vermeule, *Why Do We Care*; see especially "The Fictional Among Us," 1-20.
[77] Stouck, "*The Great Gatsby* as Pastoral," 69.
[78] R. W. Stallman, "Gatsby and the Hole in Time," in *Gatsby: Major Literary Characters*, ed. Harold Bloom (New York: Chelsea House, 1991), 62.
[79] Roger Lewis, "Money, Love, and Aspiration in *The Great Gatsby*," in *New Essays on "The Great Gatsby,"* ed. Matthew J. Bruccoli (Cambridge: Cambridge University Press, 1985), 49.
[80] Weinstein, "Fiction as Greatness," 139, 140.

procreative impulses and self-serving illusions. Comparing Gatsby to European explorers and Daisy's attractions to "the siren song of the American continent," Nick draws attention to the acquisitive awe inspired by resources with direct or indirect reproductive worth.[81] Gatsby hoped to enrich his individual fitness by claiming exclusive rights to an ideal woman: young and sexually loyal, with maximum reproductive potential. European explorers and settlers similarly hoped to enrich themselves and their posterity, increasing the chances for their lineages to survive and thrive, by laying claim to bountiful natural resources in a brand-new place. That place typically has been described as a "virgin" land, moreover, its untapped potential, like that of a virginal woman, promising great value. Fitzgerald uses figurative language to heighten his comparison, equating collective expectations awakened by discovery of the "fresh, green breast" of the New World with individual desires aroused by an incomparably beautiful, fertile young woman (140).[82] Both virginal girl and virgin land signal fecundity: they represent wondrous possibility; they offer inestimable benefits; they excite wishes for exclusive ownership.

In both instances, idealized images are shattered and utopian hopes disappointed. Both Daisy Buchanan and the New World fall short of their would-be possessors' "fantastic conceits": the endlessly faithful "golden girl," like fabled cities of gold and fountains of youth, are self-serving fabrications (77). Resources prove exhaustible, and there are challenges to rights of possession. Acquisitive efforts are severed from biological purpose, with corrupting and destructive consequences. Once the validity of glorious imaginings is contradicted by reality, both girl and place assume a different mythic identity, that of "lost paradise": a utopian vision all the more nostalgic because it never existed and never belonged to the hopeful claimants.[83] Like the lost, ideal woman, the lost, ideal land intensifies human longings to re-wind time: to return to Edenic beginnings, to start over without penalty. With its metaphoric reach and historical resonance, the conclusion to *Gatsby* emphasizes the extent to which

---

81 Joyce A. Rowe, "Delusions of American Idealism," in *Readings on "The Great Gatsby,"* ed. Katie De Koster (San Diego, CA: Greenhaven Press, 1998), 93.
82 Christiane Johnson provides careful analysis of parallels in diction, grammar, syntax, and metaphor that support the comparison of Gatsby (and his "dream" of Daisy) to European explorers (and their "dream" of a new world). "*The Great Gatsby*: The Final Vision," in *Critical Essays on F. Scott Fitzgerald's "The Great Gatsby,"* ed. Scott Donaldson (Boston: G. K. Hall,1984).
83 Ibid., 117.

fitness-driven goals dominate the interior life of every human being. Operating largely through proximate mechanisms inaccessible to conscious awareness, procreative energies exert powerful shaping influence on individual aspirations, preconceptions, rationalizations, and regrets. These same energies also animate fantastically falsified narratives—of self and of tribe—activating the symbol-making propensities peculiar to our species.

CHAPTER 9

Female Sexual Strategies in the Poetry of Edna St. Vincent Millay

Notable for its uninhibited depictions of women's ardency, the poetry of Edna St. Vincent Millay invites readers to reconsider culturally ingrained assumptions about human sexuality. Many of her best-known poems feature female speakers who acknowledge fervent desire: they take pleasure in physical intimacies; they pursue partners actively; they enjoy short-term liaisons; they resist attempts to restrict their erotic experience. Challenging images of women as sexually passive and disinterested beings, Millay's unconventional portraits earned recognition—indeed, notoriety—in a favorable sociopolitical climate. Published largely in the 1920s and 1930s, her work emerged in the wake of a Women's Movement that by 1920 had achieved the goal of universal suffrage. Concern with other kinds of gender-based inequities emerged concomitantly, and women's demands for expanded educational, vocational, and economic opportunities were accompanied by agitation for change in the social sphere. Millay's poetry seemed to support a redefinition of gender roles and expectations, including male-female relationships within and outside of marriage.[1] Resonating with contemporary social and political issues, Millay's poetry draws attention to important, often unacknowledged, biological facts about female human nature. Worldwide and cross-culturally, strategic interference by men has done much to obscure the full range of women's reproductive behavior by forcibly limiting its expression. In her poetry, Millay highlights some of the preferences women might choose to exercise if male interference, codified in legal and social systems around the globe, ceased to be enforced.

---

[1] She was "a public, contemporary figure who came to represent the new woman and who came to seem the voice of a rebellious generation." Suzanne Clark, "Uncanny Millay," in *Millay at 100: A Critical Reappraisal*, ed. Diane P. Freedman (Carbondale and Edwardsville: Southern Illinois University Press, 1995), 9. In particular, as Karen L. Kilcup observes, that "rebellious" generation of women "sought freedom from gender roles." *Robert Frost and Feminine Literary Tradition* (Ann Arbor: University of Michigan Press, 2001), 203.

Although she sometimes writes in the voice of a specifically named persona (e.g., a character drawn from history or mythology), Millay more often employs unidentified speaking voices whose intimate tones and disclosures tempt readers to assign them autobiographical significance.[2] From the outset, her fame encouraged readers to interpret her poems as a record of actual experience: she burst upon the scene as an uncommonly attractive and talented young woman seizing sexual freedom in an excitingly Bohemian, post-war world. Her striking physical beauty, which included unusual vocal powers and dramatic gifts, lent extra glamour to her art. Simultaneously scandalized and titillated, her audience tended to confuse her notorious lifestyle with her published work, searching texts of poems to complete their impressions of a charismatic celebrity and, conversely, using information about the poet's life (accurate or otherwise) to annotate and interpret her art. Biographers and critics have to some extent encouraged this tendency, offering evidence gleaned from letters and diaries to identify individual poems, if only speculatively, with romantic partners and events in Millay's life. It is doubtless the case that many of her poems were written in response to real persons and happenings—as is true of many, perhaps most, works of imaginative literature—but autobiographical transparency is not Millay's aim. She does not name her paramours in her poems (there are precious few titles or epigraphs along the lines of "For Ralph" or "To My Husband," for example), nor does she provide contextual clues ("critical particulars of names, dates, and locations") enabling readers—in the absence of research—to locate most of her compositions in place and time.[3] It is reasonable to suppose that, in common with other writers, she exercises artistic liberty in transforming the raw materials of life into art: interpreting, synthesizing, emphasizing, summarizing—in short, distilling "essence" from "Chaos," as she herself puts it, and lending "Order" to the "amorphous shape" of experience ("I will put Chaos," lines, 1, 7, 6).[4] In exploring the evolutionary biological implications of her work, it is particularly important not to confound art with biography. The speakers in Millay's poems are carefully

---

2   Elissa Zellinger discusses prevailing assumptions that women poets, in particular, were exposing their private selves in their art: these encouraged "the conflation of the woman poet with her poem." "Edna St. Vincent Millay and the Poetess Tradition," *Legacy* 29, no. 2 (2012): 240.

3   Ann K. Hoff, "'How Love May Be Acquired': Prescriptive Autobiography in Millay's *Fatal Interview*," *CEA Critic* 68, no. 3 (2006): 2.

4   Edna St. Vincent Millay, "I will put Chaos into fourteen lines," in *Collected Poems*, ed. Norma Millay (New York: Harper and Row, 1956). All citations to Millay's poems refer to this edition. Where first lines serve as titles, these have been abbreviated.

crafted elements in her lyric design. She does not seek to report objectively on the motives and behavior of an actual living woman; rather, she is casting female experience in an imaginative light for purposes of comment and interpretation.

Illustrative disparity between author and speaker can be located very easily in the often anthologized poem "What lips my lips have kissed." In this sonnet Millay speaks in the voice of an older woman in the last stage of her life history, a stage the speaker equates, metaphorically, with "winter" (line 9). It is a cold and "lonely" time, since the amorous adventures of youth, the "summer" of her life, now lie behind her: "summer ... / in me sings no more (lines 13-14). Millay composed this poem in 1919 when she was still a comparatively young woman, twenty-seven years old, and by no means finished with her active sex life.[5] Creating the figure of an aging, post-sexual woman, she is engaged in a deliberate act of imaginative projection rather than recounting personal history. Written early in her career, "What Lips My Lips Have Kissed" provides clear evidence that Millay consciously crafted literary personae, utilizing "multiple identities" to help shape mood, tone, and theme.[6] She did not confuse her autobiographical self with the speakers in her poems, although she profited from the inclination of her audience to do just that.[7]

Women's Libido

In creating speakers and characters of her own sex, Millay insists upon the physically ardent nature of woman. Terms such as "passion," "fever," "burning," and "desire" characterize presentations of women throughout

---

5 Daniel Mark Epstein, *What Lips My Lips Have Kissed: The Loves and Love Poems of Edna St. Vincent Millay* (New York: Henry Holt, 2001), 139-40.

6 Clark, "Uncanny Millay," 12. With poems like "What lips my lips have kissed," Cheryl Walker points out, Millay "so shocked and delighted her readers that she became the figurehead of free love culture, a position she exploited for her own use." "The Female Body as Icon: Edna Millay Wears a Plaid Dress," in *Millay at 100: A Critical Reappraisal*, ed. Diane P. Freedman (Carbondale and Edwardsville: Southern Illinois University Press, 1995), 89.

7 Clark argues that in her public readings Millay invited audiences to view her as the "embodiment" of her poetry and thus to overlook distinctions between "artist and person." "Uncanny Millay," 5. Ann K Hoff makes a similar argument, providing a fascinating account of the relationship between life and art reflected in *Fatal Interview*. The romance described in this book was, as Hoff's timeline demonstrates, "largely epistolary until after the sonnet sequence was ... published." Millay not only encouraged "the world to question and doubt whether the poems were 'real' accountings of an affair," she endowed that affair in advance with "mythical dimensions," then did "her best to live it as it was written." "'How Love May Be Acquired,'" 4.

her oeuvre. Female speakers in her poems describe "the desirous body's heat and sweat," for example, "the fever in the vein," "passion pounding all day long in me," and "love" that resembles "a burning city" ("Yet in an hour to come," line 10; "Peril upon the paths," line 12; "Since I cannot persuade you," line 14; "Women have loved before," line 8). They luxuriate in intimate caresses suggestive of sexual congress: "Enraptured in his great embrace I lie," one speaker proclaims, while another remembers "arms [that] have lain / Under my head till morning" and "lads ... / [who] turn to me at midnight with a cry" ("Olympian gods," line 6; "What lips my lips have kissed," lines 2-3, 7-8). "Almighty Sex," emphasized with a capital "S," sends one poem's speaker "forth at nightfall crying like a cat," eager to indulge admittedly animalistic impulses ("I too beneath your moon," lines 1, 2). Comparing herself to a female cat in heat, a breathtakingly defiant analogy, this speaker dissociates herself radically from conventional ideas of female reserve, laying claim instead to sexual impulses of unembarrassed urgency. She goes on to argue that her intellectual or spiritual qualities, no matter how "noble" and "complex," are inextricably intertwined with the physical, erotic side of her nature—namely, her "lust" (lines 8, 14). She makes the case, in sum, that sexuality is a foundational element of female human identity, that it plays a contributing role, however indirectly, in every enterprise.

Millay not only contends that women experience erotic desire, she also indicates that there are no important distinctions between male and female libido. In "Not with libations" she presents a sexually super-charged couple (a "woman and a man"), the "we" of the poem (lines 1, 14). The two are equally "impatient" to enjoy love's "fruits," equally caught up in love's "flame," and equally responsible for permitting physical desire to overwhelm "the altars" of love: together they transform "Love's sacred grove" into "a pasture to the shaggy goats of Pan" (lines 3, 10, 2, 13). They have yielded hastily to the urgency of their desire, seizing "*green* fruits" without waiting for them to ripen, (line 3, emphasis added). They enjoy a "banquet" instead of more "frugal" pleasures (line 8). Millay does not present the woman conventionally, as the partner with a more idealized conception of attachment or the one whose reticence exercises a braking function on the expression of desire. Rather, the poet makes no distinction between the female speaker and her male companion: she is equally responsible for their headlong plunge into physical intimacy, an intimacy marked as premature and unwise by images and allusions throughout. The poem presents sexual symmetry as a simple fact; there is no suggestion that this is an unusual idea or one for which a case must be made.

Such depictions of highly sexed women very obviously contradict the feminine ideal persisting in American culture as a legacy of Victorian prudery. Criticizing "her own sexually constricted society," as Holly Peppe observes, Millay contends that "a male monopoly on sexual activity is not only unfair but unnatural."[8] At the same time, moreover, her portrayal of women may appear to undermine the validity of truisms emerging from the field of evolutionary biology. Bateman's Principle posits that sexual reticence tends to serve women's reproductive interests, just as sexual ardor tends to serve men's.[9] The difference in potential lifetime reproductive success between males and females is used to explain this divergence in sexual behavior. Since women must invest heavily in each reproductive effort, while men's investment is highly variable, women would be expected to be sexually cautious and choosy, waiting for propitious environmental conditions and selecting the highest quality partners available. Because male reproductive success is largely contingent upon access to fertile women, men would be expected to seek out as many reproductive opportunities as possible. Sexual eagerness is a trait that would likely maximize the number of offspring a man might sire: the more partners, the more potential children. This is clearly not true for women: beyond a certain minimum, no increase in partners will increase the maximum number of offspring a woman can produce during her lifetime. An eagerness for many and varied sexual opportunities, consequently, would seem to benefit a woman's fitness much less than a man's.[10]

To avoid oversimplification, it must be remembered that Bateman's analysis of gender differences is used to discuss a wide continuum of behaviors and phenotypes. The variety of sexual strategies available to individuals of either sex necessarily suggests that the stereotypic division of humans into "ardent males" and "reticent females" represents an easy shorthand, intended to summarize a general set of tendencies rather than to draw a line of absolute demarcation between the two sexes. "There is not one reproductive strategy for women and another for men," David C. Geary points out, "as the strategies

---

8 Holly Peppe, "Rewriting the Myth of the Woman in Love: Millay's *Fatal Interview*," in *Millay at 100: A Critical Reappraisal*, ed. Diane P. Freedman (Carbondale and Edwardsville: Southern Illinois University Press, 1995), 58.
9 Buss, *Evolution of Desire*, 76-78.
10 David A. Frederick, Tania A. Reynolds, and Maryanne L. Fisher, "The Importance of Female Choice: Evolutionary Perspectives on Female Mating Strategies," in *Evolution's Empress: Darwinian Perspectives on the Nature of Women*, ed. Maryanne L. Fisher, Justin R. Garcia, and Rosemarie Sokol Chang (Oxford: Oxford University Press, 2013), 307-08.

adopted by women and by men often vary across contexts and across historical periods."[11] "Evolutionary accounts that emphasize the sexually indiscriminate male and the sexually coy female overstate the case," Buss cautions.[12] Pointing to recent research, David A. Frederick and his colleagues note that "the strongly held view that females were passive and coy" has begun "to fall to the wayside" in contemporary evolutionary thinking.[13] Like men, women can and do employ short-term sexual strategies. Men's tendency toward promiscuity may be more pronounced than women's, but, as researchers have been quick to point out, men could not engage in fleeting liaisons or extramarital affairs without a sufficient supply of women available to serve as short-term partners.[14] When considering the notion of female reticence, moreover, it is crucial to realize that sexual cautiousness does not necessarily indicate either an absence of desire or the inability to feel sexual pleasure. As David J. Buller and others observe, a complete disinterest in sexual activity could scarcely serve the evolutionary interest of members of any mammalian species. For women, as well as for men, "the 'sex drive' ... is an adaptation" designed to promote reproductive success.[15] Investigating sexual assertiveness in human and non-human primates, Sarah Hrdy has gathered compelling evidence that females are far less "coy" than often is assumed.[16] Almost certainly there has been some "selection in women for sexual desire": it is associated with evolutionary advantage.[17]

Hrdy goes on to argue that male interference, motivated by the wish to monopolize female fertility and ensure paternal certainty, has played a large role in shaping the myth of women's sexual disinterestedness. Physical violence and coercion, reinforced by social prescriptions, operate as effective constraints on the expression of female desire.[18] The lengths to which men have gone to restrain female sexuality indicate very clearly that there is something to

---

11 David. C. Geary, *Male, Female: The Evolution of Human Sex Differences* (Washington, D.C.: American Psychological Association, 1998), 151.
12 Buss, *Evolution of Desire*, 215.
13 Frederick, Reynolds, and Fisher, "The Importance of Female Choice," 310.
14 Buss, *Dangerous Passion*, 159.
15 David J. Buller, *Adapting Minds: Evolutionary Psychology and the Persistent Quest for Human Nature* (Cambridge, MA: The MIT Press, 2006), 294.
16 Hrdy, *Mother Nature*: 42, Sarah Blaffer Hrdy, *The Woman That Never Evolved* (Cambridge, MA and London: Harvard University Press, 1981), 172-80.
17 Hrdy, *Mother Nature*, 224.
18 Ibid., 258-63; Hrdy, *Woman That Never Evolved*, 177-80.

be restrained—that is, that women are not nearly so passionless as husbands or harem-holders might wish. Sequestration, veiling, foot-binding, and clitoridectomy, along with less extreme tactics utilized by men to suppress women's sexuality, would not be needed if women truly lacked libido, or if they seldom indulged in extramarital affairs.[19] "Women's readiness to engage in sexual activity is great enough," Hrdy points out, "that the majority of the world's cultures—most of which determine descent through the male line—have made some effort to control it."[20] The *"expectation* of female promiscuity"—an expectation that belies socially promulgated views of womanly reserve—has exercised a critical shaping effect on social institutions historically and cross-culturally.[21]

David M. Buss summarizes the situation, noting that "men tend to control resources and power worldwide"; they use their economic and political advantage to exercise domination over women, with special emphasis on women's sexual behavior.[22] Aggression figures heavily in men's efforts to dominate women, "not because men are inherently aggressive and women inherently submissive," as Barbara Smuts argues, but because physical force has proven to be an especially reliable tactic, given human sexual dimorphism, in men's ongoing struggle to "enhance their reproductive opportunities."[23] Men compete with one another for access to women, who represent the limiting resource in human reproduction. Those men who acquire and defend exclusive rights to fertile females tend to leave the largest genetic legacies. As Buss states, "we come from a long and unbroken line of ancestral fathers who succeeded in obtaining mates, preventing their infidelity, and providing enough benefits (or inflicting enough deterrent costs) to keep them from leaving."[24] In the arena of mating, male control frequently is enforced by legal codes and social penalties, as well as by physical coercion. The internalized restraints forged in modern Western societies by defining women as inherently chaste, faithful, and passionless—interested in emotional rather than

---

19 See Hrdy, *Mother Nature*, 262-63 as well as discussion by Smuts, "Male Aggression," 255.
20 Hrdy, *Woman That Never Evolved*, 177; Frederic, Reynolds, and Fisher, "The Importance of Female Choice," 321.
21 Hrdy, *Mother Nature*, 177 (Hrdy's emphasis).
22 David M. Buss, "Sexual Conflict: Evolutionary Insights into Feminism and the 'Battle of the Sexes,'" in *Sex, Power Conflict: Evolutionary and Feminist Perspectives*, ed. David M. Buss and Neil M. Malamuth (New York and Oxford: Oxford University Press, 1996), 297, 299.
23 Smuts, "Male Aggression," 256.
24 Buss, "Sexual Conflict," 309.

physical manifestations of attachment—operate with especial subtlety to limit women's sexual activity.

In this context of long-standing denial and suppression, Millay's portraits of sexually assertive women assume biological as well as political interest. Deliberately and, indeed, provocatively challenging notions of female sexual reticence, the poet offers important correctives to reductive theorizing as well as to cultural stereotyping. Her work lends the not inconsequential weight of art to the "numerous pieces of evidence" now emerging in the fields of evolutionary anthropology, zoology, and psychology to support "the idea that females are very active players in the mating game, contrary to assumed wisdom."[25] "It is in works of imagination," Joseph Carroll points out, "that people articulate the quality of their experience, make sense of it, and feel its significance and value."[26] To underline her chosen themes—the "sense" she makes of human experience—Millay favors hyperbole, frequently supported by irony and wit. In character and in situation, she exploits the power of exaggeration to command audience attention. Her recklessly passionate female personae pose defiant contrast to the ethereal conceptions of womanliness prevailing in her social environment.

The well-known sonnet beginning "I, being born a woman" epitomizes Millay's hyperbolic approach to her subject matter. The speaker lays claim to feelings and intentions precisely like those associated with male seducers of the Don-Juan type. She enters into sexual intimacy with "zest," allowing passion temporarily to dominate her sensations, that is, to "cloud the mind" and "leave [her] undone" (lines 4, 7, 8). Even as she yields to sexual ecstasy, the "treason / Of my stout blood against my staggering brain," however, she assures her partner that the shared pleasures lack emotional content (lines 9-10). "Think not for this," she cautions, that "I shall remember you with love" (lines 9, 11). She rejects the possibility of any meaningful aftermath to the "frenzy" that momentarily has united them: sexual bonding supplies "insufficient reason" for continuing social intercourse, including even the niceties of "conversation" (lines 13, 14). This sonnet is justly famous for its breathtaking reversal of traditional ideas about women. Its speaker not only revels in physical passion but

---

25 Christopher J. Wilbur and Lorne Campbell, "Swept off Their Feet? Females' Strategic Mating Behavior as a Means of Supplying the Broom," in *Evolution's Empress: Darwinian Perspectives on the Nature of Women*, ed. Maryanne L. Fisher, Justin R. Garcia, and Rosemarie Sokol Chang (Oxford: Oxford University Press, 2013), 341.

26 David Sloan Wilson and Joseph L. Carroll, "Darwin's Bridge to the Humanities: An Interview with Joseph L. Carroll," *This View of Life* (The Evolution Institute: 2016). Web.

ruthlessly dissociates sex from love, treating her partner with offhanded contempt. He serves as an instrument of her sexual satisfaction and nothing more. Instead of letting him down gently, moreover, the speaker delights in telling him exactly how little he means to her.

If these sentiments had been articulated by a male speaker, they would seem unusual only because of their brutal honesty. When men exploit women sexually, typically they express affection or gratitude even if they have no intention of pursuing the relationship: the man who promises to "call" but never does is a familiar stereotype. Millay's speaker does not comply with the custom of empty assurances, going out of her way instead to humiliate her partner. Thus she underlines via exaggeration the scantily disguised selfishness with which men often exploit women. The sarcasm directed toward the male addressee effectively counters expectations familiar from literature and opera, as well as from folklore, that women will cling desperately, and "with love," to any man with whom they have enjoyed physical intimacy (line 11). Here it is the female partner who feels "scorn" (almost but not quite tinged with "pity") for a man she is heartlessly discarding (line 12). Sex itself is presented wholly without reverence: the term "frenzy" suggests a maddened lust stripped of redeeming significance or exaltation. Readers encounter a woman who regards sex neither as terrifying contamination nor as romantic fantasy. She has the temerity to claim, furthermore, that her susceptibility to sexual passion occurs *because* of her gender, rather than despite it. "Being born a woman," she finds herself responding, irresistibly, to the physical "propinquity" of a man, yearning to feel his "body's weight upon [her] breast" (lines 1, 3, 5). She cannot help being stirred by "the needs" of her female "kind" (line 2).

Thematic statement in the poem is highlighted by Millay's parodic appropriation of the love sonnet, a genre used by male speakers to woo beautiful, sexually reticent women.[27] Traditional expectations of gallantry are subverted as Millay's speaker articulates motives that typically remain unspoken by male counterparts: she is sexually hungry, intent upon physical gratification rather than emotional

---

27 Stacy Carson Hubbard points out that the "various roles" Millay "mimics and manipulates are the rhetorical products of a specific discourse (lyric poetry, and more specifically ... the tradition of the *carpe diem* sonnet)." "Love's 'Little Day': Time and the Sexual Body in Millay's Sonnets," in *Millay at 100: A Critical Reappraisal*, ed. Diane P. Freedman (Carbondale and Edwardsville: Southern Illinois University Press, 1995), 101-102. For further analysis of Millay's purposes as she "inverts the usual place of the woman in Petrarchism," see Natasha Distiller's commentary in *Desire and Gender in the Sonnet Tradition* (Houndsmills, England and New York: Palgrave Macmillan, 2008), 154.

investment or future commitment, and she uses her gender to excuse her lustfulness. Sex does not bind her: she is in no way dependent upon her partner and his future good will. Behind the speaker's disdain, readers sense a certain auctorial glee: Millay appears to enjoy ascribing to a woman sexual appetites and prerogatives typically defined as male. More important than this speaker's ardor, even, is the dominant role she plays. There is a triumphant, 'ha ha, gotcha' element in the poem that goes far to explain its powerful effect. Its speaker overturns popular ideas about women's sexual nature with cool detachment.

Putting forward the proposition that women can function as sexually active and autonomous agents, a poem like this one courts intense reactions: readers may be horrified, offended, or thrilled, but response scarcely will be bland. In addition to questioning socially approved views of female sexuality, Millay targets for attention a fundamental source of conflict between men and women: autonomy per se. From an evolutionary biological perspective, men's domination of women appears to be "part of a psychological profile derived from their normative reproductive strategy," but that strategy comes into direct conflict with "the basic human desire for autonomous individuality."[28] Millay creates a fictive situation in which the tables are turned, and it is a woman who exercises dominance over a man. Female sexual appetite, combined with deliberately short-term involvement, is the only explanation (direct or indirect) that the poem offers for this reversal. By implication, the poem identifies the myth of women's sexual disinterestedness as fraudulent, a tool of wide-ranging political and social oppression.

Short-term Strategies

Unsurprisingly, Millay extends her presentation of female agency into the realm of sexual promiscuity. She composes numerous poems from the perspective of women engaged in short-term mating strategies. "To the Not Impossible Him" suggests, wittily but decisively, that women's much-vaunted predilection for sexual loyalty is not innate, but rather a byproduct of their limited experience. Those who never travel are unable to make comparative judgments, the speaker points out. "How shall I know, unless I go / To Cairo and Cathay," whether opportunities in my immediate environment are indeed "blesséd"? (lines 1-2, 3).

---

28 Nancy Easterlin, "From Reproductive Resource to Autonomous Individuality? Charlotte Bronte's *Jane Eyre*," in *Evolution's Empress: Darwinian Perspectives on the Nature of Women*, ed. Maryanne L. Fisher, Justin R. Garcia, and Rosemarie Sokol Chang (Oxford: Oxford University Press, 2013), 391.

A provincial outlook fosters local preference, obviously, and such preference is relatively meaningless so long as it remains untested. Until she smells "the Carthaginian rose," how can the speaker be certain that the right "flower" for her is the one here "beneath [her] nose"? (lines 8, 5, 6). In the third and final quatrain, the speaker expands her metaphor explicitly into the realm of "faithful love," which "no power shall dim or ravel / Whilst I stay here" (lines 9, 10-11). If, however, she "should ever travel," she saucily declines to answer for her future fidelity (line 12).

Geography and travel serve as metaphors in this poem for a host of customs and norms restricting women's experience. Their physical, intellectual, social, and sexual activities are limited by gender-specific rules and prohibitions. Such culturally imposed constraints prevent women from making comparisons among men and exercising selective discrimination in their mating efforts. They are satisfied, and hence faithful, because they are denied access to varied and possibly more attractive mating options or strategies. Mention of exotic destinations like Cathay highlights the freedom with which men move in the world, physically and socially. If women were permitted comparable adventuring, Millay's poem suggests, they might behave as promiscuously as men. The right to an unfettered, autonomous existence might mean that women would move from "flower" to "flower," enjoying a variety of partners. Empowerment in the social sphere, this poem implicitly argues, might well undermine female fidelity. Women who are allowed to "travel," sexually speaking, will discover an ever-changing array of alternatives to explore.

Continuing to question the stereotype of female constancy, another of Millay's female personae emphasizes the appeal of novelty. She describes her eroticism in crudely powerful terms as a "beast that rends me," but the strength of her desire does not lend it endurance ("This beast that rends me," line 1). Soon, as past experience evidently informs her, this passion "will glut, will sicken, will be gone"; "the fever will abate" (lines 4, 5). She will "forget" her current lover, even though "today" he is mightily important: her "east and west" (lines 7, 8). Another character, similarly aware of her restless sex drive, declares that she is "faithful" to its gratification rather than to any individual partner ("Oh, think not I am faithful," line 1). She stays with her current paramour, she tells him, only because he "still" represents "hunger's rarest food," sexually speaking, and can slake her "wildest thirst" (lines 5, 6). If he ceased to meet her erotic needs, she declares, "I would desert you ... / And seek another as I sought you first" (lines 7-8). She defines herself unblushingly as a woman for whom sexual satisfaction is paramount. Because her temporary partner is as "wanton, light and false" as she, the speaker furthermore argues that her departure, once their passion is spent, will serve his needs as much as hers. Loyal to the shifting object-choice of human lust, she is, paradoxically, "most faithless when ... most ... true" (line 14).

In the already mentioned "What lips my lips have kissed," Millay presents a short-term strategist who has led an active sex life devoid of long-term attachment. She has "forgotten" individual details about the many "unremembered lads" with whom she has shared sexual pleasures (lines 2, 7). Because they are so numerous, and emotionally so unimportant to her, she cannot recall "where, and why" she happened to take up with any of them (line 1). In the first line of the poem these short-term partners are reduced to body parts ("lips"), emphasizing their role in providing physical satisfaction. Here Millay employs hyperbole to stress the erotic component of female identity. Her female speaker's powerful libido defies conventional assumptions, as does her inclination to seek sexual gratification in brief encounters. Depicting a woman who conducts her sex life along lines typically regarded as masculine, the poet indirectly affirms sexual symmetry.

The sonnet's sestet, which introduces the analogy between aging woman and "lonely" tree, is particularly significant because it places the speaker's experience in the context of natural processes. The tree is "lonely" in winter because the birds that sang in its boughs all summer have "vanished" (lines 9, 10). (Like the human speaker, tellingly, the tree does not remember individuals: "nor knows what birds" have come and gone [line 10].) It is natural for birds to migrate in winter; it is equally natural for humans to reduce their sexual activity as they age. These are normal effects of seasonal progression, including progression of the metaphoric seasons typically invoked to characterize phases in human life history. The speaker's loneliness in later life is not a penalty for promiscuity, Millay's chosen analogy indicates, but a natural result of the passage of time. As Suzanne Clark points out, the poet typically describes "the shape of a love affair" as "a repeated cycle, from beginning to inevitable end."[29] Although tone in the poem's final lines is gently regretful, the speaker's regrets are focused on the loss of youth and its lusty pleasures; she expresses no dissatisfaction with her earlier behavior or strategic choices.

Numerous poems similarly defend short-term strategies by comparing sexual passion to biological inevitability: growth followed by decay. Organic life moves through developmental stages, each generally brief in duration. Human

---

29 Clark, "Uncanny Millay," 22.

passion similarly will flourish, temporarily, then decline. Such considerations lead to a philosophical rejection of long-term expectations. What makes sense, in the face of continuous change, is to maximize the pleasures of the moment. "Mark the transient butterfly, / How he hangs upon the flower," the speaker in "Mariposa" advises her companion (lines 7-8). The short lifespan of the insect does not diminish the intensity with which it enjoys present gratification of its appetite. The human lovers should model themselves on this example by acting on their physical impulses, the speaker counsels; "suffer me to take your hand" (line 3). Repeating, hyperbolically, that "death comes in a day or two," she advocates the immediate consummation of desire: "Suffer me to cherish you / Till the dawn is in the sky" (lines 4, 10-11). Her arguments recall those articulated by male poet-speakers trying to shock reticent women into abandoning sexual reserve: Marvell's "To His Coy Mistress" with its threats of tombs and worms, comes at once to mind. Here in "Mariposa" (yet another poem in which Millay affirms sexual symmetry) it is the woman who emphasizes that "all the things we ever knew / Will be ashes" soon, and who offers the imminence of death as a reason to indulge in casual sex (lines 5-6). In the face of life's brevity, she avers, questions of obligation and fidelity are irrelevant: "Whether I be false or true, / Death comes in a day or two" (lines 12-13).

Millay's understanding and acceptance of change is cosmic in its reach. In "O Earth, unhappy planet," for example, she emphasizes the process of evolution over time, referring to the extinction of species as inevitable. In the larger scheme of things, the human race will occupy only a tiny fraction of planetary time, "an hour" (line 6). No matter how "bright" his achievements, or how "high" his destiny, Homo sapiens will go "down into the sea" like a setting sun, unremembered (lines 6, 4, 7). Earth itself eventually will disintegrate, since it was "born to die" (line 1). Tempting though it is to regard man as special because of his emotional, technological, moral, and aesthetic capacities ("his singular laughter, his droll tears, / His engines and his conscience and his art"), in the end he is simply one "animal" among many (lines 11-12, 14). Emerging from "the catholic slime" that once "cradled" a host of now-fossilized creatures, the human race soon will disappear into the "ooze" from which it "but lately crawled" ("Cretaceous bird," lines 5, 13, 14). Millay demonstrates conscious awareness of nature's indifference to the survival of individuals and of kinds, including the dispassionate workings of natural selection. She grounds her ideas about human sexuality in these larger, evolutionary understandings, implicitly arguing that short-term strategies make philosophical, emotional, and practical sense in the face of death and extinction.

Her focus on the transience of all earthly things provides Millay with a doubly useful philosophical framework: justification for promiscuity and infidelity as well as consolation for any suffering such behaviors may cause. Her readers seldom encounter the warmly hopeful feelings typically associated with love poetry. The pervasiveness of multiple, simultaneous involvements adds to uncertainties posed by the evanescence of desire:

> We meet and part;
> Our talk is all of heres and nows,
> Our conduct likewise; in no act
> Is any future, any past;
> Under our sly, unspoken pact,
> I know with whom I saw you last,
> But I say nothing; and you know
> At six-fifteen to whom I go.
>
> ("Theme and Variations" IV, lines 3-10)

"Tell me, can love go on like that?" this speaker demands of her partner (line 19). The result of so much casual promiscuity, she avers, is a "bored, insulted heart" (line 20). Even as she lays claim to gender parity, she is inclined to disparage the jading effects of the equal-opportunity infidelity she reports. Another speaker admits that the experience of "a love turned ashes" represents a terrible disappointment, far worse than seasonally imposed endings ("April ... shattered" or "August ... levelled"): it proves much more difficult to recognize that "a dream can die" ("Here is a wound," lines 3, 9, 10, 13).

Since the principal characters in the poems almost invariably are female, the experiences of disappointment some of them acknowledge suggest at times that men's ardor may be more fleeting, even, than women's. The much-anthologized sonnet beginning "Pity me not" offers support for that supposition. In its reassuringly rhythmic presentation of earthly transience, it focuses first on elemental phenomena: gravitational forces affecting astronomical bodies, like the ebb and flow of oceanic tides, illustrate unremitting change. The moon is "waning"; "the year goes by"; all is "shifting" (lines 5, 4, 11). The octave concludes with an unanticipated reference to human feeling, which is slipped into the list as yet another manifestation of evanescence. Initially the poem appears to be an impersonal meditation on the theme of change, but suddenly it grows more subjective in focus. An addressee emerges, the man whose "desire is hushed so soon," and the speaker reveals herself as the former recipient of his affections: "you no longer look with love on me" (lines 7, 8). Here Millay singles out "a man's desire," rather than a woman's, to illustrate the impermanence of human passion. His inconstancy must be regarded, the poem's speaker nevertheless concludes, as simply one more instance of a larger ruling principle. She admits she finds it hard to shape her wishes in conformance with nature's ways, to accept the inexorable progression from "blossom" to "wreckage" (lines 10, 12). It is easier to recognize than to welcome the inevitable transience of all things, including erotic desire. Intellectual understanding does not guarantee emotional acquiescence: "the heart is slow to learn / What the swift mind beholds at every turn" (lines 13-14).

As such examples show, the yearning for a longer lasting "love" sometimes emerges despite the carpe diem philosophy permeating the poetry. Such yearning appears to indicate that woman's evolved potential for implementing long-term mating strategies cannot be completely suppressed. Vestiges remain, sometimes casting a shadow on the short-term strategies presented in the poems as natural and workable alternatives. For the most part, Millay's female characters do not permit themselves to expect what they acknowledge to be impossible. Elizabeth P. Perlmutter observes that "at the very moment of heartbreak" (following "reckless" surrender to "some heartless lad"), Millay's personae draw on reserves of "a terrible strength."[30] When their emotional equilibrium is threatened, the provisional nature of all organic and elemental phenomena provides them with consoling context and chin-up corrective:

> The love that stood a moment in your eyes,
> The words that lay a moment on your tongue,
> Are one with all that in a moment dies,
> A little under-said and over-sung.
>
> ("I shall go back again," lines 9-12)

Thrown off balance by the abrupt departure of a lover, the speaker in this poem defends herself from pain with biting wit, squelching her disappointment with a jibe at high-flown praise of experiences destined to be momentary. Reluctantly or mockingly, Millay's women nearly always insist on the irremediably temporal limits to desire. Thus they profit from the liberating "momentum" inherent

---

30 Elizabeth P. Perlmutter, "A Doll's Heart: The Girl in the Poetry of Edna St. Vincent Millay and Louise Bogan," *Twentieth Century Literature* 23, no. 2 (May 1977): 160.

in a "feminist embrac[ing] of the ephemeral."[31] Their avowed goal is to experience the joy of passion stripped of demands for continuance or exclusiveness: "love in the open hand" ("Not in a silver casket," line 9).

"I shall forget you presently, my dear," one speaker impudently assures her lover ("I shall forget you presently," line 1). There is discernible disdain in her voice as she advises him to "make the most of this, your little day" (line 2). Meanwhile the two of them will exchange protestations of commitment, though both know these are meaningless: "your loveliest lie" and "my favourite vow" (lines 7, 8). She wishes, the speaker continues, that "love were longer-lived / And oaths not so brittle," but since "nature has contrived" otherwise she accepts the inevitable: "so it is" (lines 9-10, 11). "Biologically speaking" she remarks at the sonnet's conclusion, their happiness is "idle," or irrelevant (line 14). Here Millay comes close to articulating Darwinian insights in twenty-first-century terms, observing that nature's contrivances (e.g., adaptations) are designed to promote evolutionary ends (i.e., fitness) rather than personal contentment. She recognizes, in effect, that sexual activity represents a response to proximate impulses keyed to reproduction, that is, sensations of desire flourish even in the absence of a conscious intention to create offspring. The pleasures these lovers "presently" share are inspired by biological forces over which they have no control. By making sex irresistibly appealing, "nature" has managed "to struggle on without a break" (lines 11, 12). Millay does not go on to ask whether yearnings for long-term commitment also might prove adaptive but focuses instead on sexual desire itself, which is limited in duration and intensity, fluctuating in object-choice. The recognition in the poem's final line that there is a biological purpose to sex is, in itself, rare in her work. The women she portrays do not appear to have or anticipate offspring, nor is conception mentioned as a possible byproduct of the erotic "frenzy" in which they indulge.

---

31 Geffrey Davies, "Edna St. Vincent Millay's *A Few Figs from Thistles,*" *Textual Cultures* 9, no. 1 (2014): 88. As Janet Gassman accurately points out, "the poems in which she is abandoned are not ... nearly so numerous as those in which she is fleeing some over-possessive admirer or ... cautioning a lover not to magnify the permanence and significance of a passionate physical attachment." "Edna St. Vincent Millay: 'Nobody's Own,'" *Colby Library Quarterly* 9, no. 6 (June 1971): 305.

Costs and Benefits

Readers cannot help noticing that in the fictive world of Millay's poems there is no mention of the costs women ordinarily incur, or risk incurring, when they employ short-term sexual strategies.[32] Most obviously, none of Millay's women become pregnant, nor do they express worry about such an eventuality. This eliminates at a stroke the most serious of the possible costs to women associated with commitment-free liaisons, namely, the prospect of bearing and rearing a child without paternal assistance. The risk of sexually transmitted diseases, which increases exponentially with numbers of casual sex partners, likewise garners no mention. Millay's women express no fear of violent retaliation at the hands of rejected or discarded partners or, for that matter, at the hands of jealous wives, girlfriends, or ex.'s. The potential loss of a long-term partner, together with the resources he provides, frequently deters women from promiscuous behavior, but Millay's characters typically describe a lifestyle predicated upon brief and uncommitted relationships; hence, they view frequent turnover in partners as natural and unavoidable. They show no eagerness to obtain access to the material resources or social advantages that affairs with prosperous, high-status men could provide.

Millay lived and wrote, of course, before truly reliable forms of contraception became available to women, yet she never acknowledges that she is ignoring biological facts. If women played no role in reproduction, men would have no need to control or coerce them, sexually or otherwise. Most of the gender-based problems women experience would be eliminated: no longer would they represent a resource to be exploited and hoarded. If women's sexual freedom exerted no impact on men's genetic legacy, it follows that men would gain nothing by inhibiting it. The liberty Millay's characters enjoy is predicated, at least in part, upon counterfactual suppositions, and these are neither explained nor discussed in the poems. There is, likewise, no mention of possible connections between the sexual freedoms the poet celebrates and the goals of birth-control activists like Margaret Sanger.[33]

When sexual activity *is* closely tied to reproduction—as in real life— much of men's controlling behavior, vis-à-vis women, is motivated by the desire

---

32 For a summary of these costs, see Buss, *Evolution of Desire*, 235.
33 Biographer Daniel Mark Epstein comments that Millay offered the embattled Sanger, "patron saint of birth control," neither public nor private support during critical legal battles in 1917. *What Lips My Lips Have Kissed*, 123.

to avoid misplaced paternal investment.[34] Women with long-term mates often are subjected to elaborate mate-guarding tactics, including abuse or desertion by jealous partners. "In virtually all the world's cultures," as Smuts observes, "mating rights entail ... the exclusion of other men from sexual access to a man's wife."[35] Virtually none of the women depicted by Millay submit to such suffocating conditions. Her most elaborate portrait of a married woman can be found in the sequence of sonnets comprising *Fatal Interview*. The female speaker recounts a history of adulterous passion, focusing chiefly on her lover. Directly and indirectly, she reveals that the threats her infidelity poses to her marriage are, in her view, negligible. Although she anticipates that the affair will disturb her relationship with her husband ("this encounter like a sword / Will lie between me and my troubled lord"), she expresses no worry that he will abandon her or resort to violence ("This beast that rends me," lines 13-14). She describes a long-term union unencumbered by male jealousy and possessiveness, an unusual arrangement that evidently grants her more sexual freedom than most wives enjoy.[36]

She boasts, in Sonnet #26 from the sequence, that she lives and loves in the manner of legendary, high-status women like Helen and Guinevere. Acting on what she describes as "unregenerate passions," she compares herself to "treacherous queens" who "took their knights to bed" with no regard to consequences ("Women have loved before," lines 12, 13). Like powerful women of mythic stature, she is "heedless and wilful" in her extramarital adventuring; she abandons herself to "love" in an "utter, ancient way" (lines 14, 8, 10). Through this voice, Millay emphasizes the untamable nature of erotic desire, which can override religious ethics or personal integrity—as terms such as "unregenerate" and "treacherous" indicate. Sexual urgency appears to foster an uncompromising focus on self, a determination to assign priority to the "burning" in one's own "breast" (line 8). The persona in this sonnet does not acknowledge that the female figures to whom she alludes did, in fact, pay a price for marital infidelity, or that their "heedless" behavior triggered collective violence and

---

34 Steven W. Gangestad, "Evidence for Adaptations for Female Extra-Pair Mating in Humans: Thoughts on Current Status and Future Directions," in *Female Infidelity and Paternal Uncertainty" Evolutionary Perspectives on Male Anti-Cuckoldry Tactics*," ed. Steven M. Platek and Todd K. Shackelford (Cambridge and New York: Cambridge University Press, 2006), 42.
35 Smuts, "Male Aggression," 246. See also 239.
36 Pratto discusses the physical punishments, up to and including murder, that form part of traditional male mate-guarding tactics. "Sexual Politics: The Gender Gap," 203.

cultural upheaval. Certainly she foresees no harsh consequences in the case of her own adultery. She does not fear physical harm to herself or to her extra-pair partner, nor does she anticipate that her husband will restrict her personal freedom in future by stepping up his mate-guarding efforts. Her suffering, noted intermittently throughout the sonnet sequence, is occasioned solely by desperate wishes that the affair, always defined as impermanent, might last longer—perhaps "a summer more"—than it does ("Well, I have lost you," line 10).

The possibility of sexual assault, inherent in the greater physical strength of men and abetted by sociopolitical power structures favoring male prerogatives, does not worry women in Millay's poetry, as modifications she makes to a classical myth in the poem "Daphne" illustrate. In the original version, Daphne is a young woman fleeing from the god Apollo, a high-status male intent on coercive sex. The transformation of girl into tree, an act of rescue performed at the last minute by her father, is presented as an unexpected resolution to her predicament. In Millay's new version, Daphne shows foreknowledge of her escape: at "any moment," she taunts Apollo, she can frustrate him by becoming "nothing but a laurel-tree" (lines 2, 3). This is not the desperately frightened girl from classical mythology. Millay's Daphne is certain from the outset that she will not be forced into sexual submission. Because of this certainty, the chase holds no terrors for her; she treats it as a game that she is bound to win. Her final words to Apollo indicate that she takes some pleasure in leading "over hill and hollow" a foolishly lust-driven man who fails to realize that he never can possess her (line 7). In response to his obstinate "will to follow," she sets forth, calling to him as if he were a dog: "I am off;—to heel, Apollo!" (lines 8, 9).

Here Millay has incorporated obviously wish-fulfilling elements into familiar materials, depicting a woman who does not depend upon others to rescue her from a sexual predator. This new Daphne emphasizes her own power ("I can," "I can") rather than any need for a father's protective intervention (lines 2, 5).[37] Transformation into a relatively insensate life form, a tree, may serve as the metaphoric equivalent of the emotional detachment so many of Millay's women cultivate as part of their strategy to retain control in their relations with men. Otherwise, the poem does not point to any real-world mechanisms or

---

37 See Geffrey Davies and also Catherine Keyser for related analysis of feminist themes in this poem. "Edna St. Vincent Millay's *A Few Figs from Thistles*," 85-86; *Playing Smart: New York Women Writers and Modern Magazine Culture* (New Brunswick, NJ: Rutgers University Press, 2011), 40.

conditions that would render young women invulnerable to sexual attack from physically and socially powerful men. It succeeds admirably in communicating how much women would stand to gain if such unreal conditions in fact prevailed. In a world where men did not threaten their sexual choice or autonomy, women could move about at will, calling men "to heel" as necessary.

Just as there are no physical costs in Millay's poetry to uncommitted sex, in terms of pregnancy, disease, coercion, or assault, there are no social costs. Her female characters express no anxiety about damage to their reputations or diminished support from family and friends. They say nothing about possible community shunning or reduced status. Such penalties, as discussed earlier, have been employed historically and cross-culturally to control women's sexual behavior. Women who engage in premarital or extramarital sex of any kind typically reduce their chances of marrying well. If already married or otherwise committed, they risk the loss of current partners along with violently jealous retaliation. Typically, they forfeit access to resources, which threatens their survival and that of offspring. They are liable to become objects of public opprobrium and familial condemnation.[38] Outside the realm of wish-fulfillment, as Millay's readers necessarily recognize, women who engage recklessly or repeatedly in short-term affairs are apt to wind up with offspring they cannot support, impoverished and reviled, possibly victims of physical battering or venereal infection as well. None of these consequences are experienced or, indeed, even anticipated by women portrayed in Millay's works. Socially, as well as biologically, the poems silently ignore the risks associated with casual sex.

Although the poems focus on benefits women stand to realize from short-term strategies, they concentrate on a select few of those potentially available. They disregard two of those frequently mentioned by evolutionary researchers and theorists, namely, resource extraction and mate switching.[39] As already observed, her women express no anxiety about their material welfare, and they do not regard temporary partners as sources of money or gifts. Generally unattached, they demonstrate no interest in future long-term commitment. Hence, they do not use short-term sex as a means of attracting permanent mates, securing backup mates, or replacing current long-term partners with more appealing alternatives.[40] Instead, they focus on benefits unrelated to commitment: mate quality (and variety), sexual gratification, self-esteem, and autonomy.

---

38 Buss, *Dangerous Passion*, 176-79.
39 Buss, *Evolution of Desire*, 235, 237.
40 Buss, *Dangerous Passion*, 163-69.

Millay's women stress the physical appeal of the men they choose. Despite their evident disinterest in procreation, they are selecting affair partners with characteristics associated with genetic quality: men likely to contribute to their fitness if insemination should occur. Their preference for physically superior specimens is motivated by adaptative considerations they do not consciously contemplate. According to the so-called good genes hypothesis, women often select as short-term partners genetically superior men who would be unavailable to them on a long-term basis. The costs to women of these brief encounters may be offset, evolutionary theorists suggest, by the possibility of bearing offspring who carry some of those genes. Since men typically lower their standards when seeking temporary partners—women to whom they make no commitment and in whose offspring they will invest minimally, if at all—such liaisons can promote the reproductive goals of both participants.[41] Uncommitted sex allows a man to increase his fitness, at least in terms of quantity, without paternal investment; it allows a woman access to genetically more desirable men than those she is likely to attract as long-term mates. For members of both sexes, additionally, a multiplicity of mates secures genetic diversity in offspring, a "bet hedging" advantage "in the face of changing environments."[42] Studies of misassigned paternity indicate that women employ a mixed strategy relatively frequently, obtaining enduring commitment from one man, then cuckolding him with short-term partners manifesting better—or at least different—phenotypic characteristics.[43]

Women identify genetic quality by relying on a variety of cues. Physical symmetry, a "heritable marker of fitness," is particularly important. Symmetrical men "tend to be more muscular, vigorous, larger in size, more physically healthy, more mentally healthy" than less symmetrical rivals.[44] A woman's decision to risk uncommitted sex with a facially and physically well-endowed man indicates that she is responding to such cues, almost certainly without conscious analysis of the underlying genetic logic. The women Millay portrays in her poems conform to this pattern, choosing short-term partners they describe as extraordinarily good-looking. One extols, for example, the "unimpeachable body" of her lover, together with his facial "loveliness" ("What's this of death,"

---

41 Buss, *Evolution of Desire*, 90.
42 Gangestad, "Evidence for Adaptations for Female Extra-Pair Mating," 40.
43 Buss, *Evolution of Desire*, 235-35; *Dangerous Passion*, 171.
44 Buss, *Evolution of Desire*, 236. See also David C. Schmitt, "Fundamentals of Human Mating Strategies," in *The Handbook of Evolutionary Psychology*, ed. David M. Buss (Hoboken, NJ: John Wiley and Sons, 2005), 273.

lines 7, 12). As she and other female personae emphasize, a partner's outstanding physical appearance is a source of pleasure; it stimulates desire. Clearly it functions as an important criterion in their selection of temporary partners.

Examples abound throughout Millay's oeuvre. The speaker in "And you as well must die" rhapsodizes over her partner's "beauty": his hand is "flawless," his head "perfect" (lines 2, 3). He possesses "a body of flame and steel": muscular and well-conditioned (line 4). In "Theme and Variations," a woman intent upon discarding a lover confesses that his extreme good looks present an obstacle to her intended departure: enchanted still by "that face," she can let him go only by courting "blindness"—that is, deliberately disregarding his exterior appeal (II, lines 17, 18). She concedes that his appearance, rather than other traits, motivated her to take up with him in the first place; thus she confirms that physical attractiveness functions as an important element in short-term female choice. "These eyes ... let him in," she laments, "not you, my guiltless heart" (II, lines 15, 16). In order to release herself from an unsatisfactory relationship, she must somehow exorcise awareness of his appearance: "these eyes, let them erase / His image," she commands (II, lines 17-18).

Continuing this theme from a slightly different perspective, another speaker informs her temporary partner that his physical attractiveness is essential to her passionate response to him: "Were you not lovely I would leave you now," she blithely assures him, deliberately emphasizing disinterest in his qualities of character as well as disdain for mutual long-term commitment ("Oh, think not I am faithful," line 3). Physical appearance, she announces, is a primary consideration in her selection of partners: "after the feet of beauty fly my own" (line 4). Here, again, hyperbole functions in part to satirize male tendencies and strategies. Millay's personae mimic men's well-known, often criticized high standards for physical beauty in women by making equally rigorous demands for good looks in their male partners, including threats to leave if and when those looks should fade.

In preferring facial beauty and a low waist-to-hip ratio in the women they court, men are responding, of course, to important cues to youth and fertility: they make mating choices that tend to promote reproductive success.[45] Despite conspicuous disregard of the topic of pregnancy, female preferences presented in Millay's poems similarly implement a potentially beneficial reproductive strategy. Analysis of "dad and cad mating strategies" indicates that mating with "bad boys" (i.e., non-investing and unreliable men) generally represents a bid

---

45 Buss, *Evolution of Desire*, 51-58

for genetic fitness.[46] Like men who command special status and resources, unusually attractive men obtain sexual access to women much more easily than do their average-looking competitors. Handsome men's appeal to women offers them frequent opportunities for short-term sex, opportunities which research shows they tend to exploit.[47] If conception should occur, the temporary female partners of these much-prized men may reap benefits in the shape of high-quality offspring. Such offspring may include so-called "sexy sons": male offspring whose above-average physical attractions will enable them, in turn, to implement short-term sexual strategies effectively, thus enhancing their mother's genetic legacy.[48] Female partners of "cads" risk incurring heavy costs, of course, since the men they prefer are unlikely to linger or to invest. Women who reject long-term commitment for themselves, as so many of those depicted in Millay's poems conspicuously do, are free to disregard such costs. With their often-stated demand for male "loveliness," Millay's women are choosing men whose mate value is high and whose motivation for commitment accordingly is low. Short-term strategists by personal inclination, philosophical conviction, or both, they revel freely in the erotic intensity inspired by extraordinarily handsome partners.

The speaker in "She Is Overheard Singing" forthrightly explains the attractions of the stereotypical caddish male. She contrasts her partner with those of other women, emphasizing the dullness of the men her acquaintances have selected. Agatha's man is "a hug-the-hearth"; Mig's man is "good as cheese"; Joan's man is "a putterer" (lines 3, 5, 37). Prue's man is "patient," and "asks not when or why"; Sue's man is "like good jell— / All one colour," while Mig's man doesn't "think at all / What's to come" (lines 33-34, 17-18, 19-20). The homely analogies used to describe these men underline the dreariness of their virtues. They are dependably committed, to be sure, but devoid of physical energy and mental keenness. Though they are "honest" and "gentle," qualities their women appreciate and laud, these men lack the ability to excite or intrigue their female partners (6, 21). The speaker rejoices in her own choice, a man who is neither home-loving nor reliable. "My true love's a rover!" she exults; "my dear lad's a liar!"; "my true love is false!" (lines 4, 8, 40). Combining endearments with ostensibly

---

46 Daniel J. Kruger, Maryanne Fisher, and Ian Jobling, "Proper Hero Dads and Dark Hero Cads: Alternate Mating Strategies Exemplified in British Romantic Literature," in *The Literary Animal: Evolution and the Nature of Narrative*," ed. Jonathan Gottschall and David Sloan Wilson (Evanston, IL: Northwestern University Press, 2005), 226, 228.
47 Kruger, Fisher, and Jobling, "Proper Hero Dads"; Schmitt, "Fundamentals of Human Mating," 273-74.
48 Buss, *Dangerous Passion*, 163-64; Kruger, Fisher, and Jobling, "Proper Hero Dads," 227.

negative characterizations, she highlights the paradoxical appeal of the outrageously handsome, notoriously inconstant men Buss dubs "'studly' charmers."[49]

Although the poem provides no physical description of the speaker's partner, his obviously high genetic quality is the source, implicitly, of his pop-star-like effect on the opposite sex. The speaker avers that all the women she knows, no matter how much they claim to value the staid devotion of their mates, "would give the life they live / For a look from the man I kiss" (lines 23-24). The reference to kissing indicates that the man's bad-boy traits stimulate passionate response, possibly against many women's better judgment and conscious wishes, promising erotic fulfillment. To have been chosen by him, moreover, validates the speaker's own mate value: desired by many women, he casts "his eyes about" with "cold" calculation, selecting only a "few" as worthy of his attention (lines 25, 26). She accepts his inconstancy as further proof of his quality, admitting without reproach that "he'd slip me clean for a nun, or a queen, / Or a beggar," (lines 27-28). This man has no need to sit at home devotedly and putter. To enjoy the sexual attentions of such a man, however briefly, is indisputably worthwhile, Millay's persona concludes: she chooses erotic excitement over domestic tranquility. The poem provides remarkably explicit illustration of the dad-cad dichotomy Darwinian researchers have identified in human mating strategies. Very evidently, it is not necessary for women to think consciously about the *genetic* superiority of men they find sexually exciting. The characters in Millay's poem are oblivious to ultimate ends, such as the high-quality offspring a handsome rogue might sire. They concentrate, rather, on the pleasures of his "kiss," i.e., his ability to satisfy proximate desires.

As foregoing examples indicate, a preference for short-term partners manifesting high genetic quality goes hand-in-hand with another benefit prized by women depicted in Millay's poetry: sexual gratification in and of itself. Because cultural norms have operated to suppress and deny women's sexuality, including any predilection for sexual variety, a frisson of the forbidden marks Millay's portrayal of lusty adventuresses. Recent research supports the conclusion, however, that though her depictions may be deliberately hyperbolic, they are essentially accurate. Studying "women's perceptions of the benefits of affairs," Buss reports, "sexual gratification was at the top of the list."[50] The women in Millay's poems similarly identify "passion" as the primary motivation for temporary liaisons ("We talk of taxes," line 9). "The desirous body's

---

49 Buss, *Dangerous Passion*, 164.
50 Ibid., 170.

heat" propels them into relationships promising sexual fulfillment ("Yet in an hour to come," line 10).

Another benefit associated with short-term sex, often observed in Millay's poetry, is enhanced self-esteem. From a Darwinian perspective, the utility of positive self-assessment in the social environment is clear. Because "self-esteem makes you behave in ways befitting an esteemed primate," it may inspire confidence and win respect (particularly, perhaps, if the affair precipitating a rise in self-esteem is not discovered).[51] Affairs provide women with opportunities for upward re-evaluation of their personal attributes, Buss reports. The novelty and intensity of an affair-partner's attentions reassure a woman that she is "beautiful," "important," "intelligent," and "sexy."[52] Buss speculates that boredom with a relationship or a routine "grown stale" may explain this "surge" in feelings of self-worth, which he likens to the effect of "a wonder drug."[53] In Part V of "Theme and Variations," the speaker compares herself to a "hall," now vacant because no lovers remain to populate it (line 5). She emphasizes the high quality of men whom she has by turns "loved badly" or "too soon," claiming nevertheless that "the very rafters of this room /Are honored by the guests it had" (lines 3, 4, 11-12). Brief and imperfect though they may have been, the affairs have exalted her: she has been partnered with "gentry" (line 15). Having increased the value she places on herself, these previous relationships enable her to dismiss her current paramour, the "only" one out of so many to prove "unworthy" (line 13). He is a peon, figuratively, in comparison with her more elite "guests," and the self-assurance she has won from their attentions proves enduringly beneficial (line 12). Other poems generate similar analogies between high self-esteem and aristocratic status. Frequently comparing themselves to queens or goddesses, Millay's female personae confirm the association between short-term sex and feelings of self-worth. Love affairs can generate a sense of importance equivalent to that accompanying social and political prestige.

The higher the quality of the short-term partner, evidently, the more powerful a jolt to self-esteem an affair can provide. It appears that the benefits available to female short-term strategists may be mutually reinforcing. A preference for exceptionally good-looking men, such as Millay's women exhibit, not only secures probable genetic payoffs for potential offspring (Benefit Number

---

51 Wright, *Moral Animal*, 244.
52 Buss, *Evolution and Desire*, 238-39.
53 Ibid., 239.

One), it promotes erotic fulfillment (Benefit Number Two), since these irresistibly handsome, universally desired men stimulate arousal and generate sexual excitement. Additionally, the attentions of such men foster feelings of confidence and self-worth (Benefit Number Three), a psychologically uplifting and socially useful effect. Millay's women stand to enjoy a constellation of smoothly intertwined benefits from their predilection for flings with heartbreakingly attractive men.

Tightly interwoven into this constellation of advantages is a final, crucial benefit women can obtain from short-term strategies: personal autonomy. Eschewing commitment, women in Millay's poetry escape the proprietary domination typically imposed by men on their long-term female partners. Temporary involvements offer them scope for assertive behavior and sexual fulfillment, including choice in partners. Although history and literature are rife with examples of women who are duped and exploited by short-term seducers, Millay's women regularly seize control, frequently dominating the men with whom they are sexually involved. Even when affairs end sooner than anticipated and against their wishes, they avoid positions of helplessness or vulnerability. The few wives depicted in the poems likewise refrain from submissive compliance with husbandly possessiveness; instead, they affirm their autonomy by indulging freely in extramarital liaisons.

Throughout Millay's work, female agency appears as a consistently important theme.[54] That agency is well served, she implicitly argues, by short-term affairs. These discourage emotional investment, permitting women to extricate themselves easily, control the timing of break-ups, and elude subjugating entanglement. "And if I loved you Wednesday, / Well, what is that to you?" one speaker demands. By Thursday she has withdrawn that love ("Thursday," lines 1-2). She chides her erstwhile partner for "complaining" about her abrupt defection, making plain that his reaction is of no concern to her whatsoever (line 5). She has moved on, emotionally, and the "love" of yesterday means nothing to her now: "what / Is that to me?" (lines 7-8). Here readers watch a woman toying with a man's affections much as men traditionally have done with women's. She is the one whose emotional detachment wins her control in the relationship. Her capacity for switching feelings rapidly on and off enables her to dominate her partner, and she revels in her role, deriding her lover's

---

54 "Of greater importance than any particular ethic of Edna Millay's—e.g., a woman's right to be as inconstant in love as a man—is the larger concept of freedom implicit in her work." Janet Gassman, "Edna St. Vincent Millay: 'Nobody's Own,'" 310.

clinginess.[55] Like the speaker in "I, being born a woman," she treats her partner with an exaggerated heartlessness, underlining her high-spirited celebration of female control.

As poem after poem illustrates, concentrating on the time-limited nature of a relationship helps a woman to retain the upper hand in it. Anticipating the end of an affair even in the "pearled and roseate" days of its beginning discourages the development of long-term expectations ("What thing is this," line 7). Thus guarded from anxieties, women can yield to romantic "bliss" while remaining in charge of their own destinies (line 12). They can cherish freely the ecstasy inherent in "fleeting" romance, no matter how "clandestine" or "brief" that ecstasy may prove, praising it in the highest terms: "I do cry holy, holy" ("When did I ever deny," lines 8, 10, 9). When necessary, they remind themselves that any affair, prolonged beyond its pre-ordained limits, is as off-putting as "stale patchouli" ("I know the face of Falsehood," line 14). They reject the "unwelcome" crumbs of a partner's cooling affection: "Love's bitter crust" ("That Love at length," line 7). Faced with the "ebb of love" and imminent conclusion of an affair, consequently, a woman is well advised to end it herself, retaining power in a deteriorating relationship by being the first to defect ("Theme and Variations" VII, line 6).

The speaker-protagonist in *Fatal Interview*, who fears from the outset that she will be abandoned by her extramarital partner, thus insists that his departure is her "choice" rather than his: "not from your temper does my doom depend" ("I know my mind," lines 1, 2). She speeds her increasingly restless lover on his way out the door instead of pleading with him to remain, a tactic that secures her a say in events. "Love me no more," she commands him, when she begins to "surmise" that her "kisses" no longer thrill him ("Love me no more," lines 1, 6, 7). Shrewdly she orders him to do what she suspects he already intends, thus replacing his volition with hers. Like so many of the short-term strategists Millay portrays, this character values her power in the relationship at least as much as the sexual fulfillment it provides. Her goal is to act rather than to be acted upon. Announcing the break-up as her decision, she avoids assuming an abject role.

The Darwinian significance of Millay's focus on autonomy is clear. All animals seek, as permitted by their varying intelligence levels, to direct their

---

55 "One of Millay's strategies for subverting the traditional love lyric," Ernest J. Smith rightly observes, "is to have the woman speaker emerge from the affair whole, rather than in a state of disintegration." "'How the Speaking Pen Has Been Impeded': The Rhetoric of Love and Selfhood in Millay and Rich," in *Millay at 100: A Critical Reappraisal*, ed. Diane P. Freedman (Carbondale and Edwardsville: Southern Illinois University Press, 1995), 48.

individual quests for survival and reproduction—deciding, for example, what to eat, when to mate, when to fight, when to run, or where to hide. Each such decision affects the ultimate genetic legacy of the creature making it. Given highly developed brains, multifaceted behavioral options, and complex cultural environments, human beings command more conscious decision-making powers than any other animal. Poised to take charge of their life histories within the bounds of their physical and social environments, individual members of the species struggle mightily to retain freedom of choice and action. From an evolutionary psychological perspective, understandably, "the desire for control is the fundamental motivation underlying the behavioral and psychological development of human beings."[56] The systematic domination of women by men contradicts this basic human desire. Patriarchal compulsion and custom radically restrict women's ability to shape their own destinies, their sexual destinies in particular.[57] Resistance to such restriction is inevitable.[58]

Millay's deliberately provocative presentation of sexually assertive, strong-willed women is a literary manifestation of such resistance.[59] Delighting and appalling her readers, she peoples her poetry with women who orchestrate their sexual lives as they see fit, unequivocally announcing and expressing their innate ardency. They utilize short-term strategies, by preference, because these maximize sexual fulfillment while minimizing threats to personal liberty. Highlighting proximate influences on behavior (the pleasure of erotic activity) while shearing these from their ultimate function (the passing on of genes through children), Millay brazenly draws attention to benefits available to women who reject long-term, exclusive commitment. With her bold, often exaggerated depictions of erotically vital, commanding women, she ridicules conventional images of feminine submission and sexual reserve. Her poems expand and correct prevailing conceptions of female human

---

56 Geary, *Male, Female*, 161.
57 Hrdy addresses the "evolutionary implications" of curtailment of female sexual activity. Research indicates that restriction of female mate choice proves dangerously disadvantageous to a species, thereby confirming the "importance of female autonomy in reproductive decisions." *Mother Nature*, 41, 42.
58 Hrdy, *Mother Nature*, 87; Frederick, Reynolds, and Fisher, "The Importance of Female Choice," 318-24; Buss, *Evolution of Desire*, 13.
59 Clark notes that Millay "seems quite conscious of the political ramifications of her work." "Uncanny Millay," 25. Colin Falck, too, discusses her conscious "repudiation of the conventionally institutionalized subjection of women." "Introduction: The Modern Lyricism of Edna Millay," in *Edna St. Vincent Millay: Selected Poems*, ed. Colin Falck (New York: HarperCollins, 1991), xxiii.

nature in important ways, undermining the rationale for gender-based sociopolitical discrimination.

At the same time, unobtrusively yet unmistakably, her poems protest biological obstacles to women's sexual freedom and personal autonomy. Chief among these are sexual dimorphism (the relatively greater physical strength enabling men to coerce women), intersexual conflict (with emphasis on strategic interference by men), and reproduction itself (pregnancy and offspring). Millay's celebratory presentation of female agency presupposes elimination of these and related impediments to its full expression. Insofar as these impediments are ineradicable, achievement of her most deeply cherished goals must remain imperfect. Only in the imaginative realm of art can proximal satisfactions be altogether decoupled from ultimate functions, or behavioral choices from evolved adaptations. Like many other writers, Millay invokes the power of imagination to construct an alternative environment, satisfyingly counterfactual in significant details. In so doing, she illustrates the unique capacity of the human animal "to rebel against the dictates of the genes."[60] Because her repudiation of biological realities is covert, taking the form of silent denial rather than open complaint, it may not be recognized by readers for what it is: tacit admission that social change alone, however necessary and desirable, would be insufficient to secure women the idealized sexual freedom and personal autonomy she so passionately imagines.

---

60 Dawkins, *Selfish Gene*, 59-60.

CHAPTER 10

Philosophy and Fitness: Hemingway's "A Clean, Well-Lighted Place" and *The Sun Also Rises*

In both his 1933 story, "A Clean, Well-Lighted Place," and his 1926 novel, *The Sun Also Rises*, Ernest Hemingway presents narrative dilemmas with reproductive implications. Thematic and symbolic features of both texts rely upon correlation between procreative circumstance and philosophical orientation. From an evolutionary perspective, it is inevitable that ruminations about life's largest questions—the purpose of human existence, for example, or the relationship between individual history and universal design—would be influenced by prospects for biological continuity. The principle of replication drives organic life on earth. For genes (the replicating agents) as well as for the "survival machines" in which they are housed, the undeniable purpose of existence is propagation.[1] Many of the behavioral adaptations characterizing any animal, including the human animal, are geared, consequently, toward reproductive goals: proximate satisfactions (such as sexual pleasure) reward activities that promote fitness (conception). Such rewards encourage individuals who succeed in achieving "evolutionarily significant goals" (i.e., "acquiring and retaining ... resources needed to survive and reproduce") to maintain more positive emotions and more sanguine spirits than do those who fail to achieve them.[2] Hemingway depicts these psychological effects in his fiction, not merely to illustrate them but as a means of investing philosophical themes with emotional intensity. The two works under discussion present worldviews consonant with the procreative environments in which action takes

---

1 As Dawkins explains, "DNA molecules are replicators. They generally ... gang together into large communal survival machines or 'vehicles.' The vehicles we know best are individual bodies like our own. ... Vehicles don't replicate themselves; they work to propagate their replicators." *Selfish Gene*, 254.
2 Geary, *Male, Female*, 170.

place. Optimistic philosophies are associated with fecundity, philosophical pessimism with barrenness. When the quest for fitness is foiled, the universe as a whole assumes an emptiness of purpose corresponding to the reproductive vacuum. Genetic death serves as a psychological and symbolic source of cosmic nihilism.[3]

"A Clean, Well-Lighted Place"

Mating and reproduction contribute significantly to the principal action and thematic core of "A Clean, Well-Lighted Place." The motivating force of sexuality is mentioned in connection with all the story's characters, major and minor. In a work notable for its narrative leanness, such iteration stands out. The subject of sex emerges almost immediately, when the two waiters—the story's nameless main characters—notice a soldier pass by the café. The soldier is accompanied by a "girl," and the couple's pace is described as "hurried."[4] Comments that he should "get off the street" to elude "the guard" suggest that the soldier is violating a military curfew (379). The waiters clearly are not surprised to see a soldier, and they seem well informed, too, about the patrolling guard. No background information is provided, so readers are left to wonder what this military presence might signify. Is there a war in progress? Does a conquering or defending army occupy a garrison in the town? Evidently such details are not centrally important, although associations triggered by the appearance of a soldier (enemies, weapons, danger, fear) may contribute tension and anxiety to the story's emotional ambiance.

The exchange between the two waiters focuses solely on the soldier's immediate (and ultimately reproductive) objective. His desire to spend time with a girl—a local girl he has picked up, perhaps, or a prostitute—appears to be sexually motivated, given the lateness of hour: approximately 2:00 a.m., as readers shortly discover. His willingness to risk punishment in order to enjoy a furtive and doubtlessly brief sexual encounter serves to highlight the urgency of the male sex drive—an adaptation very obviously designed to promote reproductive activity. From an evolutionary perspective, it is more

---

3 Günther Schmigalle places *The Sun Also Rises* in "the tradition of philosophical pessimism by its emphasis on the transitory and insignificant nature of all human action" but without reference to stymied procreative energies. "'How People Go to Hell': Pessimism, Tragedy, and Affinity to Schopenhauer in *The Sun Also Rises*," *The Hemingway Review* 25, no. 1 (2005): 19.
4 Ernest Hemingway, "A Clean, Well-Lighted Place," in *The Short Stories* (New York: Charles Scribner's Sons, 1966), 379. All citations refer to this edition.

important to pass on genes than to obey institutional regulations. "If he gets what he wants," as the younger waiter comments, penalties after the fact might "matter" very little (379). This is especially true for a man identified as a soldier, whose window of reproductive opportunity may prove to be small. Given "environmental unpredictability" and high "extrinsic risk" of mortality, in particular, "it is adaptive to favor current reproduction by starting mating early, even at a cost."[5] The soldier is assigned no dialogue and plays no further role in the story; readers are granted no interior access to his mental or emotional processes. His philosophical stance therefore remains unknown. The incident featuring him serves chiefly to underline the power of reproductive impulses, which prove strong enough to override institutionally enforced deterrents.

Reproductive impulses also trigger the main action of the story's plot: the early closing of the café. In a narrative devoid of exciting events, this is the point of action toward which the story builds. Readers observe the younger waiter's mounting impatience to be gone, evident in his conversation with the other waiter and in his brusque treatment of the café's single customer, who is elderly and deaf. Against the wishes of his coworker, "the waiter who was in a hurry" shoos this customer away, closing the café more than half an hour earlier than usual (381). From a business point of view, this early closing appears disadvantageous: had he not been forced to leave, the old man would have stayed and bought more brandies. From an interpersonal point of view, it is unkind: a "lonely" old man has been driven prematurely from the solace provided by the café (380). What overrides both business and social considerations is the waiter's mating impulse: he is "in a hurry" to get home to his wife, who is "waiting in bed" for him (382, 380). When his coworker jokes that arriving home early might prove awkward, in case his wife receives a lover during her husband's normal work hours, the younger man shows a bit of temper ("Are you trying to insult me?") but quickly states that he has no fear of being cuckolded: "I have confidence" (382).

Insofar as the younger waiter lays claim to a philosophical position, this is it: "confidence" is the leitmotif of his existence. He bases his optimistic view of himself and his future, predictably, on the access he has achieved to "resources

---

5 Marco Del Giudice and Jay Belsky, "The Development of Life History Strategies: Toward a Multi-Stage Theory," in *The Evolution of Personality and Individual Differences*, ed. David M. Buss and Patricia H. Hawley (Oxford: Oxford University Press, 2011), 155.

needed to survive and reproduce."[6] In addition to "youth," he has "a job" and a wife—a wife, tellingly, whose sexual fidelity he trusts (382). Because he is so eager to take advantage of the mating opportunities marriage offers him, he behaves impatiently, rudely, even crassly, to the customer whose presence interferes with his sexual agenda for this night. He derides the old man's presumable decline in sexual prowess, for example; he even wishes aloud that the old man had succeeded in a recent suicide attempt, reasoning that if the man were dead he couldn't patronize the café and waste the waiter's time. Hearing such sentiments, readers are bound to deplore the young man's self-absorption and lack of empathy. More crucially, however, this is a second demonstration, in the space of less than half an hour of narrative time, of the power of reproductive energy to shape behavior. First, a soldier risks punishment to pursue a one-time sexual opportunity. Shortly thereafter, a husband defies his coworker and turns out a paying customer in order to join his mate "in bed" as quickly as possible. He resents postponement of erotic fulfillment so much, in fact, that he directs a joking death-wish toward the person who unwittingly compels him to defer gratification.

The older waiter represents a contrast to his younger, married colleague. They have the same "work," but his personal situation differs in reproductively significant features (382). He has no wife, and since he is "not young" apparently has no expectation of acquiring one. There is no hint that he ever has employed short-term reproductive strategies—no mention, for example, of mistresses, affairs, or illegitimate children. For reasons never explained to readers, his life history has taken a course that excluded mating, offspring, and parental investment: the very fitness-enhancing factors currently lending motivation and purpose to the life of his younger colleague. Although the younger man does not mention children as a probable or hoped-for consequence of his marital eagerness, the proximal satisfactions he takes in bedding his wife very obviously serve reproductive ends. He is rewarded, in sexual pleasure and in "confidence," for behavior designed to pass on genes. "You have everything," the older man assures him, adding that "we are of two different kinds" (382). From an evolutionary standpoint, this distinction could not be more accurate. The younger man is poised to become an ancestor, to send his genes on through generations to come; the older man, never having reproduced and unlikely now to do so, has reached a genetic dead-end.

---

6 Geary, *Male, Female*, 170.

In the passage of interior monologue following the younger waiter's hasty departure, his more thoughtful colleague continues his musings. If the younger man has "everything"—most obviously, a long-term mate and the prospect of offspring—he himself—childless, mateless, and older—is confronted with "a nothing" (382, 383). He extends personal reproductive failure into the realm of metaphysics, inventing on the spot a cynical parody of the two principal Roman Catholic prayers: the "Our Father" and the "Hail Mary." Insistently blasphemous in their rejection of religious values and comforts, his anti-prayers substitute for content-bearing verbs and nouns in both originals the terms "nothing" or "nada," thereby obliterating the original meaning. There is no God ("our nada"), no heaven ("who art in nada"), and neither material nor spiritual sustenance ("our daily nada") (383). The substitutions point to "a series of significant absences" as Steven K. Hoffman observes.[7] Many intellectual and cultural currents in the early twentieth century contribute to the emergence of nihilistic philosophies like that expressed here, of course (and to concomitant dismantling of traditional religious beliefs), not least Darwinian theory itself. The evolutionary psychological significance of this character's metaphysical cynicism is in any case unmistakable; his perception of the cosmos as a meaningless void corresponds to his prospects of a genetic legacy, which are, so far as readers can judge, nil.

Biological parallels to cosmic nothingness become especially clear in revisions of the "Hail Mary," a prayer that celebrates fecundity and birth. Repeated again and again as part of the Rosary, it glorifies Mary's motherhood: the "fruit" of her "womb" is a valuable child whose birth will save the whole human race from death (Luke 1: 42). In terms of individual fitness, for similar if less exalted reasons, the birth of any child is valuable: it secures, or saves, the genes of its parents from annihilation. Backhandedly, the waiter's scathing parodies acknowledge parallels between the continuity of life on earth (achieved by organic propagation) and the spiritual immortality promised by orthodox religion (achieved by miraculous conception). Declaring that Mary, a sacred image of maternity, is pregnant "with nothing," Hemingway's fictional character strips from the universe all hope of a future: the womb is empty; no child will be born; life will not go on (383). The waiter's vituperative string of nothing's expresses anger with broken promises. Church doctrine assures believers, after all, that there will be *something*—"fruit,"

---

7 Steven K. Hoffmann, "*Nada* and the Clean, Well-Lighted Place: The Unity of Hemingway's Short Fiction," in *Modern Critical Views: Ernest Hemingway*, ed. Harold Bloom (New York: Chelsea House, 1985), 175.

resurrection, new life—but he finds that assurance illusory. What is true for him, personally, he expresses as universal truth. He lacks evolutionary biological consolations for his own death (descendents bearing copies of his genes), and he doubts religious consolations (eternal life of the spirit). He himself is not a father; there is likewise, for him, no supernatural Father to prevent a relentless drift "into nada" (383). He projects onto the whole human enterprise the pointlessness weighing down his own spirits ("I have never had confidence"), asserting that individual existence, per se, lacks meaning and value: "a man was nothing" (382, 383).

It should go without saying that the connections between procreation and metaphysics implicit in this character's monologue and life history—and, indeed, in the story as a whole—ought not to be interpreted narrowly. Readers certainly are not expected to come away from the story with the simplistic notion that childless people are doomed to misery or that those with offspring invariably are contented. Reproductive failure here serves, above all else, as the objective correlative for existential hopelessness, grounding abstract philosophy firmly in adapted human nature. Implied causal connections between reproductive circumstance and philosophical viewpoint, as in the case of the older-waiter character, help to launch wider symbolic signification. An author wishing to depict cosmic purposelessness can find no more emotionally resonant parallel than biological barrenness. The procreative "nothing" provides psychological ballast for metaphysical nothingness.

Presentation of the older waiter's bitter philosophical contemplations functions as the crux of the narrative, which accords primary importance to the workings of mind rather than to external action. Revealing, close-up, the principal character's emotional and mental apparatus at work in an intensely gripping scene, the narrative also implies that uninterrupted contemplation of a cosmic "nada" would be psychologically insupportable.[8] The older waiter distances himself from desperate meaninglessness in two ways. He resists continuous immersion in negative ideation, for one. The story's conclusion shows him redefining his confrontation with "nothing" as "probably only insomnia," thereby minimizing its ability to instill "fear" or "dread" (383, 382). Telling himself it is not existential panic that keeps him awake at night, but a common sleep disorder ("many must have it"), he engages in a protective act of self-deception (383).[9] Robert Trivers observes that

---

8 Hoffman argues that the story concerns "the various available human responses" to nada even more that the idea of nada itself. "*Nada* and the Clean, Well-Lighted Place," 174.
9 Hoffman interprets this character's insomnia very differently, as part of his "metaphysical courage" in embracing of nothingness: "his vision is too clear, his sense of self too firm, to

there can be "intrinsic benefit" in "positive illusions."[10] In this instance, an illusion encourages emotional equanimity and thus supports day-to-day survival. Hemingway's character shields himself from "the nothing he knew too well" in a second way by interpreting his employment at the café as a mission (383). By keeping this "clean and pleasant" place open late, he manages "to humanize both himself and his environment," offering "necessary" refuge to others who suffer from contemplation of the void: those "who do not want to go to bed" and "who need a light for the night" (382).[11] Although the literal illumination provided by a small "electric light" may seem a poor substitute for the symbolic light of truth, goodness, or salvation, it can prevent collapse into utter hopelessness (379).

It is such collapse, the narrative indicates, that caused the "old man" who patronizes the café to attempt suicide the preceding week. About eighty, according to the two waiters' estimate, and with "plenty of money," he is a "lonely" widower (379, 380). The comment that he had a wife "once" suggests that she died some time ago (381). Since it is "a niece" who looks after him, evidently he has no children. The younger waiter's dismissive comment that "a wife would be no good to him now," focusing on the old man's probable impotence, is countered by his more kindly colleague's assertion that the old man might "be better" with a spouse (381). Unsupported by intimate companionship, he has succumbed to "despair" and tried to hang himself (379). Now he sits late every night at the café, anesthetizing his miseries with brandy: "he's drunk every night" (380).

The younger, married waiter unwittingly provides an all-important clue to the old man's state of mind at the time of his suicide attempt. He was "in despair" about "nothing," the younger man avers, adding that he knows it was "nothing" because the old man "has plenty of money" (379).[12] This comment, occurring in the opening scene of the story, appears at first merely to offer evidence of the younger waiter's insensitivity: he is too shallow to recognize

---

allow him the ease of insensate slumber." This assertion attributes more conscious awareness to the character than close reading of the passage in question appears to encourage. "Nada and the Clean, Well-Lighted Place," 185, 186.

10 Robert Trivers, "Self-Deception," 273.
11 Annette Benert, "Survival through Irony: Hemingway's 'A Clean, Well-Lighted Place,'" *Studies in Short Fiction* 11 (1974), 187.
12 An astonishing amount of scholarly comment on this story addresses the sometimes confusing assignment of dialogue. David Kerner has argued ably for the correctness of the unemended text, which forms the basis, accordingly, of the present discussion. "Hemingway's Attention to 'A Clean, Well-Lighted Place,'" *The Hemingway Review* 13, no. 1 (1993).

that economic resources do not guarantee contentment. Retrospectively, after the older waiter's long interior monologue on nothingness, the earlier comment takes on a new and unanticipated weight of meaning. The old man is not in despair "about ... nothing" in the sense of despairing without cause. He despairs, evidently, because for him, as for the older waiter, the universe itself is "all a nothing" (383). The impact of this heavily ironic double entendre is all the greater for being delayed. The term "nothing" has been loaded with metaphysical import that grounds the old man's suicidal frame of mind in a worldview with wide-ranging implications. He is one of "all those" who cannot sleep at night, who seek refuge in a "well-lighted place" from isolation (social and mental), from darkness (literal and symbolic), and from nihility (natural and supernatural).

The Sun Also Rises

Plot, theme, setting, and characterization in *The Sun Also Rises* all point to connections between reproductive failure and pessimistic worldviews. Barrenness is a pronounced feature of the human environment in which the narrative unfolds. With the exception of Robert Cohn, the father of three children who live very much elsewhere and who survive, evidently, without paternal attention, none of the novel's principal characters have reproduced. Although action throughout the narrative is sexually motivated (e.g., courtship, competition, liaisons, jealousy, mate guarding), the ultimate purpose of these proximate behaviors—the passing on of genes—is not fulfilled. Except for Frances, who tells Jake (perhaps insincerely) that she had planned to have children with Robert once they were married, characters do not introduce the topic of procreation. Contraception in the relevant time period (early 1920s) certainly was far from reliable, but pregnancy is not discussed as a possible outcome of the sexual yearning that drives the plot. Brett Ashley, the focus of male attention, is desired, pursued, bedded, and fought over. She engages in sexual activity with three men in the course of the novel—Robert Cohn, Mike Campbell, and Pedro Romero—and her previous sexual history is extensive: a fiancé killed in the war (her "true love"), an unnamed first husband, Lord Ashley, to whom she still is legally married, and an apparently long list of short-term partners.[13] "Brett's gone off with men" and

---

13 Ernest Hemingway, *The Sun Also Rises* (New York: Charles Scribner's Sons, 1926; New York: Macmillan, 1988), 39. All citations refer to the 1988 edition.

"had affairs," evidently, with some regularity (143). Like Mary (as described by the older waiter in "A Clean, Well-Lighted Place"), however, Brett will bring forth no "fruit."

Every man who sees Brett immediately desires her: she is regarded as a woman with undeniably high mate value. Praise of her intrinsic "quality" and "breeding" implies indicators of both genetic and social worth (38). She exudes "class" that does not depend upon the status-enhancing aristocratic title she has acquired through marriage; she radiates self-assurance and social ease (58). She is "damned good-looking," in addition, and dresses to show off her excellent figure, "built with curves like the hull of a racing yacht" (22). Her fashion-forward attire and hairstyle are suggestively daring; they set her apart, distinguishing her from more ordinary, less exciting women. Men as radically different in background, age, and temperament as Robert Cohn and Pedro Romero desire her as a long-term mate. Local dancers at the festival for San Fermin detach her from the crowd of onlookers and encircle her in playful homage "as an image to dance around" (155). Treating Brett as a kind of female deity, these street dancers acknowledge her almost supernatural appeal to men. Naming her "Circe," with emphasis on her ability to transform "men into swine," Robert Cohn reinforces the idea that Brett is woman, writ large (144). She incarnates the female capacity to stimulate male ardor, an ardor so intense it can overpower judgment and civility—hence the "terrible" baiting and arguments in Pamplona, all spurred by male jealousy and mate-guarding, culminating in violence when Cohn uses his fists against three rivals for Brett's attentions (144).[14]

All this evidence of Brett's high mate value, a value instantly and universally apprehended, is contradicted by factors that her lovers and suitors overlook, namely, her age (thirty-four) and her childlessness. Men are drawn to good-looking, high-status, socially confident, exciting partners, true, but these attractive characteristics must be packaged with fertility. Fertility in women, indubitably, is age-dependent: it "declines steadily ...

---

14 In his Darwinian analysis of male competition in the novel, James A. Puckett points out that "whether through a display of ornaments, battle scars, physical beauty, humor, or actual fighting, the men are performing, and they are performing primarily to be seen and validated by Brett." "'Sex Explains It All': Male Performance, Evolution, and Sexual Selection in Ernest Hemingway's *The Sun Also Rises*," *Studies in American Naturalism* 8, no. 2 (2013): 138. Bender also provides discussion in Darwinian terms of "the sexual jealousy and combativeness of the male characters," including Hemingway's views of "the sexual struggle in nature." *The Descent of Love*, 353, 357.

after twenty. By the age of forty, a woman's reproductive capacity is low, and by fifty it is close to zero."[15] For this reason, "youth is a critical cue" to a woman's reproductive value and a sine qua non in male mating preferences.[16] Whether or not they consciously want offspring, men choose women whose low waist-hip ratio, facial symmetry, radiant skin, and physical vitality indicate youth—and thus the capacity to conceive and bear children.[17] It seems likely that Brett's extraordinarily attractive qualities, both physical and social, make a deceptively youthful impression. The fact remains, nevertheless, that more than half of her reproductive years already are behind her. If her childless state, at age thirty-four, is the result of deliberate contraceptive measures, those measure have proven suspiciously effective. She has risked impregnation with numerous partners and, so far as readers know, never conceived. Her sexually active lifestyle necessarily puts her fertility per se in question. Given her age, her reproductive potential—if any—is, necessarily, rapidly dwindling. Thus the novel portrays men competing with one another for sexual access to a woman of doubtful reproductive worth: libidinous energy is expended with little likelihood of positive procreative outcome. The overwhelming sense of futility permeating the novel (of things already being over), ascribed in large part to physical and psychological damage inflicted by World War I, is mirrored in the evolutionary biological futility of the sexual activity so prominently foregrounded in the novel's plot.[18]

Brett Ashley's markedly high sex drive, which serves as catalyst for much of the novel's action, further emphasizes the oxymoronic conjunction of sexuality and sterility. She yields to ardent impulses without hesitation, describing intensely physical responses to men. She turns "all to jelly" at Jake's touch (26). "Mad about the Romero boy," she is "a goner," unable to resist the urgency of desire (183). When Jake advises against the affair, she protests that she "can't help it": "I've never been able to help anything" (183).[19] She engages simultaneously in short-term and long-term mating strategies, bedding Robert Cohn and

---

15 Buss, *Evolution of Desire,* 51.
16 Ibid., 51.
17 Ibid., 53-57.
18 As Linda Wagner-Martin observes, the novel's "plotline" consists almost entirely of "a great many sexual liaisons." Introduction to *Ernest Hemingway's "The Sun Also Rises": A Casebook,* ed. Linda Wagner-Martin (Oxford: Oxford University Press, 2002), 3-4.
19 Bender notes the emphasis Hemingway places on female ardor and female choice, "the female's power to select the sexual partners she desires—for their strength (physical, financial, or social) and beauty." *The Descent of Love,* 357.

Pedro Romero successively, within the space of a very few weeks, while married to Ashley and newly pledged to Mike Campbell. Unembarrassed by her promiscuity, she tells the latter "all about" her flings with other men; indeed, she is actually living with Campbell when she takes up with Romero (143). She is a female protagonist whose sexual hunger is conspicuously strong, just as strong as that exhibited by the men who desire her. Her affairs with men occupy her time and attention to the exclusion of nearly everything else. The erotic motivation that propels her from one man to the next contributes significantly to the theme of futility dominating the narrative. She is a woman of unrelenting ardor—a quivering mass of proximal impulses—whose many matings serve no ultimate, reproductive purpose.

Secondary comment on the novel, though rich and wide-ranging, neglects the topic of Brett Ashley's dubious fertility, including the peculiarly bitter irony inherent in her desperate but sterile eroticism. She has been discussed as an example of the New Woman, as a transitional figure between traditional and modern femininity, as a feminist, as a feminist manqué.[20] She has been targeted as an unwomanly instance of gender role-reversal, as a predatory and emasculating threat to men individually and, more widely, to male sociopolitical dominance.[21] Some readers hail her as a pioneer claiming

---

20 For representative discussion of Brett and questions of gender, see Rena Sanderson, "Hemingway and Gender History," in *The Cambridge Companion to Ernest Hemingway*, ed. Scott Donaldson (Cambridge: Cambridge University Press, 1996); Wendy Martin, "Brett Ashley as New Woman in *The Sun Also Rises*," in *Ernest Hemingway's "The Sun Also Rises": A Casebook*, ed. Linda Wagner-Martin (Oxford: Oxford University Press, 2002); see 50-51, in particular, for a useful summary of critical commentary on Brett Ashley; James Nagel, "Brett and the Other Women in *The Sun Also Rises*," in *The Cambridge Companion to Ernest Hemingway*, ed. Scott Donaldson (Cambridge: Cambridge University Press, 1996); Mark Spilka, "The Death of Love in *The Sun Also Rises*," in *Ernest Hemingway's "The Sun Also Rises": A Casebook*, ed. Linda Wagner-Martin (Oxford: Oxford University Press, 2002).

21 John W. Aldridge notes Brett's "defeminized" gender status in "*The Sun Also Rises* Sixty Years Later," in *Readings on Ernest Hemingway*, ed. Katie De Koster (San Diego, CA: Greenhaven Press, 1997), 144-45. Sanderson considers the implication of Brett's manlike traits in "Hemingway and Gender History," 178-80. Debra A. Moddelmog places Brett in the "cat-egory of women who were crossing gender lines." "Contradictory Bodies in *The Sun Also Rises*," in *Ernest Hemingway's "The Sun Also Rises": A Casebook*, ed. Linda Wagner-Martin (Oxford: Oxford University Press, 2002), 157. Leslie Fiedler identifies "phallic" qualities in Brett, a "bitch-goddess" who leaves her lovers "unmanned and degraded." "Hemingway's Men and (the Absence of) Women," in *Readings on Ernest Hemingway*, ed. Katie De Koster (San Diego, CA: Greenhaven Press, 1997), 94, 95. Greg Forter examines Brett in the context of "a disappearing ideal of male autonomy and power." "Melancholy Modernism: Gender and the Politics of Mourning in *The Sun Also Rises*," in *Eight Decades of Hemingway Criticism*, ed. Linda Wagner-Martin (East Lansing: Michigan State University Press, 2009), 59.

female sexual independence; others castigate her for selfish immaturity and destructive promiscuity. While her sexual motives and behaviors have been subjected to repeated analysis, her reproductively null status has not. From an evolutionary biological standpoint, however, this aspect of Brett's characterization assumes importance. Despite husbands, fiancés, and lovers, in the course of fifteen or more sexually active years she has achieved a direct fitness of zero. Her procreative accomplishment to date is precisely the same as that of the sterile Jake Barnes—a widely ignored but significant fact. Even apart from his wound, this couple's reproductive future would look uncertain.

The plight of Jake Barnes dramatically increases the negative atmosphere of this sexually torrid yet procreatively dysfunctional world. A war wound has rendered him physically incapable of intercourse and insemination, leaving him tormented by desire he cannot consummate. Critical comment has focused on the psychosocial impact of Jake's injury rather than its reproductive consequences. He has been "unmanned," for instance, in terms of self-image and social dominance; he suffers from a "fractured sense of masculine identity"; he has "internalized stereotypes of disability."[22] His wounding may indicate "affiliation with the homosexual and gender role-reversal."[23] His "sexual disability" may reflect male "fear of inadequacy" or, more sweepingly, culture-wide "loss of masculine power and authority ... and social control."[24] Literal or figurative, these are descriptions of secondary effects; the primary effect of Jake's injury is the inability to sire offspring. That inability is the real source, largely unacknowledged as such, of most of the psychosocial disadvantages ascribed to his condition. His wound plays an important symbolic role in the novel because it anchors the emotional, cultural, and spiritual barrenness of the characters—the costs of World War I—in an individualized loss of procreative potential. The postwar world is

---

22 John W. Aldridge, "*The Sun Also Rises,*" 142; Ira Elliott, "Performance Art: Jake Barnes and 'Masculine' Signification" in *The Sun Also Rises,*" in *Ernest Hemingway's "The Sun Also Rises": A Casebook*, ed. Linda Wagner-Martin (Oxford: Oxford University Press, 2002), 71; Dana Fore, "Life Unworthy of Life? Masculinity, Disability, and Guilt in *The Sun Also Rises,*" in *Eight Decades of Hemingway Criticism*, ed. Linda Wagner-Martin (East Lansing: Michigan State University Press, 2009), 50.
23 Elliott, "Performance Art," 71.
24 Wendy Martin, "Brett Ashley as New Woman," 51.

characterized by "a kind of nothingness at its center, a lack—figured most clearly in Jake's wound."[25]

A discrete instance of damage wrought by World War I, the maiming of one man's genitals points implicitly to larger-scale destructive effects: the war has eradicated the source of life itself. All hope of continuity, of regeneration, is lost. On the individual level, Jake suffers the loss of his potential genetic legacy. No replication of his DNA can occur; he will leave no descendents. Evolutionarily, he has been deprived of a future. His situation is echoed in the sense of powerlessness and finality infecting most of the novel's characters—as well as, presumably, a large proportion of the postwar population. Hemingway's fictional people inhabit, Michael S. Reynolds observes, "a world not of their own making" a world tainted by "the broken promises of political leaders" and bereft of any sustaining "system of belief."[26] In one way or another, as Hemingway confided in a letter, "the people [he] wrote of were certainly burned out, hollow and smashed."[27]

Although "life is intrinsically future-oriented," as Trivers points out, the expatriate drifters in *Sun* have lost the ability to act on this fact. Thus they are deprived of the benefits associated with "perceived ability to affect an outcome," including an "optimistic view of the future."[28] Oppressed by what Jake famously describes as "a feeling of things coming that you could not prevent happening," a feeling originating in the recent war, they make little effort to shape their personal life histories beyond the immediate present (146). In a world without a future, action is drained of purpose. "Spiritual bankrupts," as Michael S. Reynolds dubs them, the characters wander from place to place and from drink to drink, leading an alcohol-blurred existence devoid of serious obligation, definitive plan, or optimistic anticipation.[29] Like the old man in "A Clean, Well-Lighted Place," they "utilize" alcohol as an anesthetic to help them "forget, for a moment, the anguish and emptiness at the heart of their existence" (128).[30] The devastation of Jake Barnes's personal procreative potential serves as vivid correlative to the overriding sense of foreclosed possibilities attributed to the war.

---

25 George Cheatham, "'Sign the Wire with Love': The Morality of Surplus in *The Sun Also Rises*," in *Ernest Hemingway's "The Sun Also Rises": A Casebook*, ed. Linda Wagner-Martin (Oxford: Oxford University Press, 2002), 103.

26 Michael S. Reynolds, *"The Sun Also Rises": A Novel of the Twenties* (Boston: Twayne, 1988), 7.

27 Ernest Hemingway to Grace Hemingway, 5 February 1927, in *Selected Letters 1917-1961*, ed. Carlos Baker (New York: Charles Scribner's Sons, 1981), 243.

28 Trivers, "Self-Deception" 285.

29 Reynolds, *"The Sun Also Rises"* 6.

30 Schmigalle, "'How People Go to Hell,'" 10.

The reproductive nada confronting the central couple, Jake and Brett, is a problem that cannot be solved. The novel's plot defies classic outlines by highlighting a never-to-be-resolved predicament. The persistence of that predicament is reflected in the circular structure of the narrative, which begins and ends with the two characters riding in a taxi, without a destination, discussing their thwarted mutual desire. Their relationship has no procreative potential, a personal manifestation of the lost future. In fact, that potential was blasted even before they met: Brett met Jake in the hospital during her wartime nursing service, after he had sustained his injury. The love they cannot consummate represents, even more conspicuously than any of the other pairings in the novel, a futile expenditure of erotic feeling. Because there is no way out of their difficulty, the novel's central action is essentially static, creating "that feeling of going through something that has all happened before" (64). Jake cycles through periods of despair, resignation, and bitterness, while Brett gets involved with one man after another. They agree to keep away from each other but continue, despite that intention, to torture themselves periodically with kisses, close body contact (such as dancing), and intimate conversation.

Jake's and Brett's inability to achieve sexual satisfaction through means other than intercourse is significant. "Isn't there anything we could do about it?" Jake asks, near the beginning of the narrative, when Brett tells him that her tormented desire for him remains unabated (26). She replies that she doesn't "want to go through that hell again," implying that they have tried alternative means of erotic gratification, only to find their frustration exacerbated (26). This insistence that intercourse alone can provide the sought-for release emphasizes the psychological and symbolic centrality of procreation in the novel. It is biological continuity (an ultimate goal) more than sexual passion (a proximate mechanism) that is missing. The suffering caused by unquenched and forever unquenchable erotic desire underlines the sense of futility permeating the book, and the inability of the protagonists to create new life together adds a note of finality to the sweeping depiction of irretrievable waste.[31]

As the character whose injury dramatizes the devastating after-effects of war, Jake offers readers considerable access to his emotional responses and

---

31 Fore analyzes the couple's sexual difficulties from the perspective of proximal pleasure, pointing out that by using nontraditional means of gratification "Brett and Jake *can* end their torment and be together in all senses of the work: sex is not impossible between them." Such a solution to their problems would not, of course, render their relationship reproductively viable. Fore, "Life Unworthy of Life?" 50.

mental outlook. Shortly after the initial taxi ride with Brett, he lies on his bed thinking about his "grievance," a term that suggests he regards himself as the victim of injustice (31). He has been cheated, unexpectedly and ironically, in a war theatre not thought to be particularly perilous: "a joke front like the Italian" (31). From the start, he attempts to distance himself from his predicament with morbid humor: "what happened to me is supposed to be funny" (26).[32] While recovering in the hospital, "all bandaged up," he laughs at the visiting officer who commiserates with his "mala fortuna" and who thanks him for having "given more than [his] life" (31). This visit, he claims, was "the first funny thing" that occurred: "what a speech!" (31). He plans to start "a society" with "a funny name" for all those injured in the same way (31). The usefulness of this harsh, self-directed humor is clear. In addition to keeping grief and self-pity at bay, he makes himself less vulnerable to jokes about castration, impotence, and emasculation by agreeing, in advance, with their premise: "I suppose it was funny" (30).

Jake is not always able to sustain this impervious, self-mocking posture. Stating that his goal is to divert sympathy and attention from his condition ("play along and just not make trouble for people"), he claims it is his overwhelming desire for Brett that has caused him to "realize" fully what he has lost (31). There are times when he can't "keep away" from thinking about her and their never-to-be-fulfilled mutual passion: alone in the dark, he weeps, yielding in private to overwhelming sadness (31). To avoid the pain of such high-pitched emotion (feeling "like hell"), he strives "to be hard-boiled" (34). Like the older waiter in "A Clean, Well-Lighted Place," Jake communicates in this context a jaundiced view of traditional religion. Describing himself as "technically" a Roman Catholic and even "pretty religious," he reveals notable ambivalence toward his supposed faith (124, 209). On the one hand, he visits various cathedrals, churches, and chapels during his trip to Spain; he tells Brett he sometimes has "gotten" things he prayed for; he asserts that Catholicism is "a grand religion" (209, 97). On the other

---

[32] Reynolds notes that "irony and humor are Jake's main defenses." *"The Sun Also Rises,"* 28. For discussion of Jake's "ironic mode" of humor in the context of the many "submerged jokes" in the novel, see James Hinkle's essay, "What's Funny in *The Sun Also Rises*," in *Ernest Hemingway's "The Sun Also Rises": A Casebook* ed. Linda Wagner-Martin (Oxford: Oxford University Press, 2002), 122, 107. Paul Fussell describes how survivors of World War I employed "the mechanism of irony-assisted recall," to lend coherence and significance to their wartime recollections and post-war situations. *The Great War and Modern Memory* (New York: Oxford University Press, 1975), 30.

hand, he questions the genuineness of his faith. In the cathedral at Bayonne, for instance, he recognizes that he is not engaged in true prayer but only "thinking of [himself] as praying" (97). He regrets being "such a rotten Catholic" but concludes there is "nothing to do" about the fact that he does not *feel* "religious" (97).

Jake acknowledges the true cause of his disaffection with his religion in an emotionally intense moment, when he reflects on the counsel the Church offers for dealing with extreme adversity, his own injury serving as a case in point: "The Catholic Church had an awfully good way of handling all that. Good advice, anyway. Not to think about it. Oh it was swell advice. Try and take it sometime. Try and take it" (31). With this sarcastic outburst, he indicts his religion for hypocrisy as well as ineffectualness. The Church has nothing to offer people experiencing catastrophic loss except hollow directives. It does not identify any meaning in suffering or provide solace for it; it recommends instead that sufferers simply attempt to evade their pain: exercise willpower; don't think about it. The uselessness of such "advice" explains why Jake's efforts to continue practicing the religion with which he remains "technically" affiliated bring him no real benefits. The Church has reneged on promises of metaphysical meaning, cosmic justice, and spiritual nourishment.

Disconnected from religious interpretations of human experience, Jake develops a personal philosophy congruent with the self-protective image he cultivates. He analyzes human life in economic terms, embracing an unforgiving pay-as-you-go principle. Everything comes down to "exchange of values": "you gave up something and got something else" (148). Payment can take the form of "work" or "experience" as well as money (148). Living well entails paying the price for "everything that [is] any good" and "learning to get your money's worth" (148). Elevated to a universal principle, "exchange" offers a reassuring, if limited, potential for reciprocity: "You could get your money's worth. The world was a good place to buy in" (148). Applied to the realm of human emotions and relationships, however, this "fine philosophy," as Jake sarcastically dubs it, appears deeply cynical. Even in matters involving love and friendship, as he makes clear, strict rules of "exchange" prevail: empathy, generosity, and affection, for example, play no role. No one ever gets "something for nothing"; in the most intimate of human relationships, "presentation of the bill" is inevitable (148). Jake explains his own case in these terms: because he cannot give Brett what she needs, sexually, he has failed to make proper remuneration for her "friendship" (148). "Delayed" payment is exacted from him in the jealous torments he suffers when Brett satisfies her ardor with other men (99).

Jake is aware that this ruthlessly economic model of behavior, which eliminates emotion from human interaction, flies in the face of psychological reality. Even as he justifies Brett's promiscuity in objective terms, explaining that he has "not been thinking about her side," he displays anger that is incompatible with impersonal principles of exchange. The explosive reproach he utters in the privacy of his room ("To hell with you, Brett Ashley") indicates that the complexities of human emotions cannot be reduced to transactions. Spelling out details of his "fine" philosophy, he invokes sarcasm to mock its supposed fairness, for example "the swell things you could count on" (148). He directs more satiric energy toward his "exchange of values" theory late in the novel, when he offers ironic praise for the "clear financial basis" of life in France (233). In France, he explains, "if you want people to like you" it is necessary "only to spend a little money" (233). Lavish tips, for example, induce recipients to appreciate the giver's "valuable qualities"; they enable the tipper "to make more friends" (233). Friendship is gratifyingly "simple" there because no one ever offers friendship for any "obscure reason" (233).

Redefining genuine liking as an unpleasantly "complicated" and "obscure" phenomenon, Jake employs the satiric technique of false praise to criticize the transactional principles he has claimed to espouse. He acknowledges, even initially, that his pay-as-you-go worldview is merely the most recent in a series of "philosophies" he has employed to assist him in navigating the world and making sense of it. "In five years, I thought, it will seem just as silly as all the other fine philosophies I've had" (148). Questioning the validity of not just one but all possible philosophical systems, including religious orthodoxy, Jake communicates a pessimistic view of the universe, together with human attempts to explain its workings.[33] He has discovered no comprehensive theories or enduring principles to guide his behavior or to sustain him in his personally wretched circumstances.[34] Existentially and philosophically, he is left with nothing, although he does not name it as such. He is another Hemingway protagonist "obsessed by ... the meaninglessness of the world, by nothingness, by nada."[35]

---

33 Bender points out that "Jake Barnes's loneliness derives equally from his sexual and spiritual isolation" but does not suggest a cause-and-effect relationship between the two. *The Descent of Love*, 358.

34 Scott Donaldson offers a more sympathetic analysis of the pay-as-you-go principle, arguing that Hemingway does not share Jake Barnes's disillusionment: "Hemingway, however, did not abandon the code of compensation." "Hemingway's Morality of Compensation," in *Ernest Hemingway's "The Sun Also Rises": A Casebook*, ed. Linda Wagner-Martin (Oxford: Oxford University Press, 2002), 96.

35 Robert Penn Warren, "Hemingway's World," in *Readings on Ernest Hemingway*, ed. Katie De Koster (San Diego, CA: Greenhaven Press, 1997), 38.

Thus Jake disagrees with Brett in the final scene of the novel, when she laments the accidental course of events that has prevented fulfillment of their love: "we could have had such a damned good time together" (247). Jake's sarcastic response, "isn't it pretty to think so?" first of all reflects his disillusioned assessment of Brett's attachment to him.[36] Her avowed love for him persists, as he speculates earlier, chiefly because it cannot be tested: "she only wanted what she couldn't have" (31). Second, and more important, Jake's cynical words, spoken in the final moments of the novel, express a negative view of human psychology and of cosmic design: his pessimism encompasses more than the chance obliteration of his personal sex life and reproductive future. Spelled out more fully, his message is harsh: *Not only have things not turned out according to your wishes, there never was any possibility that they could have; those who harbor the illusion that happier outcomes might have been achieved under different circumstances are simply kidding themselves.* The universe, in Jake's estimate, manifests a marked disinterest in human goals and happiness.

Like the older waiter in "Well-Lighted Place," Jake finds ways to ward off despair. His job as a journalist lends structure and purpose, however mundane, to his daily life. Characters without regular employment, like Brett Ashley or Mike Campbell, fall into more self-destructive patterns of drifting and drinking. Jake's "aficion" for bull-fighting offers a more significant locus of meaning, furthermore, almost the equivalent of a religion (132). He is accepted as an "aficionado" because he has passed "a sort of oral spiritual examination" (131, 132). Aficion is characterized by mystery, like a "very deep secret"; it encompasses respect for the bulls to be killed, as well as for the special bull-fighters who share this quasi-faith (131, 132). Jake immerses himself in its lore and its rites. He subscribes to bull-fighting magazines; he books rooms at the Hotel Montoya, where "all the good bull-fighters stayed"; he accepts the blood sacrifice of horses and steers; he experiences the ritualistic laying-on-of-hands reserved for aficionados: "they wanted to touch" (131, 132). More important, the fight between matador and bull presents Jake with opportunity for sublimation as he watches an artistically crafted, heavily symbolic version of the sexual act he cannot perform.[37]

---

36 Spilka offers explicit paraphrase of Jake's cynical message to Brett: the "damned good time" she imagines they could have enjoyed together is not just something that "can't happen now" but something that "could *never* have happened." "The Death of Love," 43.

37 Reynolds reminds readers that the bull "with his prominent phallus, was and remains the symbol of male virility." Hence "the irony ... of the man without a phallus wedding his identity so closely to a phallic ritual becomes blatant." "*The Sun Also Rises*," 35.

Descriptions of the action in the ring are suggestively erotic, replete with "images of sexual foreplay and consummation."[38] "Getting so close," the matador uses "his body" to entice the bull, "offering the body ... again ... again," but always remaining "unattainable" (218, 168). Teasing the bull with his cape-work, the matador "dominate[s] the bull"; he engages in beautifully compelling foreplay, pleasurably prolonged: "each pass gave you a sudden ache inside" so that "the crowd did not want it ever to be finished" (168, 220). When finally he plunges his sword, phallic-like, into the animal, "for just an instant he and bull were one" (218). Spectators experience a "disturbed emotional feeling," followed by "elation," a combination of tension and release mimicking sexual arousal and climax (164). Jake's intense personal investment in bull-fighting, religious overtones and all, indicates its importance to his psychological equilibrium. The conjunction of sex and death, implicit in a phallic thrust that kills instead of inseminating, speaks to the inevitable preoccupations of a man in his predicament. He derives meaning and satisfaction, however limited or temporary, from the elaborately ritualized act of penetration taking place in the bullring.

Auctorial sympathy in this novel, as in "A Clean, Well-Lighted Place," is directed toward the characters whose philosophical outlook is most pessimistic.[39] Hemingway encourages readers to admire characters with cynical worldviews by endowing them with more admirable qualities than those around them. The older waiter in "A Clean, Well-Lighted Place" demonstrates a more fully developed humanity, for example, than his "confident" junior colleague: he shows sympathy for the deaf old man who wants to sit drinking, urging his colleague to treat their unhappy customer with consideration and respect. Jake Barnes likewise displays a more empathetic nature than do his various friends and acquaintances. He treats people better, on average, than they treat him, displaying a high degree of tolerance for the unpleasantly self-indulgent conduct he frequently encounters. He creates no fuss about Mike Campbell's drunken boorishness or Robert Cohn's physical violence, for instance; he puts up with Brett's forgetfulness and perpetual lateness, not

---

38 Moddelmog, "Contradictory Bodies," 159.

39 Samuel Shaw points out that "the recognition of nothingness, *nada*—the loss of ultimate meaning in life—is Hemingway's starting point not just in *The Sun Also Rises* or "A Clean, Well-Lighted Place," but throughout the body of his work. "Hemingway, Nihilism, and the American Dream," in *Readings on Ernest Hemingway*, ed. Katie De Koster (San Diego, CA: Greenhaven Press, 1997), 74. Hoffman also discusses this issue, observing that "the shadow of *nada* looms behind much of Hemingway's fiction." "*Nada* and the Clean, Well-Lighted Place," 175.

to mention her affairs with other men. Ironically, it is his poor opinion of the human species that accounts for Jake's generally agreeable response to the self-absorbed antics of those around him. "Everybody behaves badly," he explains to Brett when she complains of the "depressing" squabbling between Robert Cohn and Mike Campbell (181). Given "the proper chance," and motivated by strong enough feeling, almost everyone will pursue personal agendas at the expense of kindness and civility (181). Jake's low expectations for his fellow creatures fit well with his cynical weltanshauung. In an inexplicable universe, why would people behave rationally or unselfishly? Anticipating altruism from members of one's social group would be as "silly" as demanding an explanation for cosmic indifference. In creating characters like Jake and the older waiter, Hemingway indirectly provides inducement for readers to align themselves with negative worldviews.

In *The Sun Also Rises*, additionally, title and epigraphs position the author philosophically near to Jake Barnes. The lines quoted from *Ecclesiastes* emphasize human mortality. In contrast to the endless cycling of astronomical and elemental phenomena, organic life is finite: every generation "passeth away" (1:4). Wind and water are described as making "circuits"; they "return again," but this is not true for living beings (1: 6, 7). The finality of death renders all human endeavor pointless: "all *is* vanity" (1:1).[40] Since the strivings and sufferings of each living generation are nullified by death, the emotions that fuel those strivings and sufferings prove mere "vexation of spirit" and likewise serve no enduring purpose (1: 14). Rebuking human self-importance, the opening verses of *Ecclesiastes* communicate a sternly stoic view of human life, a view that hovers on the brink of nihilism. The image of generations succeeding one another (one ... passeth away, and another ... cometh") assumes ironic significance in retrospect: once having finished the novel, readers recognize that generational continuity is precisely what is lacking in the barren environment of *The Sun Also Rises* (1: 4). There is, as already observed, plenty of reproductively motivated activity at the center of the novel's plot—lustful pursuit, sexual intimacy, intrasexual rivalry, masculine jealousy, and intrusive mate guarding—activity that signally fails to accomplish the reproductive ends it evolved to serve.

Picking up on the term "generation," the epigraph attributed to Gertrude Stein underlines the idea that procreative processes have been fatally disrupted.

---

40 Hemingway initially included this verse in the epigraph. In a letter to Maxwell Perkins he directs Perkins to "delete" an unspecified number of verses before and after those he chose to retain (i.e., 4, 5, 6, and 7). Ernest Hemingway to Maxwell Perkins, 19 November 1926, in *Selected Letters 1917-1961*, ed. Carlos Baker (New York: Charles Scribner's Sons, 1981), 229.

She describes the postwar generation as "lost," a comment that lends itself to varied interpretation. Psychosocially, for example, Stein may be referring to widespread loss of moral bearings, of economic security, of shared norms, of religious faith, or of emotional equanimity. In a more literal, biological sense, her comment underlines dismayingly obvious facts: if a whole generation is "lost," in the sense of failing to reproduce, complete extinction of the species must follow. Loss of one generation necessarily entails loss of all. Stein's remark aptly sums up the principal problem in the fictional environment Hemingway portrays: radically diminished prospects for ongoing life.

Together, the two epigraphs to *The Sun Also Rises* compel readers to contemplate death on an increasingly vast scale: individual, generational, and species-wide. The sun may continue to rise and set with dependable regularity, but the human characters confront a procreative dead-end; all sense of forward progression is missing. Instead, they linger in what Jake calls a "nightmare" of repetition (64). This futureless limbo necessarily encompasses loss of the past, since modes of continuance and connection no longer function. Paul Fussell explains that "the Great War took place in what was, compared to ours, a static world, where the values appeared stable and where the meanings of abstractions seemed permanent and reliable."[41] The radically destabilizing effects of the war were social, moral, and metaphysical. Hemingway locates the failure of traditional certainties, figuratively, in procreative failure. Because the fictional characters manifest no explicit interest in descendents, there is no obtrusive insistence on the symbolically central role of propagation. Characters describe their problems and frustrations chiefly in terms of proximal motives: erotic desire postponed, contested, or thwarted. In this respect they behave realistically, since the ultimate purposes of human behavior often elude conscious awareness.[42] Jake and Brett bemoan their inability to achieve sexual satisfaction, for example, rather than their inability to conceive offspring.

Hemingway's readers typically have shared this preoccupation with proximate goals, subjecting characters' sexual yearnings, strategies, and relationships to close scrutiny. Such scrutiny is justified to the extent that sexuality, including an array of adaptive mechanisms and functions, does form a portion of Hemingway's subject matter in *The Sun Also Rises*. Intriguing though that subject matter is, sociopolitically as well as psychologically, it is insufficient by

---

41 Fussell, *The Great War and Modern Memory*, 21.
42 Wright, *Moral Animal*, 388.

itself to support the novel's philosophically bleak thematic center. It is the *fruitlessness* of desire, in all senses of the word, that suffuses the story with bitter irony: the specter of procreative energies expended in vain. The existential despair permeating the fictional environment reflects more than a loss of sexual pleasure: it reflects an irreversible loss of fecundity and thus "the death of value."[43]

In *The Sun Also Rises* Hemingway relies on dramatic exaggeration of both character and situation to communicate a pessimistic worldview. The central predicament in the novel, the stymied union between a sexually insatiable woman and a genitally wounded man, posits macabre extremes. Brett's many affairs, together with the erotically suggestive bull-fights, serve to keep reproductively oriented activity at the forefront of a novel in which there is a complete absence of reproductive results: this contrast similarly verges on the ludicrous. The reason for the focus on extremes is clear: working with the terms of his central metaphor, Hemingway is striving for equivalence between vehicle (sexual frustration and reproductive failure) and tenor (metaphysical frustration and cosmic emptiness). Biological nihility will support philosophical nihilism adequately only if the sexual and reproductive problems experienced by the fictional characters are extraordinary. The result is a plot in which a woman who can't get enough sex falls in love with a sexually nonfunctional man, subplots in which an amorous woman sleeps with almost every man in sight yet never conceives a child. When there is no conception or birth, and no prospect of any, all human enterprise, including mating efforts and sexual competition, is rendered pointless. Thus the older waiter in "A Clean, Well-Lighted Place" anchors his nihilistic metaphysics in the image of Mary's empty womb, "full of nothing." Failure of biological continuity voids all human purpose; it signals, literally, the end of the line. The reproductive nada at the heart of plot and theme in both narratives conveys, as no other symbolic figuration could, a sense of overriding futility. Evolutionary analysis does not offer reasons for Hemingway's despairing philosophical stance; it demonstrates, rather, how he gives literary shape and force to his existential themes. Grounding cultural and cosmic discontents in the most basic of human concerns—procreation—he maximizes their impact.

---

43 Sam S. Baskett, "'An Image to Dance Around': Brett and Her Lovers in *The Sun Also Rises*," *Centennial Review*, 22 (1978), 69.

CHAPTER 11

Paternal Confidence in Hurston's "The Gilded Six-Bits"

Zora Neal Hurston's 1933 short story, "The Gilded Six-Bits," highlights male mating behavior. The plot addresses a husband's reactions to his wife's infidelity, emphasizing the importance of paternal confidence in long-term commitment. The possibility that an unfaithful wife will give birth to a child sired by her extramarital partner represents an evolutionarily grave risk for her husband: if he provides care and resources for a child to whom he is not biologically related, he helps to perpetuate another's genes rather than his own.[1] Existing commentary on the story has not focused on the evolutionary implications of female adultery, however. Readers instead have emphasized tensions the story explores between variously defined oppositions: between "real" and "false" values,[2] for example, between appearance and reality,[3] between country and city,[4] between material and non-material wealth,[5] between Caucasian and

---

1   Buss, *Evolution of Desire*, 10, 67; Dawkins, *Selfish Gene*, 148; Trivers, "Parental Investment and Reproductive Success," 76.
2   Pearlie Mae Fisher Peters, "Missie May in 'The Gilded Six-Bits,'" in *The Assertive Woman in Zora Neale Hurston's Fiction, Folklore, and Drama*, (New York: Garland Publishing, 1998), 89-95.
3   Norman German, "Counterfeiting and a Two-Bit Error in Zora Neale Hurston's 'The Gilded Six-Bits,'" *Xavier Review* 19, no. 2 (1999).
4   Nancy Chinn and Elizabeth E. Dunn, "'The Ring of Singing Metal on Wood': Zora Neale Hurston's Artistry in 'The Gilded Six-Bits,'" *Mississippi Quarterly: The Journal of Southern Cultures* 49, no. 4 (1996). http://web.ebscohost.com.online.library.marist.edu.htm, accessed February 2, 2008; Evora W. Jones, "The Pastoral and Picaresque in Zora Neale Hurston's 'The Gilded Six-Bits,'" *College Language Association Journal* 35, no. 3 (1992).
5   Henry Louis Gates, Jr. and Sieglinde Lenke, "Zora Neale Hurston: Establishing the Canon," in *Zora Neale Hurston: The Complete Stories* (New York: Harper Perennial, 2008); Cheryl A. Wall, introduction to *"Sweat": Zora Neale Hurston*, ed. Cheryl A. Wall (New Brunswick, NJ: Rutgers University Press, 1997).

African-American systems of valuation.[6] Though presentation of such themes likely forms part of Hurston's auctorial intention, she clearly signals paternity as the central concern in her narrative. Insights from evolutionary biological theory enable readers to explore that concern, together with its implications.

As David M. Buss points out, human males are confronted "with a unique paternity problem not faced by other primate males"; concealed ovulation in the human female means there is no overtly recognizable cause-and-effect connection between copulation and pregnancy.[7] Lacking observable proof that his mating efforts, rather than another man's, have caused impregnation, the individual male possesses no definitive evidence that he is the biological father of a partner's offspring. (Since gestation occurs within their own bodies, women, obviously, harbor no equivalent doubts about their genetic relationship to offspring.) To reduce the degree of paternal uncertainty inherent in their situation, and to maximize the evolutionary appropriateness of their parental investment, human males demand female sexual fidelity, since it offers the best possible guarantee that a woman's acknowledged mate has in fact sired her children.[8] Consequently, evidence that a woman has allowed sexual access to other men tends to dilute or end her partner's mating commitment.[9] Exploring the psychology of the betrayed husband, Hurston's narrative offers insight into the workings of adaptive mechanisms designed to counteract the threat to male fitness posed by female adultery.

The featured couple is working-class: Joe Banks brings home weekly wages from the G and G Fertilizer company, where he works the night shift. Small details sufficiently indicate that the job involves hard manual labor in filthy conditions, for Joe is tired when he returns home and in need of a bath; periodically he complains of pains in his back. Resources are not plentiful, clearly, and this is an important factor in the development of character and plot. The interaction Hurston selects to demonstrate the vitality of this young marriage (Joe and Missie May have been married just over a year) is a ritual in which Joe hands over all his pay to his wife. He first flings silver dollars through

---

6   Hildegard Hoeller, "Racial Currency: Zora Neale Hurston's 'The Gilded Six-Bits' and the Gold-Standard Debate," *American Literature* 77, no. 4 (2005); Wall, introduction.
7   Buss, *Evolution of Desire*, 66.
8   Ibid., 67; Trivers, "Parental Investment and Reproductive Success," 170.
9   Buss, *Evolution of Desire*, 67; Daly and Wilson, "Evolutionary Psychology," 16.

the doorway, "for her to pick up and pile beside her plate."[10] She responds with mock reproach, which ends in a joyful, erotically charged scuffle as she searches his pockets for small gifts he pretends to withhold from her, "things he had hidden there for her to find" (88). "A furious mass of male and female energy," they engage in "tussling" and "tickling," a "friendly battle" that bears witness to the couple's energetic sexual relationship (87, 88).

Introducing readers to Joe and Missie May, this lovingly described encounter illustrates with great clarity the evolutionary psychology of long-term mating, from the point of view of both sexes. The man invests his resources in his mate, indicating the intensity and enthusiasm of his commitment by the manner in which he transfers wealth to her. This is no cut-and-dried, 'here's your housekeeping money for the week' exchange. Joe's behavior emphasizes that there are no limits to his willingness to invest in Missie May. Playfully prodigal, he in effect announces to her, 'here is all my money; I throw it at your feet; I reserve nothing; I put it entirely at your disposal.' By supplying her with some resources in the shape of gifts with particular appeal to her femininity (small luxuries such as chewing gum or scented soap), he further underlines his desire to please her. The most important luxury item he purchases for her is a bag of "candy kisses," which metaphorically links the proffered resources with the sexual satisfactions the relationship so obviously provides (88). Joe supplements material generosity with verbal expressions of his devotion. "So long as Ah be yo' husband, Ah don't keer 'bout nothin' else," he assures her, for example (91). His strategy for preserving his marriage combines the "provision of resources" with the expression of "love and kindness," features that Buss identifies as key ingredients in the enterprise of long-term mating.[11]

The plot proper begins with a new outlay of expense intended to please Missie May, when Joe proposes an outing to a "real swell" new ice cream parlor (89). Its proprietor, Mr. Otis D. Slemmons, has impressed Joe and other local men with his fine clothes, gold teeth, and prosperous, cosmopolitan air. A combination of conspicuous wealth and success with women makes him the object of general male envy. He wears gold coins (five- and ten-dollar pieces) as personal adornment, on his stick-pin and watch chain, at the same time letting it be known that "all de womens is crazy 'bout him" and that this is the source of his wealth: "womens give it all to 'im" (90). Slemmon's self-presentation appeals

---

10 Zora Neale Hurston, "The Gilded Six-Bits," in *Zora Neale Hurston: The Complete Stories*, with an introduction by Henry Louis Gates, Jr. and Sieglinde Lenke (New York: Harper Perennial, 2008), 87. All citations refer to this edition.
11 Buss, *Evolution of Desire*, 132.

very obviously to male fantasies, for it blatantly reverses the usual relationship between male wealth and female willingness. Instead of having to invest resources in order to enjoy sexual intimacy with women, Slemmons avers that women supply the resources in compensation for sexual access to *him*. The picture he paints compels his listeners' belief, if only temporarily, because it represents male wish-fulfillment. *Midnight Cowboy* offers another variation on this fantasy, as readers may recall, and that film's plot hinges on the unrealistic nature of the protagonist's expectations. Not participating in the collective desire of Slemmons's male audience to give credence to his boasts, Missie May responds with telling skepticism to the tales her husband has accepted so uncritically. "How you know dat, Joe?" she demands, arguing that Slemmons's mere word "don't make it so .... He kin lie jes' lak anybody else" (90).

It is difficult—if not, indeed, impossible—to think of any human culture in which fertile young women offer material inducements in order to enjoy erotic encounters with men. (Dowry systems pose an exception, not relevant here, of course, and Slemmons seems in any case to be referring to short-term mating opportunities rather than to the long-term, contractual relationships regulated by female dowries; see Daly and Wilson.[12]) Because of their biological role in reproduction, including critical facts about egg size, gestation period, and lifetime reproductive potential, females command uniquely "valuable resources."[13] Except in unusual instances, therefore, they do not need to offer men any inducement beyond sexual opportunity itself, which is in and of itself precious.[14] Joe and his fellows nonetheless are hoodwinked by Slemmons's improbable claims. Overwhelmed by his show of wealth to a degree that prevents them from criticizing its manifest boastfulness, they are disposed to take the impressive stranger at his own value. They are further dazzled by the irresistible appeal of the fantasy he represents, a scenario in which women eagerly offer themselves—and their resources—to a uniquely attractive man. Each one of them would like to be that man and enjoy such advantages—to be freed, in short, from the usual rules of the Darwinian game and find himself holding all the cards.

Hildegard Hoeller argues that since Slemmons has been receiving money from white women in exchange for sex, he has in effect sold himself in a

---

12 Daly and Wilson, *Sex, Evolution*, 289-290, 322.
13 Buss, *Evolution of Desire*, 20.
14 Ibid., 20, 86.

humiliating, perhaps parodistic, re-enactment of slavery.[15] The fraudulence of Slemmons's claims constitutes an important obstacle to Hoeller's interpretation, however, on two different counts. First, if he had been successful in selling his sexual services to wealthy women, he would not be so quick to alter his tactics with Missie May—to whom he promises "gold" in return for *her* favors. Second, if large numbers of women had been giving him money, his boast that he has "money 'cumulated" would be true (90); his prosperity would be genuine rather than pretended. Once his wealth is revealed as sham, his claims that women—of any race or ethnicity—have given him money are exposed as false.

Joe escorts Missie May to the new ice cream parlor with more than one motive. In addition to wishing to give her pleasure, he desires to show her off to the shop's apparently high-status proprietor. Presenting his attractive wife to Slemmons is an act of competitive male display on Joe's part, proof that he has been able to attract an enviable mate of his own.[16] "He talkin' 'bout his pretty women—Ah wants 'im to see *mine*" (90-91). He appears to achieve that goal, for Slemmons expresses admiration for Missie May and, implicitly, for the man who can clam long-term access to her: "Ah have to hand it to you, Joe" (91). Joe's triumph is tinged with irony, however, for he has drawn the interest of a womanizer to his wife's attractions. Slemmons begins an intensive pursuit of Missie May, a pursuit he conducts along more ordinary lines than those he has boasted of to the men in town. Indeed, the tactics Slemmons employs in his pursuit of Missie May effectively give the lie to his earlier bragging. It is evident that he does not expect her to supplement her personal charms with anything of material value; rather, he frankly offers her his money in return for sexual favors. "He said he wuz gointer give me dat gold money," she later explains, "and he jes' kep on after me—" (94). In this brief affair, readers observe evolved adaptations at work: courted by a man who appears to offer vastly more resources than her current mate, a woman decides it is in her interest to accept his attentions. As Buss points out, "immediate extraction of resources is a key adaptive benefit that women secure through affairs".[17]

---

15   Hoeller, "Racial Currency," 772, 775.
16   Ibid., 771.
17   Buss, *Evolution of Desire*, 87.

Newcomers to evolutionary biological theory may be disconcerted by the idea of women exchanging sexual favors for resources. Initially, certainly, the notion can seem retrograde and anti-feminist, presenting an unpleasantly acquisitive picture of women. A number of readers have expressed discomfort with Missie May's apparent "prostitution" of herself, either within her marriage (as witnessed by the silver coins Joe tosses in her direction every week) or in the context of her affair, undertaken for the sake of "gold money" (94).[18] Even a cursory consideration of women's situation in the ancestral environment, however, suggests why women had to consider a potential mate's resources before engaging in sexual activity. A single sexual encounter might lead to conception, and a woman left to survive pregnancy, lactation, and child-rearing on her own, without resources in the shape of assistance, provisions, shelter, and the like, would be unlikely to succeed in the reproductive enterprise. Throughout most of human history, the connection between available resources and offspring survival has been incontrovertible. If the politically and economically pernicious effects of evolved sexual strategies are to be effectively counteracted in a contemporary, post-industrial environment, moreover, they must be recognized and acknowledged. As Buss explains, "an evolutionary perspective on sexual strategies provides valuable insights into the origins and maintenance of men's control of resources and men's attempts to control women's sexuality."[19] Elsewhere Buss describes "possible points of congruence between feminist and evolutionary perspectives," and Anne Campbell has undertaken a careful, point-by-point comparative analysis of feminist and evolutionary theory.[20] Barbara Smuts explores intellectual and political tensions between the two theoretical systems, as do Kenrich, Trost, and Sheets.[21] Griet Vandermassen's detailed consideration of feminism in the context of evolutionary biology also is illuminating in this context.[22]

---

18 See, for instance, Chinn and Dunn, "The Ring of Singing Metal," 3; Hoeller, "Racial Currency," 772-73; German, "Counterfeiting," 5, 11-12.
19 Buss, *Evolution of Desire*, 212.
20 Buss, "Sexual Conflict," 296; Campbell, *A Mind of Her Own*, 12-33.
21 Smuts, "Male Aggression"; Douglas T. Kenrick, Melanie R. Trost, and Virgil L. Sheets. "Power, Harassment, and Trophy Mates: The Feminist Advantages of an Evolutionary Perspective," in *Sex, Power, Conflict: Evolutionary and Feminist Perspectives*, ed. David M. Buss and Neil M. Malamuth, (New York and Oxford: Oxford University Press, 1996).
22 Griet Vandermassen, *Who's Afraid of Charles Darwin? Debating Feminism and Evolutionary Theory* (Lanham, MD: Rowan and Littlefield, 2005).

Because readers do not watch the progress of the courtship but are presented, like Joe, with a sudden fait accompli when Slemmons and Missie May are discovered in bed, it is difficult to assess her motives step-by-step. From the outset she expresses doubts about the newcomer's self-proclaimed prowess with women ("Whyn't he stay up dere where dey so crazy 'bout 'im?") and hints at vague plans for procuring some of his wealth: "Us might find some [gold] goin' long de road some time" (90, 91). Such remarks leave readers with the impression that her affair may be motivated by the desire to transfer Slemmons's wealth to her husband. This explanation of her behavior is supported by her grief-stricken tears when Joe catches her in the act of adultery and by her subsequent remorseful conduct. Insisting that she loves Joe "so hard," she appears genuinely devastated by the loss of his trust and affection (94). There is evidence, in sum, that she has not been infatuated by Slemmons's apparent wealth and status, that she feels no love for him and never aspired to become his long-term partner. Instead, she may be exchanging her sexual favors quite deliberately for "dat gold money," intending to present it to her husband; at one point she avers that the gold coins would "look a whole heap better" on Joe (91). Thus she perhaps justifies her adulterous behavior, in her own mind, as an act intended to enrich her marriage rather than imperil it, "a sin committed out of her love for Joe."[23] Trivers's analysis of self-deception is relevant here, as readers attempt to sort out the tangled layers of Missie May's conscious and unconscious intentions.[24]

There is no getting around the fact that if she grants secret sexual access to a short-term partner in order to bring new resources to her marriage, Missie May risks lowering her husband's lifetime reproductive success. If Slemmons fathers her first child, the total number of children Joe might conceive with her will have been reduced by one. No matter how generously her motives are interpreted, the consequences of Missie May's infidelity—in terms of fitness—are not nearly so damaging for her as for her husband. The logic of her intentions, very likely not consciously articulated, seems clear when examined from a Darwinian perspective. If she becomes pregnant by Slemmons, she risks giving birth to a lower-quality child than she could have conceived with Joe, perhaps, but the child will still be hers. Self-interest therefore might suggest to her that the risk of impregnation by Slemmons is outweighed by the advantage of access to his money. If her affair is not discovered, Joe is likely to

---

23 Peters, "Missie May," 93.
24 Trivers, "Self-Deception," 271-86.

acknowledge and support the child without suspecting that he might not be its father—a course of action obviously "contrary to [his] own interest" but highly "adaptive" from Missie May's point of view.[25] Meanwhile that child, along with any others later sired by Joe, will enjoy the benefits of the unexpected resources Missie May has extracted from a short-term affair. If Slemmons's wealth had been real, rather than feigned, her decision to seize this opportunity to ensure a more financially secure future for her offspring might have made a positive difference in her fitness and that of her progeny.

As long as the affair remains undetected, and so long as her short-term partner gives a woman otherwise unavailable resources, she stands to reap benefits in fitness. The poorer the woman, the more true this is: a larger percentage of her children is likely to survive and thrive if more food, better shelter, enhanced medical care, or improved vocational opportunities flow to her family through a wealthy extramarital partner. Missie May and Joe belong to the class of the working poor, after all; a woman compelled to dry herself after bathing with a "meal sack" might with reason prove susceptible to the blandishments of a prosperous suitor (87). Disclosure of the affair threatens the stability of the marriage (and this is the principal risk Missie May assumes in accepting Slemmons's attentions) precisely because a wife's adultery stands to decrease her husband's fitness. Missie May's cost-benefit analysis, as she weighs the pros and cons of an affair with a supposedly rich suitor, scarcely will coincide with Joe's. Even a small risk that his wife might conceive a child with another man would be unacceptable from a husband's point of view.[26] He is unlikely to regard resource-extraction from her partner in adultery as adequate compensation for the loss he will suffer in numbers of copies of genes passed on to the next generation.

In terms of plot development, Missie May's strong desire to preserve her marriage is crucial. Once detected in an adulterous liaison, she assumes a posture of dignified remorse, cooking and cleaning with energetic dedication while hoping her husband will accept her contrition and renew his trust in her. After the discovery scene, in which Joe strikes Slemmons and wrests the gold piece from his watch chain, the omniscient narrator shifts the focus of attention to Missie May. In consequence, readers observe the operation of male jealousy, defined by Buss as the psychological mechanism "our ancestors evolved ... for solving the paternity problem" through the eyes of the woman at whom it is

---

25 Trivers, "Parental Investment and Reproductive Success," 76.
26 Buss, *Evolution of Desire*, 66-67.

directed.[27] Joe's initial reaction to the sight of another man in bed with his wife is a stunned incredulity ("the great belt in the wheel of Time slipped"), followed closely by "fury" (93): "he had both chance and time to kill ... but he was too weak to take action" (93). He lands a couple of punches and sends the man on his way, caught in a kind of emotional paralysis, "feeling so much and not knowing what to do with all his feelings" (94). The powerful emotions Joe experiences in this moment illustrate the essential elements of male sexual jealousy, including rage and aggression.[28]

In the weeks and months following this confrontation with Slemmons, Joe says nothing to his wife about his feelings or plans. Consistently "polite," but "aloof," he refrains from questioning her about the affair, just as he reveals nothing about his future intentions (95). He maintains the "outside show" of their marriage, going through the motions of ordinary chores and activities with two significant exceptions (96): he ceases their sexual relations and he stops handing over resources. "There were no more Saturday romps. No ringing silver dollars to stack beside her plate" (95). With the passage of time, he finds himself unable to maintain his sexual reserve: a backrub after "three months" of abstinence leads to further intimacy, and "youth triumphed" (95). Missie May anticipates that sexual contact will facilitate reconciliation but finds herself mistaken: Joe maintains emotional distance. He makes his position painfully clear by leaving the gold coin he has yanked off his rival's watch chain underneath her pillow, as if in payment for the sexual encounter.

Only at this point does Missie May learn what Joe has known ever since he acquired the trophy: it is not a real ten-dollar gold coin at all but merely a gilded fifty-cent piece. Given the story's composition date in 1933, some readers are inclined to interpret the gilded coin in the context of the Great Depression and the gold-standard debate.[29] "Making money and the desire for money became national concerns," Chinn and Dunn argue. "Popular songs, fiction, and movies throughout the 1930's celebrated the lives of the rich and the famous," they point out, suggesting that Hurst uses "gilded money and Otis T. Slemmons to explore the misguided belief that material goods would bring happiness."[30] Hoeller explores the possibility that Hurston forges the emphatic silver-gold contrast in the story in order to voice her critique of the "the gold standard and

---

27 Ibid., 126.
28 Buss, *Evolutionary Psychology*, 294-95.
29 Chinn and Dunn, "The Ring of Singing Metal"; Hoeller, "Racial Currency."
30 Chinn and Dunn, "The Ring of Singing Metal," 3.

its insistence on the supremacy and universality of white values (and white civilization)."[31] These readers make a well-wrought case that Hurston is taking on broad-based sociopolitical and economic issues in her story. The presence of such concerns does not, of course, alter the biosocial implications of the gilded coins as a male resource. Any political or economic statement is secondary to the biologically fundamental issues that so clearly dominate the story's content and shape its plot.

Since Missie May's affair with Slemmons was motivated, on her own admission, by the resources he promised her ("he was gointer give me dat gold money"), it is humiliating for her to find that those resources were all sham. There never was any benefit to be gained by an involvement with Slemmons, and she has jeopardized her marriage to Joe for nothing. Slemmons's success in impressing her with his supposedly magnificent resources illustrates the "evolutionary arms race between deception perpetrated by one sex and detection accomplished by the other."[32] In this instance, a woman has been insufficiently alert to deceptive male tactics. Readers infer that Joe takes some satisfaction in passing on this ironic information to Missie May; he assuages his anger with his wife by demonstrating how she has been duped. Presenting her with the counterfeit coin also enables him to express his resentment of her disloyalty via insult, since by offering payment for sex he implies that he regards her as a promiscuous woman whose favors are for sale. "He had come home to buy from her as if she were any woman in the long house. Fifty cents for her love. As if to say that he could pay as well as Slemmons" (96). Joe's unflattering message is that Missie May has ceased to belong to the Madonna-like category of women, characterized by premarital chastity and post-marital sexual fidelity, to whom men make long-term commitments. Her adulterous behavior positions her, instead, in the ranks of promiscuous women with whom men seek only short-term liaisons.[33]

Missie May returns the counterfeit gold coin as wordlessly as it is given, by placing it in Joe's clothing. Her message to him is as clear as his to her: she indicates that she is providing him with sexual intimacy out of marital love rather than for pay. The coin looms large in her imagination, an object inspiring fear and loathing; it is "a monster hiding in the cave of his pockets to destroy her" (95). She interprets Joe's use of it to torment her as "her punishment" (96). An important effect of Joe's punitive action, clearly, is to

---

31 Hoeller, "Racial Currency," 780.
32 Buss, *Evolution of Desire*, 155.
33 Smuts, "Male Aggression," 252; Trivers, "Parental Investment and Reproductive Success," 74.

convince his wife that he will not tolerate sexual transgressions. If he were to offer her quick or easy forgiveness, he would risk licensing future extramarital escapades on her part. In any cooperative alliance, as Dawkins points out in his analysis of tit-for-tat strategies, it is necessary that individuals be "punished for defection" or cheating will become rampant.[34] Another effect of Joe's behavior is to test the degree of Missie May's commitment to him. Without resorting to either rudeness or violence, he nevertheless succeeds in making his wife extremely uncomfortable. She has no idea when, if ever, his withholding behavior and silent rebukes will end. By putting up with an extended period of coldness and by suffering the insults represented by the coin, she acknowledges fault, communicates remorse, and affirms loyalty. The longer Joe tests her, the more convincingly she proves that the marriage is valuable to her and that she is willing to endure discomfort to win back his trust. Both partners in the marriage are engaged in a waiting game. Joe is waiting to see whether Missie May will offer adequate proof of ongoing commitment, while she in turn is waiting to see when and if his resentment of her fault will be healed. Psychologically, this waiting makes sense on both sides: the rift caused by Joe's mistrust can be repaired only gradually, as Missie May's "displays of fidelity" over time provide persuasive evidence of her renewed commitment to sexual exclusiveness.[35]

The plot takes another turn at this point, as Hurston introduces an evolutionarily critical complication: Joe observes that his wife is showing signs of pregnancy. Before the incident with Slemmons, he had been wishing for exactly this state of affairs: "He thought about children. ... A little boy child would be about right" (92). Now, of course, his wife's pregnancy is a source of great ambivalence for him. Whose child is she carrying? Neither Joe nor the reader knows for certain whether Missie May's affair with Slemmons involved more than the single sexual encounter that Joe interrupts. There is no evidence, certainly, that they were together often or long. It is possible, of course, that conception occurred on the one occasion when Joe found her in bed with Slemmons. His wife's pregnancy therefore poses a fitness-related dilemma for Joe. If the baby is his, he longs to nurture it and its mother; if it is Slemmons's baby, he has no such wishes. Joe takes over the heavy chores ("you ain't got no business choppin' wood, and you know it," he avers), a precautionary move to safeguard the health of a fetus that may well be his (96). At the same time,

---

34 Dawkins, *Selfish Gene*, 227.
35 Buss, *Evolution of Desire*, 114.

however, he lets his wife know that he remains wary of investing in this pregnancy. Questioning her assertion that the baby will be sure to resemble him ("You reckon?"), he fingers the gilded coin he still keeps in his pocket. This serves as a deliberate reminder of her infidelity, making his reservations, and their cause, unmistakably plain.

From readers' point of view, it should be noted, there is a frustrating element of imprecision in the timeline of Missie May's pregnancy. Joe notices the pregnancy at about the three-and-a-half-month mark, since she gives birth "almost six months later" (96). A vague reference to passage of time between the resumption of their conjugal relations and his observation of her condition introduces a slight question as to whether more than nine months elapse between her affair and the birth of the child: "the sun swept around the horizon, trailing its robes of weeks and days" (95-96). Joe's openly expressed doubts about the child's paternity offer evidence that readers are expected to interpret those "trailing ... robes" of time as a relatively brief period—that is, less than a month. Joe can do the arithmetic for himself, obviously, and his continued worries indicate that numerical calculations alone will not suffice to eliminate Slemmons from the running as father. Quite apart from any nine-month countdown, moreover, the suspicions awakened by his wife's infidelity work to create a generalized distrust on Joe's part: a wife guilty on one occasion of sexual disloyalty may prove so again. For the best of reasons Joe's anxieties about paternity loom large.

German reads the "trailing ... robes of weeks and days" as a fairly extensive period of time, and he concludes that Joe is sure Slemmons *cannot* be the baby's father (10).[36] Such a reading is undermined by Joe's openly articulated concerns about the child's paternity; it introduces a further temporal complication, moreover. If the vaguely denoted "weeks and days" represent any amount of time between four and ten weeks, then Joe absolutely cannot be the father, since conception would have occurred during the three-month period of conjugal abstinence. It seems likely, on balance, that the confusion generated by the narrator's reference to "weeks and days" is accidental and that the more definitely noted time periods (e.g., three months, six months) are those to which readers are expected to attend.

Hurston assigns to Joe's mother the central role in relieving his doubts. Because a man's relatives also stand to lose if he invests in offspring not his own, it is adaptive for them to maintain a watchful, even suspicious attitude

---

36 German, "Counterfeiting," 10.

in response to the problem of paternal uncertainty. After all, Joe's relatives will suffer decreased inclusive fitness if he spends years supporting a child conceived by Otis T. Slemmons. Because they share genes with Joe, if he sires fewer children as a result of being cuckolded they, too, suffer a loss. Any assistance to that child given by grandparents, aunts or uncles on Joe's side of the family (and such assistance from extended family is, of course, common in human societies) similarly would be misplaced, if Joe accepts as his own another man's child.[37] One commonplace response to the adaptive problem faced by paternal relatives is the tendency of maternal relatives to suggest that an infant resembles its father, or some member of the father's family, presumably with the unconscious hope of allaying fears that might short-circuit paternal investment.[38]

Just as it is in the interest of relatives on the maternal side to insist that there can be no possible question about the identity of the father, however, it is in the interest of relatives on the paternal side to remain vigilant to the possibility of cuckoldry. Because Joe's mother belongs to the naturally suspicious set of paternal relatives, her announcement to him that the newborn baby is "'de spittin' image of yuh, son'" carries weight (97). She underlines her conviction with notable insistence, telling him "if you never git another one, dat un is yourn" (97). Similar statements from Missie May's mother would lack the persuasive force of this testimony from Joe's. There is no reason for Joe's mother to imagine a resemblance that is not there; indeed, she has a genetic stake in remaining objective in her assessment of the baby's appearance. Hurston also has provided evidence in her text that Missie May's mother-in-law was displeased from the start by her son's choice of a wife, judging her to be potentially promiscuous—for example, to "fan her foot around" and "get misput on her road" (97). Very evidently, her statements about the child are not motivated by any personal affection for her daughter-in-law, or by more generalized loyalty to her sex. Rather, the doubts she harbors about Missie May's character make her particularly apt to question the paternity of a putative grandchild. Her pre-existing bias against her daughter-in-law renders her assurances to Joe all the more convincing.

Gayl Jones's comment that "the story is perhaps resolved too simply at this point, the '*baby chile*' being a kind of *deus ex machina*," misses the point.[39]

---

37 Buss, *Evolutionary Psychology*, 236, 249; Dawkins, *Selfish Gene*, 186.
38 D. Kelly McLain et al., "Ascription of Resemblance of Newborns by Parents and Nonrelatives," *Evolution and Human Behavior* 21 (2000): 21-22.
39 Gayl Jones, "Breaking out of the Conventions of Dialect: Dunbar and Hurston," *Présence Africaine: Revue Culturelle du Monde Noir* 144 (1987): 41.

The birth of a baby resembling Joe resolves the plot for good reason: it resolves as, indeed, nothing else can, the paternal uncertainty which constitutes the major source of conflict in the story. Joe is in conflict with Slemmons, who has diverted his wife's sexual attentions and reproductive potential away from her marriage. Joe also is in conflict with Missie May, who has been sexually disloyal and who now may be trying to trick him into supporting another man's child. Finally, Joe is in conflict with himself: desperately ambivalent, he yearns to forgive but seethes with mistrust. The child is no narrative contrivance but an essential means of relieving Joe's doubts and enabling him to continue his long-term commitment to Missie May. If there is a hint of artifice in the story's conclusion, it is Joe's mother, rather than the baby, who plays the role of deus ex machina. Her assurances of Joe's paternity make it possible for him to accept his wife's child as his own and renew his marital commitment. His mother's unsought testimony, offered at just the right moment to allay Joe's painful suspicions, may strike some readers as a little too convenient.

Confirmation of paternity thus serves as the resolution of the story's plot. In the starkest biological terms, what is at stake, more than individual happiness or the sanctity of marriage, is the passing on of genes. Readers can only speculate about what might have happened to Joe's and Missie May's relationship if his mother had not volunteered such a strong conviction that Joe is the father of his wife's baby. In the absence of certainty on that point, his commitment to the marriage might be expected to waver. The happy ending Hurston depicts is possible only because the husband is confident that he will be investing in a child carrying his genes. Hildegard Hoeller argues that Joe has no "essential proof [of paternity] that goes beyond the surface appearance," dismissing the testimony of Joe's mother. Hoeller goes on to voice admiration for Joe's willingness to accept the baby "as his own"; he "makes the baby his own currency."[40] While it is true that his mother's pronouncement does not constitute absolute proof of Joe's paternity, he accepts it as such. The movement of the plot strongly supports her assurances, moreover, reaching its climax in the moment when she avers that the baby is "de spittin' image" of Joe. Only then, encouraged by a close kinswoman who also has a vested interest in unmasking false candidates for his investment, does he effect a reconciliation with his wife. Hurston provides ample evidence of Joe's conviction that he is the biological father—behavioral indicators as well as verbal testimony. His certainty on this point is necessarily subjective, but it is unmistakable. Storyline and plot

---

40 Hoeller, "Racial Currency," 777.

development lose their meaning if readers interpret Joe's parental pride at the story's conclusion as altruism rather than as fitness-enhancing behavior.

The importance of this issue is clear: readers must notice, for instance, that Missie May is guilty of adultery no matter who fathered her child. The fact that Joe, rather than Slemmons, impregnated her is irrelevant, ethically speaking. Joe can forgive her, evidently, if her sexual disloyalty will have no negative impact on his genetic legacy. Readers must suspect that if the baby had looked like a tiny Otis, Joe's forgiveness would not have been forthcoming. If Joe is biding his time, as noted earlier, for adequate proof of Missie May's remorse and commitment, he is also awaiting the outcome of the pregnancy. If Missie May were to miscarry, or if the child were to be stillborn, for example, then its paternity would be irrelevant. In such a case, if he were sufficiently convinced of his wife's future loyalty Joe might continue in his marriage without worrying about Slemmons's threat to his lineage. In the case of a live birth, there is hope, but no guarantee, that the child's appearance will settle the issue of paternity. In an era before genetic testing was available, the most convincing proofs of kinship were provided by signs of physical resemblance.

Once his mother has come forward to settle the question of paternity, Joe resumes investing resources in his wife. In addition to bringing home a large supply of groceries ("all the staples"), he once again flings his pay, fifteen silver dollars, through the doorway (97). He cashes in Slemmon's counterfeit coin, furthermore, spending the fifty cents on "candy kisses" for Missie May (98). This act signals his wish for a full reconciliation. Disposing of the evidence of Missie May's adultery, he indicates that he will no longer use the coin as an instrument of reproach. Purchasing "gifts of eroticized food" with that same coin, he expresses his desire to renew their sexual intimacy, in all its joyful vitality.[41] When the store clerk suggests that fifty cents worth of molasses kisses is an absurdly large quantity, advising Joe to "take some chocolate bars too," Joe refuses; only an extravagant gesture will do (98). All of Slemmons's money must be spent on "kisses" that illustrate the connection between female reproductive energies and the expenditure of male resources. Like Ado Annie's suitor in *Oklahoma,* Joe indicates that he is an all-or-nothing man: the prodigality of his outlay communicates the message that he will put *all* available resources at his wife's disposal, with the expectation that she, for her part, will channel *all* her reproductive energy toward him.

---

41 Ibid., 774.

Joe's conversation with the store clerk from whom he purchases the candy and other provisions also shows him making efforts to deflect the social humiliation associated with cuckoldry. He describes Slemmons as "a stray nigger" who offended Joe with his boastful manners and pretensions to wealth (97). He even adds that Slemmons was "tryin' to tole off folkses wives from home," a detail he might have suppressed unless he fears that word of Slemmons's womanizing has spread (98). The clerk responds by asking, "did he fool you, too?" raising the possibility that Joe has been deceived by Slemmons's mate-poaching activities as well as by his phony gold (98). Joe offers an emphatic denial, claiming that he "knocked 'im down" and seized the gilded coin simply because he was irritated by the stranger's braggadocio, or "smart talk" (98). He makes a point, as well, of affirming paternity of the new baby: "Ah got a li'l boy chile home now" (98).

Readers perceive that Joe is misrepresenting his interactions with Slemmons calculatingly, in order to avoid the reputational damage typically suffered by a man who fails to keep his mate's sexual loyalty.[42] Insisting that he distrusted Slemmons from the outset, Joe hopes to squelch any gossip linking the stranger with Missie May. At the same time he attempts to present himself as a forceful and aggressive male, well able to fend off challenges from other men. Such masculine "displays of bravado ... are directed toward other men in an attempt to elevate status and prestige."[43] As part of this effort, Joe even adopts some of Slemmons's posturing, telling the store clerk that he has been away in "spots and places" (97). Echoing Slemmons's phrasing to suggest that he is well traveled and sophisticated, Joe imitates the strategy the newcomer used so successfully to impress new acquaintances. The knowledge that Slemmons achieved status and respect (however temporary) by means of fraudulent claims does not deter Joe from making use of similarly deceptive tactics in the hope of bolstering his own image in the community.[44]

The impact of race on the characters' situation emerges most clearly in the white store clerk's comment after Joe's departure: "these darkies ... laughin' all the time. Nothin' worries 'em" (98). Interpreting Joe's laughing deprecation of Slemmons as the sign of a carefree nature, the clerk reads Joe as "a type," revealing his conviction that individual psychology is racially determined.[45] To say

---

42 Buss, *Evolution of Desire*, 126.
43 Ibid., 10.
44 Chinn and Dunn, "The Ring of Singing Metal," 8; German, "Counterfeiting," 11.
45 John Lowe, *Jump at the Sun: Zora Neale Hurston's Classic Comedy*, excerpted in *"Sweat": Zora Neale Hurston*, ed. Cheryl A. Wall (New Brunswick, NJ: Rutgers University Press, 1997), 191.

that Joe never "worries" is to deny his full humanity and, by extension, that of all African Americans. Readers are acquainted firsthand with the suffering Joe has experienced in previous months, moreover, and they also understand the attitude of easy confidence he projects while mocking Slemmons as a function of intrasexual competition (here the attempt to assert dominance over a rival). Hurston has arranged for readers to realize how utterly mistaken the white man's racially based assumptions are and thus to reject their underlying bigotry. The irony evoked by the clerk's remark is directed, very obviously, toward him. Adaptationist analysis of the story supports Hurston's point fully, as the characters' behavior is shown to be consistent with "universal psychological mechanisms."[46]

As Lillie P. Howard states, one of Hurston's recurring messages is "that people, regardless of their color or their peculiar burdens, must inevitably struggle with some of the same life problems." In confronting problematic and conflict-ridden situations, fraught with "infidelity, jealousy, violence, and hatred," her characters express their humanness in all its complexity.[47] Further evidence that Hurston regards her characters' feelings and behavior as normative can be found in her chosen narrative strategies. The omniscient narrator keeps readers at some distance from the characters' inner reflections at several critical points in the story. Readers obtain no direct access to Missie May's motives in yielding to Slemmons's courtship, for instance, or to Joe's plans in the months following his wife's adultery. As Gayl Jones points out, "Hurston handles all the emotional reversals and complications in narrative summary rather than in active dramatic scenes."[48] Assuming that readers will understand the two protagonists' motives, reactions, and calculations on the basis of general human experience, she implies that her story is an old one, with universal application. In this way, her narrative method appears to reflect her background as folklorist and ethnographer. She utilizes dialect, rituals, and folkways to locate her characters in an identifiable environment, simultaneously pointing toward psychological mechanisms transcending the local.[49]

Certainly men's apprehensions of misplacing parental effort is universal, as countless examples from popular culture and literature bear witness. The final song in Shakespeare's *Love's Labor Lost*, for instance, declares that the

---

46 Buss, *Evolution of Desire*, 185.
47 Lillie P. Howard, "Marriage: Zora Neale Hurston's System of Values," *College Language Association Journal* 21 (1977): 256, 257.
48 Jones, "Breaking out of the Conventions," 41.
49 Chinn and Dunn, "The Ring of Singing Metal," 4; Hoeller, "Racial Currency," 778.

spring call of the cuckoo "mocks married men."[50] Not only does the bird's call mimic the word "cuckold," warning men of their wives' possible infidelity, the brood parasitism for which this species is notorious exemplifies reproductive deceit and exploitation at its most extreme. The cuckoo's victims take care of another bird's offspring because they are unable to distinguish the cuckoo's eggs or chicks from their own. In contrast to the bird world, in which both parents are equally prone to deception, the prospect of being so tricked threatens only males in the human realm:

> The cuckoo then, on every tree
> Mocks married men; for thus sings he—
> Cuckoo,
> Cuckoo, cuckoo! O, word of fear
> Unpleasing to a married ear![51]

It is highly fitting that such words conclude a play titled *Love's Labor's Lost*. Shakespeare's lyrics remind us that the emotion of "love" is a proximate mechanism driving humans toward reproductive efforts that constitute the central "labor" of most individual lives. To lose the genetic payoff from that labor by lavishing energy on genetic impostors represents an irretrievable loss, indeed.

Like Hurston's story, Shakespeare's song assumes familiarity with the problem female infidelity poses for men: cuckoldry is presented as a widely understood human concern, not restricted to any one historical moment or social context. Hurston states in her autobiography that her attention as a writer is drawn to commonalities in human nature that underlie surface distinctions:

> My interest lies in what makes a man or a woman do such-and-so, regardless of his color. It seemed to me that the human beings I met reacted pretty much the same to the same stimuli. Different ideas, yes. Circumstances and conditions having power to influence, yes. Inherent difference, no.[52]

Clearly, her perspective is very like that of an evolutionary psychologist. The store clerk's racist assumptions, like Joe's and Missie May's ritualized games

---

50 William Shakespeare, *Love's Labor's Lost*, in *Shakespeare: The Complete Works*, ed. G. B. Harrison (New York: Harcourt, Brace, World, 1948), 5.2.909.
51 Ibid., 5.2.908-12.
52 Zora Neale Hurston, *Dust Tracks on a Road* (Philadelphia: Lippincott, 1942), Reprint. (New York: Arno Press, 1969), 214.

and richly metaphoric verbal exchanges, form part of the particularized cultural context in which the protagonists' evolutionary heritage expresses itself.[53]

With the restoration of resource-provisioning and sexual vitality to Joe's and Missie May's relationship, their story comes full circle. The breach in their marriage is healed, and its future prospects are strengthened by a joint parental commitment to a child in which both partners claim genetic interest. Hurston's plot illustrates with striking clarity the centrality of paternal confidence in male mating decisions: indeed, it may be read as a case study of this particular adaptive problem. It offers an illuminating portrait of male jealousy, identifying fear of misplaced parental investment as a principal source of this powerful emotion. Readers observe that Joe's ability to forgive an adulterous act is tied inextricably to the genetic consequences of the deed. Above all else, the adaptationist perspective cuts through any tendency to wrest sentimental or didactic meaning from the story. Often it is read as a record of maturation and forgiveness: marital discord is overcome; false values are rejected; reconciliation is achieved.[54] Neither ethical principles nor romantic ideals dictate Joe's decision to remain in his marriage, however; his chief concern is the safeguarding of his own fitness. If confronted with another instance of infidelity on his wife's part, he can be expected to demonstrate at least as much coldness and anger as he did the first time, very probably more. He has not become more altruistic, or more forgiving of human frailty; rather, he has reaped the adaptive benefits of jealousy.

To locate the story's meaning in vague ideas about the power of love or the ethics of reconciliation does great disservice to the tough-mindedness of its statement. "The Gilded Six-Bits" is not a vapid tale of error and forgiveness but an unsparing delineation of Darwinian realities: men practice deceit to gain social status and access to women; happily married women can be tempted to sexual disloyalty if sufficiently impressive resources are on offer; a man can forgive his wife's infidelity if—and only if—he is sure she has not foisted alien genes upon him. The author who crafted a fictional situation to test and illustrate these realities is not surprised by the outcomes she depicts, nor does she encourage readers to condemn the portrait of human psychology that emerges.

---

53 Jones, "Breaking out of the Conventions," 44-45; Wall, Introduction, 14.
54 See Rosalie Murphy Baum, "The Shape of Hurston's Fiction," in *Zora in Florida*, ed. Steve Glassman and Kathryn Lee Seidel (Orlando: University of Central Florida Press, 1991); Gates and Lenke, Introduction; Robert E. Hemenway, *Zora Neale Hurston: A Literary Biography* (Urbana: University of Illinois Press, 1980); Howard, "Marriage"; Jones, "Pastoral and Picaresque"; Jones, "Breaking out of the Conventions"; Lowe, *Jump at the Sun*; Peters, "Missie May."

Zora Neale Hurston's narrative quietly accepts genetic self-interest as an inevitable component of our common human nature, a sine qua non that, with luck and a modicum of good will, need not be incompatible with tender and lasting relationships. "Tremendous benefits flow to couples who remain committed," after all.[55] Missie May and Joe have much to gain if they continue their marriage, so long as they can do so without jeopardizing the reproductive success of either partner.

---

55 Buss, *Evolution of Desire*, 123.

CHAPTER 12

The Role of the Arts in Male Courtship Display: Billy Collins's "Serenade"

Research in the field of evolutionary psychology underlines the importance of masculine display in the mate-selection process. Men seek opportunities to exhibit qualities women find desirable; hence they invite inspection of their resources and status, their physical and mental prowess. They also advertise specialized skills and abilities, including artistic performance and creativity. Men seeking to impress potential mates hope to benefit not only from displaying survival-oriented skills as toolmakers or hunters but also from publishing adeptness in less utilitarian realms such as storytelling, drumming, or carving.[1] Exhibition of aesthetic achievement is relevant, therefore, to current inquiries into the adaptive value of art. The poem "Serenade" (2001) by recent Poet Laureate Billy Collins offers indirect reinforcement of the hypothesis that female preference encompasses achievement in the arts. The poem introduces a male speaker who bases his courtship, including his expectation of besting rivals, on musical virtuosity.

Evolutionary theorists generally agree that sexual selection provides one of the most plausible explanations for the evolution of art in human populations: a cross-culturally ubiquitous, costly, and pleasurable activity, art is "unlikely to be a biological accident."[2] In addition to the potentially status-serving function of the arts (including but not limited to enhancement of mate value) the ability to create and appreciate aesthetic designs of varied types very possibly contributes to fitness in other ways. The social value of the arts, for example, has received considerable attention: dance, song, drawing, sculpture, and narrative may promote social cohesion and foster transmission of community norms.[3]

---

1 Geoffrey Miller, *The Mating Mind: How Sexual Choice Shaped the Evolution of Human Nature* (New York: Random, 2001), 196.
2 Miller, *The Mating Mind*, 157.
3 Useful discussion of this topic is provided by Miller, *The Mating Mind*, 159-61, and by Ellen Dissanayake, *Art and Intimacy: How the Arts Began* (Seattle: University of Washington Press, 2000), 72-85.

A related benefit, particularly evident in dramatic and narrative arts, is the opportunity to practice mindreading skills, to rehearse behavioral options, and to hone interpersonal problem-solving skills.[4] In consequence, the arts might assist in "generating adaptive flexibility," a heightened ability to cope with stressors in physical, mental, and social environments.[5] As evolutionary explanations of the arts grow in sophistication and draw on emergent research from such relevant fields as cognition, ethnography, and psychology, it seems certain that findings will prove multifarious: the evolutionary advantages of human art cannot be reduced to a single fitness benefit.

In sum, enhancement of mate value appears to supply one clearly demonstrable adaptive motive—though surely not the sole motive—for human art-making activity. Even if aesthetic pleasure should prove to be a fascinating byproduct of human mental functioning, as Steven Pinker has argued, rather than an adaptation in its own right, it is a byproduct that has been regularly harnessed in service of courtship behavior and thus rendered adaptive, in effect, through the back door.[6] As Geoffrey Miller points out, "seemingly useless ... ornamentation" serves throughout the natural world as a discriminating factor in sexual choice. He compares human art-making activity to the male bowerbird's patient construction of a symmetrically and colorfully designed nest from grasses, twigs, leaves, and feathers. Like images pecked into rock or sounds arranged in patterns, this avian bower makes no direct contribution to the survival and rearing of offspring. No chicks are sheltered or raised in it. Its only function is to attract females and induce them to mate with those males whose architectural accomplishments elicit most admiration.[7] It is easy to show that much human art is similarly inspired by a mating impulse: love and courtship consistently provide opportunities for showcasing artistic effort.[8] Like bowerbirds, humans appreciate achievements that require exceptional talent, energy, and persistence. High-cost products and performance come to be regarded

---

4 See Sugiyama, "Reverse-Engineering Narrative," 186-87; Denis Dutton, *The Art Instinct: Beauty, Pleasure, and Human Evolution* (New York: Bloomsbury Press, 2009), 105-106; Steven Pinker, *How the Mind Works* (New York: W. W. Norton, 2009), 540-43.
5 Joseph Carroll, *Reading Human Nature: Literary Darwinism in Theory and Practice* (Albany: State University of New York Press, 2011), 5. See also John Tooby and Leda Cosmides, "Does Beauty Build Adapted Minds? Toward an Evolutionary Theory of Aesthetics, Fiction, and the Arts," in *Evolution, Literature, and Film: A Reader*, ed. Brian Boyd, Joseph Carroll, and Jonathan Gottschall (New York: Columbia University Press, 2010), 181-82, and Wilson, *Consilience*, 224-25.
6 Pinker, *How the Mind Works*, 534-35.
7 Miller, *The Mating Mind*, 262-65, 267-70.
8 Ibid., 272-74.

as beautiful precisely because they demonstrate hard-won mastery of technique, medium, and form. Every artist attempts to win admiration by exhibiting a level of excellence that less gifted or less dedicated competitors fail to reach.[9]

The situation presented in "Serenade" is a case in point: Collins's speaker launches the poem by disparaging the banal tastes and mediocre abilities of "other boys from the village," employing the familiar tactic of derogating rivals.[10] These rivals communicate their "longing" using the most ordinary of instruments ("bean-shaped guitars"), relying on "three simple chords" to communicate their passion (lines 6, 3, 8). Their singing is dismissed as an unrefined, unromantic "yodeling" (line 8). Addressing the unnamed woman who is the object of all this masculine desire, the speaker announces his intention to win her by aspiring to a superior standard of artistic excellence. He will undertake serious "study" of unusual or difficult musical instruments such as the zither and the miniature bassoon, devoting years to "lessons" and "practice" (lines 12, 11, 16). Recognizing that many "hours of life" are required to achieve a high performance level, he commits himself to a long musical apprenticeship and, by extension, to a protracted courtship: he is willing to "bide [his] time" (lines 17, 10). Because he is motivated by a determination to outperform competitors by mastering musical instruments others cannot play, the aspiring suitor confronts the special challenges posed by a "double-reed" and "a row of wakeful strings," perhaps reaping advantage from the handicap principle (lines 9, 21).[11] The zealousness of his dedication to music, together with his capacity for comprehending and reproducing intricate sound patterns in more than one medium, will display to prospective mates a number of qualities associated with fitness: prominent among these are "health, energy, endurance, hand-eye coordination, fine motor control, intelligence, creativity, access to rare materials, the ability to learn difficult skills, and lots of free time."[12]

The multidimensional investment of effort required to achieve technical excellence in the realm of music also may suggest a capacity for long-term commitment in the interpersonal realm. Collins's speaker manifests an unwavering devotion to his musical goals that surely will appeal to female

---

9 Ibid., 281, 282.
10 Billy Collins, "Serenade," in *Sailing Alone Around the Room: New and Selected Poems* (New York: Random, 2001), 152-53, line 1. Citations refer to this edition. For discussion of derogation as a courtship tactic, see Buss, *Evolution of Desire*, 97-98.
11 See Pinker, *How the Mind Works*, 500, and Miller, *The Mating Mind*, 221-22.
12 Miller, *The Mating Mind*, 281.

preference for faithful and dependable partners.[13] He hints briefly, too, at family status and resources, obviously important fitness indicators, when he refers to practicing in the "music room" of a home containing a "corridor" filled with "the fierce portraits of my ancestors" (lines 14, 13, 15).[14] Such details remind potential mates that artistic activity correlates strongly with socioeconomic privilege.[15] So far as readers know, the sole purpose of his artistic endeavors is to impress a much-sought-after female. Music provides a venue for showcasing his genetic quality and socioeconomic assets. All his choices and actions are guided by the unstated premise that musical accomplishment, particularly when focused on the rare and the demanding, constitutes evidence of high mate value.

As the poem continues, readers observe that the speaker is prepared to make increasingly spectacular musical displays if his initial endeavors should prove insufficient to win the woman's regard. "If this is not enough," he assures her, "I will apply myself to the pyrophone, / the double-lap dulcimer, / the glassarina, and the tiny thumb piano" (lines 22, 25-27). The increasingly far-fetched line-up of musical instruments he is ready to learn in order to ensure the success of his "serenade" emphasizes his determination to distinguish himself at all costs from other suitors—those ordinary guitar players. The most exotic instruments he names are the pyrophone and the glassarina, eighteenth-century inventions with properties that prove suggestive when considered in conjunction with courtship. The pyrophone is an especially telling choice, since it utilizes fire to create sound. Resembling an organ or calliope, it features a set of pipes. The combustive power of heated gas produces vibrations in these pipes, creating "singing-flames": a "serenade" driven literally by fire.[16] In outdoor, night-time performances, pyrophonic music may be enhanced by visual effects such as cascading flames.[17] The explosive heat associated with this instrument aptly communicates the sexual ardor driving the speaker's courtship efforts.

The glassarina, presumably a reference to the water harmonica or water organ, provides an elemental contrast to the pyrophone: it uses water, rather

---

13 See discussion in Buss, *Evolution of Desire,* 33, 41-43.
14 Buss analyzes the importance of status and resources in mate selection in *Evolution of Desire,* 24-26.
15 Pinker, *How the Mind Works,* 126.
16 See M. Dunant, "The Pyrophone," *Popular Science Monthly,* vol. 7 (August 1875): 444-53, and G. E. Kastner, "Improvement in Pyrophones," Patents: US 164458A (June 15, 1875); IFI Claims Patent Services. https://www.google/patents/US/64458.
17 Allan Milnes, "Valley Fiesta in Brisbane, Australia," *Demotix: The Network for Freelance Photojournalists* (September 10, 2010).

than fire, to produce sound. In the version invented by Benjamin Franklin in the 1760's, "a set of glass bowls is mounted concentrically on a spindle."[18] As the spindle turns, it moistens the rims of the bowls continuously in a trough of water positioned beneath them. Working the spindle with a foot-treadle, the instrumentalist can use the fingers to touch several glass-rims simultaneously, playing chords as well as individual notes. This instrument has a historically distinguished history: a number of important composers, most notably Mozart, wrote pieces especially designed for it.[19] Its cool, ethereal fragility stands in obvious juxtaposition to the fiery heat powering the music of the pyrophone. In choosing two such different instruments to convey his feelings, the speaker reveals that his beloved stimulates a wide range of emotional responses—from the forceful to the delicate, from the sensual to the spiritual. The polar oppositions in his ambitiously shifting choice of musical medium indicate that he desires her, and hence will woo her, in every possible way. A related point concerning the water harmonica is that the "continual friction of the edge of the glass on the fingertips ... combined with the singing whine of the glasses, sent many of its practitioners mad."[20] Collins's speaker is willing to endure nerve-shattering agitation and even put his sanity at risk, evidently, in order to create musical effects that might please the woman of his dreams.

He caps his enumeration of future accomplishments by promising to create uniquely new music, "sounds no woman has ever heard," to be played on a musical apparatus of his own devising: "a nameless instrument / it took so many days and nights to invent" (lines 36, 42-43). He will take aesthetic novelty to the highest possible level, devoting his "days and nights" not only to the mastery of existing forms and vehicles of of musical art but to the invention of new ones. Making extraordinary music—the something "special" that constitutes art, as Ellen Dissayanake compellingly argues[21]—he hopes to demonstrate that he himself, in his role as suitor, is as special as the music he creates. There is unmistakable hyperbole in his selection of increasingly esoteric means of musical expression: he insists that he will play obscure instruments, difficult instruments, long forgotten instruments, a yet-to-be invented instrument. He vows to make utterly new patterns of sound. All this aesthetic eccentricity and elaborate ambition he dedicates, with great enthusiasm, to the woman who is

---

18 Jeremy Montagu, *The World of Baroque and Classical Musical Instruments* (Woodstock, New York: Overlook Press 1979), 124.
19 Ibid., 124-25.
20 Ibid., 124-25.
21 Dissanayake, *Homo Aestheticus*, 49-63.

the object of his desire. "I will be the strange one," he tells her, "the irresistible misfit" (lines 28, 34).

His attitude toward the addressee is characterized throughout by reverent admiration, his pursuit of her by seriousness of purpose, but he is amazed, even amused, by the extravagance of his own behavior. *See what bizarre things men will do to win a woman*, he seems to say, inviting readers to laugh at his unremitting quest to set himself apart from rivals. His witty self-portrait anchors what Stephen Pinker calls "the otherwise inexplicable oddities of the arts" in the drive to defeat sexual rivals. To win fame, fortune and, not least of all, women, artists in every medium strive for aesthetic novelty: they "avoid the hackneyed" and "challenge jaded tastes."[22] The introduction of new forms, techniques, and theories enables them to enjoy the attention (and potential mating benefits) that elite, high-cost creative achievement attracts.

The final, ironic twist in Collins's poem is that its speaker's musical accomplishments remain unrealized. He woos his beloved with declarations of future intent: "I will … ," "I will … ," I will …" (lines 10, 13, 25, 28, 34) Since he has not mastered even one of the musical instruments he names, the "serenade" with which he hopes to win his lady love cannot yet be performed. He occupies the entire space of the poem, forty-two lines in all, describing a virtuosity he has not even begun to attain. In the present moment of the poem, readers recognize, there is no evidence that he possesses the creative talents to which he lays such confident claim. Because his courtship display relies on hypothetical rather than actual achievement, the extravagance of his stated ambitions appears even more ridiculous. He is a show-off with nothing to show. With his dramatic promises and improbable plans, he illustrates a familiar masculine display tactic, projecting a self-assurance that emphasizes braggadocio over substance.[23]

It is the poet, Billy Collins, rather than the fictional character he creates, who succeeds in exhibiting artistic flair. The as yet untrained musician's "serenade" remains unsung, but the poem recounting the tale of his immoderate ambition is complete. It demonstrates its maker's mastery of literary language and form; it displays exhilarating intelligence and wit. The aesthetic satisfactions and novelty it offers are fully realized; it delights the reader with unexpected content just as the speaker means to delight his beloved with unusual musical effects. The poem is as "irresistible" as its speaker boldly hopes to become (line 34). Humor is positively associated with intelligence and creativity, as emerging

---

22 Pinker, *How the Mind Works*, 522, 523.
23 See Buss, *The Evolution of Desire*, 107-109.

research shows, and this constellation of traits plays a role in sexual selection.[24] Working in a different medium, and indirectly acknowledging the roots of poetry in song, the poet rescues his speaker's indefinitely deferred, wholly hypothetical courtship display, converting it into a successful exhibition of verbal fluency and creative intelligence. While it remains entertaining in spirit and jocular in tone, the poem succeeds in communicating serious reflection on a topic of enduring human interest, namely, the intersection of art and desire. Leavened by self-deprecating wit directed toward masculine boastfulness, the poem illustrates an indisputably important evolutionary motive for aesthetic striving.

Fitness benefits Billy Collins, the human artificer, might hope to reap from his exertions cannot be ascertained by examination of textual content. Such benefits are surely more varied than those aspired to by the speaker in the poem, more subtly linked to the passing on of genes. Some evolutionarily significant profit is likely to be garnered by readers as well. The poem clearly provides opportunity for analysis and rehearsal of behavioral options, as well as practice in mindreading. Readers are prompted to consider an intriguing behavioral cluster of intersexual competition, female choice, male courtship display, mate value, and false—or hyperbolic—self-presentation. Recognizing recurring human aspirations and conflicts in the stuff of the poem, a content rendered more potent by the playful originality of its presentation, readers may engage in adaptively advantageous reflection or projection. Any pleasure they derive from such engagement typically elicits admiration, boosting the author's reputation and status. Since fame tends to enhance mate value, it follows that the poem may be regarded, indirectly, as a courtship display on the part of the poet. It functions as a generalized rather than a targeted display, and its accomplished virtuosity sets it apart from the unrealized ambitions of the poem's speaker. Employing the same means chosen by the fictive "I" of his poem—namely, extraordinary achievement in the arts—the poet is poised to win social rewards, potentially including the romantic success still eluding his counterpart in the imaginary universe of the poem. This disparity between poet and speaker constitutes a final amusing irony for readers to savor.

---

24 Scott Barry Kaufman, Aaron Kozbelt, Melanie L. Bromley, and Geoffrey F. Miller, "The Role of Creativity and Humor in Human Mate Selection," in *Mating Intelligence: Sex, Relationships, and the Mind's Reproductive System*, ed. Glenn Geher and Geoffrey Miller (New York: Taylor and Francis, 2007).

Conclusion

A dozen examples of Literary Darwinism at work should suffice to suggest the wide variety of concerns it can address. A common misperception of the evolutionary approach is that it confines itself to a small number of topics directly connected to mating and reproduction; a related erroneous assumption is that it is limited in practical application and reductive in its interpretive conclusions. Since human physical and mental design is the result of natural selection over time, however, every aspect of human physiological and psychological experience necessarily invites evolutionary examination. Literary investigation based on evolutionary principles encompasses the whole range of human motivation and activity, as does evolutionary science itself. "The idea that the evolutionary causation of behavior would lead to rigid, inflexible behavior is the opposite of the truth," as research in psychology, ethnography, and cognition has demonstrated.[1] In literature, as in life, "richly contingent systems" for making choices and decisions can be observed operating "in different combinations to elicit a dazzling variety of behavioral responses."[2]

The myriad possible permutations on human behavior are particularly evident in literary art, where the psychological makeup of authors and readers, as well as that of fictional characters, comes into play. There are likely to be at least three distinct mental identities busy observing, assessing, and interpreting any narrative situation: the author's and the reader's, plus one or more mental identities embedded in the text as character, speaker, or narrator. Indeed, literature focuses as much on the mind's interpretive endeavors—often self-deceiving, always self-interested—as much as on events and situations. Ever-recurring human aspirations and problems are situated in particular cultural contexts,

---

1 Tooby and Cosmides, "Conceptual Foundations," 13.
2 Ibid., 13, 14.

moreover: literary works show adaptive strategies and proximate mechanisms responding to pressures exerted by local customs and norms. Tension between individual goals and collectively imposed constraints is a constant in the life of a social animal dependent for survival on varying forms of cooperative enterprise and hierarchical sharing. Behavior that proves adaptive in one time or place may prove less so in another. Consciously and unconsciously, individuals tend to adjust their behavior, and even their avowed motives, so as to wrest maximum advantage from prevailing social conditions. It is not accidental that literary works so often explore conflicts between self and group, including the challenges posed to individual fitness by status struggles, shifting alliances, and community ethos.

No matter how exotic the cultural setting (real or imagined) or how eccentric the individual character, in any literary work these are susceptible to evolutionary analysis. Motive and behavior can be traced back to ultimate causes, that is, to the fitness purposes they evolved to serve; obstacles to adaptive behavior can be investigated and strategic conflicts between individual interests identified. The activity of the mind itself can be explored as it responds to external and internal pressures: protracted interior debate; delusional thinking and projection; counterfactual revisions of personal memory and life-history narratives; successful and unsuccessful efforts at mind reading; elaborate construction of alternative realities or excursions into fantasy. Considering the possible evolutionary basis and adaptive significance of settings, actions, crises, and conflicts depicted in literary works, even when these appear to be far removed from reproductive issues, nearly always leads to useful insights into auctorial purpose and design: it illumines the human and aesthetic concerns at stake in a specific story, play, or poem. Evolutionary analysis helps to explain why readers respond as they do to particular characters and their plights: how characters' seemingly bizarre behavior may serve ultimate ends, how authors allocate sympathy and judgment. Finally, literature provides a forum in which the human mind grapples with impulses and preferences that elude conscious understanding and deliberate choice—impulses and preferences that evolved to serve the replicatory imperatives of genes rather than the contentment of individual "survival machines."[3]

In sum, literary art necessarily addresses universal aspirations and dilemmas, at the same time exploring an extensive repertoire of behavioral responses, in all its "dazzling variety," to recurring human situations. Numerous works may feature the same or similar predicaments but present them from different

---

3   Dawkins, *Selfish Gene*, 254.

angles and situate them in varied cultural milieus. Readers encounter hundreds of stories focusing on sexual infidelity and jealousy, for example, without experiencing any sense of redundancy. This is so not only because these issues remain centrally important in human life history, thus attracting eager attention from readers, but because every story will differ in its handling of basic elements: phenotypical and psychological makeup of characters, relevant cultural norms, and questions of status and mate value, along with allocation of judgment and empathy. The plots in Zora Neale Hurston's "The Gilded Six-Bits" and Edith Wharton's *Ethan Frome*, for example, both place adultery, or the possibility of adultery, at the forefront of the action: in each case, the prospect of losing a mate to an interloper elicits a jealous response from the betrayed spouse. Yet the operation of that jealousy could not be more different in the two narratives and, accordingly, different reactions are elicited from readers. Joe Banks's jealousy serves a clearly adaptive purpose: it punishes his unfaithful partner, testing her marital commitment and discouraging future disloyalty. Zeena Frome's jealousy is so punitively cruel it borders on the pathological: it is intended to torment rather than to test or re-establish trust. Joe's jealous behavior toward his wife and her short-term partner fits the degree of their transgressions, moreover, whereas Zeena's jealous vengefulness is radically disproportionate to Ethan's and Mattie's wrongdoing. Readers are encouraged to assess infidelity itself (a sexual strategy typically incurring social costs if discovered) very differently in the two tales. Nothing in Hurston's story validates Missy May's affair; no matter what she planned to do with resources she hoped to extract from her extra-pair partner, readers view her sexual mis-step as an unwarranted violation of marital loyalty to a generous and loving husband. Ethan's yearning to cast off an aging, sickly, shrewish wife for a sweet and lovely younger woman, contrastingly, is viewed by readers as understandable and forgivable. These differing responses are keyed to relative mate values, intriguingly, more than to moral considerations. Joe Banks's mate value is high, Zeena Frome's is low: betrayal of a top-quality partner is condemned more than betrayal of an essentially valueless one. The unlike temperaments, situations, motives, and backgrounds of the two sets of characters further induce readers of these two tales to contemplate sexual disloyalty, together with the jealousy it inspires, from disparate standpoints.

In Benjamin Franklin's autobiography, a work focused on behavioral issues less directly linked to reproduction, readers repeatedly witness the importance of social intelligence. The narrator-protagonist presents himself as a young man assessing his immediate environment politically, economically, and interpersonally with great accuracy. Shaping his ambitions and his behavior with regard to prevailing norms, he is able to maximize opportunities to accumulate resources and raise his status. His success in analyzing and exploiting the social milieu in which he finds himself offers stark contrast to the humiliation suffered by Nathaniel Hawthorne's Robin Molineux, another young man seeking advancement in Colonial America. Hawthorne draws readers' attention to the danger of acting on insufficient information about new and possibly changing environmental conditions. Handicapped by his youth and country-bred naiveté, Robin lacks self-protective wariness. He clings with foolish stubbornness to his preconceptions when entering an unfamiliar, clearly more sophisticated environment. He fails to question his own interpretation of events, moreover, despite mounting evidence that his social analyses are deficient. He is hampered by an unshakeable belief in his own shrewdness, a point reiterated with sly frequency by the omniscient narrator: overestimation of his own abilities contributes to his obtuseness.

The necessity of interpreting social cues correctly and adjusting behavior to fit prevailing cultural conditions plays a central a role in Hawthorne's narrative, as it does in Franklin's, but the two authors approach this theme, together with its obvious implications for fitness, from different angles. Atmosphere and tone in the two works, together with variations in surrounding thematic materials, further differentiate them (e.g., Hawthorne featuring nepotistic influence on socioeconomic advancement much more centrally than Franklin). Franklin illustrates the successful operation of social intelligence, along with the benefits it brings, while Hawthorne depicts an instance of its failure, together with the causes and costs of that failure. Fitzgerald offers still another variation on this topic, pointing to the high price his protagonist pays for his flawed understanding of a single set of social facts—facts concerning the relationship between material resources and social class. Gatsby is mistaken in thinking that wealth alone, no matter how great, provides automatic entrée into the upper stratum of early twentieth-century American society. This miscalculation plays a major role in the humiliation he suffers during a pivotal showdown with his sexual rival. An extravagantly conceived mate quest, a plan demanding years of patient and laborious preparation, comes to grief largely because the author of that plan acts on an insufficiently nuanced conception of social hierarchy.

Social discernment is far from the only fitness-oriented concern in Franklin's *Autobiography*. Another central preoccupation, namely, the relationship between individual and community, offers an interesting study in comparison and contrast with Henry David Thoreau's exploration of that relationship in *Walden*. Both authors offer autobiographical descriptions of their activities and lifestyles. Both proclaim success in achieving life goals; both profess contentment. Either explicitly or implicitly, each presents his life as a possible model, or launching point, for readers. A pivotal contention in both books is that self-interest overlaps with collective interest: what benefits the private self also benefits a larger community. Franklin concentrates his attention on the human community, however, whereas Thoreau focuses on the biosphere, a much vaster community comprising all organic life on earth. The experience of reading the two books could scarcely be more different: Thoreau describes the flora and fauna of his native New England with detailed precision and affection, while Franklin reports on employer-employee relations, family conflicts, business deals, self-improvement projects, financial setbacks and opportunities. Thoreau keeps "appointments" with trees and enjoys the "company" of wasps, squirrels, loons, and hares; Franklin spends time with people who can advance his commercial reputation and success, such as customers, investors, and legislators.

When Franklin argues that what is good for the self is good for the whole, he means that altruistic enterprises (devoted, say, to establishing libraries or fire departments) benefit the altruist along with everyone else. He means, too, that prosocial behaviors, including integrity in reciprocal exchange and other forms of cooperative striving, prove more advantageous, in the long run, than do strategies based on cheating or aggression. When Thoreau argues that the interest of self and community are congruent, he is pointing to the genetic relatedness uniting all forms of life and thus, indirectly, to the operations of inclusive kinship. Sharing genes, relatives have a stake in one another's welfare: the reproductive success of one contributes to the genetic legacy of all. Claiming kinship with "leaves and vegetable mold," birds, worms, and woodchucks allows Thoreau to assert that what is good for any and all living things ultimately is good for Henry Thoreau.

Franklin's *Autobiography* does not discuss the natural world as such: action takes place in eighteenth-century urban environments. The only sphere of activity that interests him is human—a social community in which alliances are forged, goods and services exchanged, agreements made or broken, reputations made and lost. In *Walden*, of course, Thoreau has plenty to say about human social communities, almost none of it good. Arguing that wealth and status, along with struggles to achieve them, constitute a major source of human unhappiness, he explicitly rejects the objects of Franklin's ambitious labors. Franklin, for his part, considers the value of status and wealth self-evident: he spends no time seeking to convince readers of their appeal. Since the idea of global kinship appears not to have entered his mind, he says nothing about the potentially liberating effects of universal relatedness as described in *Walden*. Thoreau has set himself the more difficult persuasive task. Franklin need only convince his readers that evolved tendencies to assume the roles of cheater, free-rider, or bully should be curbed, since these behaviors will prove unsuccessful (at least in his immediate social environment). Thoreau must convince readers to expand their sense of kinship, consciously and deliberately, far beyond their nearest relatives to include a multitude of life forms. He contends that nepotistic loyalty, rightly understood, will prevent human animals from resenting a partial loss of crops to marauding birds and insects. Once these creatures are accepted as relatives, self-interest commands concern for their welfare. When, finally, *all life on earth* is regarded as one comprehensive family, competition for wealth and reputation in the tiny human arena appears petty and irrelevant. Unlike Franklin, Thoreau is asking readers to re-examine goals and values whose importance they rarely question. He attempts to make his ideas attractive by associating them with fundamental adaptive principles, namely, inclusive fitness and nepotistic loyalty. Encouraging family feeling for far-flung relatives, he is urging readers to focus on an evolutionarily direct goal—their genetic legacy—instead of wasting time on mere strategies. Resources and status are only means to an end, after all: proliferation of genes is an end in itself.

Both authors bring good news: it is possible to satisfy personal and collective needs simultaneously. It is not necessary to quash competitors, whether rival newspaper publishers or leaf-eating insects: the world can sustain us all. Both writers predicate this generous view of competition on an environment of plenitude: Franklin relies on a boom economy when he states that there is room for any number of businessmen, that everyone who works industriously can make a good living. Thoreau relies on the apparently boundless fecundity of nature when he asserts that there is enough food, wild and cultivated, for all. As even cursory comparison demonstrates, these two books provide fascinating examples of authors who assert nearly identical claims, claims with discernibly fitness-based implications, yet present the relationship between personal contentment and evolved adaptations from distinctly dissimilar viewpoints.

Literary works depicting clearly procreative activities also handle what might seem to be similar subjects in markedly differing ways. Walt Whitman, Edna St. Vincent Millay, and Ernest Hemingway, for example, all depict characters who conduct active sex lives yet never sire or conceive children. Not one of the three authors acknowledges or explains that anomaly. Whitman and Millay allow their protagonists to act on amorous impulses without biological or social hindrances in order to suggest how men or women might behave if proximate desires could be dissociated from ultimate goals. Relieved of demands for long-term commitment and paternal investment, for instance, the speaker-self in Whitman's "Song" inhabits a sexual paradise: there is nothing to restrain his ardency. Female characters in many of Millay's poems similarly are liberated from sexual restraint. Since they never conceive, they are free to indulge in short-term, uncommitted relationships, free to choose highly attractive but unreliable partners without risking pregnancy and unassisted childrearing. Taking advantage of these freedoms, moreover, her characters offer bold defiance to societal regulation of female sexuality. Whitman and Millay sweep readers along with them in their unimpeded pursuit of proximate pleasures. Immersed in the poets' utopian visions, everyone can enjoy, for a space of time, freedoms real life does not offer—or did not before the invention of reliable contraception, a very recent development in the history of the species.

Based largely on the same premises as Whitman's, Millay's portrayal of proximate gratifications remains less idyllic, less consistently upbeat, than his. This reflects, very possibly, women's greater investment in human reproduction (large egg, gestation, and lactation, for starters). Because of that disproportionately greater investment, women's evolved tendency to value paternal commitment and resources in the mate-selection process is strong. No matter how much Millay may wish to liberate her female characters from worry about unforeseen pregnancy and mating mistakes, she does not entirely eliminate from her protagonists' psychological make-up a wistful yearning for long-term commitment. Since men make a much smaller initial investment in reproduction, male philandering (including abandonment of short-term partners and their offspring) often has proven to be advantageous from the perspective of male fitness. As Dawkins observes, "males are in general likely to be biased towards promiscuity and lack of paternal care."[4] Thus the ideal of cheerfully short-term, unencumbered sex endorsed by both Whitman and Millay is more fully congruent with evolved male sexuality than with evolved female sexuality. Attempting to depict the pleasure of erotic activity disconnected from material and emotional resources, Millay takes on a more difficult task than does her male counterpart: she is asking women to validate behavior that over evolutionary history frequently would have contradicted their best interests. Put another way, she is fighting against long-standing female mating styles, which favor choosiness and caution. Whitman, in contrast, makes a direct appeal to

---

4   Ibid., 161.

equally long-standing male mating styles, which favor eagerness, numbers and variety. This contrast accounts for some, at least, of the difference in emotional tone readers discern in these two presentations of immediate gratification divorced from long-term consequences.

The disconnection of sex from reproduction serves no idyllic purposes whatsoever in *The Sun Also Rises*. Brett Ashley's infertility, no matter its cause, does render her sexually independent, free to pursue her every erotic whim; she moves rapidly from affair to affair, changing partners with casual unconcern. If any of her liaisons had resulted in offspring, the responsibilities of motherhood presumably would have rendered her unable to conduct her life as she does. Despite her personal liberty, however, she does not radiate contentment, nor is the post-war environment of the novel presented as a carefree sexual playground. Brett's acerbic comments, vacillating moods, and non-stop drinking suggest an underlying bitterness of spirit. Her frenzied yet sterile eroticism, epitomized by her frustrated passion for the genitally wounded Jake Barnes, contributes to the larger sense of futility characterizing the world of the novel. The disjunction between sexuality and procreation assumes symbolic proportions in the novel, conveying cosmic irony and metaphysical frustration. Beginning with a situation very like that envisioned by Whitman and Millay (sex that, inexplicably, never leads to procreation), Hemingway uncouples proximate impulses from ultimate causes to express a very different set of ideas about humans, their history, and their mental universe.

When writers portray sexual acts that do result in conception and offspring (consequences occurring frequently in art, as in life), an array of dissimilar preoccupations and purposes crowds the literary landscape. Paternal investment, for example, serves as a source of conflict in many works of fiction. Hurston focuses on the problem of paternal confidence: Joe Banks forgives his wife's adultery and makes full paternal commitment only when he is persuaded that her child is also his. Readers see how genetic self-interest guides his marital and parental investment strategy, together with his ethical stance. It is fitness-based selfishness rather than religious teachings, moral strictures, or sentimentalized conceptions of love that makes a happy ending possible for both the child and its parents. If genetic self-interest emerges as a benign force in Hurston's story, it looks still more benign in Mark Twain's *Adventures of Huckleberry Finn*. Flouting such self-interest, Pap's brutal and exploitative treatment of his only child clearly undermines his fitness. Capturing readers' attention with the specter of radically maladaptive parenting, Twain makes use of readers' inevitable disapprobation and horror—biologically rooted and socially reinforced—

to associate Pap with vicious social institutions and ideologies. Condemnation of bad parenting positions readers to affirm thematically central sociopolitical values in Twain's novel.

Parental investment plays a vital but clearly different role in the fictional history of Sherwood Anderson's Ray Pearson. Ray's problem is not paternal uncertainty but paternal commitment. Readers observe him lamenting the forces that have lured him into energy-sapping, life-depleting parental responsibility that never was his object. As the overworked father of numerous children, earning a meager living by hard physical labor, Ray is inclined to castigate the proximate cause of his premature aging and permanent entrapment: irresistible erotic desire "tricked" him into becoming a father. He vaguely discerns the hormonal triggers and related adaptive mechanisms that inspired his youthful behavior, behavior that subsequently circumscribes his personal freedom and life choices. Instead of rejoicing in the high degree of direct fitness secured to him by his children, Ray bemoans the all-consuming burden they represent. At this moment of rebellious reflection, no doubt he would accept with enthusiasm an offer to be transported into the imaginary realm of Whitman's "Song of Myself." The opportunity to engage in sexual activity devoid of reproductive consequences is exactly what he is wishing for himself and, indeed, for everyone—particularly for men: "Why should I pay? Why should Hal pay? Why should anyone pay?"

Ray's disillusioned view of his predicament as male provider underlines the appeal of Whitman's poem, which frees men—guiltlessly—from a host of interpersonal demands, high among them parental investment. Anderson's story offers more psychological realism than does Whitman's "Song" (expectedly, given the differing historical frameworks) in that his protagonist clearly articulates the disparity between his motive (lust) and its consequence (procreation). Ray's comprehension of his plight is neither static nor simplistic, moreover, as readers observe. Once he decides to advise his younger companion to evade marital and parental commitment, Ray finds himself recalling his children with some affection: indirect and unexpected acknowledgement, in the end, of the fitness benefits they represent. His key insight is that any piece of advice he might offer another man would represent only a partial truth. The multiplicity of reproductive strategies available, together with the ability to contemplate and assess alternatives, undermines the satisfactions any choice might bring. No one strategy can prove ideal from every possible point of view or in every set of phenotypic or environmental circumstances. Protesting the paternal investment to which proximate desires have led, Ray Pearson gives voice to an evolutionarily and socially critical male predicament. It is a predicament Whitman's "Song" never directly explains, but obliquely concedes, by effacing it in utopian fantasy.

Ray Pearson's outrage encompasses more than the specifically masculine dilemma he describes: he suffers, as he dimly realizes, because the adaptations influencing his conscious and unconscious decision-making have not evolved to serve his individual happiness. His anguished musings illustrate the human ability to entertain past, future, alternative, and counterfactual circumstances; his accusatory anger against his female partner highlights the human capacity to engage in creative rationalization and narcissistic self-deception. Looking at the evolutionary basis of motivation and behavior, in this instance and in others, helps readers probe the complexities of human nature, together with the abundantly varied manifestations of behavioral responses to species-typical challenges. An understanding of natural selection and its workings, including its slow but relentless shaping of mental and emotional processes, anchors Darwinian critical methodology in interdisciplinary science without limiting the scope of its investigation. Evolutionary theory and research provide solid foundation for studying literary representations of any and every aspect of the human condition—physiological, emotional, and social—with special emphasis on the painfully perplexed, playfully inventive, self-scrutinizing and self-justifying activity of "the never-resting mind."[5]

---

5   Wallace Stevens, "The Poems of Our Climate," in *The Palm at the End of the Mind: Selected Poems and a Play*, ed. Holly Stevens (New York: Vintage Books, 1972), 158, line 18.

Works Cited

Adams, Joseph D. "The Societal Initiation and Hawthorne's 'My Kinsman, Major Molineux.'" *English Studies* 1, no. 1 (1976): 1-19.

Adams, Richard P. "The Unity and Coherence of *Huckleberry Finn*." In *Twentieth Century Interpretations of "Adventures of Huckleberry Finn"*, edited by Claude M. Simpson, 41-53. Englewood Cliffs, NJ: Prentice-Hall, 1968.

Aldridge, John W. "*The Sun Also Rises*, Sixty Years Later." In *Readings on Ernest Hemingway*, edited by Katie De Koster, 138-45. San Diego, CA: Greenhaven Press, 1997.

Alkana, Joseph. "Disorderly History in 'My Kinsman, Major Molineux.'" *ESQ: A Journal of the American Renaissance* 53 (2007): 1-30.

Allen, Gay Wilson. "Mutations in Whitman's Art." In *Walt Whitman: A Collection of Criticism*, edited by Arthur Golden, 37-49. New York: McGraw-Hill, 1974.

———. *A Reader's Guide to Walt Whitman*. New York: Farrar, Straus and Giroux, 1970.

Allison, Alexander W. "The Literary Contexts of 'My Kinsman, Major Molineux'" *Nineteenth-Century Fiction* 3 (1968): 304-11.

Ammons, Elizabeth. *Edith Wharton's Argument with America*. Athens: University of Georgia Press, 1980.

———. "The Myth of Imperiled Whiteness in *Ethan Frome*." *New England Quarterly* 81, no. 1 (2008): 5-33.

Anderson, Sherwood. "The Untold Lie." 1919. In *"Winesburg, Ohio": Text and Criticism*, edited by John H. Ferres, 202-209. New York: Viking Press, 1966.

Aspiz, Harold. "Sexuality and the Language of Transcendence." *Walt Whitman Review* 5, no. 2 (1987): 1-7.

———. "Walt Whitman: The Spermatic Imagination." *American Literature* 56, no. 3 (1984): 379-95.

Asya, Ferda. "Edith Wharton's Dream of Incest: *Ethan Frome*." *Studies in Short Fiction* 35, no. 1 (1998): 23-40.

Autrey, Max L. "'My Kinsman, Major Molineux': Hawthorne's Allegory of the Urban Movement." *College Literature* 12, no. 3 (1985): 211-21.

Baskett, Sam S. "'An Image to Dance Around': Brett and Her Lovers in *The Sun Also Rises*." *Centennial Review* 22 (1978): 45-69.

Baum, Rosalie Murphy. "The Shape of Hurston's Fiction." In *Zora in Florida*, edited by Steve Glassman and Kathryn Lee Seidel, 94-109. Orlando: University of Central Florida Press, 1991.

Baym, Nina. "Thoreau's View of Science." *Journal of the History of Ideas* 26, no. 2 (1965): 221-34.

Beaver, Harold. "Huck and Pap." In *Huck Finn: Major Literary Characters*, edited by Harold Bloom, 174-183. New York: Chelsea House, 1990.

Bell, Millicent. "*Huckleberry Finn* and the Sleights of the Imagination." In *Huck Finn: Major Literary Characters*, edited by Harold Bloom, 108-25. New York: Chelsea House, 1990.

Bellis, Peter J. "Representing Dissent: Hawthorne and the Drama of Revolt." *ESQ: A Journal of the American Renaissance* 41, no. 2 (1995): 97-119.

Bender, Bert. *The Descent of Love: Darwin and the Theory of Sexual Selection in American Fiction, 1871-1926*. Philadelphia: University of Pennsylvania Press, 1996.

———. *Evolution and "the Sex Problem": American Narratives during the Eclipse of Darwinism*. Kent, OH and London: Kent State University Press, 2004.

Benert, Annette. "Survival through Irony: "Hemingway's 'A Clean, Well-Lighted Place.'" *Studies in Short Fiction* 11 (1974): 181-87.

Bewley, Marius. "Scott Fitzgerald's Criticism of America." In *Twentieth Century Interpretations of "The Great Gatsby,"* edited by Ernest Lockridge, 37-53. Englewood Cliffs, NJ: Prentice-Hall, 1968.

Bird, John. "Gauging the Value of Nature: Thoreau and His Woodchucks." *The Concord Saunterer*, n.s., 2, no. 1 (1994): 139-47.

Blair, Walter. "'So Noble … and So Beautiful a Book.'" In *Twentieth Century Interpretations of "Adventures of Huckleberry Finn"*, edited by Claude M. Simpson, 61-70. Englewood Cliffs, NJ: Prentice-Hall, 1968.

Bloom, Harold. Introduction to *Huck Finn: Major Literary Characters*, edited by Harold Bloom, 1-3. New York: Chelsea House, 1990.

Boehm, Christopher. *Hierarchy in the Forest: The Evolution of Egalitarian Behavior*. Cambridge, MA and London: Harvard University Press, 1999.

Boudreau, Gordon V. *The Roots of "Walden" and the Tree of Life*. Nashville, TN: Vanderbilt University Press, 1990.

Boyd, Brian. *On the Origin of Stories: Evolution, Cognition, and Fiction*. Cambridge, MA and London: Harvard University Press, 2009.

Boyd, Brian, Joseph Carroll, and Jonathan Gottschall. *Evolution, Literature, and Film: A Reader*. New York: Columbia University Press, 2010.

Boyer, Pascal and H. Clark Barrett. "Domain Specificity and Intuitive Ontology." In *The Handbook of Evolutionary Psychology*, edited by David M. Buss, 96-118. Hoboken, NJ: John Wiley and Sons, 2005.

Bremer, Sydney H. "Exploding the Myth of Rural America and Urban Europe: 'My Kinsman, Major Molineux' and 'The Paradise of Bachelors and the Tartarus of Maids.'" *Studies in Short Fiction* 18, no. 1 (1981): 49-57.

Brennan, Joseph X. "*Ethan Frome*: Structure and Metaphor." *Modern Fiction Studies* 7, no. 4 (1961): 347-56.

Bridgman, Richard. *Dark Thoreau*. Lincoln and London: University of Nebraska Press, 1982.

Brodwin, Stanley. "Mark Twain in the Pulpit: The Theological Comedy of *Huckleberry Finn*." In *One Hundred Years of "Huckleberry Finn": The Boy, His Book, and American Culture*, edited by Robert Sattelmeyer and J. Donald Crowley, 371-85. Columbia: University of Missouri Press, 1985.

Broes, Arthur T. "Journey into Moral Darkness: 'My Kinsman, Major Molineux' As Allegory." *Nineteenth-Century Fiction* 19, no. 2 (1964): 171-84.

Bruccoli, Matthew J. "Explanatory Notes" to *The Great Gatsby*, edited and reprinted by Matthew J. Bruccoli, 180-204. Cambridge: Cambridge University Press, 1991.

Budick, Emily Miller. "American Literature's Declaration of Independence: Stanley Cavell, Nathaniel Hawthorne, and the Covenant of Consent." In *Summoning: Ideas of the Covenant and Interpretive Theory*, edited by Ellen Spolsky, 211-27. Albany: State University of New York Press, 1993.

Buell, Lawrence. *The Environmental Imagination: Thoreau, Nature Writing, and the Formation of American Culture*. Cambridge, MA and London: Harvard University Press, 1995.

———. "Thoreau and the Natural Environment." In *The Cambridge Companion to Henry David Thoreau*, edited by Joel Myerson, 171-93. Cambridge and New York: Cambridge University Press, 1995.

Buller, David J. *Adapting Minds: Evolutionary Psychology and the Persistent Quest for Human Nature*. Cambridge, MA: The MIT Press, 2006.

Burbick, Joan. *Thoreau's Alternative History: Changing Perspectives on Nature, Culture, and Language*. Philadelphia: University of Pennsylvania Press, 1987.

Burghardt, Gordon M., and Harold A. Herzog, Jr. "Beyond Conspecifics: Is Brer Rabbit Our Brother?" *BioScience* 30 (1980): 763-68.

Burnstein, Eugene. "Altruism and Genetic Relatedness." In *The Handbook of Evolutionary Psychology*, edited by David M. Buss, 528-51. Hoboken, NJ: John Wiley and Sons, 2005.

Buss, David M. *The Dangerous Passion: Why Jealousy Is as Necessary as Love and Sex*. New York: Free Press / Simon and Schuster, 2000.

———. *The Evolution of Desire: Strategies of Human Mating*. Rev. ed. New York: Basic Books, 2003.

———. *Evolutionary Psychology: The New Science of the Mind*. 2nd ed. Boston: Pearson, 2004.

———. "Sexual Conflict: Evolutionary Insights into Feminism and the 'Battle of the Sexes'." In *Sex, Power, Conflict: Evolutionary and Feminist Perspectives*, edited by David M. Buss and Neil M. Malamuth, 296-318. New York and Oxford: Oxford University Press, 1996.

———. *The Murderer Next Door: Why the Mind Is Designed to Kill*. New York: Penguin, 2005.

Buss, David M. and David P. Schmitt. "Sexual Strategies Theory: An Evolutionary Perspective on Human Mating." *Psychological Review* 100 (1993): 204-32.

Cameron, Sharon. *Writing Nature: Henry Thoreau's "Journal."* New York and Oxford: Oxford University Press, 1985.

Campbell, Anne. *A Mind of Her Own: The Evolutionary Psychology of Women.* Oxford: Oxford University Press, 2002.

Carlyle, Thomas. *Sartor Resartus.* In *"Sartor Resartus" and "On Heroes and Hero Worship,"* 1-236. New York: E. P. Dutton, 1959.

Carroll, Joseph. *Evolution and Literary Theory.* Columbia: University of Missouri Press, 1995.

———. "An Evolutionary Paradigm for Literary Study, with Two Sequels." In *Reading Human Nature: Literary Darwinism in Theory and Practice,* 3-54. Albany: State University of New York Press, 2011.

———. *Literary Darwinism: Evolution, Human Nature, and Literature.* New York and London: Routledge, 2004.

———. "Literature and Evolutionary Psychology." In *The Handbook of Evolutionary Psychology,* edited by David M. Buss, 931-52. Hoboken, NJ: John Wiley and Sons, 2005.

———. *Reading Human Nature: Literary Darwinism in Theory and Practice.* Albany: State University of New York Press, 2011.

———. "Wilson's *Consilience* and Literary Study." In *Literary Darwinism: Evolution, Human Nature, and Literature,* 69-84. New York and London: Routledge, 2004.

Cheatham, George. "'Sign the Wire with Love': The Morality of Surplus in *The Sun Also Rises.*" In *Ernest Hemingway's "The Sun Also Rises": A Casebook,* edited by Linda Wagner-Martin, 99-106. Oxford: Oxford University Press, 2002.

Chinn, Nancy and Elizabeth E. Dunn. "'The Ring of Singing Metal on Wood': Zora Neale Hurston's Artistry in 'The Gilded Six-Bits.'" *Mississippi Quarterly: The Journal of Southern Cultures* 49, no. 4 (1996): 2-10. 2 Feb. 2008 http://web.ebscohost.com.online.library.marist.edu.htm

Christie, John Aldrich. *Thoreau as World Traveler.* New York and London: Columbia University Press, 1965.

Clark, Stuart. "Inversion, Misrule and the Meaning of Witchcraft." *The Witchcraft Reader.* 2nd ed., edited by Darren Oldridge. London and New York: Routledge, 2008. 120-30.

Clark, Suzanne. "Uncanny Millay." In *Millay at 100: A Critical Reappraisal,* edited By Diane P. Freedman, 3-26. Carbondale and Edwardsville: Southern Illinois University Press, 1995.

Clasen, Mathias. "'Can't Sleep, Clowns Will Eat Me': Telling Scary Stories." In *Telling Stories / Geschichten Erzählen: Literature and Evolution / Literatur und Evolution,* edited by Carsten Gansel and Dirk Vanderbeke, 324-46. Berlin: De Gruyter, 2012.

Colacurcio, Michael J. "The Matter of America: 'My Kinsman, Major Molineux.'" In *Nathaniel Hawthorne: Modern Critical Views,* edited by Harold Bloom, 197-221. New York: Chelsea House, 1986.

Collins, Billy. "Serenade." In *Sailing Alone Around the Room: New and Selected Poems,* 152-53. New York: Random House, 2001.

Cooke, Brett. "Biopoetics: The New Synthesis." In *Biopoetics: Evolutionary Exploration in the Arts*, edited by Brett Cooke and Frederick Turner, 3-25. Lexington, KY: International Conference on the Unity of the Sciences, 1999.

Cooke, Brett and Clinton Machann, eds. Applied Evolutionary Criticism: *Style* 46, special issue, no. 3-4 (2012).

Coviello, Peter. "Intimate Nationality: Anonymity and Attachment in Whitman." *American Literature* 73, no. 1 (2001): 85-119.

Cowley, Geoffrey. "The Biology of Beauty." *Newsweek* (June 3, 1996): 61-66.

Cowley, Malcolm. "Introduction to *Winesburg, Ohio*." In *"Winesburg, Ohio": Text and Criticism*, edited by John H. Ferres, 357-68. New York: Viking Press, 1966. First published in *Winesburg, Ohio*, edited by Malcolm Cowley. New York: Viking Press, 1960.

Cox, James M. "A Hard Book to Take." In *Mark Twain's "Adventures of Huckleberry Finn,"* edited by Harold Bloom, 87-108. New York: Chelsea House, 1986.

———. "Remarks on the Sad Initiation of Huckleberry Finn." In *Huck Finn among the Critics: A Centennial Selection* edited by M. Thomas Inge, 141-55. Frederick, MD: University Publications of America, 1985.

Crews, Frederick C. *The Sins of the Fathers: Hawthorne's Psychological Themes*. New York: Oxford University Press, 1966.

D'Avanzo, Mario L. "The Literary Sources of 'My Kinsman, Major Molineux.'" *Studies in Short Fiction* 10 (1973): 121-36.

Daly, Martin and Margo Wilson. "Evolutionary Psychology and Marital Conflict: The Relevance of Stepchildren." In *Sex, Power, Conflict: Evolutionary and Feminist Perspectives*, edited by David M. Buss and Neil M. Malamuth, 9-28. New York and Oxford: Oxford University Press, 1996.

———. *Sex, Evolution, and Behavior*. 2nd ed. Belmont, CA: Wadsworth Publishing Company, 1983.

Davies, Geffrey. "Edna St. Vincent Millay's *A Few Figs from Thistles*." *Textual Cultures* 9, no. 1 (2014): 66-94. DOI: 10/4434/tc.v9i1.2117.

Dawkins, Richard. *River Out of Eden: A Darwinian View of Life*. New York: Harper Collins, 1995.

———. *The Selfish Gene*, New ed. Oxford and New York: Oxford University Press, 1989.

Del Giudice, Marco and Jay Belsky. "The Development of Life History Strategies: Toward a Multi-Stage Theory." In *The Evolution of Personality and Individual Differences*, edited by David M. Buss and Patricia H. Hawley, 154-76. Oxford: Oxford University Press, 2011.

Dennis, Carl. "How to Live in Hell: The Bleak Vision of Hawthorne's 'My Kinsman, Major Molineux.'" *University Review* 37 (1971): 250-58.

DeVoto, Bernard. "The Artist as American," in *Twentieth Century Interpretations of "Adventures of Huckleberry Finn"*, edited by Claude M. Simpson, 7-15. Englewood Cliffs, NJ: Prentice-Hall, 1968.

Dissanayake, Ellen. *Art and Intimacy: How the Arts Began*. Seattle: University of Washington Press, 2000.

———. *Homo Aestheticus: Where Art Comes From and Why*. Seattle: University of Washington Press, 1992.

———. *What Is Art For?* Seattle: University of Washington Press, 1988.

Donaldson, Scott. "Hemingway's Morality of Compensation." In *Ernest Hemingway's "The Sun Also Rises": A Casebook*, edited by Linda Wagner-Martin, 81-98. Oxford: Oxford University Press, 2002.

Donovan, Josephine. *After the Fall: The Demeter-Persephone Myth in Wharton, Cather, and Glasgow*. University Park: Pennsylvania State University Press, 1989.

Downes, Paul. "Democratic Terror in 'My Kinsman, Major Molineux' and 'The Man of the Crowd.'" *Poe Studies* 37 (2004): 31-35.

Drake, William. "Walden." In *Thoreau: A Collection of Critical Essays*, edited by Sherman Paul, 71-91. Englewood Cliffs, NJ: Prentice Hall, 1962.

Dunant, M. "The Pyrophone." *Popular Science Monthly* Vol 7 (August 1875): 444-53. https: en.m.wikisource org/wiki/Popular_Science_Monthly/Volume 7_The Pyrophone.

Dutton, Denis. *The Art Instinct: Beauty, Pleasure and Human Evolution*. New York: Bloomsbury Press, 2009.

Dutton, Geoffrey. *Whitman*. New York: Grove, 1961.

Easterlin, Nancy. *A Biocultural Approach to Literary Theory and Interpretation*. Baltimore, MD: Johns Hopkins University Press, 2012.

———. "From Reproductive Resource to Autonomous Individuality? Charlotte Bronte's *Jane Eyre*." In *Evolution's Empress: Darwinian Perspectives on the Nature of Women*, edited by Maryanne L. Fisher, Justin R. Garcia, and Rosemarie Sokol Chang, 390-405. Oxford: Oxford University Press, 2013.

Egan, Michael. *Mark Twain's Huckleberry Finn: Race, Class and Society*. London: Sussex University Press, 1977.

Eble, Kenneth. "*The Great Gatsby*." *College Literature* 1, no. 1 (1974): 34-47.

Elliott, Ira. "Performance Art: Jake Barnes and 'Masculine' Signification in *The Sun Also Rises*." In *Ernest Hemingway's "The Sun Also Rises": A Casebook*, edited by Linda Wagner-Martin, 63-80. Oxford: Oxford University Press, 2002.

Ellis, Bruce J., and Donald Symons. "Sex Differences in Sexual Fantasy: An Evolutionary Psychological Approach", *Journal of Sex Research* 27 (1990): 527-56.

Emerson, Ralph Waldo. "The Poet." In *The Collected Works of Ralph Waldo Emerson*. Vol. 3. Essays: Second Series. Edited by Joseph Slater, Alfred R. Ferguson and Jean Ferguson Carr, 1-24. Cambridge, MA and London: Harvard University Press, 1983.

Epstein, Daniel Mark. *What Lips My Lips Have Kissed: The Loves and Love Poems of Edna St. Vincent Millay*. New York: Henry Holt, 2001.

Erkkila, Betsy. "Whitman and the Homosexual Republic," in *Walt Whitman: The Centennial Essays*, edited by Ed Folsom, 153-71. Iowa City: University of Iowa Press, 1994.

Falck, Colin. "Introduction: The Modern Lyricism of Edna Millay." In *Edna St. Vincent Millay: Selected Poems*, edited by Colin Falck, xv-xxx. New York: HarperCollins, 1991.

Fass, Barbara. "Rejection of Paternalism: Hawthorne's 'My Kinsman, Major Molineux' and Ellison's *Invisible Man*." *College Language Association Journal* 14 (1971): 317-23.

Fertel, R. J. "Spontaneity and the Quest for Maturity in *Huckleberry Finn*." In *Huck Finn: Major Literary Characters*, edited by Harold Bloom, 82-98. New York: Chelsea House, 1990.

Fetterley, Judith. "*The Great Gatsby*: Fitzgerald's *droit de seigneur*." In *The Resisting Reader: A Feminist Approach to American Fiction*, 72-100. Bloomington and London: Indiana University Press, 1978.

Fiedler, Leslie. "Hemingway's Men and (the Absence of) Women." In *Readings on Ernest Hemingway*, edited by Katie De Koster, 90-95. San Diego, CA: Greenhaven Press, 1997.

Fisher, Benjamin K. "Transitions from Victorian to Modern: The Supernatural Stories of Mary Wilkins Freeman and Edith Wharton." *American Supernatural Fiction from Edith Wharton to the "Weird Tales" Writers*, edited by Douglas Robillard, 3-42. New York: Garland, 1996.

Fitzgerald, F. Scott. *The Great Gatsby*. New York: Charles Scribner's Sons, 1925, edited and reprinted by Matthew J. Bruccoli. Cambridge and New York: Cambridge University Press, 1991.

Fore, Dana. "Life Unworthy of Life? Masculinity, Disability, and Guilt in *The Sun Also Rises*." In *Eight Decades of Hemingway Criticism*, edited by Linda Wagner-Martin, 37-54. East Lansing: Michigan State University Press, 2009.

Forter, Greg. "Melancholy Modernism: Gender and the Politics of Mourning in *The Sun Also Rises*." In *Eight Decades of Hemingway Criticism*, edited by Linda Wagner-Martin, 55-73. East Lansing: Michigan State University Press, 2009.

Frank, Waldo. "*Winesburg, Ohio* After Twenty Years." In *The Achievement of Sherwood Anderson: Essays in Criticism*, edited by Ray Lewis White, 116-21. Chapel Hill: University of North Carolina Press, 1966. First published in *Story* 19 (1941): 29-33.

Franklin, Benjamin. "The Autobiography." In *Benjamin Franklin's Autobiography: An Authoritative Text, Backgrounds, Criticism*, edited by J. A. Leo Lemay and P. M. Zall, 1-146. New York and London: Norton, 1986.

———. "Information to Those Who Would Remove to America." In *The Norton Anthology of American Literature*. Vol A: *Beginnings to 1820*. 7th ed., edited by Nina Baym, Wayne Franklin, Philip F. Gura, and Arnold Krupat, 463-468. New York and London: Norton, 2007.

Frederick, David A., Tania A. Reynolds, and Maryanne L. Fisher. "The Importance of Female Choice: Evolutionary Perspectives on Female Mating Strategies." In *Evolution's Empress: Darwinian Perspectives on the Nature of Women*, edited by Maryanne L. Fisher, Justin R. Garcia, and Rosemarie Sokol Chang, 304-29. Oxford: Oxford University Press, 2013.

Fryer, Judith. *Felicitous Space: The Imaginative Structures of Edith Wharton and Willa Cather*. Chapel Hill: University of North Carolina Press, 1986.

Fussell, Edwin. "*Winesburg, Ohio*: Art and Isolation." In *The Achievement of Sherwood Anderson*, edited by Ray Lewis White, 104-13. Chapel Hill: University of North Carolina Press, 1966. First published in *Modern Fiction Studies* 6 (1960): 106-14.

Fussell, Edwin S. "Fitzgerald's Brave New World." *English Literary History* 19, no. 4 (1952): 291-306.

Fussell, Paul. *The Great War and Modern Memory*. New York: Oxford University Press, 1975.

Gangestad, Steven W. "Evidence for Adaptations for Female Extra-Pair Mating in Humans: Thoughts on Current Status and Future Directions." In *Female Infidelity and Paternal Uncertainty: Evolutionary Perspectives on Male Anti-Cuckoldry Tactics*, edited by Steven M. Platek and Todd K. Shackelford, 37-57. Cambridge and New York: Cambridge University Press, 2006.

Gassman, Janet. "Edna St. Vincent Millay: 'Nobody's Own.'" *Colby Library Quarterly* 9, no. 6 (June 1971): 297-310.

Gates, Henry Louis, Jr. and Sieglinde Lenke. "Zora Neale Hurston: Establishing the Canon." In *Zora Neale Hurston: The Complete Stories*, ix-xxiii. New York: Harper Perennial, 2008.

Geary, David. C. *Male, Female: The Evolution of Sex Differences*. Washington, DC: American Psychological Association, 1998.

Gentile, Kathy Justice. "Supernatural Transmissions: Turn-of-the-Century Ghosts in American Women's Fiction: Jewett, Freeman, Wharton, and Gilman." *Approaches to Teaching Gothic Fiction*, edited by Diana Long Hoeveler and Tamar Heller, 208-14. New York: Modern Language Association, 2003.

German, Norman. "Counterfeiting and a Two-Bit Error in Zora Neale Hurston's 'The Gilded Six-Bits.'" *Xavier Review* 19, no. 2 (1999): 5-15.

Gilmore, Michael T. "*Walden* and the 'Curse of Trade.'" In *Critical Essays on Henry David Thoreau's Walden*, edited by Joel Myerson, 177-92. Boston: G.K. Hall, 1988.

Gollin, Rita K. *Nathaniel Hawthorne and the Truth of Dreams*. Baton Rouge and London: Louisiana State University Press, 1979.

Goodman, Susan. *Edith Wharton's Women: Friends and Rivals*. Hanover, NH: University of New England Press, 1990.

Grayson, Robert C. "The New England Sources of 'My Kinsman, Major Molineux.'" *American Literature: A Journal of Literary History, Criticism, and Bibliography* 54, no. 4 (1982): 545-59.

Griffith, John. "Franklin's Sanity and the Man Behind the Masks." In *The Oldest Revolutionary*, edited by J. A. Leo Lemay, 123-38. Philadelphia: University of Pennsylvania Press, 1976.

Gross, Barry Edward. *Critical Extracts*. In *Gatsby: Major Literary Characters*, edited by Harold Bloom, 23-25. New York: Chelsea House, 1991.

Gross, Seymour L. "Hawthorne's 'My Kinsman, Major Molineux': History as Moral Adventure." *Nineteenth-Century Fiction* 12, no. 2 (1957): 97-109.

Gunn, Giles F. "F. Scott Fitzgerald's *Gatsby* and the Imagination of Wonder." In *Critical Essays on F. Scott Fitzgerald's "The Great Gatsby,"* edited by Scott Donaldson, 228-42. Boston: G. K. Hall, 1984.

Harding, Walter. *The Days of Henry Thoreau*. Rev. ed. Princeton, NJ: Princeton University Press, 1982.

Harris, Susan K. "Huck Finn." In *Huck Finn: Major Literary Characters*, edited by Harold Bloom, 73-81. New York: Chelsea House, 1990.

Hart, Jeffrey. "Anything Can Happen: Magical Transformation in *The Great Gatsby*," *South Carolina Review* 25, no. 2 (1993): 37-50.

Harvey, W. J. "Theme and Texture in *The Great Gatsby*." In *Critical Essays on F. Scott Fitzgerald's "The Great Gatsby*," edited by Scott Donaldson, 75-84. Boston: G. K. Hall, 1984.

Hawthorne, Nathaniel. "My Kinsman, Major Molineux." In *The Snow-Image and Uncollected Tales*. The Centenary Edition of the Works of Nathaniel Hawthorne. Vol. 11. Edited by William Charvat, Roy Harvey Pearce, Claude M. Simpson, and J. Donald Crowley, 208-31. Columbus: Ohio State University Press, 1974.

———. *The Scarlet Letter*. The Centenary Edition of the Works of Nathaniel Hawthorne. Vol. 1. Edited by William Charvat, Roy Harvey Pearce, Claude M. Simpson, Fredson Bowers, and Matthew J. Bruccoli. Columbus: Ohio State University Press, 1962.

Hays, Peter L. "Oxymoron in *The Great Gatsby*." *Papers on Language and Literature* 47, no. 3 (2011): 318-25.

Heerwagen, Judith H. and Gordon H. Orians. "Humans, Habitats, and Aesthetics." In *The Biophilia Hypothesis*, edited by Stephen R. Kellert and Edward O. Wilson, 138-72. Washington, DC: Island Press, 1993.

Helms, Alan. "Whitman's 'Live Oak with Moss.'" In *The Continuing Presence of Walt Whitman: The Life after the Life*, edited by Robert K. Martin, 185-205. Iowa City: University of Iowa Press, 1992.

Hemenway, Robert E. *Zora Neale Hurston: A Literary Biography*. Urbana: University of Illinois Press, 1980.

Hemingway, Ernest. "A Clean, Well-Lighted Place." New York: Scribner's, 1933. Reprinted in *The Short Stories*, 379-83. New York: Charles Scribner's Sons, 1966. Citations refer to the 1966 edition.

———. *Selected Letters 1917-1961*, edited by Carlos Baker. New York: Charles Scribner's Sons, 1981.

———. *The Sun Also Rises*. New York: Charles Scribner's Sons, 1926. Reprint New York: Macmillan, 1988. Citations refer to the 1988 edition.

Hinkle, James. "What's Funny in *The Sun Also Rises*?" In *"The Sun Also Rises": A Casebook,* edited by Linda Wagner-Martin, 107-23. Oxford: Oxford University Press, 2002.

Hoag, Ronald Wesley. "Thoreau's Later Natural History Writings." In *The Cambridge Companion to Henry David Thoreau*, edited by Joel Myerson, 152-70. Cambridge and New York: Cambridge University Press, 1995.

Hoeller, Hildegard. "Racial Currency: Zora Neale Hurston's 'The Gilded Six-Bits' and the Gold-Standard Debate." *American Literature* 77, no. 4 (2005): 761-85.

Hoff, Ann K. "'How Love May Be Acquired': Prescriptive Autobiography in Millay's *Fatal Interview*." *CEA Critic* 68, no. 3 (2006): 1-15.

Hoffman, Steven K. "*Nada* and the Clean, Well-Lighted Place: The Unity of Hemingway's Short Fiction." In *Modern Critical Views: Ernest Hemingway*, edited by Harold Bloom, 173-192. New York: Chelsea House, 1985.

Howard, Lillie P. "Marriage: Zora Neale Hurston's System of Values." *College Language Association Journal* 21 (1977): 256-68.

Howe, Irving. "The Book of the Grotesque." In *"Winesburg, Ohio": Text and Criticism*, edited by John H. Ferres, 405-20. New York: Viking Press, 1966.

———. "Introduction: The Achievement of Edith Wharton." In *Edith Wharton: A Collection of Critical Essays*, edited by Irving Howe, 1-18. Englewood Cliffs, NJ: Prentice-Hall, 1962.

Hrdy, Sarah Blaffer. *Mother Nature: A History of Mothers, Infants, and Natural Selection*. New York: Pantheon Books, 1999.

———. *The Woman That Never Evolved*. Cambridge, MA and London: Harvard University Press, 1981.

Hubbard, Stacy Carson. "Love's 'Little Day': Time and the Sexual Body in Millay's Sonnets." In *Millay at 100: A Critical Reappraisal*, edited by Diane P. Freedman, 100-16. Carbondale and Edwardsville: Southern Illinois University Press, 1995.

Hungerford, Edward. "Walt Whitman and his Chart of Bumps." *American Literature* 2, no. 4 (1931): 350-84.

Hurston, Zora Neale. *Dust Tracks on a Road*. Philadelphia: Lippincott, 1942. Reprint, New York: Arno Press, 1969.

———."The Gilded Six-Bits." 1933. *Zora Neale Hurston: The Complete Stories*, with an introduction by Henry Louis Gates, Jr. and Sieglinde Lenke, 86-98. New York: Harper Perennial, 2008.

Hyman, Stanley Edgar. "Henry Thoreau in Our Time." In *Thoreau: A Collection of Critical Essays*, edited by Sherman Paul, 23-36. Englewood Cliffs, NJ: Prentice-Hall, 1962.

Jackson, Louise. "Witches, Wives and Mothers." *The Witchcraft Reader*. 2nd ed. Edited by Darren Oldridge, 311-23. London and New York, Routledge, 2008.

Jennings, Francis. *Benjamin Franklin: Politician*. New York and London: Norton, 1996.

Johnson, Christiane. "*The Great Gatsby*: The Final Vision." In *Critical Essays on F. Scott Fitzgerald's "The Great Gatsby,"* edited by Scott Donaldson, 112-17. Boston: G. K. Hall, 1984.

Jones, Evora W. "The Pastoral and Picaresque in Zora Neale Hurston's 'The Gilded Six-Bits.'" *College Language Association Journal* 35, no. 3 (1992): 316-24.

Jones, Gayl. "Breaking out of the Conventions of Dialect: Dunbar and Hurston." *Présence Africaine: Revue Culturelle du Monde Noir* [Cultural Review of the Negro World] 144 (1987): 32-46.

Kastner, G. E. "Improvement in Pyrophones." Patents: US 164458A: 15 June 1875. IFI Claims Patent Services. https://www.google/patents/US/64458.

Katcher, Aaron and Gregory Wilkins. "Dialogue with Animals: Its Nature and Culture." In *The Biophilia Hypothesis*, edited by Stephen R. Kellert and Edward O. Wilson, 173-97. Washington, DC: Island Press, 1993.

Kaufman, Scott Barry, Aaron Kozbelt, Melanie L. Bromley, and Geoffrey F. Miller. "The Role of Creativity and Humor in Human Mate Selection." In *Mating Intelligence: Sex, Relationships, and the Mind's Reproductive System*, edited by Glenn Geher and Geoffrey F. Miller, 227-62. New York: Taylor and Francis, 2007.

Kazin, Alfred. "The New Realism: Sherwood Anderson." In *"Winesburg, Ohio": Text and Criticism*, edited by John H. Ferres, 321-30. New York: Viking Press, 1966. Excerpted from "The New Realism: Sherwood Anderson and Sinclair Lewis." First published in *On Native Grounds: An Interpretation of Modern American Prose Literature*, edited by Alfred Kazin, 162-73. New York: Reynal and Hitchcock, 1942.

Kellert, Stephen R. "The Biological Basis for Human Values of Nature." In *The Biophilia Hypothesis*, edited by Stephen R. Kellert and Edward O. Wilson, 42-69. Washington, DC: Island Press, 1993.

Kenner, Hugh. "The Promised Land." In *Gatsby: Major Literary Characters*, edited by Harold Bloom, 74-80. New York: Chelsea House, 1991.

Kenrick, Douglas T., Melanie R. Trost and Virgil L. Sheets. "Power, Harassment, and Trophy Mates: The Feminist Advantages of an Evolutionary Perspective." In *Sex, Power, Conflict: Evolutionary and Feminist Perspectives*, edited by David M. Buss and Neil M. Malamuth, 29-53. New York and Oxford: Oxford University Press, 1996.

Keyser, Catherine. *Playing Smart: New York Women Writers and Modern Magazine Culture*. New Brunswick, NJ: Rutgers University Press, 2011.

Kilcup, Karen L. *Robert Frost and Feminine Literary Tradition*. Ann Arbor: University of Michigan Press, 2001.

Killingsworth, M. Jimmie. "Whitman and the Gay American Ethos." In *A Historical Guide to Walt Whitman*, edited by David S. Reynolds, 121-151, Oxford and New York: Oxford University Press, 2000.

———. "Whitman's Physical Eloquence." In *Walt Whitman: The Centennial Essays*, edited by Ed Folsom, 68-78. Iowa City: University of Iowa Press, 1994.

Kruger, Daniel J., Maryanne Fisher, and Ian Jobling. "Proper Hero Dads and Dark Hero Cads: Alternate Mating Strategies Exemplified in British Romantic Literature." In *The Literary Animal: Evolution and the Nature of Narrative*, edited by Jonathan Gottschall and David Sloan Wilson, 199-243. Evanston, IL: Northwestern University Press, 2005.

Krutch, Joseph Wood. *Henry David Thoreau*. New York: William Sloane Associates, 1948.

Kurland, Jeffrey A., and Steven J. C. Gaulin. "Cooperation and Conflict Among Kin." In *The Handbook of Evolutionary Psychology*, edited by David M. Buss, 447-82. Hoboken, NJ: John Wiley and Sons, 2005.

Lane, Lauriat, Jr. "On the Organic Structure of *Walden*." In *Critical Essays on Henry David Thoreau's "Walden,"* edited by Joel Myerson, 68-77. Boston: G.K. Hall, 1988.

Leibowitz, Herbert. "'That Insinuating Man': *The Autobiography of Benjamin Franklin*." In *Fabricating Lives: Explanations in American Autobiography*, edited by Herbert Leibowitz, 29-70. New York: Alfred A. Knopf, 1989.

Lemay, J. A. Leo. "Franklin's *Autobiography* and the American Dream." In *Benjamin Franklin's Autobiography: An Authoritative Text, Backgrounds, Criticism*, edited by J. A. Leo Lemay and

P. M. Zall, 349-60. New York and London: Norton, 1986. Excerpted from *The Renaissance Man in the Eighteenth Century*. Los Angeles: William Andrews Clark Memorial Library, 1978.

Lenz, William E. "Confidence and Convention in *Huckleberry Finn*." In *One Hundred Years of "Huckleberry Finn": The Boy, His Book, and American Culture*, edited by Robert Sattelmeyer and J. Donald Crowley, 186-200. Columbia: University of Missouri Press, 1985.

Lesser, Simon O. "The Image of the Father: A Reading of 'My Kinsman, Major Molineux' and 'I Want to Know Why.'" *Partisan Review* 22 (1955): 372-90.

Levin, David. "The Autobiography of Benjamin Franklin: The Puritan Experimenter in Life and Art." *Yale Review* 53, no. 2 (1964): 258-75.

Lewis, R.W.B. *Edith Wharton: A Biography*. New York: Harper Row, 1975.

Lewis, Roger. "Money, Love, and Aspiration in *The Great Gatsby*." In *New Essays on "The Great Gatsby,"* edited by Matthew J. Bruccoli 41-57. Cambridge: Cambridge University Press, 1985.

Lhamon, Jr., W. T. "The Essential Houses of *The Great Gatsby*." In *Critical Essays on F. Scott Fitzgerald's "The Great Gatsby,"* edited by Scott Donaldson, 166-75. Boston: G. K. Hall, 1984.

Lovecraft, H. P. *Supernatural Horror in Literature*. New York: Dover, 1973. Originally published in *The Recluse* 1 (1927).

Lovelock, James. *Gaia: A New Look at Life on Earth*. Rpt. with new Preface, New York: Oxford University Press, 1987.

Lowe, John. *Jump at the Sun: Zora Neale Hurston's Classic Comedy*. Excerpted in *"Sweat": Zora Neale Hurston*, edited by Cheryl A. Wall, 183-92. New Brunswick, NJ: Rutgers University Press, 1997.

Lynn, Kenneth S. "Critical Extracts." In *Huck Finn: Major Literary Characters*, edited by Harold Bloom, 22-27. New York: Chelsea House, 1990.

Marchand, Mary V. "Cross Talk: Edith Wharton and the New England Women Regionalists." *Women's Studies* 30 (2001): 369-95.

Martin, Robert K. *The Homosexual Tradition in American Poetry*. Austin and London: University of Texas Press, 1979.

Martin, Terence. *Nathaniel Hawthorne*. United States Authors Series. Edited by Lewis Leary, Rev. ed. Boston: Twayne, 1983.

Martin, Wendy. "Brett Ashley as New Woman in *The Sun Also Rises*." In *Ernest Hemingway's "The Sun Also Rises": A Casebook*, edited by Linda Wagner-Martin, 47-62. Oxford: Oxford University Press, 2002.

Marx, Leo. "Mr. Eliot, Mr. Trilling, and *Huckleberry Finn*." In *Twentieth Century Interpretations of "Adventures of Huckleberry Finn"* edited by Claude M. Simpson, 26-40. Englewood Cliffs, N.J., 1968.

———. *The Machine in the Garden: Technology and the Pastoral Ideal in America*. London and Oxford: Oxford University Press, 1964.

Marzec, Marcia Smith. "'My Kinsman, Major Molineux's Theo-Political Allegory." *American Transcendental Quarterly* 1, no. 4 (1987): 273-89.

Maugham, W. Somerset. *Books and You*. New York: Doubleday, Doran, and Company, 1940.

McGowan, Philip. "The American Carnival of *The Great Gatsby*." *Connotations* 13, no. 1-2 (2003 / 2004): 143-58.
McGregor, Robert Kuhn. *A Wider View of the Universe: Henry Thoreau's Study of Nature*. Urbana and Chicago: University of Illinois Press, 1997.
McLain, D. Kelly, Deanna Setters, Michael P. Moulton, and Ann E. Pratt. "Ascription of Resemblance of Newborns by Parents and Nonrelatives." *Evolution and Human Behavior* 21 (2000): 11-23.
McMurry, Andrew. *Environmental Renaissance: Emerson, Thoreau, and the Systems of Nature*. Athens and London: University of Georgia Press, 2003.
McVay, Scott. Prelude: "A Siamese Connexion with a Plurality of Other Mortals." In *The Biophilia Hypothesis*, edited by Stephen R. Kellert and Edward O. Wilson, 3-19. Washington, DC: Island Press, 1993.
Michelson, Bruce. "Huck and the Games of the World." In *Huck Finn among the Critics: A Centennial Selection*, edited by M. Thomas Inge, 211-29. Frederick, MD: University Publications of America, 1985.
Millay, Edna St. Vincent. *Collected Poems*, edited by Norma Millay. New York: Harper and Row, 1956.
Miller, Edwin Haviland. *Walt Whitman's "Song of Myself": A Mosaic of Interpretations*. Iowa City: University of Iowa Press, 1989.
———. *Walt Whitman's Poetry: A Psychological Journey*. Boston: Houghton Mifflin, 1968.
Miller, Geoffrey. *The Mating Mind: How Sexual Choice Shaped the Evolution of Human Nature*. New York: Random, 2001.
Miller, James E., Jr. *A Critical Guide to "Leaves of Grass."* Chicago and London: University of Chicago Press, 1957.
———. "Fitzgerald's *Gatsby*: The World as Ash Heap." In *Critical Essays on F. Scott Fitzgerald's "The Great Gatsby,"* edited by Scott Donaldson, 242-58. Boston: G. K. Hall, 1984.
Miller, John N. "The Pageantry of Revolt in 'My Kinsman, Major Molineux.'" *Studies in American Fiction* 17, no. 1 (1989): 51-64.
Milnes, Allan. "Valley Fiesta in Brisbane, Australia." *Demotix: The Network for Freelance Photojournalists*. September 10, 2010.
Moddelmog, Debra A. "Contradictory Bodies in *The Sun Also Rises*." In *Ernest Hemingway's "The Sun Also Rises": A Casebook*, edited by Linda Wagner-Martin, 155-165. Oxford: Oxford University Press, 2002.
Montagu, Jeremy. *The World of Baroque and Classical Musical Instruments*. Woodstock, NY: Overlook Press, 1979.
Nagel, James. "Brett and the Other Women in *The Sun Also Rises*." In *The Cambridge Companion to Ernest Hemingway*, edited by Scott Donaldson, 87-108. Cambridge: Cambridge University Press, 1996.
Nevius, Blake. "On *Ethan Frome*." In *Edith Wharton: A Collection of Critical Essays*, edited by Irving Howe, 130-36. Englewood Cliffs, NJ: Prentice-Hall, 1962.
Oelschlager, Max. *The Idea of Wilderness*. New Haven: Yale University Press, 1982.

Ornstein, Robert. "Scott Fitzgerald's Fable of East and West." In *Twentieth-Century Interpretations of "The Great Gatsby,"* edited by Ernest Lockridge, 54-60. Englewood Cliffs, NJ: Prentice-Hall, 1968.

Orr, David W. "Love It or Lose It: The Coming Biophilia Revolution." In *The Biophilia Hypothesis*, edited by Stephen R. Kellert and Edward O. Wilson, 415-40. Washington, DC: Island Press, 1993.

Parker, Hershel. "The Real 'Live Oak, with Moss': Straight Talk about Whitman's 'Gay Manifesto.'" *Nineteenth-Century Literature* 51, no. 2 (1996): 145-60.

Paul, Sherman. "A Fable of the Renewal of Life." In *Thoreau: A Collection of Critical Essays*, edited by Sherman Paul, 100-16. Englewood Cliffs, NJ: Prentice-Hall, 1962.

Pearce, Roy Harvey. *The Continuity of American Poetry*. Princeton, NJ: Princeton University Press, 1961.

———. "Hawthorne and the Sense of the Past or, the Immortality of Major Molineux." *English Literary History* 21, no. 4 (1954): 327-49.

Peck, H. Daniel. *Thoreau's Morning Work: Meaning and Perception in "A Week on the Concord and Merrimack Rivers," the Journal, and "Walden."* New Haven and London: Yale University Press, 1990.

Perlmutter, Elizabeth P. "A Doll's Heart: The Girl in the Poetry of Edna St. Vincent Millay and Louise Bogan." *Twentieth Century Literature* 23, no. 2 (May 1977): 157-79.

Peppe, Holly. "Rewriting the Myth of the Woman in Love: Millay's *Fatal Interview*." In *Millay at 100: A Critical Reappraisal*, edited by Diane P. Freedman, 52-65. Carbondale and Edwardsville: Southern Illinois University Press, 1995.

Peters, Pearlie Mae Fisher. "Missie May in 'The Gilded Six-Bits.'" In *The Assertive Woman in Zora Neale Hurston's Fiction, Folklore, and Drama*, 89-95. New York: Garland Publishing, 1998.

Pinker, Steven. *The Blank Slate: The Modern Denial of Human Nature*. New York: Penguin, 2002.

———. *How the Mind Works*. New York: Norton, 2009.

Pitofsky, Alex. "Pap Finn's Overture: Fatherhood, Identity, and Southwestern Culture in *Adventures of Huckleberry Finn*." *Mark Twain Annual* 4, no. 1 (2006): 55-70.

Poirier, Richard. "Huck Finn and the Metaphors of Society." In *Twentieth Century Interpretations of "Adventures of Huckleberry Finn,"* edited by Claude M. Simpson, 95-101. Englewood Cliffs, NJ: Prentice-Hall, 1968.

Posnock, Ross. "'A New World, Material Without Being Real': Fitzgerald's Critique of Capitalism in *"The Great Gatsby."* In *Critical Essays on F. Scott Fitzgerald's "The Great Gatsby,"* edited by Scott Donaldson, 201-13. Boston: G. K. Hall, 1984.

Powys, Llewelyn, "Thoreau: A Disparagement." In *Critical Essays on Henry David Thoreau's "Walden,"* edited by Joel Myerson, 53-56. Boston: G.K. Hall, 1988.

Pratto, Felicia. "Sexual Politics: The Gender Gap in the Bedroom, the Cupboard, and the Cabinet." In *Sex, Power, Conflict: Evolutionary and Feminist Perspectives*, edited by David M. Buss and Neil M. Malamuth, 179-230. New York and Oxford: Oxford University Press, 1996.

Puckett, James A. "'Sex Explains It All': Male Performance, Evolution, and Sexual Selection in Ernest Hemingway's *The Sun Also Rises*." *Studies in American Naturalism* 8, no. 2 (2013): 125-49.

Pughe, Thomas. "Brute Neighbors: The Modernity of a Metaphor." In *Thoreauvian Modernities: Transatlantic Conversations on an American Icon*, edited by François Specq, Laura Dassow Walls, and Michel Granger, 249-64. Athens and London: University of Georgia Press, 2013.

Reesman, Jeanne Campbell. "Bad Fathering in *Adventures of Huckleberry Finn*." In *The Turn Around Religion in America: Literature, Culture, and the Work of Saven Bercovitch*, edited by Nan Goodman and Michael P. Kramer, 157-81. Surrey, England: Ashgate Publishing, 2011.

Reynolds, David S. *Walt Whitman's America: A Cultural Biography*. New York: Alfred A. Knopf, 1995.

Reynolds, Michael S. *"The Sun also Rises": A Novel of the Twenties*. Boston: Twayne, 1988.

Robinson, David M. "Thoreau, Modernity, and Nature's Seasons." In *Thoreauvian Modernities: Transatlantic Conversations on an American Icon*, edited by François Specq, Laura Dassow Walls, and Michel Granger, 69-81. Athens and London: University of Georgia Press, 2013.

Rodewald, Fred A. and Neal B. Houston. "'My Kinsman, Major Molineux': A Re-Evaluation." *Real: A Journal of the Liberal Arts* 21, no. 1 (1996): 40-44.

Rolston, Holmes, III,. "Biophilia, Selfish Genes, Shared Values." In *The Biophilia Hypothesis*, edited by Stephen R. Kellert and Edward O. Wilson, 381-414. Washington, DC: Island Press, 1993.

Rossi, William. "Thoreau's Transcendental Ecocentrism." In *Thoreau's Sense of Place: Essays in American Environmental Writing*, edited by Richard J. Schneider, 28-43. Iowa City: University of Iowa Press, 2000.

Rowe, Joyce A. "Delusions of American Idealism." In *Readings on "The Great Gatsby,"* edited by Katie De Koster, 87-95. San Diego, CA: Greenhaven Press, 1998.

Russell, John. "Allegory and 'My Kinsman, Major Molineux.'" *New England Quarterly* 40, no. 3 (1967): 432-40.

Sagan, Dorion and Lynn Margulis. "God, Gaia, and Biophilia." In *The Biophilia Hypothesis*, edited by Stephen R. Kellert and Edward O. Wilson, 345-364. Washington, DC: Island Press, 1993.

San Juan, Epifanio, Jr. "Vision and Reality: A Reconsideration of Sherwood Anderson's *Winesburg, Ohio*." In *"Winesburg, Ohio": Text and Criticism*, edited by John H. Ferres 468-81. New York: Viking Press, 1966. First published in *American Literature* 35 (1963): 137-55.

Sanderson, Rena. "Hemingway and Gender History." In *The Cambridge Companion to Ernest Hemingway*, edited by Scott Donaldson, 170-96. Cambridge: Cambridge University Press, 1996.

Sattelmeyer, Robert. "'Interesting, but Tough': *Huckleberry Finn* and the Problem of Tradition." In *One Hundred Years of "Huckleberry Finn": The Boy, His Book, and American Culture*, edited by Robert Sattelmeyer and J. Donald Crowley, 354-70. Columbia: University of Missouri Press, 1985.

———. *Thoreau's Reading: A Study in Intellectual History*. Princeton, NJ: Princeton University Press, 1988.

Sayre, Robert F. *The Examined Self: Benjamin Franklin, Henry Adams, Henry James*. Madison: University of Wisconsin Press, 1988.

———. "The Worldly Franklin and the Provincial Critics." *Texas Studies in Literature and Language* 4 (1963): 512-24.

Schmidgall, Gary. *Walt Whitman: A Gay Life*. New York: Dutton, 1997.

Schmigalle, Günther. "'How People Go to Hell': Pessimism, Tragedy, and Affinity to Schopenhauer in *The Sun Also Rises*." *The Hemingway Review* 25, no. 1 (2005): 7-21.

Schmitt, David P. "Fundamentals of Human Mating Strategies." In *The Handbook of Evolutionary Psychology*, edited by David M. Buss, 258-91. Hoboken, NJ: John Wiley and Sons, 2005.

Schulz, Dieter. "Sherwood Anderson: 'The Untold Lie.'" In *Amerikanische Short Stories des 20. Jahrhunderts*, edited by Michael Hanke, 18-26. Stuttgart: Reclam, 1998.

Schyberg, Frederik. *Walt Whitman*. Trans. Evie Alison Allen. New York: Columbia University Press, 1951.

Scigaj, Leonard M. and Nancy Craig Simmons. "Ecofeminist Cosmology in Thoreau's *Walden*." *Interdisciplinary Studies in Literature and Environment* 1, no. 1 (1993): 121-29.

Scott, Robert Ian. "Entropy vs. Ecology in *The Great Gatsby*." In *Gatsby: Major Literary Characters*, edited by Harold Bloom, 81-92. New York: Chelsea House, 1991.

Seavey, Ormond. *Becoming Benjamin Franklin: The Autobiography and the Life*. University Park and London: Pennsylvania State University Press, 1988.

Seshachari, Neila. "*The Great Gatsby*: Apogee of Fitzgerald's Mythopoeia." In *Gatsby: Major Literary Characters*, edited by Harold Bloom, 93-102. New York: Chelsea House, 1991.

Shakespeare, William. *Love's Labor's Lost*. In *Shakespeare: The Complete Works*, edited by G. B. Harrison, 394-429. New York: Harcourt, Brace, World, 1948.

Shaw, Peter. "Fathers, Sons, and the Ambiguities of Revolution in 'My Kinsman, Major Molineux.'" *New England Quarterly* 49, no. 4 (1976): 559-76.

Shaw, Samuel. "Hemingway, Nihilism, and the American Dream." In *Readings on Ernest Hemingway*, edited by Katie De Koster, 71-77. San Diego, CA: Greenhaven Press, 1997.

Shields, John C. "Hawthorne's 'Kinsman' and Vergil's *Aeneid*." *Classical and Modern Literature: A Quarterly* 19, no. 1 (1998): 35-51.

Shulman, Robert. "Fathers, Brothers, and 'the Diseased': The Family, Individualism, and American Society in *Huck Finn*." In *One Hundred Years of "Huckleberry Finn": The Boy, His Book, and American Culture*, edited by Robert Sattelmeyer and J. Donald Crowley, 325-40. Columbia: University of Missouri Press, 1985.

Shurr, William H. "Whitman's Omnisexual Sensibility." *Soundings: An Interdisciplinary Journal* 74, no. 1-2 (1991): 101-28.

Simpson, Louis. "Strategies of Sex in Whitman's Poetry." In *Walt Whitman of Mickle Street: A Centennial Collection of Essays*, edited by Geoffrey M. Sill, 28-37. Knoxville: University of Tennessee, 1994.

Singley, Carol J. "Calvinist Tortures in Edith Wharton's *Ethan Frome*." *The Calvinist Roots of the Modern Era*, edited by Aliki Barnstone, Michael Tomasek Manson, and Carol J. Singley, 162-80. Hanover, NH: University Press of New England, 1997.

Singley, Carol J. and Susan Elizabeth Sweeney. "Forbidden Reading and Ghostly Power in Wharton's 'Pomegranate Seed.'" *Women's Studies* 20 (1991): 177-203.

Smith, David L. "Huck, Jim, and American Racial Discourse." In *Huck Finn among the Critics: A Centennial Selection*, edited by M. Thomas Inge, 247-65. Frederick, MD: University Publications of America, 1985.

Smith, Henry Nash. "A Sound Heart and a Deformed Conscience." In *Twentieth Century Interpretations of "Adventures of Huckleberry Finn,"* edited by Claude M. Simpson 71-81. Englewood Cliffs, NJ: Prentice-Hall, 1968.

Smith, Ernest J. "'How the Speaking Pen Has Been Impeded': The Rhetoric of Love and Selfhood in Millay and Rich." In *Millay at 100: A Critical Reappraisal*, edited by Diane P. Freedman, 43-51. Carbondale and Edwardsville: Southern Illinois University Press, 1995.

Smuts, Barbara. "Male Aggression Against Women: An Evolutionary Perspective." In *Sex, Power, Conflict: Evolutionary and Feminist Perspectives*, edited by David M. Buss and Neil M. Malamuth, 231-68. New York and Oxford: Oxford University Press, 1996.

Soulé, Michael E. "Biophilia: Unanswered Questions." In *The Biophilia Hypothesis*, edited by Stephen R. Kellert and Edward O. Wilson, 441-55. Washington, DC: Island Press, 1993.

Specq, François and Laura Dassow Walls. "Introduction: The Manifold Modernity of Henry D. Thoreau." In *Thoreauvian Modernities: Transatlantic Conversations on an American Icon*, edited by François Specq, Laura Dassow Walls, and Michel Granger, 1-17. Athens and London: University of Georgia Press, 2013.

Spilka, Mark. "The Death of Love in *The Sun Also Rises*." In *Ernest Hemingway's "The Sun Also Rises": A Casebook*, edited by Linda Wagner-Martin, 33-45. Oxford: Oxford University Press, 2002.

Stallman, R. W. "Gatsby and the Hole in Time." In *Gatsby: Major Literary Characters*, edited by Harold Bloom, 55-63. New York: Chelsea House, 1991.

Stapleton, Lawrence. "Introduction." In *Thoreau: A Collection of Critical Essays*, edited by Sherman Paul, 161-179. Englewood Cliffs, NJ: Prentice-Hall, 1962.

Stevens, Wallace. "The Poems of Our Climate." In *The Palm at the End of the Mind: Selected Poems and a Play*, edited by Holly Stevens, 158. New York: Vintage Books, 1972.

Stoller, Leo. *After "Walden": Thoreau's Changing Views on Economic Man*. Stanford, CA: Stanford University Press, 1957.

Storey, Robert. *Mimesis and the Human Animal: On the Biogenetic Foundations of Literary Representation*. Evanston, IL: Northwestern University Press, 1996.

Stouck, David. "*The Great Gatsby* as Pastoral." In *Gatsby: Major Literary Characters*, edited by Harold Bloom, 64-73. New York: Chelsea House, 1991.

Sugiyama, Michelle Scalise. "Reverse-Engineering Narrative: Evidence of Special Design." In *The Literary Animal: Evolution and the Nature of Narrative*, edited by Jonathan Gottschall and David Sloan Wilson, 177-96. Evanston, IL: Northwestern University Press, 2005.

Symons, Donald. *The Evolution of Human Sexuality*. Oxford: Oxford University Press, 1979.

Thoreau, Henry David. *The Writings of Henry D. Thoreau: Walden*. 1854. Edited by J. Lyndon Shanley. Princeton, NJ: Princeton University Press, 1971.

Thorpe, Dwayne. "'My Kinsman, Major Molineux': The Identity of the Kinsman." *Topic* 18 (1969): 53-63.

Tooby, John and Leda Cosmides. "Conceptual Foundations of Evolutionary Psychology." In *The Handbook of Evolutionary Psychology*, edited by David M. Buss, 5-67. Hoboken, NJ: John Wiley and Sons, 2005.

———. "Does Beauty Build Adapted Minds? Toward an Evolutionary Theory of Aesthetics, Fiction, and the Arts." In *Evolution, Literature, and Film: A Reader*, edited by Brian Boyd, Joseph Carroll, and Jonathan Gottschall, 174-183. New York: Columbia University Press, 2010.

Trachtenberg, Alan. "The Form of Freedom in *Huckleberry Finn*." In *Huck Finn: Major Literary Characters*, edited by Harold Bloom, 48-60. New York: Chelsea House, 1990.

Travis, Jennifer. "Pain and Recompense: The Trouble with *Ethan Frome*." *Arizona Quarterly* 53, no. 3 (1997): 37-64.

Trilling, Lionel. "The Morality of Inertia." In *Edith Wharton: A Collection of Critical Essays*, edited by Irving Howe, 137-46. Englewood Cliffs, NJ: Prentice-Hall, 1962.

Trivers, Robert. *Natural Selection and Social Theory: Selected Papers of Robert Trivers*. Oxford: Oxford University Press, 2002.

———. "Parental Investment and Reproductive Success." In *Natural Selection and Social Theory: Selected Papers of Robert Trivers*, 56-110. Oxford: Oxford University Press, 2002.

———. "Self-Deception in Service of Deceit." In *Natural Selection and Social Theory: Selected Papers of Robert Trivers*, 255-93. Oxford: Oxford University Press, 2002.

Troy, William. "Scott Fitzgerald — the Authority of Failure." In *F. Scott Fitzgerald: A Collection of Critical Essays*, edited by Arthur Mizener, 20-24. Englewood Cliffs, NJ: Prentice-Hall, 1963.

Twain, Mark. *Adventures of Huckleberry Finn*. In *The Works of Mark Twain*. Vol. 8, edited by Walter Blair and Victor Fischer. Berkeley: University of California Press, 1988. First published 1884 by Chatto and Windus / Charles L. Webster. Citations refer to the 1988 edition.

———. *The Adventures of Tom Sawyer*. In *The Works of Mark Twain*. Vol. 4, edited by John C. Gerber, Paul Baender, and Terry Firkin, 31-237. Berkeley: University of California Press, 1980. First published 1876 by Bliss. Citations refer to the 1980 edition.

Ulrich, Roger S. "Biophilia, Biophobia, and Natural Landscapes." In *The Biophilia Hypothesis*, edited by Stephen R. Kellert and Edward O. Wilson, 73-137. Washington, DC: Island Press, 1993.

Vandermassen, Griet. *Who's Afraid of Charles Darwin? Debating Feminism and Evolutionary Theory*, Lanham, MD: Rowman and Littlefield, 2005.

Vermeule, Blakey. *Why Do We Care about Literary Characters?* Baltimore, MD: Johns Hopkins University Press, 2010.

Waggoner, Hyatt H. *The Presence of Hawthorne*. Baton Rouge and London: Louisiana State University Press, 1979.

Wagner-Martin, Linda. Introduction to *Ernest Hemingway's "The Sun Also Rises": A Casebook*, edited by Linda Wagner-Martin, 3-14. Oxford: Oxford University Press, 2002.

Waid, Candace. *Edith Wharton's Letters from the Underworld: Fictions of Women and Writing*. Chapel Hill: University of North Carolina Press, 1991.

Walcutt, Charles Child. "Sherwood Anderson: Impressionism and the Buried Life." In *The Achievement of Sherwood Anderson: Essays in Criticism*, edited by Ray Lewis White, 156-71.

Chapel Hill: University of North Carolina Press, 1966. First published in *Sewanee Review* 60 (1952): 28-47.

Walker, Cheryl. "The Female Body as Icon: Edna Millay Wears a Plaid Dress." In *Millay at 100: A Critical Reappraisal*, edited by Diane P. Freedman, 85-99. Carbondale and Edwardsville: Southern Illinois University Press, 1995.

Walker, Nancy. "Reformers and Young Maidens: Women and Virtue." In *Mark Twain's "Adventures of Huckleberry Finn": Modern Critical Interpretations*, edited by Harold Bloom, 69-85. New York: Chelsea House, 1986.

Wall, Cheryl A. Introduction to *"Sweat": Zora Neale Hurston,* edited by Cheryl A. Wall, 3-19. New Brunswick, NJ: Rutgers University Press, 1997.

Wallins, Roger P. "Robin and the Narrator in 'My Kinsman, Major Molineux.'" *Studies in Short Fiction* 12 (1975): 173-79.

Walls, Laura Dassow. "Believing in Nature: Wilderness and Wildness in Thoreauvian Science." In *Thoreau's Sense of Place: Essays in American Environmental Writing*, edited by Richard J. Schneider, 15-27. Iowa City: University of Iowa Press, 2000.

———. *Seeing New Worlds: Henry David Thoreau and Nineteenth-Century Natural Science*. Madison: University of Wisconsin Press, 1995.

Ward, John William. "Who Was Benjamin Franklin?" *American Scholar* 32 (1963): 541-53.

Warren, Robert Penn, "Hemingway's World." In *Readings on Ernest Hemingway*, edited by Katie De Koster, 34-38. San Diego, CA: Greenhaven Press, 1997.

Way, Brian. "*The Great Gatsby*." In *F. Scott Fitzgerald's "The Great Gatsby,"* edited by Harold Bloom, 87-108. New York: Chelsea House, 1986.

Weinstein, Arnold. "Fiction as Greatness: The Case of Gatsby." In *Gatsby: Major Literary Characters*, edited by Harold Bloom, 137-53. New York: Chelsea House, 1991.

Weinstock, Jeffrey Andrew. *Scare Tactics: Supernatural Fiction by American Women*. New York: Fordham University Press, 2008.

Wershoven, Carol. *The Female Intruder in the Novels of Edith Wharton*. Rutherford, NJ and London: Associated University Presses, 1982.

Wharton, Edith. *Ethan Frome*. New York: Charles Scribner's Sons, 1911.

———. "A Little Girl's New York." 1938. *Edith Wharton: The Uncollected Critical Writings*, edited by Frederick Wegener, 274-88. Princeton, NJ: Princeton University Press, 1996.

———. "Pomegranate Seed." *The World Over*, 53-110. New York and London: Appleton-Century, 1936.

———. Preface to *The Ghost Stories of Edith Wharton*, 1-4. Illus. Laszlo Kubinyi. New York: Scribner/Macmillan, Hudson River Ed. 1986.

———. "Roman Fever." *Collected Stories, 1911-1937,* edited by Maureen Howard, 749-61. New York: Library of America, 2001.

White, Charles Dodd. "Hawthorne's 'My Kinsman, Major Molineux.'" *Explicator* 65, no. 4 (2007): 215-17.

White, Ray Lewis. *"Winesburg, Ohio": An Exploration*. Boston: Twayne Publishers, 1990.

Whitman, Walt. "Song of Myself." In *Leaves of Grass*, edited by Sculley Bradley and Harold W. Blodgett, 28-89. New York and London: Norton, 1973.

Wilbur, Christopher J. and Lorne Campbell. "Swept off Their Feet? Females' Strategic Mating Behavior as a Means of Supplying the Broom." *Evolution's Empress: Darwinian Perspectives on the Nature of Women*, edited by Maryanne L. Fisher, Justin R. Garcia, and Rosemarie Sokol Chang, 330-344. Oxford: Oxford University Press, 2013.

Wilson, David Sloan and Joseph L. Carroll. "Darwin's Bridge to the Humanities: An Interview with Joseph L. Carroll." *This View of Life*. The Evolution Institute: 2016. Web.

Wilson, Edward O. *Biophilia*. Cambridge, MA and London: Harvard University Press, 1984.

———. "Biophilia and the Conservationist Ethic." In *The Biophilia Hypothesis*, edited by Stephen R. Kellert and Edward O. Wilson, 31-41. Washington, DC: Island Press, 1993.

———. *Consilience: The Unity of Knowledge*. New York: Alfred A. Knopf, 1998.

———. "Prologue: A Letter to Thoreau." In *The Future of Life*, xi-xxiv. New York: Vintage Books, 2002.

Wolff, Cynthia Griffin. *A Feast of Words: The Triumph of Edith Wharton*. New York: Oxford University Press, 1977.

Wright, Robert. *The Moral Animal: Evolutionary Psychology and Everyday Life*. New York: Vintage Books, 1994.

Young, Judy Hale. "The Repudiation of Sisterhood in Edith Wharton's 'Pomegranate Seed.'" *Studies in Short Fiction* 33 (1996): 1-11.

Zall, P. M. "A Portrait of the Artist as an Old Artificer." In *The Oldest Revolutionary*, edited by J. A. Leo Lemay, 53-65. Philadelphia: University of Pennsylvania Press, 1976.

Zellinger, Elissa. "Edna St. Vincent Millay and the Poetess Tradition." *Legacy* 29, no. 2 (2012): 240-62.

Zuckert, Catherine H. "Law and Nature in the *Adventures of Huckleberry Finn*." In *Huck Finn among the Critics: A Centennial Selection*, edited by M. Thomas Inge, 231-46. Frederick, MD: University Publications of America, 1985.

Zunshine, Lisa. *Why We Read Fiction: Theory of Mind and the Novel*. Columbus: Ohio State University Press, 2006.

Index

A

Adaptation/Adaptive, viii, xii–xiii, 1, 2–3, 7, 18, 21, 28, 32, 33, 35, 37–38, 40, 53, 56, 57, 60, 61, 63, 65, 68, 71, 76, 78, 80, 82, 86, 87, 97, 102–03, 108, 134, 136, 148, 152, 158, 159, 161–62, 170, 180, 190, 193–94, 203, 204, 205, 209, 224, 247, 258, 262

Aggression, 9–11, 12, 14, 19, 21, 27, 28–32, 36, 88–89, 128, 138, 140, 143, 158–59, 160, 161, 180, 181, 191, 192, 193, 194, 212, 222, 242

Alliances, 8, 11, 12, 16–17, 21, 34, 52, 55, 110, 156, 254

Alloparent, viii, 86, 91

Altruism, viii, 1, 18, 31, 32, 34–36, 46, 79, 80, 86, 223, 244, 257

Ancestral Environment/EEA, 39, 40, 43, 57, 128

Anthropocentrism, 45, 51, 59

Apollo, 193

Ardor, 61–67, 69–70, 70–71, 74, 76–77, 81, 117, 121–28, 164–65, 175, 177–79, 182–86, 188–89, 192, 202–03, 205, 207, 211, 212, 213–14, 217, 219, 223, 249

Autonomy, 108, 184–85, 193, 194, 200, 201, 202, 203

B

Bateman's Principle, 61–63, 65, 179–80
Biophilia, 37–38, 40, 41, 46, 54, 56–69, 60
Brood Parasitism, 243

C

Carlyle, Thomas, 65–66
Casaubon, Edward (Elliot), 108
Cheating, 7, 11, 12, 20, 236, 258
Chillingworth, Roger (Hawthorne), 30
Cognition, xi, 37, 38, 43
Coefficient of Relatedness, viii, 24–25, 48, 79
Contraception, 191, 211, 213

Cooperation, 1, 6–7, 11–13, 18–19, 20, 21, 159, 236

Costs and Benefits/Cost–Benefit Calculations, 7, 14–15, 22, 24, 29, 31, 34, 36, 70, 81, 114, 135, 144–47, 152, 181, 191–202, 233

Courtship, 10, 69, 81, 118, 149–55, 163, 211, 246–48

Cuckoldry, 144, 206, 241, 243

D

Daphne, 193–194
Dads–Cads, 196–98
Darwin, Charles, xi, xii, 42, 44, 50n54, 51n58, 58
Darwinian/Evolutionary Literary Theory, x–xiv, 21–22, 108–09, 123–24, 172, 253–55, 262

Deception, x, 6, 12, 14, 15, 20, 98, 134, 143, 144, 145, 149, 150, 153, 190, 197, 241, 244, 252

Desertion, 67, 101, 104, 110, 113, 119, 121–22, 124, 129, 132, 138, 143, 145, 156, 158, 160, 166–68, 169, 192, 200, 201

Dominance, 1, 3, 8, 10, 17, 26, 28, 86, 123, 128, 139, 144, 146, 151, 153n36, 184, 215, 242

Dorset, Bertha (Wharton), 97

E

Ecology/Ecocriticism, 37, 46, 50, 52, 56, 59
Emerson, Ralph Waldo, 45, 65
Error Management Theory, 152
Evolution/Evolutionary Theory, xi–xiii, 2, 3, 36, 44, 46, 49, 50n54, 52, 57, 59n89, 60, 61, 63, 78, 80, 86, 96, 97, 104, 107, 110, 123, 126, 131, 138, 144, 147, 149, 150, 152, 160, 162, 163, 164, 167, 168, 170, 180, 187, 195, 204, 205, 207, 216, 225, 253

Evolutionary Biology, 12, 23, 29, 31, 32, 37, 62, 66, 78, 176, 179, 184, 190, 209, 213, 215

Index

Evolutionary Psychology, xii–xiii, 43, 77, 137, 151, 166, 202, 208, 228, 243
Extinction, 187, 224

F

Female Choosiness and Reserve, 63, 131–32, 148, 168, 175, 178, 179, 180, 181–82, 187, 202–03, 235, 259–60
Female Mating Preferences
    General and Long-term: 3, 66, 68, 69, 71, 112, 128–29, 138, 143, 151, 153, 154–55, 158, 161, 193, 246, 248–49, 259–60
    Short-term: 129–30, 142–43, 194–98
Female Mating Strategies
    General and Long-term: 63, 66, 70, 175, 180, 185, 186–87, 189, 213, 231
    Mixed: 195
    Short-term: 71, 129, 143, 155, 175, 184, 186–87, 189–90, 194, 196–97, 198–201, 202, 213, 229–30, 233
Fertility/Infertility, 51, 67, 74, 110–12, 115, 120, 122, 131, 138, 143, 148, 151, 155, 165, 173, 180, 181, 196–97, 205, 208, 209, 211, 212–14, 225
Fidelity/Infidelity, 67, 97–98, 103, 111, 113, 118, 122, 134, 138, 140, 141, 143, 144, 145, 146, 147, 155, 156, 158, 159, 167, 168, 169, 170, 181, 183–85, 186, 187–88, 191–92, 197–98, 200, 207, 226, 227, 232, 238, 240, 241, 244, 255
Fitness
    General, viii, x, 3, 23, 24, 31, 32, 37, 53, 59, 60, 62, 66, 78, 79, 81, 82, 87, 96, 98, 103, 104, 105, 109, 111, 113, 120, 121, 122, 124, 126, 131, 133, 134, 136, 140, 143, 148, 159, 160, 161, 162, 163, 165, 167, 170, 173, 174, 190, 194, 195, 196, 204, 207, 233, 236, 244, 247, 248–49
    Direct, viii, 46, 51, 52, 53, 59–60, 69, 81, 105, 112, 113, 123, 127, 129, 152, 215, 261
    Indirect, viii, 23, 24, 79, 113, 114
    Inclusive, viii, 4, 23–26, 32, 36, 46–49, 51–54, 60, 114, 238, 257–58

G

Genes/Genetic (DNA), 3, 4, 23, 26, 28, 32, 36, 38, 44, 46, 48, 49, 50, 51, 53, 67, 78–80, 86, 103, 105, 106, 107, 110, 114, 122, 129, 131, 133, 136, 140, 141, 148, 152, 165, 168, 170, 181, 191, 195–96, 197–99, 201, 202, 203, 204, 205, 206, 207, 208–09, 211, 212, 216, 239–40, 243, 244, 252, 254, 258
Guinevere, 192

H

Handicap Principle, 248
Health/Illness, 15, 24, 30, 65, 81, 82, 86, 109, 110–12, 114, 122, 165
Helen of Troy, 192
Homoeroticism/Homosexuality, 52, 75–76, 215
Hume, David, 22
Hypergamy, ix, 143
Hypogamy, ix, 143

I

Intersexual Competition, 73, 105, 107, 121, 148, 161, 184, 203, 239, 252
Intrasexual Competition, 23, 66, 68–69, 76, 97, 105, 107, 108, 121, 138, 145–46, 148, 158–59, 160, 161, 164, 181, 212, 217, 239, 242, 249–51

J

Jealousy, x, 97, 102, 105, 107, 108–09, 117, 119, 121, 124, 148n28, 158, 159, 160, 161, 167, 168, 169, 191–92, 194, 211, 212, 219, 223, 233–34, 241, 244, 255
Jefferson, Thomas, 22
Jellyby, Mrs. (Dickens), 81

K

Kin Selection, ix, 23, 28, 29–31, 32, 35–36, 54
Kinship, 4, 23, 27, 28, 33, 35, 36, 37, 44–49, 52–54, 59, 82, 96, 240, 258

L

Life History, x, 41, 52, 123, 169, 170, 171, 172, 177, 186, 202, 206n5, 207, 216
Love's Labor's Lost (Shakespeare), 243

M

Maladaptive, 60, 78, 87, 105, 135, 163, 260–61
Male Mating Preferences
    General, 75, 110, 179, 196, 213
    Long-term, 131, 138, 141, 167, 171, 173, 235
    Short-term, 140–41, 194
Male Mating Strategies
    General, 126, 132–36, 162–63, 179, 246, 251–52, 261–62

Long-term, 131, 132–33, 138, 149, 153–55, 157–58, 228–30, 240, 249–51
Short-term, 61–70, 73–76, 230, 259–60
Mixed, 66–67, 130–31, 140–41, 144–46
Masculine Display, 127–28, 153–54, 241, 246, 251–52
Masculinity, 64, 68n26, 74, 127–28, 139, 146, 158, 164, 215
Mate Guarding, 69, 97–99, 104, 105–06, 109, 114–15, 119, 121, 124, 145, 158, 159, 161, 192, 192n36, 211, 223
Mate Poaching, 97, 113, 118, 119, 122, 124, 138, 158, 160, 166, 167, 170, 241
Mate Retention, 97–99, 100–104, 108, 121, 124–25, 138, 156, 161
Mate Switching, 113, 114, 138, 156, 194
Mate Value, 14–15, 26, 98, 109, 110, 111–12, 113–14, 120, 139, 143, 148, 149, 151, 158, 167, 168, 197, 198, 211, 246–47, 249, 255
Mating Commitment, 66–67, 97, 104, 105, 106, 108, 112, 113, 115, 131, 132, 134, 140, 141, 143–44, 145, 149, 150, 151, 154–55, 156, 158, 162, 166–67, 168, 169, 183, 188–89, 191, 194–95, 196, 197–98, 200–02, 227, 236, 239, 245, 259
Middlemarch (Elliot), 108

N
Natural Selection, 44, 50, 170, 187, 262
Nepotism, ix, 4, 23, 25, 27, 29, 31–36, 46, 48, 49, 59, 79, 84, 96, 104, 258

O
Offspring, 3, 4, 24–25, 52–54, 66–68, 78–80, 82–86, 95–96, 98, 103–04, 111, 127, 130, 168
The Odyssey (Homer), 100
Osmond, Gilbert (James), 81

P
Parental Investment, ix, 3, 24–25, 32, 52, 66, 78–82, 86, 96, 98, 117, 127, 129, 130, 135, 191, 195, 207
Paternal Confidence, 67, 69, 76, 98, 107n19, 131, 145, 158, 167, 180, 191–92, 226–27, 236–40, 242, 244, 260
Paternal Investment, 63, 66–68, 76, 78, 85–88, 98, 104, 113, 129, 130, 132–34, 136, 140, 143, 145, 154, 167, 191–92, 227, 238, 259–61

Persephone, 100–01
Personal Narrative, 16, 106, 112, 113–14, 124, 166, 168, 171, 174
Phenotype, ix, 22, 27, 133, 179, 195
Physical Environment, 22, 29, 37–44, 49, 53–59, 66, 81, 98, 111–12, 116, 123–24, 201, 206, 257
Pluto, 100
Pontifex, Theobald (Butler), 80
Primogeniture, 26
Promiscuity, 61, 63–64, 67, 70, 73, 75, 133, 134, 180–81, 184–88, 191, 214, 215, 220, 235, 238
Proximate Mechanisms, ix, 3, 52, 61, 68, 76, 80, 105, 123, 124, 126–27, 135, 136, 149, 174, 190, 198, 202, 204, 207, 211, 214, 217, 224, 243, 259–61

R
Reciprocity, 1, 6–8, 11, 12, 19, 20, 21, 46, 135, 219
Reproduction/Reproductive Success, x, 32, 51, 52–54, 59–60, 61, 62–63, 67, 79, 80, 81, 86, 93, 97, 101, 103, 104, 105, 106, 108, 110, 111, 113, 114, 120, 121, 122, 123, 124, 126, 128, 133, 143, 146, 152, 159, 160, 161, 162–63, 168, 170, 171, 173–74, 179, 180, 181, 190, 191, 195, 201–02, 204, 205, 206, 207–08, 209, 211, 213, 215, 216, 217, 221, 223, 224, 225
Reproductive Value/Residual Reproductive Value, ix, 25, 32, 79, 110, 122, 143, 149, 151, 165, 213
Reputation, 5–6, 7, 8, 12–13, 17, 18, 21, 52, 93, 98, 113, 114, 120, 122, 127, 129, 131, 145, 194, 252
Resources (Wealth), 1, 2–5, 7, 8, 12, 17, 19, 21, 24, 25, 52, 54–56, 59–60, 68, 81, 85–86, 94, 98, 102–03, 109, 114, 124, 138–39, 141, 142, 145, 146, 148, 151, 152, 153–55, 157, 160, 162, 165, 173, 181, 191, 194, 196, 204, 227–29, 234–35
Revenge/Retaliation, 9, 9–11, 12, 19, 21, 28, 30, 87, 103, 159–61
Role-Playing, 13–14, 21–22

S
Sanger, Margaret, 191
The Scarlet Letter (Hawthorne), 30
Self-Deception, 14–16, 18, 134–35, 136–37, 138, 149, 150, 166, 169, 171–74, 209–10, 232, 262

Selfishness/Self-Interest, ix, 1, 18–19, 29, 31–32, 36, 49, 53, 74, 76, 78, 86, 97, 105, 106, 113, 114, 123, 124, 135, 136, 156, 169, 171, 173, 182, 192, 215, 222–23, 232, 245, 257–58, 260
Sexual Dimorphism, 181, 202
Sexual Selection, 162, 246, 252
Sexy-Sons Theory, 130, 197
Sharp, Becky (Thackeray), 80
Siren, 164–65, 173
Slade, Alida (Wharton), 97, 99
Social Environment, 1, 12, 16, 18, 20–22, 23, 27, 28, 29, 32, 33–35, 37, 46, 60, 68, 73, 77, 79, 80, 82, 95, 112, 128, 162, 182, 202, 242, 244, 254, 257
Social Norms, 21–22, 29, 30, 32, 37, 52, 60, 61, 71–72, 73, 76, 79–80, 81, 84, 87, 91–96, 98, 112, 117, 118–19, 124, 130, 131, 134, 135, 167, 175, 180, 181–82, 184, 185, 193, 194, 198, 202, 203, 215, 224, 254
Social Hierarchy, 3, 8–9, 17, 27, 34, 36, 84, 86, 138–39, 163
Social Intelligence, 5, 21, 34, 131, 255–56
Spragg, Undine (Wharton), 80–81
Status, 1, 2–3, 5, 12, 17, 21, 24, 25, 28, 30, 33, 52, 60, 86–87, 94, 98, 108, 110, 113, 115, 131, 138, 141, 145, 148, 151, 154, 155, 156, 157, 161, 162, 165, 191, 193, 194, 197, 199, 212, 241, 246
Strategic Interference, 66–67, 75–76, 106, 121, 123, 124, 175, 180, 203
Symmetry (bodily, facial), 110, 165, 195, 213

T
Theory of Mind, 247, 252, 254
Tit for Tat (also see Reciprocity), 7, 236
Transcendentalism, 45, 59n89, 61, 65–66, 70, 72, 77

U
Ultimate Explanations of Behavior, ix, 3, 52, 68, 127, 162, 198, 202, 205, 211, 214, 217, 254, 259–60
Universal Human Nature, x, xii–xiii, 1, 21, 22, 28, 29–30, 37–38, 59, 77, 96, 122, 175, 201–02, 209, 242–43, 245

V
Venereal Disease, 15, 191, 194
Voltaire, 22

W
Waist-Hip Ratio, 110, 165, 196, 213